Johnson, Allen
    Stephen A. Douglas

DATE DUE

MAY 1 0 7			
DEC 14 7			
OCT 2 9 '80			
NOV 26 '80			

STEPHEN A. DOUGLAS

A Study in American Politics

A Da Capo Press Reprint Series

THE AMERICAN SCENE
Comments and Commentators

GENERAL EDITOR: WALLACE D. FARNHAM
University of Illinois

STEPHEN A. DOUGLAS

A Study in American Politics

BY ALLEN JOHNSON

DA CAPO PRESS • NEW YORK • 1970

A Da Capo Press Reprint Edition

This Da Capo Press edition of *Stephen A. Douglas: A Study in American Politics* is an unabridged republication of the first edition published in New York in 1908.

Library of Congress Catalog Card Number 77-98690
SBN 306-71836-7

Published by Da Capo Press
A Division of Plenum Publishing Corporation
227 West 17th Street
New York, N.Y. 10011

Manufactured in the United States of America

STEPHEN A. DOUGLAS:
A STUDY IN AMERICAN POLITICS

THE MACMILLAN COMPANY
NEW YORK · BOSTON · CHICAGO
ATLANTA · SAN FRANCISCO

MACMILLAN & CO., LIMITED
LONDON · BOMBAY · CALCUTTA
MELBOURNE

THE MACMILLAN CO. OF CANADA, LTD.
TORONTO

STEPHEN A. DOUGLAS:

A STUDY IN AMERICAN POLITICS

By

ALLEN JOHNSON

PROFESSOR OF HISTORY IN BOWDOIN COLLEGE; SOMETIME
PROFESSOR OF HISTORY IN IOWA COLLEGE

New York

THE MACMILLAN COMPANY

1908

PREFACE

To describe the career of a man who is now chiefly remembered as the rival of Abraham Lincoln, must seem to many minds a superfluous, if not invidious, undertaking. The present generation is prone to forget that when the rivals met in joint debate fifty years ago, on the prairies of Illinois, it was Senator Douglas, and not Mr. Lincoln, who was the cynosure of all observing eyes. Time has steadily lessened the prestige of the great Democratic leader, and just as steadily enhanced the fame of his Republican opponent.

The following pages have been written, not as a vindication, but as an interpretation of a personality whose life spans the controversial epoch before the Civil War. It is due to the chance reader to state that the writer was born in a New England home, and bred in an anti-slavery atmosphere where the political creed of Douglas could not thrive. If this book reveals a somewhat less sectional outlook than this personal allusion suggests, the credit must be given to those generous friends in the great Middle West, who have helped the writer to interpret the spirit of that region which gave both Douglas and Lincoln to the nation.

The material for this study has been brought together from many sources. Through the kindness of Mrs. James W. Patton of Springfield, Illinois, I have had access to a valuable collection of letters written by Douglas to her father, Charles H. Lanphier, Esq., editor of the Illinois *State Register*. Judge Robert M. Douglas of North Carolina has permitted me to use an autobiographical sketch of his father, as well as other papers in the possession of the family. Among those who have lightened my labors, either by copies of letters penned by Douglas or by personal recollections, I would mention with particular gratitude the late Mrs. L. K. Lippincott ("Grace Greenwood"); Mr. J. H. Roberts and Stephen A. Douglas, Esq. of Chicago; Chief Justice Melville W. Fuller and the late Hon. Robert R. Hitt of Washington. With his wonted generosity, Mr. James F. Rhodes has given me the benefit of his wide acquaintance with the newspapers of the period, which have been an invaluable aid in the interpretation of Douglas's career. Finally, by personal acquaintance and conversation with men who knew him, I have endeavored to catch the spirit of those who made up the great mass of his constituents.

Brunswick, Maine,
   November, 1907.

CONTENTS

BOOK I. THE CALL OF THE WEST

BOOK II. THE DOCTRINE OF POPULAR SOVEREIGNTY

BOOK I
THE CALL OF THE WEST

CHAPTER I

From the Green Mountains to the Prairies

The dramatic moments in the colonizing of coastal New England have passed into song, story, and sober chronicle; but the farther migration of the English people, from tide-water to interior, has been too prosaic a theme for poets and too diverse a movement for historians. Yet when all the factors in our national history shall be given their full value, none will seem more potent than the great racial drift from the New England frontier into the heart of the continent. The New Englanders who formed a broad belt from Vermont and New York across the Northwest to Kansas, were a social and political force of incalculable power, in the era which ended with the Civil War. The New Englander of the Middle West, however, ceased to be altogether a Yankee. The lake and prairie plains bred a spirit which contrasted strongly with the smug provincialism of rock-ribbed and sterile New England. The exultation born of wide, unbroken, horizon lines and broad, teeming, prairie landscapes, found expression in the often-quoted saying, "Vermont is the most glorious spot on the face of this globe for a man to be born in, *provided* he emigrates when he is very young." The career of Stephen Arnold Douglas is intelligible only as it is viewed against the background of a New England boyhood, a young manhood passed on the prairies of Illinois, and a wedded life pervaded by the gentle culture of Southern womanhood.

3

In America, observed De Tocqueville two generations ago, democracy disposes every man to forget
his ancestors. When the Hon. Stephen A. Douglas
was once asked to prepare an account of his career
for a biographical history of Congress, he chose to omit
all but the barest reference to his forefathers.[1] Possibly he preferred to leave the family tree naked, that
his unaided rise to eminence might the more impress
the chance reader. Yet the records of the Douglass
family are not uninteresting.[2] The first of the name to
cross the ocean was William Douglass, who was born in
Scotland and who wedded Mary Ann, daughter of
Thomas Marble of Northampton. Just when this
couple left Old England is not known, but the birth of
a son is recorded in Boston, in the year 1645. Soon
after this event they removed to New London, preferring, it would seem, to try their luck in an outlying
settlement, for this region was part of the Pequot
country. Somewhat more than a hundred years later,
Benajah Douglass, a descendant of this pair and grandfather of the subject of this sketch, pushed still farther
into the interior, and settled in Rensselaer County, in
the province of New York. The marriage of Benajah
Douglass to Martha Arnold, a descendant of Governor
William Arnold of Rhode Island, has an interest for
those who are disposed to find Celtic qualities in the
grandson, for the Arnolds were of Welsh stock, and
may be supposed to have revived the strain in the
Douglass blood.

[1] There can be little doubt that he supplied the data for the sketch
in Wheeler's Biographical and Political History of Congress.

[2] See Transactions of the Illinois State Historical Society, 1901, pp.
113-114.

Tradition has made Benajah Douglass a soldier in the war of the Revolution, but authentic records go no farther back than the year 1795, when he removed with his family to Brandon, Vermont. There he purchased a farm of about four hundred acres, which he must have cultivated with some degree of skill, since it seems to have yielded an ample competency. He is described as a man of genial, buoyant disposition, with much self-confidence. He was five times chosen selectman of Brandon; and five times he was elected to represent the town in the General Assembly. The physical qualities of the grandson may well have been a family inheritance, since of Benajah we read that he was of medium height, with large head and body, short neck, and short limbs.[1]

The portrait of Benajah's son is far less distinct. He was a graduate of Middlebury College and a physician by profession. He married Sally Fisk, the daughter of a well-to-do farmer in Brandon, by whom he had two children, the younger of whom was Stephen Arnold Douglass, born April 23, 1813. The promising career of the young doctor was cut short by a sudden stroke, which overtook him as he held his infant son in his arms. The plain, little one-and-a-half story house, in which the boy first saw the light, suggests that the young physician had been unable to provide for more than the bare necessities of his family.[2]

Soon after the death of Dr. Douglass, his widow removed to the farm which she and her unmarried brother had inherited from her father. The children grew to love this bachelor uncle with almost filial affec-

[1] Vermont Historical Gazetteer, III, p. 457.
[2] Transactions of the Illinois State Historical Society, 1901, p. 115.

tion. Too young to take thought for the morrow, they led the wholesome, natural life of country children. Stephen went to the district school on the Brandon turnpike, and had no reason to bemoan the fate which left him largely dependent upon his uncle's generosity. An old school-mate recalls young Douglass through the haze of years, as a robust, healthy boy, with generous instincts though tenacious of his rights.[1] After school hours work and play alternated. The regular farm chores were not the least part in the youngster's education; he learned to be industrious and not to despise honest labor.[2]

This bare outline of a commonplace boyhood must be filled in with many details drawn from environment. Stephen fell heir to a wealth of inspiring local traditions. The fresh mountain breezes had also once blown full upon the anxious faces of heroes and patriots; the quiet valleys had once echoed with the noise of battle; this land of the Green Mountains was the Wilderness of colonial days, the frontier for restless New Englanders, where with good axe and stout heart they had carved their home plots out of the virgin forest. Many a legend of adventure, of border warfare, and of personal heroism, was still current among the Green Mountain folk. Where was the Vermont lad who did not fight over again the battles of Bennington, Ticonderoga, and Plattsburg?

Other influences were scarcely less formative in the life of the growing boy. Vermont was also the land of

---

[1] Mr. B. F. Field in the *Vermonter*, January, 1897.

[2] For many facts relating to Douglas's life, I am indebted to an unpublished autobiographical sketch in the possession of his son, Judge R. M. Douglas, of Greensboro, North Carolina.

the town meeting. Whatever may be said of the efficiency of town government, it was and is a school of democracy. In Vermont it was the natural political expression of social forces. How else, indeed, could the general will find fit expression, except through the attrition of many minds? And who could know better the needs of the community than the commonalty? Not that men reasoned about the philosophy of their political institutions: they simply accepted them. And young Douglass grew up in an atmosphere friendly to local self-government of an extreme type.

Stephen was nearing his fourteenth birthday, when an event occurred which interrupted the even current of his life. His uncle, who was commonly regarded as a confirmed old bachelor, confounded the village gossips by bringing home a young bride. The birth of a son and heir was the nephew's undoing. While the uncle regarded Stephen with undiminished affection, he was now much more emphatically *in loco parentis.* An indefinable something had come between them. The subtle change in relationship was brought home to both when Stephen proposed that he should go to the academy in Brandon, to prepare for college. That he was to go to college, he seems to have taken for granted. There was a moment of embarrassment, and then the uncle told the lad, frankly but kindly, that he could not provide for his further education. With considerable show of affection, he advised him to give up the notion of going to college and to remain on the farm, where he would have an assured competence. In after years the grown man related this incident with a tinge of bitterness, averring that there had been an understanding in the family that he was to attend college.[1] Momentary disappointment he may have felt, to be sure, but he could hardly have been led to believe that he could draw indefinitely upon his uncle's bounty.

Piqued and somewhat resentful, Stephen made up his mind to live no longer under his uncle's roof. He would show his spirit by proving that he was abundantly able to take care of himself. Much against the wishes of his mother, who knew him to be mastered by a boyish whim, he apprenticed himself to Nahum Parker, a cabinet-maker in Middlebury.[2] He put on his apron, went to work sawing table legs from two-inch planks, and, delighted with the novelty of the occupation and exhilarated by his newly found sense of freedom, believed himself on the highway to happiness and prosperity. He found plenty of companions with whom he spent his idle hours, young fellows who had a taste for politics and who rapidly kindled in the newcomer a consuming admiration for Andrew Jackson. He now began to read with avidity such political works as came to hand. Discussion with his new friends and with his employer, who was an ardent supporter of Adams and Clay, whetted his appetite for more reading and study. In after years he was wont to say that these were the happiest days of his life.[3]

Toward the end of the year, he became dissatisfied with his employer because he was forced to perform "some menial services in the house."[4] He wished his employer to know that he was not a household servant, but an apprentice. Further difficulties arose, which

---

[1] Wheeler, Biographical History of Congress, p. 61; also MS. Autobiography.

[2] Troy *Whig*, July 6, 1860.   [3] MS. Autobiography.   [4] *Ibid.*

terminated his apprenticeship in Middlebury. Returning to Brandon, he entered the shop of Deacon Caleb Knowlton, also a cabinet-maker; but in less than a year he quit this employer on the plea of ill-health.[1] It is quite likely that the confinement and severe manual labor may have overtaxed the strength of the growing boy; but it is equally clear that he had lost his taste for cabinet work. He never again expressed a wish to follow a trade. He again took up his abode with his mother; and, the means now coming to hand from some source, he enrolled as a student in Brandon Academy, with the avowed purpose of preparing for a professional career.[2] It was a wise choice. Vermont may have lost a skilled handworker—there are those who vouch for the excellence of his handiwork[3]—but the Union gained a joiner of first-rate ability.

Wedding bells rang in another change in his fortunes. The marriage of his sister to a young New Yorker from Ontario County, was followed by the marriage of his mother to the father, Gehazi Granger. Both couples took up their residence on the Granger estate, and thither also went Stephen, with perhaps a sense of loneliness in his boyish heart.[4] He was then but seventeen. This removal to New York State proved to be his first step along a path which Vermonters were wearing toward the West.

Happily, his academic course was not long interrupted by this migration, for Canandaigua Academy, which offered unusual advantages, was within easy reach from his new home. Under the wise instruction of Professor Henry Howe, he began the study of Latin

[1] MS. Autobiography; see Wheeler, Biographical History, p. 62.
[2] Ibid. [3] Vermonter, January, 1897. [4] MS. Autobiography.

and Greek; and by his own account made "considerable improvement," though there is little evidence in his later life of any acquaintance with the classics. He took an active part in the doings of the literary societies of the academy, distinguishing himself by his readiness in debate. His Democratic proclivities were still strong; and he became an ardent defender of Democracy against the rising tide of Anti-Masonry, which was threatening to sweep New York from its political moorings. Tradition says that young Douglass mingled much with local politicians, learning not a little about the arts and devices by which the Albany Regency controlled the Democratic organization in the State. In this school of practical politics he was beyond a peradventure an apt pupil.

A characteristic story is told of Douglass during these school days at Canandaigua.[1] A youngster who occupied a particularly desirable seat at table had been ousted by another lad, who claimed a better right to the place. Some one suggested that the claimants should have the case argued by counsel before a board of arbitration. The dispossessed boy lost his case, because of the superior skill with which Douglass presented the claims of his client. "It was the first assertion of the doctrine of squatter sovereignty," said the defeated claimant, recalling the incident years afterward, when both he and Douglas were in politics.

Douglass was now maturing rapidly. His ideals were clearer; his native tastes more pronounced. It is not improbable that already he looked forward to politics as a career. At all events he took the proximate step

[1] This story was repeated to me by Judge Douglas, on the authority, I believe, of Senator Lapham of New York.

toward that goal by beginning the study of law in the office of local attorneys, at the same time continuing his studies begun in the academy. What marked him off from his comrades even at this period was his lively acquisitiveness. He seemed to learn quite as much by indirection as by persevering application to books.[1]

In the spring of 1833, the same unrest that sent the first Douglass across the sea to the new world, seized the young man. Against the remonstrances of his mother and his relatives, he started for the great West which then spelled opportunity to so many young men. He was only twenty years old, and he had not yet finished his academic course; but with the impatience of ambition he was reluctant to spend four more years in study before he could gain admission to the bar. In the newer States of the West conditions were easier. Moreover, he was no longer willing to be a burden to his mother, whose resources were limited. And so, with purposes only half formed and with only enough money for his immediate needs, he began, not so much a journey, as a drift in a westerly direction, for he had no particular destination in view.[2]

After a short stay in Buffalo and a visit to Niagara Falls and the battle ground of Chippewa, the boy took a steamboat to Cleveland, where happily he found a friend in Sherlock J. Andrews, Esquire, a successful attorney and a man of kindly impulses. Finding the city attractive and the requirements for the Ohio bar less rigorous, Douglass determined to drop anchor in this pleasant port. Mr. Andrews encouraged him in

[1] This is the impression of all who knew him personally, then and afterward. See Arnold, Reminiscences of the Illinois Bar.

[2] MS. Autobiography.

this purpose, offering the use of his office and law library. In a single year Douglass hoped to gain admission to the bar. With characteristic energy, he began his studies. Fate ruled, however, that his career should not be linked with the Western Reserve. Within a few days he was prostrated by that foe which then lurked in the marshes and lowlands of the West—foe more dreaded than the redman—malarial typhoid. For four weary months he kept his bed, hovering between life and death, until the heat of summer was spent and the first frosts of October came to revive him. Urgent appeals now came to him to return home; but pride kept him from yielding. After paying all his bills, he still had forty dollars left. He resolved to push on farther into the interior.[1]

He was far from well when he took the canal boat from Cleveland to Portsmouth on the Ohio river; but he was now in a reckless and adventurous mood. He would test his luck by pressing on to Cincinnati. He had no well-defined purpose: he was in a listless mood, which was no doubt partly the result of physical exhaustion. From Cincinnati he drifted on to Louisville, and then to St. Louis. His small funds were now almost all spent. He must soon find occupation or starve. His first endeavor was to find a law office where he could earn enough by copying and other work to pay his expenses while he continued his law studies. No such opening fell in his way and he had no letters of introduction here to smooth his path. He was now convinced that he must seek some small country town. Hearing that Jacksonville, Illinois, was a thriving settlement, he resolved to try his luck in this quarter.

[1] MS. Autobiography.

With much the same desperation with which a gambler plays his last stake, he took passage on a river boat up the Illinois, and set foot upon the soil of the great prairie State.[1]

A primitive stage coach plied between the river and Jacksonville. Too fatigued to walk the intervening distance, Douglass mounted the lumbering vehicle and ruefully paid his fare. From this point of vantage he took in the prairie landscape. Morgan County was then but sparsely populated. Timber fringed the creeks and the river bottoms, while the prairie grass grew rank over soil of unsuspected fertility. Most dwellings were rude structures made of rough-hewn logs and designed as makeshifts. Wildcats and wolves prowled through the timber lands in winter, and game of all sorts abounded.[2] As the stage swung lazily along, the lad had ample time to let the first impression of the prairie landscape sink deep. In the timber, the trees were festooned with bitter-sweet and with vines bearing wild grapes; in the open country, nothing but unmeasured stretches of waving grass caught the eye.[3] To one born and bred among the hills, this broad horizon and unbroken landscape must have been a revelation. Weak as he was, Douglass drew in the fresh autumnal air with zest, and unconsciously borrowed from the face of nature a sense of unbounded capacity. Years afterward, when he was famous, he testified, "I found my mind liberalized and my opinions enlarged, when I got on these broad prairies, with only the heavens to bound my vision, instead of having

[1] MS. Autobiography.

[2] Kirby, Sketch of Joseph Duncan in Fergus Historical Series No. 29; also Historic Morgan, p. 60.   [3] *Ibid.*

them circumscribed by the little ridges that surrounded the valley where I was born.''[1]   But of all this he was unconscious, when he alighted from the stage in Jacksonville.   He was simply a wayworn lad, without a friend in the town and with only one dollar and twenty-five cents in his pocket.[2]

Jacksonville was then hardly more than a crowded village of log cabins on the outposts of civilized Illinois.[3]   Comfort was not among the first concerns of those who had come to subdue the wilderness.   Comfort implied leisure to enjoy, and leisure was like Heaven,—to be attained only after a wearisome earthly pilgrimage.   Jacksonville had been scourged by the cholera during the summer; and those who had escaped the disease had fled the town for fear of it.[4]   By this time, however, the epidemic had spent itself, and the refugees had returned.   All told, the town had a population of about one thousand souls, among whom were no less than eleven lawyers, or at least those who called themselves such.[5]

A day's lodging at the Tavern ate up the remainder of the wanderer's funds, so that he was forced to sell a few school books that he had brought with him. Meanwhile he left no stone unturned to find employment to his liking.   One of his first acquaintances was Murray McConnell, a lawyer, who advised him to go to Pekin, farther up the Illinois River, and open a law office.   The young man replied that he had no license to practice law and no law books.   He was assured

---

[1] Speech at Jonesboro, in the debate with Lincoln, Sept. 15, 1858.
[2] MS. Autobiography.   [3] Kirby, Joseph Duncan.
[4] James S. Anderson in Historic Morgan.
[5] Peck, *Gazetteer of Illinois*, 1834.

that a license was a matter of no consequence, since anyone could practice before a justice of the peace, and he could procure one at his leisure. As for books, McConnell, with true Western generosity, offered to loan such as would be of immediate use. So again Douglass took up his travels. At Meredosia, the nearest landing on the river, he waited a week for the boat upstream. There was no other available route to Pekin. Then came the exasperating intelligence, that the only boat which plied between these points had blown up at Alton. After settling accounts with the tavern-keeper, he found that he had but fifty cents left.[1]

There was now but one thing to do, since hard manual labor was out of the question: he would teach school. But where? Meredosia was a forlorn, thriftless place, and he had no money to travel. Fortunately, a kind-hearted farmer befriended him, lodging him at his house over night and taking him next morning to Exeter, where there was a prospect of securing a school. Disappointment again awaited him; but Winchester, ten miles away, was said to need a teacher. Taking his coat on his arm—he had left his trunk at Meredosia—he set off on foot for Winchester.[2]

Accident, happily turned to his profit, served to introduce him to the townspeople of Winchester. The morning after his arrival, he found a crowd in the public square and learned that an auction sale of personal effects was about to take place. Everyone from the administrator of the estate to the village idler, was eager for the sale to begin. But a clerk to keep record of the sales and to draw the notes was wanting. The eye of the administrator fell upon Douglass; some-

[1] MS. Autobiography.   [2] *Ibid.*

thing in the youth's appearance gave assurance that he could "cipher.". The impatient bystanders "'lowed that he might do," so he was given a trial. Douglass proved fully equal to the task, and in two days was in possession of five dollars for his pains.[1]

Through the good will of the village storekeeper, who also hailed from Vermont, Douglass was presented to several citizens who wished to see a school opened in town; and by the first Monday in December he had a subscription list of forty scholars, each of whom paid three dollars for three months' tuition.[2] Luck was now coming his way. He found lodgings under the roof of this same friendly compatriot, the village store-keeper, who gave him the use of a small room adjoining the store-room.[3] Here Douglass spent his evenings, devoting some hours to his law books and perhaps more to comfortable chats with his host and talkative neighbors around the stove. For diversion he had the weekly meetings of the Lyceum, which had just been formed.[4] He owed much to this institution, for the the debates and discussions gave him a chance to convert the traditional leadership which fell to him as village schoolmaster, into a real leadership of talent and ready wit. In this Lyceum he made his first political speech, defending Andrew Jackson and his attack upon the Bank against Josiah Lamborn, a lawyer from Jacksonville.[5] For a young man he proved himself astonishingly well-informed. If the chronology of his autobiography may be accepted, he had already read

[1] MS. Autobiography.   [2] *Ibid.*

[3] Letter of E. G. Miner, January, 1877, in Proceedings of the Illinois Association of Sons of Vermont.

[4] *Ibid.*   [5] *Ibid.;* MS. Autobiography.

the debates in the Constitutional Convention of 1787, the *Federalist,* the works of John Adams and Thomas Jefferson, and the recent debates in Congress.

Even while he was teaching school, Douglass found time to practice law in a modest way before the justices of the peace; and when the first of March came, he closed the schoolhouse door on his career as pedagogue. He at once repaired to Jacksonville and presented himself before a justice of the Supreme Court for license to practice law. After a short examination, which could not have been very searching, he was duly admitted to the bar of Illinois. He still lacked a month of being twenty-one years of age.[1] Measured by the standard of older communities in the East, he knew little law; but there were few cases in these Western courts which required much more than common-sense, ready speech, and acquaintance with legal procedure. *Stare decisis* was a maxim that did not trouble the average lawyer, for there were few decisions to stand upon.[2] Besides, experience would make good any deficiencies of preparation.

[1] MS. Autobiography.
[2] Hon. J. C. Conkling in Fergus Historical Series, No. 22.

CHAPTER II

THE RISE OF THE POLITICIAN

The young attorney who opened a law office in the Court House at Jacksonville, bore little resemblance to the forlorn lad who had vainly sought a livelihood there some months earlier. The winter winds of the prairies, so far from racking the frame of the convalescent, had braced and toned his whole system. When spring came, he was in the best of health and full of animal spirits. He entered upon his new life with zest. Here was a people after his own heart; a generous, wholesome, optimistic folk. He opened his heart to them, and, of course, hospitable doors opened to him. He took society as he found it, rude perhaps, but genuine. With plenty of leisure at command, he mingled freely with young people of his own age; he joined the boisterous young fellows in their village sports; he danced with the maidens; and he did not forget to cultivate the good graces of their elders. Mothers liked his animation and ready gallantry; fathers found him equally responsive on more serious matters of conversation. Altogether, he was a very general favorite in a not too fastidious society.[1]

Nor was the circle of the young attorney's acquaintances limited to Jacksonville. As the county seat and most important town in Morgan County, Jacksonville was a sort of rural emporium. Thither came

[1] Joseph Wallace in a letter to the Illinois *State Register*, April 30, 1899.

18

farmers from the country round about, to market their
produce and to purchase their supplies. The town had
an unwontedly busy aspect on Saturdays. This was
the day which drew women to town. While they did
their shopping, the men loitered on street corners, or
around the Court House, to greet old acquaintances.
Douglass was sure to be found among them, joining
in that most subtle of all social processes, the forming
of public opinion. Moving about from group to group,
with his pockets stuffed with newspapers, he became
a familiar figure.[1] Plain farmers, in clothes soiled with
the rich loam of the prairies, enjoyed hearing the young
fellow express so pointedly their own nascent convictions.

This forum was an excellent school for the future
politician. The dust might accumulate upon his law
books: he was learning unwritten law in the hearts
of these countrymen. And yet, even at this time, he
exhibited a certain maturity. There seems never to
have been a time when the arts of the politician were
not instinctive in him. He had no boyish illusions to
outlive regarding the nature and conditions of public
life. His perfect self-possession attested this mental
maturity.

One of the first friendships which the young lawyer
formed in his new home was with S. S. Brooks, Esq.,
editor of the Jacksonville *News*. While Douglass was
still in Winchester, the first issue of this sheet had
appeared; and he had written a complimentary letter
to Brooks, congratulating him on his enterprise. The
grateful editor never forgot this kindly word of en-

[1] Illinois *State Register*, April 30, 1899.

couragement.[1] The intimacy which followed was of great value to the younger man, who needed just the advertising which the editor was in a position to give. The bond between them was their devotion to the fortunes of Andrew Jackson. Together they labored to consolidate the Democratic forces of the county, with results which must have surprised even the sanguine young lawyer.

The political situation in Morgan County, as the State election approached, is not altogether clear. President Jackson's high-handed acts, particularly his attitude toward the National Bank, had alarmed many men who had supported him in 1832. There were defections in the ranks of the Democracy. The State elections would surely turn on national issues. The Whigs were noisy, assertive, and confident. Largely through the efforts of Brooks and Douglass, the Democrats of Jacksonville were persuaded to call a mass-meeting of all good Democrats in the county. It was on this occasion, very soon after his arrival in town, that Douglass made his début on the political stage.

It is said that accident brought the young lawyer into prominence at this meeting. A well-known Democrat who was to have presented resolutions, demurred, at the last minute, and thrust the copy into Douglass' hands, bidding him read them. The Court House was full to overflowing with interested observers of this little by-play. Excitement ran high, for the opposition within the party was vehement in its protest to cut-and-dried resolutions commending Jackson. An older man with more discretion and modesty, would have hesitated to face the audience; but Douglass possessed

[1] Sheahan, Life of Douglas, pp. 16-17.

neither retiring modesty nor the sobriety which comes with years. He not only read the resolutions, but he defended them with such vigorous logic and with such caustic criticism of Whigs and half-hearted Democrats, that he carried the meeting with him in tumultuous approval of the course of Andrew Jackson, past and present.[1]

The next issue of the *Patriot,* the local Whig paper, devoted two columns to the speech of this young Democratic upstart; and for weeks thereafter the editor flayed him on all possible occasions. The result was such an enviable notoriety for the young attorney among Whigs and such fame among Democrats, that he received collection demands to the amount of thousands of dollars from persons whom he had never seen or known. In after years, looking back on these beginnings, he used to wonder whether he ought not to have paid the editor of the *Patriot* for his abuse, according to the usual advertising rates.[2] The political outcome was not in every respect so gratifying. The Democratic county ticket was elected and a Democratic congressman from the district; but the Whigs elected their candidate for governor.

A factional quarrel among members of his own party gave Douglass his reward for services to the cause of Democracy, and his first political office. Captain John Wyatt nursed a grudge against John J. Hardin, Esq., who had been elected State's attorney for the district through his influence, but who had subsequently proved ungrateful. Wyatt had been re-elected member of the

[1] Sheahan's account of this incident (pp. 18-20) is confused. The episode is told very differently in the MS. Autobiography.

[2] MS. Autobiography.

legislature, however, in spite of Hardin's opposition, and now wished to revenge himself, by ousting Hardin from his office. With this end in view, Wyatt had Douglass draft a bill making the State's attorneys elective by the legislature, instead of subject to the governor's appointment. Since the new governor was a Whig, he could not be used by the Democrats. The bill met with bitter opposition, for it was alleged that it had no other purpose than to vacate Hardin's office for the benefit of Douglass. This was solemnly denied;[1] but when the bill had been declared unconstitutional by the Council of Revision, Douglass' friends made desperate exertions to pass the bill over the veto, with the now openly avowed purpose to elect him to the office. The bill passed, and on the 10th of February, 1835, the legislature in joint session elected the boyish lawyer State's attorney for the first judicial district, by a majority of four votes over an attorney of experience and recognized merit. It is possible, as Douglass afterward averred, that he neither coveted the office nor believed himself fitted for it; and that his judgment was overruled by his friends. But he accepted the office, nevertheless.

When Douglas,—for he had now begun to drop the superfluous s in the family name, for simplicity's sake,[2]—set out on his judicial circuit, he was not an imposing figure. There was little in his boyish face to command attention, except his dark-blue, lustrous eyes. His big head seemed out of proportion to his

---

[1] In the Autobiography, Douglas makes a vigorous defense of his connection with the whole affair.

[2] Just when he dropped the final s, I am unable to say. Joseph Wallace thinks that he did so soon after coming to Illinois. See Transactions of the Illinois State Historical Society, 1901, p. 114.

stunted figure. He measured scarcely over five feet and weighed less than a hundred and ten pounds. Astride his horse, he looked still more diminutive. His mount was a young horse which he had borrowed. He carried under his arm a single book, also loaned, a copy of the criminal law.[1] His chief asset was a large fund of Yankee shrewdness and good nature.

An amusing incident occurred in McLean County at the first court which Douglas attended. There were many indictments to be drawn, and the new prosecuting attorney, in his haste, misspelled the name of the county—M Clean instead of M'Lean. His professional brethren were greatly amused at this evidence of inexperience; and made merry over the blunder. Finally, John T. Stuart, subsequently Douglas's political rival, moved that all the indictments be quashed. Judge Logan asked the discomfited youth what he had to say to support the indictments. Smarting under the gibes of Stuart, Douglas replied obstinately that he had nothing to say, as he supposed the Court would not quash the indictments until the point had been proven. This answer aroused more merriment; but the Judge decided that the Court could not rule upon the matter, until the precise spelling in the statute creating the county had been ascertained. No one doubted what the result would be; but at least Douglas had the satisfaction of causing his critics some annoyance and two days' delay, for the statutes had to be procured from an adjoining county. To the astonishment of Court and Bar, and of Douglas himself, it appeared that Douglas had spelled the name correctly. To the indescribable chagrin of the learned Stuart, the

[1] Joseph Wallace in the Illinois *State Register*, April 30, 1899.

Court promptly sustained all the indictments. The young attorney was in high feather; and he made the most of his triumph. The incident taught him a useful lesson: henceforth he would admit nothing, and require his opponents to prove everything that bore upon the case in hand. Some time later, upon comparing the printed statute of the county with the enrolled bill in the office of the Secretary of State, Douglas found that the printer had made a mistake and that the name of the county should have been M'Lean.[1]

On the whole Douglas seems to have discharged his not very onerous duties acceptably. The more his fellow practitioners saw of him, the more respect they had for him. Moreover, they liked him personally. His wholesome frankness disarmed ill-natured opponents; his generosity made them fast friends. There was not an inn or hostelry in the circuit, which did not welcome the sight of the talkative, companionable, young district attorney.

Politically as well as socially, Illinois was in a transitional stage. Although political parties existed, they were rather loose associations of men holding similar political convictions than parties in the modern sense with permanent organs of control. He who would might stand for office, either announcing his own candidacy in the newspapers, or if his modesty forbade this course, causing such an announcement to be made by "many voters." In benighted districts, where the light of the press did not shine, the candidate offered

[1] Douglas tells the story with great relish in his autobiography. The title of the act reads "An Act creating M'Lean County," but the body of the act gives the name as McLean. Douglas had used the exact letters of the name, though he had twisted the capital letters, writing a capital C for a capital L.

himself in person. Even after the advent of Andrew Jackson in national politics, allegiance to party was so far subordinated to personal ambition, that it was no uncommon occurrence for several candidates from each party to enter the lists.[1] From the point of view of party, this practice was strategically faulty, since there was always the possibility that the opposing party might unite on a single candidate. What was needed to insure the success of party was the rationale of an army. But organization was abhorrent to people so tenacious of their personal freedom as Illinoisans, because organization necessitated the subordination of the individual to the centralized authority of the group. To the average man organization spelled dictation.

The first step in the effective control of nominations by party in Illinois, was taken by certain Democrats, foremost among whom was S. A. Douglas, Esq. His rise as a politician, indeed, coincides with this development of party organization and machinery. The movement began sporadically in several counties. At the instance of Douglas and his friend Brooks of the *News*, the Democrats of Morgan County put themselves on record as favoring a State convention to choose delegates to the national convention of 1836.[2] County after county adopted the suggestion, until the movement culminated in a well-attended convention at Vandalia in April, 1835. Not all counties were represented, to be sure, and no permanent organization was effected; but provision was made for a second convention in December, to nominate presidential electors.[3] Among the delegates from Morgan County in this

---

[1] Ford, History of Illinois, pp. 285-286; see contemporary newspapers.
[2] Illinois *Advocate*, May 4, 1835.   [3] *Ibid.*, May 6, 1835.

December convention was Douglas, burning with zeal for the consolidation of his party. Signs were not wanting that he was in league with other zealots to execute a sort of *coup d'état* within the party. Early in the session, one Ebenezer Peck, recently from Canada, boldly proposed that the convention should proceed to nominate not only presidential electors but candidates for State offices as well. A storm of protests broke upon his head, and for the moment he was silenced; but on the second day, he and his confidants succeeded in precipitating a general discussion of the convention system. Peck—contemptuously styled "the Canadian" by his enemies—secured the floor and launched upon a vigorous defense of the nominating convention as a piece of party machinery. He thought it absurd to talk of a man's having a right to become a candidate for office without the indorsement of his party. He believed it equally irrational to allow members of the party to consult personal preferences in voting. The members of the party must submit to discipline, if they expected to secure control of office. Confusion again reigned. The presiding officer left the chair precipitately, denouncing the notions of Peck as anti-republican.[1]

In the exciting wrangle that followed, Douglas was understood to say that he had seen the workings of the nominating convention in New York, and he knew it to be the only way to manage elections successfully. The opposition had overthrown the great DeWitt Clinton only by organizing and adopting the convention system. Gentlemen were mistaken who feared that the people of the West had enjoyed their own opinions too long

[1] Illinois *Advocate*, Dec. 17, 1835; Sangamo *Journal*, Feb. 6, 1836.

to submit quietly to the wise regulations of a convention. He knew them better: he had himself had the honor of introducing the nominating convention into Morgan County, where it had already prostrated one individual high in office. These wise admonitions from a mere stripling failed to mollify the conservatives. The meeting broke up in disorder, leaving the party with divided counsels.[1]

Successful county and district conventions did much to break down the resistance to the system. During the following months, Morgan County, and the congressional district to which it belonged, became a political experiment station. A convention at Jacksonville in April not only succeeded in nominating one candidate for each elective office, but also in securing the support of the disappointed aspirants for office, which under the circumstances was in itself a triumph.[2] Taking their cue from the enemy, the Whigs of Morgan County also united upon a ticket for the State offices, at the head of which was John J. Hardin, a formidable campaigner. When the canvass was fairly under way, not a man could be found on the Democratic ticket to hold his own with Hardin on the hustings. The ticket was then reorganized so as to make a place for Douglas, who was already recognized as one of the ablest debaters in the county. Just how this transposition was effected is not clear. Apparently one of the nominees of the convention for State representative was persuaded to withdraw.[3] The Whigs promptly pointed

---

[1] Sangamo *Journal,* February 6, 1836.

[2] There was one exception, see Sheahan, Douglas, p. 26.

[3] Sheahan, Douglas, p. 26; Wheeler, Biographical History, p. 67; Sangamo *Journal,* May 7, 1836.

out the inconsistency of this performance. "What are good Democrats to do?" asked the Sangamo *Journal* mockingly. Douglas had told them to vote for no man who had not been nominated by a caucus![1]

The Democrats committed also another tactical blunder. The county convention had adjourned without appointing delegates to the congressional district convention, which was to be held at Peoria. Such of the delegates as had remained in town, together with resident Democrats, were hastily reassembled to make good this omission.[2] Douglas and eight others were accredited to the Peoria convention; but when they arrived, they found only four other delegates present, one from each of four counties. Nineteen counties were unrepresented.[3] Evidently there was little or no interest in this political innovation. In no wise disheartened, however, these thirteen delegates declared themselves a duly authorized district convention and put candidates in nomination for the several offices. Again the Whig press scored their opponents. "Our citizens cannot be led at the dictation of a dozen unauthorized individuals, but will act as freemen," said the Sangamo *Journal*.[4] There were stalwart Democrats, too, who refused to put on "the Caucus collar." Douglas and his "Peoria Humbug Convention" were roundly abused on all sides. The young politician might have replied, and doubtless did reply, that the rank and file had not yet become accustomed to the system, and that the bad roads and inclement weather were largely responsible for the slim attendance at Peoria.

---

[1] Sangamo *Journal*, May 7, 1836.
[2] *Ibid.*   [3] *Ibid.*, May 14, 1836.   [4] *Ibid.*

The campaign was fought with the inevitable concomitants of an Illinois election. The weapons that slew the adversary were not always forged by logic. In rude regions, where the rougher border element congregated, country stores were subsidized by candidates, and liquor liberally dispensed. The candidate who refused to treat was doomed. He was the last man to get a hearing, when the crowds gathered on Saturday nights to hear the candidates discuss the questions at issue. To speak from an improvised rostrum—"the stump"—to a boisterous throng of men who had already accepted the orator's hospitality at the store, was no light ordeal. This was the school of oratory in which Douglas was trained.[1]

The election of all but one of the Democratic nominees was hailed as a complete vindication of the nominating convention as a piece of party machinery. Douglas shared the elation of his fellow workers, even though he was made to feel that his nomination was not due to this much-vaunted caucus system. At all events, the value of organization and discipline had been demonstrated. The day of the professional politician and of the machine was dawning in the frontier State of Illinois.

During the campaign there had been much wild talk about internal improvements. The mania which had taken possession of the people in most Western States had affected the grangers of Illinois. It amounted to an obsession. The State was called upon to use its resources and unlimited credit to provide a market for their produce, by supplying transportation facilities for every aspiring community. Elsewhere State credit

[1] Ford, History of Illinois, pp. 103-105.

was building canals and railroads: why should Illinois, so generously endowed by nature, lag behind? Where crops were spoiling for a market, farmers were not disposed to inquire into the mysteries of high finance and the nature of public credit. All doubts were laid to rest by the magic phrase "natural resources."[1] Mass-meetings here and there gave propulsion to the movement.[2] Candidates for State office were forced to make the maddest pledges. A grand demonstration was projected at Vandalia just as the legislature assembled.

The legislature which met in December, 1836, is one of the most memorable, and least creditable, in the annals of Illinois. In full view of the popular demonstrations at the capital, the members could not remained unmoved and indifferent to the demands of their constituents, if they wished. Besides, the great majority were already committed in favor of internal improvements in some form. The subject dwarfed all others. For a time two sessions a day were held; and special committees prolonged their labors far into the night. Petitions from every quarter deluged the assembly.[3]

A plan for internal improvements had already taken shape in the mind of the young representative from Morgan County.[4] He made haste to lay it before his colleagues. First of all, he would have the State complete the Illinois and Michigan canal, and improve the navigation of the Illinois and Wabash rivers. Then

[1] See letter of "M—" in the Illinois *State Register*, July 29, 1836.
[2] Illinois *State Register*, October 28, 1836.
[3] *Ibid.*, December 8, 1836.
[4] Sheahan, Douglas, p. 29; MS. Autobiography.

he would have two railroads constructed which would cross the State from north to south, and from east to west. For these purposes he would negotiate a loan, pledging the credit of the State, and meet the interest payments by judicious sales of the public lands which had been granted by the Federal government for the construction of the Illinois and Michigan canal. The most creditable feature of these proposals is their moderation. This youth of twenty-three evinced far more conservatism than many colleagues twice his age.

There was not the slightest prospect, however, that moderate views would prevail. Log-rolling had already begun; the lobby was active; and every member of the legislature who had pledged himself to his constituents was solicitous that his section of the State should not be passed over, in the general scramble for appropriations. In the end a bill was drawn, which proposed to appropriate no less than $10,230,000 for public works. A sum of $500,000 was set aside for river improvements, but the remainder was to be expended in the construction of eight railroads. A sop of $200,000 was tossed to those counties through which no canal or railroad was to pass.[1] What were prudent men to do? Should they support this bill, which they believed to be thoroughly pernicious, or incur the displeasure of their constituents by defeating this, and probably every other, project for the session? Douglas was put in a peculiarly trying position. He had opposed this "mammoth bill," but he knew his constituents favored it. With great reluctance, he voted for

[1] Act of February 27, 1837.

the bill.[1] He was not minded to immolate himself on the altar of public economy at the very threshold of his career.[2]

Much the same issue was forced upon Douglas in connection with the Illinois and Michigan canal. Unexpected obstacles to the construction of the canal had been encountered. To allow the waters of Lake Michigan to flow through the projected canal, it was found that a cut eighteen feet deep would have to be made for twenty-eight miles through solid rock. The cost of such an undertaking would exceed the entire appropriation. It was then suggested that a shallow cut might be made above the level of Lake Michigan which would then permit the Calumet River or the Des Plaines, to be used as a feeder. The problem was one for expert engineers to solve; but it devolved upon an ignorant assembly, which seems to have done its best to reduce the problem to a political equation. A majority of the House—Douglas among them—favored a shallow cut, while the Senate voted for the deep cut. The deadlock continued for some weeks, until a conference committee succeeded in agreeing upon the Senate's programme. As a member of the conferring committee, Douglas vigorously opposed this settlement, but on the final vote in the House he yielded his convictions. In after years he took great satisfaction in pointing out—as evidence of his prescience—that the State became financially

---

[1] In his Autobiography Douglas says that the friends of the bill persuaded his constituents to instruct him to vote for the bill; hence his affirmative vote was the vote of his constituents.

[2] Douglas was in good company at all events. Abraham Lincoln was one of those who voted for the bill.

embarrassed and had finally to adopt the shallow cut.[1]

The members of the 10th General Assembly have not been wont to point with pride to their record. With a few notable exceptions they had fallen victims to a credulity which had become epidemic. When the assembly of 1840 repealed this magnificent act for the improvement of Illinois, they encountered an accumulated indebtedness of over $14,000,000. There are other aspects of the assembly of 1836-37 upon which it is pleasanter to dwell.

As chairman of a committee on petitions Douglas rendered a real service to public morality. The general assembly had been wont upon petition to grant divorces by special acts. Before the legislature had been in session ten days, no less than four petitions for divorces had been received. It was a custom reflecting little credit upon the State.[2] Reporting for his committee, Douglas contended that the legislature had no power to grant divorces, but only to enact salutary laws, which should state the circumstances under which divorces might be granted by the courts. The existing practice, he argued, was contrary to those provisions of the constitution which expressly separated the three departments of government. Moreover, everyone recognized the injustice and unwisdom of dissolving marriage contracts by act of legislature, upon *ex parte* evidence.[3] Without expressing an opinion on the constitutional questions involved, the assembly accepted the main recommendation of the committee, that hence-

[1] See Davidson and Stuvé, History of Illinois, Chapter 40; Wheeler, Biographical History, pp. 68-70; Sheahan, Douglas, pp. 32-33.

[2] But it was no worse than the English custom before the Act of 1857.

[3] House Journal, p. 62.

forth the legislature should not grant bills of divorce.[1]

One of the recurring questions during this session was whether the State capital should be moved. Vandalia was an insignificant town, difficult of access and rapidly falling far south of the center of population in the State. Springfield was particularly desirous to become the capital, though there were other towns which had claims equally strong. The Sangamon County delegation was annoyingly aggressive in behalf of their county seat. They were a conspicuous group, not merely because of their stature, which earned for them the nickname of "the Long Nine," but also because they were men of real ability and practical shrewdness. By adroit management, a vote was first secured to move the capital from Vandalia, and then to locate it at Springfield. Unquestionably there was some trading of votes in return for special concessions in the Internal Improvements bill. It is said that Abraham Lincoln was the virtual head of the Sangamon delegation, and the chief promoter of the project.[2]

Soon after the adjournment of the legislature, Douglas resigned his seat to become Register of the Land Office at Springfield; and when "the Long Nine" returned to their constituents and were fêted and banqueted by the grateful citizens of Springfield, Douglas sat among the guests of honor.[3] It began to be rumored about that the young man owed his appointment to the Sangamon delegation, whose schemes he had industriously furthered in the legislature.

---

[1] The assembly substituted the word "inexpedient" for "unconstitutional," in the resolution submitted by Douglas. House Journal, p. 62.

[2] Nicolay and Hay, Abraham Lincoln, I, pp. 137-138.

[3] *Ibid.*, p. 139.

Finally, the Illinois *Patriot* made the direct accusation of bargain.[1] Touched to the quick, Douglas wrote a letter to the editor which fairly bristles with righteous indignation. His circumstantial denial of the charge,—his well-known opposition to the removal of the capital and to all the schemes of the Sangamon delegation during the session,—cleared him of all complicity. Indeed, Douglas was too zealous a partisan to play into the hands of the Sangamon Whigs.[2]

The advent of the young Register at the Land Office was noted by the Sangamo Whig *Journal* in these words: "The Land Office at this place was opened on Monday last. We are told the *little man* from Morgan was perfectly astonished, at finding himself making money at the rate of from one to two hundred dollars a day!"[3] This sarcastic comment is at least good evidence that the office was doing a thriving business. In two respects Douglas had bettered himself by this change of occupation. He could not afford to hold his seat in the legislature with its small salary. Now he was assured of a competence. Besides, as a resident of Springfield, he could keep in touch with politics at the future capital and bide his time until he was again promoted for conspicuous service to his party.

The educative value of his new office was no small consideration to the young lawyer. He not only kept the records and plans of surveys within his district, but put up each tract at auction, in accordance with

[1] Transactions of the Illinois State Historical Society, 1901, p. 111.

[2] Transactions of the Illinois State Historical Society, 1901, pp. 111-112. The Sangamo *Journal*, August 5, 1837, says that Douglas owed his appointment to the efforts of Senator Young in his behalf.

[3] Sangamo *Journal*, August 29, 1837.

the proclamation of the President, and issued certificates of sale to all purchasers, describing the land purchased. The duties were not onerous, but they required considerable familiarity with land laws and with the practical difficulties arising from imperfect surveys, pre-emption rights, and conflicting claims.[1] Daily contact with the practical aspects of the public land policy of the country, seems to have opened his eyes to the significance of the public domain as a national asset. With all his realism, Douglas was gifted with a certain sort of imagination in things political. He not only saw what was obvious to the dullest clerk,—the revenue derived from land sales,—but also those intangible and prospective gains which would accrue to State and nation from the occupation and cultivation of the national domain. He came to believe that, even if not a penny came into the treasury, the government would still be richer from having parcelled out the great uninhabited wastes in the West. Beneath the soiled and uncomely exterior of the Western pioneer, native or foreigner, Douglas discerned not only a future tax-bearer, but the founder of Commonwealths.

Only isolated bits of tradition throw light upon the daily life of the young Register of the Land Office. All point to the fact that politics was his absorbing interest. He had no avocations; he had no private life, no esoteric tastes which invite a prying curiosity; he had no subtle aspects of character and temperament which sometimes make even commonplace lives dramatic. His life was lived in the open. Lodging at the

[1] Douglas describes his duties in Cutts, Const. and Party Questions, pp. 160 ff.

American Tavern, he was always seen in company with other men. Diller's drug-store, near the old market, was a familiar rendezvous for him and his boon companions. Just as he had no strong interests which were not political, so his intimates were likely to be his political confrères. He had no literary tastes: if he read at all, he read law or politics.[1] Yet while these characteristics suggest narrowness, they were perhaps the inevitable outcome of a society possessing few cultural resources and refinements, but tremendous directness of purpose.

One of the haunts of Douglas in these Springfield days was the office of the *Republican,* a Democratic journal then edited by the Webers. There he picked up items of political gossip and chatted with the chance comer, or with habitués like himself. He was a welcome visitor, just the man whom a country editor, mauling over hackneyed matter, likes to have stimulate his flagging wits with a jest or a racy anecdote. Now and then Douglas would take up a pen good-naturedly, and scratch off an editorial which would set Springfield politicians by the ears. The tone of the *Republican,* as indeed of the Western press generally at this time, was low. Editors of rival newspapers heaped abuse upon each other, without much regard to either truth or decency. Feuds were the inevitable product of these editorial amenities.

On one occasion, the *Republican* charged the commissioners appointed to supervise the building of the new State House in Springfield, with misuse of the public funds. The commissioners made an apparently

[1] Conversation with Charles A. Keyes, Esq., of Springfield, and with Dr. A. W. French, also of Springfield, Illinois.

straightforward defense of their expenditures. The
Republican doubted the statement and reiterated the
charge in scurrilous language. Then the aggrieved
commissioners, accompanied by their equally exasperated friends, descended upon the office of the *Republican* to take summary vengeance. It so happened that
Douglas was at the moment comfortably ensconced in
the editorial sanctum. He could hardly do otherwise
than assist in the defense; indeed, it is more than
likely that he had provoked the assault. In the disgraceful brawl that followed, the attacking party was
beaten off with heavy losses. Sheriff Elkins, who
seems to have been acting in an unofficial capacity as a
friend of the commissioners, was stabbed, though not
fatally, by one of the Weber brothers.[1]

From such unedifying episodes in the career of a
rising politician, public attention was diverted by the
excitement of a State election. Since the abortive
attempts to commit the Democratic party to the convention system in 1835, party opinion had grown more
favorable to the innovation. Rumors that the Whigs
were about to unite upon a State ticket doubtless
hastened the conversion of many Democrats.[2] When
the legislature met for a special session in July, the
leading spirits in the reform movement held frequent
consultations, the outcome of which was a call for a
Democratic State convention in December. Every
county was invited to send delegates. A State committee of fifteen was appointed, and each county was

---

[1] Sangamo *Journal,* July 1, 1837. The newspaper accounts of this
affair are confusing; but they are in substantial agreement as to the
causes and outcome of the attack upon the office of the *Republican.*

[2] Illinois *State Register,* July 22, 1837.

urged to form a similar committee. Another committee was also created—the Committee of Thirty—to prepare an address to the voters. Fifth on this latter committee was the name of S. A. Douglas of Sangamon.[1] The machinery of the party was thus created out of hand by a group of unauthorized leaders. They awaited the reaction of the insoluble elements in the party, with some anxiety.

The new organization had no more vigilant defender than Douglas. From his coign of vantage in the Land Office, he watched the trend of opinion within the party, not forgetting to observe at the same time the movements of the Whigs. There were certain phrases in the "Address to the Democratic Republicans of Illinois" which may have been coined in his mint. The statement that "the Democratic Republicans of Illinois propose to bring theirs [their candidates] forward by the full and consentaneous voice of every member of their political association," has a familiar, full-mouthed quality.[2] The Democrats of Sangamon called upon him to defend the caucus at a mass-meeting; and when they had heard his eloquent exposition of the new System, they resolved with great gravity that it offered "the only safe and proper way of securing union and victory."[3] There is something amusing in the confident air of this political expert aged twenty-four; yet there is no disputing the fact that his words carried weight with men of far wider experience than his own.

Before many weeks of the campaign had passed, Douglas had ceased to be merely a consultative spe-

[1] Illinois *State Register,* July 22, 1837.
[2] *Ibid.,* November 4, 1837.   [3] *Ibid.,* October 27, 1837.

cialist on party ailments. Not at all unwillingly, he was drawn into active service. It was commonly supposed that the Honorable William L. May, who had served a term in Congress acceptably, would again become the nominee of the Democratic party without opposition. If the old-time practice prevailed, he would quietly assume the nomination "at the request of many friends." Still, consistency required that the nomination should be made in due form by a convention. The Springfield *Republican* clamored for a convention; and the Jacksonville *News* echoed the cry.[1] Other Democratic papers took up the cry, until by general agreement a congressional district convention was summoned to meet at Peoria. The Jacksonville *News* was then ready with a list of eligible candidates among whom Douglas was mentioned. At the same time the enterprising Brooks announced "authoritatively" that *if* Mr. May concluded to become a candidate, he would submit his claims to the consideration of the convention.[2] This was the first intimation that the gentleman's claims were likely to be contested in the convention. Meantime, good friends in Sangamon County saw to it that the county delegation was made up of men who were favorably disposed toward Douglas, and bound them by instructions to act as a unit in the convention.[3]

The history of the district convention has never been written: it needs no historian. Under the circumstances the outcome was a foregone conclusion. Not all the counties were represented; some were

---

[1] Illinois *State Register*, October 13, 1837.

[2] Jacksonville *News*, quoted by Illinois *State Register*, Oct. 13, 1837.

[3] Illinois *State Register*, October 27, 1837.

poorly represented; most of the delegates came without any clearly defined aims; all were unfamiliar with the procedure of conventions. The Sangamon County delegation alone, with the possible exception of that from Morgan County, knew exactly what it wanted. When a ballot was taken, Douglas received a majority of votes cast, and was declared to be the regular nominee of the party for Congress.[1]

There was much shaking of heads over this machine-made nomination. An experienced public servant had been set aside to gratify the ambition of a mere stripling. Even Democrats commented freely upon the untrustworthiness of a device which left nominations to the caprice of forty delegates representing only fourteen counties out of thirty-five.[2] The Whigs made merry over the folly of their opponents. "No nomination could suit us better," declared the Sangamo Journal.[3]

The Democratic State convention met at the appointed time, and again new methods prevailed. In spite of strong opposition, a slate was made up and proclaimed as the regular ticket of the party. Unhappily, the nominee for governor fell under suspicion as an alleged defaulter to the government, so that his deposition became imperative.[4] The Democrats were in a sorry plight. Defeat stared them in the face. There was but one way to save the situation, and that was to call a second convention. This was done. On June 5th, a new ticket was put in the field, without further

---

[1] Illinois *State Register*, December 9, 1837; Sangamo *Journal*, November 25, 1837.

[2] Sangamo *Journal*, November 25, 1837; but see also Peoria *Register*, November 25, 1837. [3] *Ibid.* [4] See Illinois *State Register*, May 11, 1838.

mention of the discredited nominee of the earlier convention.[1] It so happened that Carlin, the nominee for Governor, and McRoberts, candidate for Congress from the first district, were receivers in land offices. This "Land Office Ticket" became a fair mark for wags in the Whig party.[2]

In after years, Douglas made his friends believe that he accepted the nomination with no expectation of success: his only purpose was to "consolidate the party."[3] If this be true, his buoyant optimism throughout the canvass is admirable. He was pitted against a formidable opponent in the person of Major John T. Stuart, who had been the candidate of the Whigs two years before. Stuart enjoyed great popularity. He was "an old resident" of Springfield,—as Western people then reckoned time. He had earned his title in the Black Hawk War, since which he had practiced law. For the arduous campaign, which would range over thirty-four counties,—from Calhoun, Morgan and Sangamon on the south to Cook County on the north,—Stuart was physically well-equipped.[4]

Douglas was eager to match himself against Stuart. They started off together, in friendly rivalry. As they rode from town to town over much the same route, they often met in joint debate; and at night, striking a truce, they would on occasion, when inns were few and far between, occupy the same quarters. Accommodations were primitive in the wilderness of the northern

---

[1] Illinois *State Register,* June 8, 1838.

[2] Sangamo *Journal,* July 21, 1838.

[3] Wheeler, Biographical History of Congress I, pp. 72-73; Sheahan, Douglas, p. 36.

[4] Sheahan, Douglas, pp. 36-37; Transactions of the Illinois State Historical Society, 1902, pp. 109 ff; Peoria *Register,* May 19, 1838.

counties. An old resident relates how he was awakened one night by the landlord of the tavern, who insisted that he and his companion should share their beds with two belated travelers. The late arrivals turned out to be Douglas and Stuart. Douglas asked the occupants of the beds what their politics were, and on learning that one was a Whig and the other a Democrat, he said to Stuart, "Stuart, you sleep with the Whig, and I'll sleep with the Democrat."[1]

Douglas never seemed conscious of the amusing discrepancy between himself and his rival in point of physique. Stuart was fully six feet tall and heavily built, so that he towered like a giant above his boyish competitor. Yet strange to relate, the exposure to all kinds of weather, the long rides, and the incessant speaking in the open air through five weary months, told on the robust Stuart quite as much as on Douglas. In the midst of the canvass Douglas found his way to Chicago. He must have been a forlorn object. His horse, his clothes, his boots, and his hat were worn out. His harness was held together only by ropes and strings. Yet he was still plucky. And so his friends fitted him out again and sent him on his way rejoicing.[2]

The rivals began the canvass good-naturedly, but both gave evidence of increasing irritability as the summer wore on. Shortly before the election, they met in joint debate at Springfield, in front of the Market House. In the course of his speech, Douglas used language that offended his big opponent. Stuart then promptly tucked Douglas's head under his arm, and carried him *hors de combat* around the square. In his

[1] Palmer, Personal Recollections, p. 24.
[2] Forney, Anecdotes of Public Men, II, p. 180.

efforts to free himself, Douglas seized Stuart's thumb in his mouth and bit it vigorously, so that Stuart carried a scar, as a memento of the occasion, for many a year.[1]

As the canvass advanced, the assurance of the Whigs gave way to ill-disguised alarm. Disquieting rumors of Douglas's popularity among some two thousand Irishmen, who were employed on the canal excavation, reached the Whig headquarters.[2] The young man was assiduously cultivating voters in the most inaccessible quarters. He was a far more resourceful campaigner than his older rival.

The election in August was followed by weeks of suspense. Both parties claimed the district vociferously. The official count finally gave the election to Stuart by a majority of thirty-five, in a total vote of over thirty-six thousand.[3] Possibly Douglas might have successfully contested the election.[4] There were certain discrepancies in the counting of the votes; but he declined to vex Congress with the question, so he said, because similar cases were pending and he could not hope to secure a decision before Congress adjourned. It is doubtful whether this merciful consideration for Congress was uppermost in his mind in the year 1838. The fact is, that Douglas wrote to Senator Thomas H. Benton to ascertain the proper procedure in such cases;[5] and abandoned the notion of

[1] Transactions of the Illinois Historical Society, 1902, p. 110.

[2] Sangamo *Journal*, August 25, 1838; Peoria *Register*, August 11, 1838.

[3] Election returns in the Office of the Secretary of State.

[4] See Sheahan, Douglas, p. 37; also Illinois *State Register*, October 12, 1838.

[5] MS. Letter, Benton to Douglas, October 27, 1838.

carrying his case before Congress, when he learned how costly such a contest would be.[1] He had resigned his position as Register of the Land Office to enter the campaign, and he had now no other resources than his profession.

It was comforting to the wounded pride of the young man to have the plaudits of his own party, at least. He had made a gallant fight; and when Democrats from all over the State met at a dinner in honor of Governor-elect Carlin, at Quincy, they paid him this generous tribute: "Although so far defeated in the election that the certificate will be given to another, yet he has the proud gratification of knowing that the people are with him. His untiring zeal, his firm integrity, and high order of talents, have endeared him to the Democracy of the State and they will remember him two years hence."[2] Meantime there was nothing left for him to do but to solicit a law practice. He entered into partnership with a Springfield attorney by the name of Urquhart.

By the following spring, Douglas was again dabbling in local politics, and by late fall he was fully immersed in the deeper waters of national politics. Preparations for the presidential campaign drew him out of his law office,—where indeed there was nothing to detain him,—and he was once again active in party conclaves. He presided over a Democratic county convention, and lent a hand in the drafting of a platform.[3] In November he was summoned to answer Cyrus Walker,

[1] For correspondence between Douglas and Stuart, see Illinois *State Register*, April 5, 1839.

[2] Illinois *State Register*, October 26, 1838.

[3] *Ibid.*, April 5, 1839.

a Whig who was making havoc of the Democratic programme at a mass-meeting in the Court House. In the absence of any reliable records, nothing more can be said of Douglas's rejoinder than that it moved the Whigs in turn to summon reinforcements, in the person of the awkward but clever Lincoln. The debate was prolonged far into the night; and on which side victory finally folded her wings, no man can tell.[1] Douglas made the stronger impression, though Whigs professed entire satisfaction with the performance of their protagonist. There were some in the audience who took exception to Lincoln's stale anecdotes, and who thought his manner clownish.[2]

Not long after this encounter, Douglas came in for his share of public ridicule. Considering himself insulted by a squib in the Sangamo *Journal,* Douglas undertook to cane the editor. But as Francis was large and rotund, and Douglas was not, the affair terminated unsatisfactorily for the latter. Lincoln described the incident with great relish, in a letter to Stuart: "Francis caught him by the hair and jammed him back against a market-cart, where the matter ended by Francis being pulled away from him. The whole affair was so ludicrous that Francis and everybody else, Douglas excepted, have been laughing about it ever since."[3] The Illinois *State Register* tried to save Douglas's dignity by the following account of the rencontre: "Mr. Francis had applied scurrilous language to Mr. Douglas, which could be noticed in no other way. Mr. Douglas, therefore, gave him a sound caning, which Mr. Francis took with Abolition patience, and is now

---

[1] Illinois *State Register*, November 23, 1839.   [2] *Ibid.*
[3] Nicolay and Hay, Lincoln, I, p. 181.

praising God that he was neither killed nor scathed.''

The executive talents of Douglas were much in demand. First he was made a member of the Sangamon County delegation to the State convention;[1] then chairman of the State Central Committee; and finally, virtual manager of the Democratic campaign in Illinois.[2] He was urged to stand for election to the legislature; but he steadily refused this nomination. ''Considerations of a private nature,'' he wrote, ''constrain me to decline the nomination, and leave the field to those whose avocations and private affairs will enable them to devote the requisite portion of their time to the canvass.''[3] Inasmuch as Sangamon County usually sent a Whig delegation to the legislature, this declination could hardly have cost him many hours of painful deliberation.[4] At all events his avocations did not prevent him from making every effort to carry the State for the Democratic party.

An unfortunate legal complication had cost the Democrats no end of worry. Hitherto the party had counted safely on the vote of the aliens in the State; that is, actual inhabitants whether naturalized or not.[5] The right of unnaturalized aliens to vote had never been called in question. But during the campaign, two Whigs of Galena instituted a collusive suit to test the rights of aliens, hoping, of course, to embarrass their opponents.[6] The Circuit Court had

[1] Illinois *State Register*, November 23, 1839.
[2] *Ibid.*, February 21, 1840.
[3] *Ibid.*, April 24, 1840.
[4] See Illinois *State Register*, August 7, 1840.
[5] The Constitution of 1819 bestowed the suffrage upon every white male ''inhabitant'' twenty-one years of age.
[6] Sheahan, Douglas, pp. 44-45.

already decided the case adversely, when Douglas assumed direction of the campaign. If the decision were allowed to stand, the Democratic ticket would probably lose some nine thousand votes and consequently the election. The case was at once appealed.[1] Douglas and his old friend and benefactor, Murray McConnell, were retained as counsel for the appellant. The opposing counsel were Whigs. The case was argued in the winter term of the Supreme Court, but was adjourned until the following June, a scant six months before the elections.

It was regrettable that a case, which from its very nature was complicated by political considerations, should have arisen in the midst of a campaign of such unprecedented excitement as that of 1840. It was taken for granted, on all sides, that the judges would follow their political predilections—and what had Democrats to expect from a bench of Whigs? The counsel for the appellant strained every nerve to secure another postponement. Fortune favored the Democrats. When the court met in June, Douglas, prompted by Judge Smith, the only Democrat on the bench, called attention to clerical errors in the record, and on this technicality moved that the case be dismissed. Protracted arguments *pro and con* ensued, so that the whole case finally was adjourned until the next term of court in November, after the election.[2] Once more, at all events, the Democrats could count on the alien vote. Did ever lawyer serve politician so well?

[1] The title of the case was Thomas Spraggins, appellant *vs.* Horace H. Houghton, appellee.

[2] Sheahan, Douglas, pp. 45-46; Wheeler, Biographical History of Congress, p. 76.

As Chairman of the State Central Committee, Douglas had no perfunctory position. The Whigs were displaying unusual aggressiveness. Their leaders were adroit politicians and had taken a leaf from Democratic experience in the matter of party organization. The processions, the torch-light parades, the barbecues and other noisy demonstrations of the Whigs, were very disconcerting. Such performances could not be lightly dismissed as "Whig Humbuggery," for they were alarmingly effective in winning votes. In self-defense, the Democratic managers were obliged to set on foot counter-demonstrations. On the whole, the Democrats were less successful in manufacturing enthusiasm. When one convention of young Democrats failed, for want of support, Douglas saved the situation only by explaining that hard-working Democrats could not leave their employment to go gadding. They preferred to leave noise and sham to their opponents, knowing that in the end "the quiet but certain influence of truth and correct principles" would prevail.[1] And when the Whigs unwittingly held a great demonstration for "Tippecanoe and Tyler too," on the birthday of King George III, Douglas saw to it that an address was issued to voters, warning them against the chicane of unpatriotic demagogues. As a counter-blast, "All Good Democrats" were summoned to hold mass-meetings in the several counties on the Fourth of July. "We select the Fourth of July," read this pronunciamento, "not to desecrate it with unhallowed shouts . . . . but in cool and calm devotion to our country, to renew upon the altars of its liberties, a sacred oath of fidelity to its principles."[2]

[1] Illinois *State Register*, May 15, 1840.   [2] *Ibid.*, June 12, 1840.

Both parties now drew upon their reserves. Douglas went to the front whenever and wherever there was hard fighting to be done.[1] He seemed indefatigable. Once again he met Major Stuart on the platform.[2] He was pitted against experienced campaigners like ex-Governor Duncan and General Ewing of Indiana. Douglas made a fearless defence of Democratic principles in a joint debate with both these Whig champions at Springfield.[3] The discussion continued far into the night. In his anxiety to let no point escape, Douglas had his supper brought to him; and it is the testimony of an old Whig who heard the debate, that Duncan was "the worst used-up man" he ever saw.[4] Whether Douglas took the field as on this occasion, or directed the campaign from headquarters, he was cool, collected, and resourceful. If the sobriquet of "the Little Giant" had not already been fastened upon him, it was surely earned in this memorable campaign of 1840. The victory of Van Buren over Harrison in Illinois was little less than a personal triumph for Douglas, for Democratic reverses elsewhere emphasized the already conspicuous fact that Illinois had been saved only by superior organization and leadership.

[1] Illinois *State Register*, July 10, 1840; Forney, Anecdotes of Public Men, II, p. 180.

[2] *Ibid.*, September 4, 1840.　　　[3] *Ibid.*, October 2, 1840.

[4] Letter of J. H. Roberts, Esq., of Chicago, to the writer; see also Illinois *State Register*, October 2, 1840.

CHAPTER III

Law and Politics

The years were passing rapidly during which Douglas should have laid broad and deep the foundations of his professional career, if indeed law was to be more than a convenient avocation. These were formative years in the young man's life; but as yet he had developed neither the inclination nor the capacity to apply himself to the study of the more intricate and abstruse phases of jurisprudence. To be sure, he had picked up much practical information in the courts, but it was not of the sort which makes great jurists. Besides, his law practice had been, and was always destined to be, the handmaid of his political ambition. In such a school, a naturally ardent, impulsive temperament does not acquire judicial poise and gravity. After all, he was only a soldier of political fortune, awaiting his turn for promotion. A reversal in the fortunes of his party might leave him without hope of preferment, and bind him to a profession which is a jealous mistress, and to which he had been none too constant. Happily, his party was now in power, and he was entitled to first consideration in the distribution of the spoils. Under somewhat exceptional circumstances the office of Secretary of State fell vacant in the autumn of 1840, and the chairman of the Democratic Central Committee entered into his reward.

When Governor Carlin took office in 1838, he sent to the Senate the nomination of John A. McClernand as

Secretary of State, assuming that the office had been vacated and that a new Governor might choose his advisers.[1] Precedent, it is true, militated against this theory, for Secretary Field had held office under three successive governors; but now that parties had become more sharply defined, it was deemed important that the Secretary of State should be of the same political persuasion as the Governor,—and Field was a Whig. The Senate refused to indorse this new theory. Whereupon the Governor waited until the legislature adjourned, and renewed his appointment of McClernand, who promptly brought action against the tenacious Field to obtain possession of the office. The case was argued in the Circuit Court before Judge Breese, who gave a decision in favor of McClernand. The case was then appealed. Among the legal talent arrayed on the side of the claimant, when the case appeared on the docket of the Supreme Court, was Douglas—as a matter of course. Everyone knew that this was not so much a case at law as an issue in politics. The decision of the Supreme Court reversing the judgment of the lower court was received, therefore, as a partisan move to protect a Whig office-holder.[2]

For a time the Democrats, in control elsewhere, found themselves obliged to tolerate a dissident in their political family; but the Democratic majority in the new legislature came promptly to the aid of the Governor's household. Measures were set on foot to terminate Secretary Field's tenure of office by legislative enactment. Just at this juncture that gentleman prudently resigned; and Stephen A. Douglas was ap-

[1] Ford, History of Illinois, pp. 213-214.
[2] Davidson and Stuvé, History of Illinois, pp. 454-455.

pointed to the office which he had done his best to vacate.[1]

This appointment was a boon to the impecunious young attorney. He could now count on a salary which would free him from any concern about his financial liabilities,—if indeed they ever gave him more than momentary concern. Besides, as custodian of the State Library, he had access to the best collection of law books in the State. The duties of his office were not so exacting but that he could still carry on his law studies, and manage such incidental business as came his way. These were the obvious and tangible advantages which Douglas emphasized in the mellow light of recollection.[2] Yet there were other, less obvious, advantages which he omitted to mention.

The current newspapers of this date make frequent mention of an institution popularly dubbed "the Third House," or "Lord Coke's Assembly."[3] The archives of state do not explain this unique institution. Its location was in the lobby of the State House. Like many another extra-legal body it kept no records of its proceedings; yet it wielded a potent influence. It was attended regularly by those officials who made the lobby a rendezvous; irregularly, by politicians who came to the Capitol on business; and on pressing occasions, by members of the legislature who wished to catch the undertone of party opinion. The debates in this Third House often surpassed in interest the formal proceedings behind closed doors across the

[1] Why McClernand was passed over is not clear. Douglas entered upon the duties of his office November 30, 1840.

[2] Wheeler, Biographical History of Congress, p. 74.

[3] Sheahan, Douglas, p. 43.

corridor. Members of this house were not held to rigid account for what they said. Many a political *coup* was plotted in the lobby. The grist which came out of the legislative mill was often ground by irresponsible politicians out of hearing of the Speaker of the House. The chance comer was quite as likely to find the Secretary of State in the lobby as in his office among his books.

The lobby was a busy place in this winter session of 1840-41. It was well known that Democratic leaders had planned an aggressive reorganization of the Supreme Court, in anticipation of an adverse decision in the famous Galena alien case. The Democratic programme was embodied in a bill which proposed to abolish the existing Circuit Courts, and to enlarge the Supreme Court by the addition of five judges. Circuit Courts were to be held by the nine judges of the Supreme Court.[1] Subsequent explanations did not, and could not, disguise the real purpose of this chaste reform.[2]

While this revolutionary measure was under fire in the legislature and in the Third House, the Supreme Court rendered its opinion in the alien case. To the amazement of the reformers, the decision did not touch the broad, constitutional question of the right of aliens to vote, but simply the concrete, particular question arising under the Election Law of 1829.[3] Judge Smith alone dissented and argued the larger issue. The admirable self-restraint of the Court, so far from stopping the mouths of detractors, only excited more unfavorable comment. The suspicion

[1] Ford, History of Illinois, p. 217.   [2] *Ibid.*, pp. 212-222.
[3] Davidson and Stuvé, History of Illinois, p. 456.

of partisanship, sedulously fed by angry Democrats, could not be easily eradicated. The Court was now condemned for its contemptible evasion of the real question at issue.

Douglas made an impassioned speech to the lobby, charging the Court with having deliberately suppressed its decision on the paramount issue, in order to disarm criticism and to avert the impending reorganization of the bench.[1] He called loudly for the passage of the bill before the legislature; and the lobby echoed his sentiments. McClernand in the House corroborated this charge by stating, "under authorization," that the judges had withdrawn the opinion which they had prepared in June.[2] Thereupon four of the five judges made an unqualified denial of the charge.[3] McClernand fell back helplessly upon the word of Douglas. Pushed into a corner, Douglas then stated publicly, that he had made his charges against the Court on the explicit information given to him privately by Judge Smith. Six others testified that they had been similarly informed, or misinformed, by the same high authority.[4] At all events, the mischief had been done. Under the party whip the bill to reorganize the Supreme Court was driven through both houses of the legislature, and unofficially ratified by Lord Coke's Assembly in the lobby.

[1] Illinois *State Register*, January 29, 1841; Ford, History of Illinois, p. 220.

[2] Davidson and Stuvé, History of Illinois, pp. 457-458.

[3] *Ibid.*, pp. 457-458.

[4] Illinois *State Register*, February 5, 1841. Judge Smith is put in an unenviable light by contemporary historians. There seems to be no reason to doubt that he misinformed Douglas and others. See Davidson and Stuvé, History of Illinois, pp. 458-459.

Already it was noised abroad that Douglas was "slated" for one of the newly created judgeships. The Whig press ridiculed the suggestion but still frankly admitted, that if party services were to qualify for such an appointment, the "Generalessimo of the Loco-focos of Illinois" was entitled to consideration. When rumor passed into fact, and Douglas was nominated by the Governor, even Democrats demurred. It required no little generosity on the part of older men who had befriended the young man, to permit him to pass over their heads in this fashion.[1] Besides, what legal qualifications could this young man of twenty-seven possess for so important a post?

The new judges entered upon their duties under a cloud. Almost their first act was to vacate the clerkship of the court, for the benefit of that arch-politician, Ebenezer Peck; and that, too,—so men said,—without consulting their Whig associates on the bench. It was commonly reported that Peck had changed his vote in the House just when one more vote was needed to pass the Judiciary Bill.[2] Very likely this rumor was circulated by some malicious newsmonger, but the appointment of Peck certainly did not inspire confidence in the newly organized court.

Was it to make his ambition seem less odious, that Douglas sought to give the impression that he accepted the appointment with reluctance and at a "pecuniary sacrifice"; or was he, as Whigs maintained, forced out of the Secretaryship of State to make way for one of the Governor's favorites?[3] He could not have been

[1] Chicago *American*, February 18, 1841.
[2] Sangamo *Journal*, March 19, 1841.
[3] Chicago *American*, February 18, 1841.

perfectly sincere, at all events, when he afterward declared that he supposed he was taking leave of political life forever.[1] No one knew better than he, that a popular judge is a potential candidate for almost any office in the gift of the people.

Before starting out on his circuit Douglas gave conspicuous proof of his influence in the lobby, and incidentally, as it happened, cast bread upon the waters. The Mormons who had recently settled in Nauvoo, in Hancock County, had petitioned the legislature for acts incorporating the new city and certain of its peculiar institutions. Their sufferings in Missouri had touched the people of Illinois, who welcomed them as a persecuted sect. For quite different reasons, Mormon agents were cordially received at the Capitol. Here their religious tenets were less carefully scrutinized than their political affiliations. The Mormons found little trouble in securing lobbyists from both parties. Bills were drawn to meet their wishes and presented to the legislature, where parties vied with each other in befriending the unfortunate refugees from Missouri.[2]

Chance—or was it design?—assigned Judge Douglas to the Quincy circuit, within which lay Hancock County and the city of Nauvoo. The appointment was highly satisfactory to the Mormons, for while they enjoyed a large measure of local autonomy by virtue of their new charter, they deemed it advantageous to have the court of the vicinage presided over by one who had proved himself a friend. Douglas at once confirmed this good impression. He appointed the commander

---

[1] Wheeler, Biographical History of Congress, p. 74.

[2] Ford, History of Illinois, pp. 263-265; Linn, Story of the Mormons, pp. 236-237.

of the Nauvoo Legion a master in chancery; and when
a case came before him which involved interpretation
of the act incorporating this peculiar body of militia,
he gave a constructive interpretation which left the
Mormons independent of State officers in military
affairs.[1] Whatever may be said of this decision in
point of law, it was at least good politics; and the
dividing line between law and politics was none too
sharply drawn in the Fifth Judicial District.

Politicians were now figuring on the Mormon vote
in the approaching congressional election. The Whigs
had rather the better chance of winning their support,
if the election of 1840 afforded any basis for calcula-
tion, for the Mormons had then voted *en bloc* for Harrison and Tyler.[2] Stuart was a candidate for re-election. It was generally believed that Ralston, whom the
Democrats pitted against him, had small chance of
success. Still, Judge Douglas could be counted on
to use his influence to procure the Mormon vote.

Undeterred by his position on the bench, Douglas
paid a friendly visit to the Mormon city in the course
of the campaign; and there encountered his old Whig
opponent, Cyrus Walker, Esq., who was also on a mission. Both made public addresses of a flattering description. The Prophet, Joseph Smith, was greatly
impressed with Judge Douglas's friendliness. "Judge
Douglas," he wrote to the Faithful, "has ever proved
himself friendly to this people; and interested himself to obtain for us our several charters, holding at
the same time the office of Secretary of State." But
what particularly flattered the Mormon leader, was the

[1] Linn, Story of the Mormons, pp. 237-238.
[2] *Ibid.*, p. 244.

edifying spectacle of representatives from both parties laying aside all partisan motives to mingle with the Saints, as "brothers, citizens, and friends."[1] This touching account would do for Mormon readers, but Gentiles remained somewhat skeptical.

In spite of this coquetting with the Saints, the Democratic candidate suffered defeat. It was observed with alarm that the Mormons held the balance of power in the district, and might even become a makeweight in the State elections, should they continue to increase in numbers.[2] The Democrats braced themselves for a new trial of strength in the gubernatorial contest. The call for a State convention was obeyed with alacrity;[3] and the outcome justified the high expectations which were entertained of this body. The convention nominated for governor, Adam W. Snyder, whose peculiar availability consisted in his having fathered the Judiciary Bill and the several acts which had been passed in aid of the Mormons. The practical wisdom of this nomination was proved by a communication of Joseph Smith to the official newspaper of Nauvoo. The pertinent portion of this remarkable manifesto read as follows: "The partisans in this county who expected to divide the friends of humanity and equal rights will find themselves mistaken,—we care not a fig for *Whig or Democrat:* they are both alike to us; but we shall go for our *friends,* our TRIED FRIENDS, and the cause of *human liberty* which is the cause of God. . . . DOUGLASS is a *Master Spirit,* and *his friends are our friends*—we are willing to cast our

[1] *Times and Seasons,* II, p. 414.
[2] Illinois *State Register,* August 13, 1841.
[3] *Ibid.,* September 24, 1841.

banners on the air, and fight by his side in the cause
of humanity, and equal rights—the cause of liberty
and the law. SNYDER and MOORE, are *his* friends—they
are *ours* . . . .Snyder, and Moore, are *known* to be our
friends; their friendship is *vouched* for by those whom
we have tried. We will never be justly charged with
the sin of ingratitude—they *have* served us, and we
will serve them.''[1]

This was a discomfiting revelation to the Whigs, who
had certainly labored as industriously as the Democrats, to placate the Saints of Nauvoo. From this
moment the Whigs began a crusade against the Mormons, who were already, it is true, exhibiting the
characteristics which had made them odious to the
people of Missouri.[2] Rightly or wrongly, public
opinion was veering; and the shrewd Duncan, who
headed the Whig ticket, openly charged Douglas with
bargaining for the Mormon vote.[3] The Whigs hoped
that their opponents, having sowed the wind, would
reap the whirlwind.

Only three months before the August elections of
1844, the Democrats were thrown into consternation
by the death of Snyder, their standard-bearer. Here
was an emergency to which the convention system was
not equal, in the days of poor roads and slow stage-
coaches. What happened was this, to borrow the account of the chief Democratic organ, ''A large number
of Democratic citizens from almost all parts of the
State of Illinois met together by a general and public

[1] *Times and Seasons,* III, p. 651.

[2] Ford, History of Illinois, p. 269.

[3] Illinois *State Register,* June 17, 1842. Douglas replied in a speech
of equal tartness. See *Register,* July 1, 1842.

call"—and nominated Judge Thomas Ford for governor.[1] It adds significance to this record to note that this numerous body of citizens met in the snug office of the *State Register*. Democrats in distant parts of the State were disposed to resent this action on the part of "the Springfield clique"; but the onset of the enemy quelled mutiny. In one way the nomination of Ford was opportune. It could not be said of him that he had showed any particular solicitude for the welfare of the followers of Joseph Smith.[2] The ticket could now be made to face both ways. Ford could assure hesitating Democrats who disliked the Mormons, that he had not hobnobbed with the Mormon leaders, while Douglas and his crew could still demonstrate to the Prophet that the cause of human liberty, for which he stood so conspicuously, was safe in Democratic hands. The game was played adroitly. Ford carried Hancock County by a handsome majority and was elected governor.[3]

It has already been remarked that as judge, Douglas was potentially a candidate for almost any public office. He still kept in touch with Springfield politicians, planning with them the moves and countermoves on the checker-board of Illinois politics. There was more than a grain of truth in the reiterated charges of the Whig press, that the Democratic party was dominated by an arbitrary clique.[4] It was a matter of common observation, that before Democratic candidates put to sea in the troubled waters of State

[1] Illinois *State Register*, June 10, 1842.
[2] Ford, History of Illinois, pp. 277-278.
[3] Gregg, History of Hancock County, p. 419.
[4] Illinois *State Register*, November 4, 1842.

politics, they took their dead-reckoning from the office of the *State Register*. It was noised abroad in the late fall that Douglas would not refuse a positive call from his party to enter national politics; and before the year closed, his Springfield intimates were actively promoting his candidacy for the United States Senate, to succeed Senator Young. This was an audacious move, since even if Young were passed over, there were older men far more justly entitled to consideration. Nevertheless, Douglas secured in some way the support of several delegations in the legislature, so that on the first ballot in the Democratic caucus he stood second, receiving only nine votes less than Young. A protracted contest followed. Nineteen ballots were taken. Douglas's chief competitor proved to be, not Young, but Breese, who finally secured the nomination of the caucus by a majority of five votes.[1] The ambition of Judge Douglas had overshot the mark.

In view of the young man's absorbing interest in politics, his slender legal equipment, and the circumstances under which he received his appointment, one wonders whether the courts he held could have been anything but travesties on justice. But the universal testimony of those whose memories go back so far, is that justice was on the whole faithfully administered.[2] The conditions of life in Illinois were still comparatively simple. The suits instituted at law were not such as to demand profound knowledge of jurisprudence. The wide-spread financial distress which followed the crisis of 1837, gave rise to many processes to collect

[1] Illinois *State Register*, December 23, 1842.

[2] Conkling, Recollections of the Bench and Bar, Fergus Historical Series, No. 22.

debts and to set aside fraudulent conveyances. "Actions of slander and trespass for assault and battery, engendered by the state of feeling incident to pecuniary embarrassment, were frequent."[1]

The courts were in keeping with the meagre legal attainments of those who frequented them. Rude frame, or log houses served the purposes of bench and bar. The judge sat usually upon a platform with a plain table, or pine board, for a desk. A larger table below accommodated the attorneys who followed the judge in his circuit from county to county. "The relations between the Bench and the Bar were free and easy, and flashes of wit and humor and personal repartee were constantly passing from one to the other. The court rooms in those days were always crowded. To go to court and listen to the witnesses and lawyers was among the chief amusements of the frontier settlements."[2] In this little world, popular reputations were made and unmade.

Judge Douglas was thoroughly at home in this primitive environment. His freedom from affectation and false dignity recommended him to the laity, while his fairness and good-nature put him in quick sympathy with his legal brethren and their clients. Long years afterward, men recalled the picture of the young judge as he mingled with the crowd during a recess. "It was not unusual to see him come off the bench, or leave his chair at the bar, and take a seat on the knee of a friend, and with one arm thrown familiarly around a friend's neck, have a friendly talk, or a legal or

[1] Conkling, Recollections of the Bench and Bar, Fergus Historical Series, No. 22.

[2] Arnold, Reminiscences of the Illinois Bar, Fergus Historical Series, No. 22.

political discussion.''[1] An attorney recently from the East witnessed this familiarity with dismay. "The judge of our circuit," he wrote, "is S. A. Douglas, a youth of 28 . . . . He is a Vermonter, a man of considerable talent, and, in the way of despatching business, is a perfect 'steam engine in breeches.' . . . He is the most democratic judge I ever knew. . . . I have often thought we should cut a queer figure if one of our Suffolk bar should accidentally drop in."[2]

Meantime, changes were taking place in the political map of Illinois, which did not escape the watchful eye of Judge Douglas. By the census of 1840, the State was entitled to seven, instead of four representatives in Congress.[3] A reapportionment act was therefore to be expected from the next legislature. Democrats were already at work plotting seven Democratic districts on paper, for, with a majority in the legislature, they could redistrict the State at will. A gerrymander was the outcome.[4] If Douglas did not have a hand in the reapportionment, at least his friends saw to it that a desirable district was carved out, which included the most populous counties in his circuit. Who would be a likelier candidate for Congress in this Democratic constituency than the popular judge of the Fifth Circuit Court?

Seven of the ten counties composing the Fifth Congressional District were within the so-called "military tract," between the Mississippi and Illinois rivers;

[1] Arnold, Reminiscences of the Illinois Bar.

[2] Davidson and Stuvé, History of Illinois, p. 698.

[3] Statute of June 25, 1842.

[4] A sheet called *The Gerrymander* was published in March 1843, which contained a series of cartoons exhibiting the monstrosities of this apportionment. The Fifth District is called "the Nondescript."

three counties lay to the east on the lower course of the
Illinois. Into this frontier region population began
to flow in the twenties, from the Sangamo country;
and the organization of county after county attested
the rapid expansion northward. Like the people of
southern Illinois, the first settlers were of Southern
extraction; but they were followed by Pennsylvanians,
New Yorkers, and New Englanders. In the later
thirties, the Northern immigration, to which Douglas
belonged, gave a somewhat different complexion to
Peoria, Fulton, and other adjoining counties. Yet there
were diverse elements in the district: Peoria had a
cosmopolitan population of Irish, English, Scotch, and
German immigrants; Quincy became a city of refuge
for "Young Germany," after the revolutionary disturbances of 1830 in Europe.[1]

No sooner had the reapportionment act passed than
certain members of the legislature, together with
Democrats who held no office, took it upon themselves to
call a nominating convention, on a basis of representation determined in an equally arbitrary fashion.[2] The
summons was obeyed nevertheless. Forty "respect-
able Democats" assembled at Griggsville, in Pike
County, on June 5, 1843. It was a most satisfactory
body. The delegates did nothing but what was expected
of them. On the second ballot, a majority cast their
votes for Douglas as the candidate of the party for
Congress. The other aspirants then graciously with-

[1] Patterson, Early Society in Southern Illinois, Fergus Historical
Series No. 14; Körner, Das deutsche Element in den Vereinigten Staaten,
pp. 245, 277; Baker, America as the Political Utopia of Young Germany; Peoria *Register*, June 30, 1838; Ballance, History of Peoria, pp.
201-202.

[2] Illinois *State Register*, March 10, 1843.

drew their claims, and pledged their cordial support to the regular nominee of the convention.[1] Such machine-like precision warmed the hearts of Democratic politicians. The editor of the *People's Advocate* declared the integrity of Douglas to be "as unspotted as the vestal's fame—as untarnished and as pure as the driven snow."

The Griggsville convention also supplied the requisite machinery for the campaign: vigilant precinct committees; county committees; a district corresponding committee; a central district committee. The party now pinned its faith to the efficiency of its organization, as well as to the popularity of its candidate.

Douglas made a show of declining the nomination on the score of ill-health, but yielded to the urgent solicitations of friends, who would fain have him believe that he was the only Democrat who could carry the district.[2] Secretly pleased to be overruled, Douglas burned his bridges behind him by resigning his office, and plunged into the thick of the battle. His opponent was O. H. Browning, a Kentuckian by birth and a Whig by choice. It was Kentucky against Vermont, South against North, for neither was unwilling to appeal to sectional prejudice. Time has obscured the political issues which they debated from Peoria to Macoupin and back; but history has probably suffered no great loss. Men, not measures, were at stake in this campaign, for on the only national issue which they seemed to have discussed—Oregon—they were in practical agreement.[3] Both cultivated the little arts

[1] Illinois *State Register*, June 16, 1843.

[2] Sheahan, Douglas, p. 55; Wheeler, Biographical History of Congress, p. 75.   [3] *Globe*, 28 Cong. 1 Sess. App. pp. 598 ff.

which relieve the tedium of politics. Douglas talked in heart to heart fashion with his "esteemed fellow-citizens," inquired for the health of their families, expressed grief when he learned that John had the measles and that Sally was down with the chills and fever.[1] And if Browning was less successful in this gentle method of wooing voters, it was because he had less genuine interest in the plain common people, not because he despised the petty arts of the politician.

The canvass was short but exhausting. Douglas addressed public gatherings for forty successive days; and when election day came, he was prostrated by a fever from which he did not fully recover for months.[2] Those who gerrymandered the State did their work well. Only one district failed to elect a Democratic Congressman. Douglas had a majority over Browning of four hundred and sixty-one votes.[3] This cheering news hastened his convalescence, so that by November he was able to visit his mother in Canandaigua. Member of Congress at the age of thirty! He had every reason to be well satisfied with himself. He was fully conscious that he had begun a new chapter in his career.

[1] Alton *Telegraph*, July 20, 1843.

[2] Sheahan, Douglas, p. 56; Wheeler, Biographical History of Congress, p. 75; Alton *Telegraph*, August 26, 1843.

[3] According to the returns in the office of the Secretary of State. The *Whig Almanac* gives 451 as Douglas's majority.

CHAPTER IV

UNDER THE AEGIS OF ANDREW JACKSON

In his own constituency a member of the national House of Representatives may be a marked man; but his office confers no particular distinction at the national capital. He must achieve distinction either by native talent or through fortuitous circumstance; rarely is greatness thrust upon him. A newly elected member labors under a peculiar and immediate necessity to acquire importance, since the time of his probation is very brief. The representative who takes his seat in December of the odd year, must stand for re-election in the following year. Between these termini, lies only a single session. During his absence eager rivals may be undermining his influence at home, and the very possession of office may weaken his chances among those disposed to consider rotation in office a cardinal principle of democracy. If a newly elected congressman wishes to continue in office, he is condemned to do something great.

What qualities had Douglas which would single him out from the crowd and impress his constituents with a sense of his capacity for public service? What had he to offset his youth, his rawness, and his legislative inexperience? None of his colleagues cared a fig about his record in the Illinois Legislature and on the Bench. In Congress, as then constituted, every man had to stand on his own feet, unsupported by the dubious props of a local reputation.

68

There was certainly nothing commanding in the figure of the gentleman from Illinois. "He had a herculean frame," writes a contemporary, "with the exception of his lower limbs, which were short and small, dwarfing what otherwise would have been a conspicuous figure. . . . His large round head surmounted a massive neck, and his features were symmetrical, although his small nose deprived them of dignity."[1] It was his massive forehead, indeed, that redeemed his appearance from the commonplace. Beneath his brow were deep-set, dark eyes that also challenged attention.[2] It was not a graceful nor an attractive exterior surely, but it was the very embodiment of force. Moreover, the Little Giant had qualities of mind and heart that made men forget his physical shortcomings. His ready wit, his suavity, and his heartiness made him a general favorite almost at once.[3] He was soon able to demonstrate his intellectual power.

The House was considering a bill to remit the fine imposed upon General Andrew Jackson at New Orleans for contempt of court. It was a hackneyed theme. No new, extenuating circumstances could be adduced to clear the old warrior of high-handed conduct; but a presidential election was approaching and there was political capital to be made by defending "Old Hickory." From boyhood Douglas had idolized Andrew Jackson. With much the same boyish indignation which led him to tear down the coffin handbills in old Brandon, he now sprang to the defense of his hero. The case had been well threshed already. Jackson

---

[1] Poore, Reminiscences, I, pp. 316-317.

[2] Joseph Wallace in the Illinois *State Register*, April 19, 1885.

[3] Forney, Anecdotes of Public Men, I, p. 146.

had been defended eloquently, and sometimes truthfully. A man of less audacity would have hesitated
to swell this tide of eloquence, and at first, it seemed
as though Douglas had little but vehemence to add to
the eulogies already pronounced. There was nothing
novel in the assertion that Jackson had neither violated the Constitution by declaring martial law at New
Orleans, nor assumed any authority which was not
"fully authorized and legalized by his position, his
duty, and the unavoidable necessity of the case." The
House was used to these dogmatic reiterations. But
Douglas struck into untrodden ways when he contended, that even if Jackson had violated the laws and
the Constitution, his condemnation for contempt of
court was "unjust, irregular and illegal." Every unlawful act is not necessarily a contempt of court, he
argued. "The doctrine of contempts only applies to
those acts which obstruct the proceedings of the court,
and against which the general laws of the land do not
afford adequate protection. . . . It is incumbent upon
those who defend and applaud the conduct of the judge
to point out the specific act done by General Jackson
which constituted a contempt of court. The mere
declaration of martial law is not of that character. . . .
It was a matter over which the civil tribunals had no
jurisdiction, and with which they had no concern, unless some specific crime had been committed or injury
done; and not even then until it was brought before
them according to the forms of law."[1]

The old hero had never had a more adroit counsel.
Like a good lawyer, Douglas seemed to feel himself
in duty bound to spar for every technical advantage,

[1] *Globe,* 28 Cong., 1 Sess., App., p. 44.

and to construe the law, wherever possible, in favor of his client. At the same time he did not forget that the House was the jury in this case, and capable of human emotions upon which he might play. At times he became declamatory beyond the point of good taste. In voice and manner he betrayed the school in which he had been trained. "When I hear gentlemen," he cried in strident tones, "attempting to justify this unrighteous fine upon General Jackson upon the ground of non-compliance with rules of court and mere formalities, I must confess that I cannot appreciate the force of the argument. In cases of war and desolation, in times of peril and disaster, we should look at the substance and not the shadow of things. I envy not the feelings of the man who can reason coolly and calmly about the force of precedents and the tendency of examples in the fury of the war-cry, when 'booty and beauty' is the watchword. Talk not to me about rules and forms in court when the enemy's cannon are pointed at the door, and the flames encircle the cupola! The man whose stoicism would enable him to philosophize coolly under these circumstances would fiddle while the Capitol was burning, and laugh at the horror and anguish that surrounded him in the midst of the conflagration! I claim not the possession of these remarkable feelings. I concede them all to those who think that the savior of New Orleans ought to be treated like a criminal for not possessing them in a higher degree. Their course in this debate has proved them worthy disciples of the doctrine they profess. Let them receive all the encomiums which such sentiments are calculated to inspire."[1]

[1] *Globe*, 28 Cong., 1 Sess., App., p. 45.

His closing words were marked with much the same perfervid rhetoric, only less objectionable because they were charged with genuine emotion: "Can gentlemen see nothing to admire, nothing to commend, in the closing scenes, when, fresh from the battlefield, the victorious general—the idol of his army and the acknowledged savior of his countrymen—stood before Judge Hall, and quelled the tumult and indignant murmurs of the multitude by telling him that 'the same arm which had defended the city from the ravages of a foreign enemy should protect him in the discharge of his duty?' Is this the conduct of a lawless desperado, who delights in trampling upon Constitution, and law, and right? Is there no reverence for the supremacy of the laws and the civil institutions of the country displayed on this occasion? If such acts of heroism and moderation, of chivalry and submission, have no charms to excite the admiration or soften the animosities of gentlemen in the Opposition, I have no desire to see them vote for this bill. The character of the hero of New Orleans requires no endorsement from such a source. They wish to fix a mark, a stigma of reproach, upon his character, and send him to his grave branded as a criminal. His stern, inflexible adherence to Democratic principles, his unwavering devotion to his country, and his intrepid opposition to her enemies, have so long thwarted their unhallowed schemes of ambition and power, that they fear the potency of his name on earth, even after his spirit shall have ascended to heaven."

"An eloquent, sophistical speech, prodigiously admired by the slave Democracy of the House," was the comment of John Quincy Adams; words of high praise,

for the veteran statesman had little patience with the
style of oratory affected by this "homunculus."[1] A
correspondent of a Richmond newspaper wrote that
this effort had given Douglas high rank as a debater.[2]
Evidence on every hand confirms the impression that
by a single, happy stroke the young Illinoisan had
achieved enviable distinction; but whether he had
qualities which would secure an enduring reputation,
was still open to question.

In the long run, the confidence of party associates
is the surest passport to real influence in the House.
It might easily happen, indeed, that Douglas, with all
his rough eloquence, would remain an impotent legis-
lator. The history of Congress is strewn with oratorical derelicts, who have often edified their auditors,
but quite as often blocked the course of legislation.
No one knew better than Douglas, that only as he
served his party, could he hope to see his wishes crystallize into laws, and his ambitions assume the guise
of reality. His opportunity to render effective service
came also in this first session.

Four States had neglected to comply with the recent
act of Congress reapportioning representation, having
elected their twenty-one members by general ticket.
The language of the statute was explicit: "In every
case where a State is entitled to more than one Representative, the number to which each State shall be
entitled under this apportionment shall be elected by
districts composed of contiguous territory equal in
number to the number of Representatives, to which
said State may be entitled, no one district electing

---

[1] J. Q. Adams, Memoirs, XI, p. 478.
[2] Richmond *Enquirer*, Jan. 6, 1844.

more than one Representative.'"[1] Now all but two of
these twenty-one Representatives were Democrats.
Would a Democratic majority punish this flagrant
transgression of Federal law by unseating the offenders?

In self-respect the Democratic members of the
House could not do less than appoint a committee to
investigate whether the representatives in question
had been elected "in conformity to the Constitution
and the law."[2] Thereupon it devolved upon the six
Democratic members of this committee of nine to construct a theory, by which they might seat their party
associates under cover of legality. Not that they held
any such explicit mandate from the party, nor that
they deliberately went to work to pervert the law; they
were simply under psychological pressure from which
only men of the severest impartiality could free themselves. The work of drafting the majority report (it
was a foregone conclusion that the committee would
divide), fell to Douglas. It pronounced the law of
1842 "not a *law* made in pursuance of the Constitution of the United States, and valid, operative, and
binding upon the States." Accordingly, the representatives of the four States in question were entitled to
their seats.

By what process of reasoning had Douglas reached
this conclusion? The report directed its criticism
chiefly against the second section of the Act of 1842,
which substituted the district for the general ticket in
congressional elections. The Constitution provides
that "the Times, Places, and Manner of holding elec-

[1] Act of June 25, 1842; United States Statutes at Large, V, p. 491.
[2] December 14, 1843. *Globe*, 28 Cong. 1 Sess. p. 36.

tions for Senators and Representatives, shall be prescribed in each State by the Legislature thereof; but
the Congress may at any time by Law make or alter
such Regulations.'' But by the law of 1842, contended
the report, Congress had only partially exercised its
power, and had attempted ''to subvert the entire system of legislation adopted by the several States of the
Union, and to compel them to conform to certain rules
established by Congress for their government.'' Congress ''may'' make or alter such regulations, but ''the
right to change State laws or to enact others which
shall suspend them, does not imply the right to compel
the State legislatures to make such change or new
enactments.'' Congress may exercise the privilege
of making such regulations, only when the State legislatures refuse to act, or act in a way to subvert the
Constitution. If Congress acts at all in fixing times,
places, and manner of elections, it must act exhaust-
ively, leaving nothing for the State legislatures to do.
The Act of 1842 was general in its nature, and inoperative without State legislation. The history of the Constitutional Convention of 1787 was cited to prove that
it was generally understood that Congress would exercise this power only in a few specified cases.[1]

Replying to the attacks which this report evoked,
Douglas took still higher ground. He was ready to
affirm that Congress had no power to district the
States. To concede to Congress so great a power was
to deny those reserved rights of the States, without
which their sovereignty would be an empty title.
''Congress may alter, but it cannot supersede these
regulations [of the States] till it supplies others in

[1] Niles' *Register*, Vol. 65, pp. 393-396.

their places, so as to leave the right of representation perfect."[1]

The argument of the report was bold and ingenious, if not convincing. The minority were ready to admit that the case had been cleverly stated, although hardly a man doubted that political considerations had weighed most heavily with the chairman of the committee. Douglas resented the suggestion with such warmth, however, that it is charitable to suppose he was not conscious of the bias under which he had labored.

Upon one auditor, who to be sure was inexpressibly bored by the whole discussion of the "everlasting general ticket elections," Douglas made an unhappy impression. John Quincy Adams recorded in his diary,— that diary which was becoming a sort of Rogues' Gallery: "He now raved out his hour in abusive invectives upon the members who had pointed out its slanders and upon the Whig party. His face was convulsed, his gesticulation frantic, and he lashed himself into such a heat that if his body had been made of combustible matter, it would have burnt out. In the midst of his roaring, to save himself from choking, he stripped off and cast away his cravat, and unbuttoned his waist-coat, and had the air and aspect of a half-naked pugilist. And this man comes from a judicial bench, and passes for an eloquent orator."[2]

No one will mistake this for an impartial description. Nearly every Democrat who spoke upon this tedious question, according to Adams, either "raved" or "foamed at the mouth." The old gentleman was too wearied and disgusted with the affair to be a fair

[1] *Globe*, 28 Cong. 1 Sess. pp. 276-277.
[2] J. Q. Adams, Memoirs, XI, p. 510.

reporter. But as a caricature, this picture of the young man from Illinois certainly hits off the style which he affected, in common with most Western orators.

Notwithstanding his very substantial services to his party, Douglas had sooner or later to face his constituents with an answer to the crucial question, "What have you done for us?" It is a hard, brutal question, which has blighted many a promising career in American politics. The interest which Douglas exhibited in the Western Harbors bill was due, in part at least, to his desire to propitiate those by virtue of whose suffrages he was a member of the House of Representatives. At the same time, he was no doubt sincerely devoted to the measure, because he believed profoundly in its national character. Local and national interests were so inseparable in his mind, that he could urge the improvement of the Illinois River as a truly national undertaking. "Through this channel, and this alone," he declared all aglow with enthusiasm, "we have a connected and uninterrupted navigation for steamboats and large vessels from the Atlantic Ocean and the Gulf of Mexico, to all the northern lakes." Considerations of war and defense, as well as of peace and commerce, counselled the proposed expenditure. "We have no fleet upon the lakes; we have no navy-yard there at which we could construct one, and no channel through which we could introduce our vessels from the sea-board. In times of war, those lakes must be defended, if defended at all, by a fleet from the naval depot and a yard on the Mississippi River." After the State of Illinois had expended millions on the Illinois and Michigan canal, was Congress to begrudge a few thousands to remove the sand-bars which impeded navigation in this "national highway by an irrevocable ordinance"?[1]

This special plea for the Illinois River was prefaced by a lengthy exposition of Democratic doctrine respecting internal improvements, for it was incumbent upon every good Democrat to explain a measure which seemed to countenance a broad construction of the powers of the Federal government. Douglas was at particular pains to show that the bill did not depart from the principles laid down in President Jackson's famous Maysville Road veto-message.[2] To him Jackson incarnated the party faith; and his public documents were a veritable, political testament. In the art of reading consistency into his own, or the conduct of another, Douglas had no equal. To the end of his days he possessed in an extraordinary degree the subtle power of redistributing emphasis so as to produce a desired effect. It was the most effective and the most insidious of his many natural gifts, for it often won immediate ends at the permanent sacrifice of his reputation for candor and veracity. The immediate result of this essay in interpretation of Jacksonian principles, was to bring down upon Douglas's devoted head the withering charge, peculiarly blighting to a budding statesman, that he was conjuring with names to the exclusion of arguments. With biting sarcasm, Representative Holmes drew attention to the gentleman's disposition, after the fashion of little men, to advance to the fray under the seven-fold shield of the Telamon

---

[1] *Globe*, 28 Cong., 1 Sess., pp. 549-550. For the trend of public opinion in the district which Douglas represented, see Peoria *Register*, September 21, 1839.

[2] *Globe*, 28 Cong., 1 Sess., pp. 527-528

Ajax—a classical allusion which was altogether lost on the young man from Illinois.

The appropriation for the Illinois River was stricken from the Western Harbors bill much to Douglas's regret.[1] Still, he had evinced a genuine concern for the interests of his constituents and his reward was even now at hand. Early in the year the Peoria *Press* had recommended a Democratic convention to nominate a candidate for Congress.[2] The *State Register,* and other journals friendly to Douglas, took up the cry, giving the movement thus all the marks of spontaneity. The Democratic organization was found to be intact; the convention was held early in May at Pittsfield; and the Honorable Stephen A. Douglas was unanimously re-nominated for Representative to Congress from the Fifth Congressional District.[3]

Soon after this well-ordered convention in the little Western town of Pittsfield, came the national convention of the Democratic party at Baltimore, where the unexpected happened. To Douglas, as to the rank and file of the party, the selection of Polk must have come as a surprise; but whatever predilections he may have had for another candidate, were speedily suppressed.[4] With the platform, at least, he found himself in hearty accord; and before the end of the session he convinced his associates on the Democratic side of the House, that he was no lukewarm supporter of the ticket.

While the Civil and Diplomatic Appropriations bill

[1] *Globe,* 28 Cong., 1 Sess., p. 534.

[2] Illinois *State Register,* February 9, 1844.

[3] *Ibid.,* May 17, 1844.

[4] It was intimated that he had at first aided Tyler in his forlorn hope of a second term.

was under discussion in the House, a desultory debate occurred on the politics of Colonel Polk. Such digressions were not unusual on the eve of a presidential election. Seizing the opportunity, Douglas obtained recognition from the Speaker and launched into a turgid speech in defence of Polk, "the standard-bearer of Democracy and freedom." It had been charged that Colonel Polk was "the industrious follower of Andrew Jackson." Douglas turned the thrust neatly by asserting, "He is emphatically a Young Hickory—the unwavering friend of Old Hickory in all his trials—his bosom companion—his supporter and defender on all occasions, in public and private, from his early boyhood until the present moment. No man living possessed General Jackson's confidence in a greater degree. . . . That he has been the industrious follower of General Jackson in those glorious contests for the defence of his country's rights, will not be deemed the unpardonable sin by the American people, so long as their hearts beat and swell with gratitude to their great benefactor. He is the very man for the times—a 'chip of the old block'—of the true hickory stump. The people want a man whose patriotism, honesty, ability, and devotion to democratic principles, have been tested and tried in the most stormy times of the republic, and never found wanting. That man is James K. Polk of Tennessee."[1]

There could be no better evidence that Douglas felt sure of his own fences, than his willingness to assist in the general campaign outside of his own district and State. He not only addressed a mass-meeting of delegates from many Western States at Nashville,

[1] *Globe,* 28 Cong., 1 Sess., pp. 598 ff.

Tennessee,[1] but journeyed to St. Louis and back again, in the service of the Democratic Central Committee, speaking at numerous points along the way with gratifying success, if we may judge from the grateful words of appreciation in the Democratic press.[2] It was while he was in attendance on the convention in Nashville that he was brought face to face with Andrew Jackson. The old hero was then living in retirement at the Hermitage. Thither, as to a Mecca, all good Democrats turned their faces after the convention. Douglas received from the old man a greeting which warmed the cockles of his heart, and which, duly reported by the editor of the Illinois *State Register*, who was his companion, was worth many votes at the cross-roads of Illinois. The scene was described as follows:

"Governor Clay, of Alabama, was near General Jackson, who was himself sitting on a sofa in the hall, and as each person entered, the governor introduced him to the hero and he passed along. When Judge Douglas was thus introduced, General Jackson raised his still brilliant eyes and gazed for a moment in the countenance of the judge, still retaining his hand. 'Are you the Mr. Douglas, of Illinois, who delivered a speech last session on the subject of the fine imposed on me for declaring martial law at New Orleans?' " asked General Jackson.

" 'I have delivered a speech in the House of Representatives upon that subject,' was the modest reply of our friend.

" 'Then stop,' said General Jackson; 'sit down here beside me. I desire to return you my thanks for that

[1] Illinois *State Register*, August 30, 1844.
[2] *Ibid.*, September 27, 1844.

speech. You are the first man that has ever relieved
my mind on a subject which has rested upon it for
thirty years. My enemies have always charged me
with violating the Constitution of my country by declaring martial law at New Orleans, and my friends
have always admitted the violation, but have contended
that circumstances justified me in that violation. I
never could understand how it was that the performance of a solemn duty to my country—a duty which,
if I had neglected, would have made me a traitor in
the sight of God and man, could properly be pronounced a violation of the Constitution. I felt convinced in my own mind that I was not guilty of such a
heinous offense; but I could never make out a legal
justification of my course, nor has it ever been done,
sir, until you, on the floor of Congress, at the late
session, established it beyond the possibility of cavil
or doubt. I thank you, sir, for that speech. It has
relieved my mind from the only circumstance that
rested painfully upon it. Throughout my whole life
I never performed an official act which I viewed as a
violation of the Constitution of my country; and I
can now go down to the grave in peace, with the perfect
consciousness that I have not broken, at any period of
my life, the Constitution or laws of my country.'

"Thus spoke the old hero, his countenance brighten-
ed by emotions which it is impossible for us to describe.
We turned to look at Douglas—he was speechless. He
could not reply, but convulsively shaking the aged
veteran's hand, he rose and left the hall. Certainly
General Jackson had paid him the highest compliment
he could have bestowed on any individual.'"[1]

[1] Sheahan, Douglas, pp. 70-71.

When the August elections had come and gone, Douglas found himself re-elected by a majority of fourteen hundred votes and by a plurality over his Whig opponent of more than seventeen hundred.[1] He was to have another opportunity to serve his constituents; but the question was still open, whether his talents were only those of an adroit politician intent upon his own advancement, or those of a statesman, capable of conceiving generous national policies which would efface the eager ambitions of the individual and the grosser ends of party.

[1] Official returns in the office of the Secretary of State.

CHAPTER V

MANIFEST DESTINY

The defeat of President Tyler's treaty in June, 1844, just on the eve of the presidential campaign, gave the Texas question an importance which the Democrats in convention had not foreseen, when they inserted the re-annexation plank in the platform. The hostile attitude of Whig senators and of Clay himself toward annexation, helped to make Texas a party issue. While it cannot be said that Polk was elected on this issue alone, there was some plausibility in the statement of President Tyler, that "a controlling majority of the people, and a majority of the States, have declared in favor of immediate annexation." At all events, when Congress reassembled, President Tyler promptly acted on this supposition. In his annual message, and again in a special message a fortnight later, he urged "prompt and immediate action on the subject of annexation." Since the two governments had already agreed on terms of annexation, he recommended their adoption by Congress "in the form of a joint resolution, or act, to be perfected and made binding on the two countries, when adopted in like manner by the government of Texas."[1] A policy which had not been able to secure the approval of two-thirds of the Senate was now to be endorsed by a majority of both houses. In short, a legislative treaty was to be enacted by Congress.

[1] Message of December 3, 1844.

The Hon. Stephen A. Douglas had taken his seat in the House with augmented self-assurance. He had not only secured his re-election and the success of his party in Illinois, but he had served most acceptably as a campaign speaker in Polk's own State. Surely he was entitled to some consideration in the councils of his party. In the appointment of standing committees, he could hardly hope for a chairmanship. It was reward enough to be made a member of the Committee of Elections and of the Committee on the Judiciary. On the paramount question before this Congress, he entertained strong convictions, which he had no hesitation in setting forth in a series of resolutions, while older members were still feeling their way. The preamble of these "Joint Resolutions for the annexation of Texas" was in itself a little stump speech: "Whereas the treaty of 1803 had provided that the people of Texas should be incorporated into the Union and admitted as soon as possible to citizenship, and whereas the present inhabitants have signified their willingness to be re-annexed; therefore" .... Particular interest attaches to the Eighth Resolution which proposed to extend the Missouri Compromise line through Texas, "inasmuch as the compromise had been made prior to the treaty of 1819, by which Texas was ceded to Spain."[1] The resolutions never commanded any support worth mentioning, attention being drawn to the joint resolution of the Committee on Foreign Affairs which was known to have the sanction of the President. The proposal of Douglas to settle the matter of slavery in Texas in the act of annexation itself, was perhaps his only contribution to the

[1] *Globe*, 28 Cong., 2 Sess., p. 85.

discussion of ways and means. An aggressive Southern group of representatives readily caught up the suggestion.

The debate upon the joint resolution was well under way before Douglas secured recognition from the Speaker. The opposition was led by Winthrop of Massachusetts and motived by reluctance to admit slave territory, as well as by constitutional scruples regarding the process of annexation by joint resolution. Douglas spoke largely in rejoinder to Winthrop. A clever retort to Winthrop's reference to "this odious measure devised for sinister purposes by a President not elected by the people," won for Douglas the good-natured attention of the House. It was President Adams and not President Tyler, Douglas remonstrated, who had first opened negotiations for annexation; but perhaps the gentleman from Massachusetts intended to designate his colleague, Mr. Adams, when he referred to "a president not elected by the people"![1] Moreover, it was Mr. Adams, who as Secretary of State had urged our claims to all the country as far as the Rio del Norte, under the Treaty of 1803. In spite of these just boundary claims and our solemn promise to admit the inhabitants of the Louisiana purchase to citizenship, we had violated that pledge by ceding Texas to Spain in 1819. These people had protested against this separation, only a few months after the signing of the treaty; they now asked us to redeem our ancient pledge. Honor and violated faith required the immediate annexation of Texas.[2] Had Douglas known, or taken pains to ascertain, who these people were, who protested against the treaty of 1819,

[1] *Globe*, 28 Cong., 2 Sess., App., p. 65.   [2] *Ibid.*, p. 66.

he would hardly have wasted his commiseration upon them. Enough: the argument served his immediate purpose.

To those who contended that Congress had no power to annex territory with a view to admitting new States, Douglas replied that the Constitution not only grants specific powers to Congress, but also general power to pass acts necessary and proper to carry out the specific powers. Congress may admit new States, but in the present instance Congress cannot exercise that power without annexing territory. "The annexation of Texas is a prerequisite without the performance of which Texas cannot be admitted."[1] The Constitution does not state that the President and Senate may admit new States, nor that they shall make laws for the acquisition of territory in order to enable Congress to admit new States. The Constitution declares explicitly, "*Congress* may admit new States." "When the grant of power is to Congress, the authority to pass all laws necessary to its execution is also in Congress; and the treaty-making power is to be confined to those cases where the power is not located elsewhere by the Constitution."[2]

With those weaklings who feared lest the extension of the national domain should react unfavorably upon our institutions, and who apprehended war with Mexico, Douglas had no patience. The States of the Union were already drawn closer together than the thirteen original States in the first years of the Union, because of the improved means of communication. Transportation facilities were now multiplying more rapidly than population. "Our federal system," he

[1] *Globe*, 28 Cong., 2 Sess., App., p. 66.   [2] *Ibid.*, p. 67.

exclaimed, with a burst of jingoism that won a round of applause from Western Democrats as he resumed his seat, "Our federal system is admirably adapted to the whole continent; and, while I would not violate the laws of nations, nor treaty stipulations, nor in any manner tarnish the national honor, I would exert all legal and honorable means to drive Great Britain and the last vestiges of royal authority from the continent of North America, and extend the limits of the republic from ocean to ocean. I would make this an ocean-bound republic, and have no more disputes about boundaries, or 'red lines' upon the maps."[1]

In this speech there was one notable omission. The slavery question was not once touched upon. Those who have eyes only to see plots hatched by the slave power in national politics, are sure to construe this silence as part of an ignoble game. It is possible that Douglas purposely evaded this question; but it does not by any means follow that he was deliberately playing into the hands of Southern leaders. The simple truth is, that it was quite possible in the early forties for men, in all honesty, to ignore slavery, because they regarded it either as a side issue or as no issue at all. It was quite possible to think on large national policies without confusing them with slavery. Men who shared with Douglas the pulsating life of the Northwest wanted Texas as a "theater for enterprise and industry." As an Ohio representative said, they desired "a West for their sons and daughters where they would be free from family influences, from associated wealth and from those thousand things which in the old settled country have the tendency of

[1] *Globe*, 28 Cong., 2 Sess., App., p. 68.

keeping down the efforts and enterprises of young
people." The hearts of those who, like Douglas, had
carved out their fortunes in the new States, responded
to that sentiment in a way which neither a John Quincy
Adams nor a Winthrop could understand.

Yet the question of slavery in the proposed State
of Texas was thrust upon the attention of Congress
by the persistent tactics of Alexander H. Stephens
and a group of Southern associates. They refused
to accept all terms of annexation which did not
secure the right of States formed south of the Missouri Compromise line to come into the Union with
slavery, if they desired to do so.[1] Douglas met this
opposition with the suggestion that not more than three
States besides Texas should be created out of the new
State, but that such States should be admitted into
the Union with or without slavery, as the people of
each should determine, at the time of their application to Congress for admission. As the germ of the
doctrine of Popular Sovereignty, this resolution has
both a personal and a historic interest. While it
failed to pass,[2] it suggested to Stephens and his friends
a mode of adjustment which might satisfy all sides.
It was at his suggestion that Milton Brown of Tennessee proposed resolutions providing for the admission of not more than four States besides Texas, out of
the territory acquired. If these States should be
formed south of the Missouri Compromise line, they
were to be admitted with or without slavery, as the
people of each should determine. Northern men demurred, but Douglas saved the situation by offering

[1] *American Historical Review*, VIII, pp. 93-94.
[2] It was voted down 107 to 96; *Globe*, 28 Cong., 2 Sess., p. 192.

as an amendment, "And in such States as shall be
formed north of said Missouri Compromise line, slavery or involuntary servitude, except for crime, shall
be prohibited."[1]   The amendment was accepted, and
thus amended, the joint resolution passed by an
ample margin of votes. In view of later developments,
this extension of the Missouri Compromise line is a
point of great significance in the career of Douglas.

Not long after Douglas had voiced his vision of "an
ocean-bound republic," he was called upon to assist
one of the most remarkable emigrations westward,
from his own State. The Mormons in Hancock County
had become the most undesirable of neighbors to his
constituents. Once the allies of the Democrats, they
were now held in detestation by all Gentiles of adjoining counties, irrespective of political affiliations. The
announcement of the doctrine of polygamy by the
Prophet Smith had been accompanied by acts of defiance and followed by depredations, which, while not
altogether unprovoked, aroused the non-Mormons to
a dangerous pitch of excitement. In the midst of
general disorder in Hancock County, Joseph Smith was
murdered. Every deed of violence was now attributed
to the Danites, as the members of the militant order
of the Mormon Church styled themselves. Early in the
year 1845, the Nauvoo Charter was repealed; and
Governor Ford warned his quondam friends confidentially that they had better betake themselves westward,
suggesting California as "a field for the prettiest enterprise that has been undertaken in modern times."
Disgraceful outrages filled the summer months of
1845 in Hancock County. A band of Mormon-haters

[1] *Globe*, 28 Cong., 2 Sess., p. 193.

ravaged the county, burning houses, barns, and grain stacks, and driving unprotected Mormon settlers into Nauvoo. To put an end to this state of affairs, Governor Ford sent Judge Douglas and Attorney-General McDougal, with a force of militia under the command of General Hardin, into Hancock County. Public meetings in all the adjoining counties were now demanding the expulsion of the Mormons in menacing language.[1] While General Hardin issued a proclamation bidding Mormons and anti-Mormons to desist from further violence, and promised that his scanty force of four hundred would enforce the laws impartially, the commissioners entered into negotiations with the Mormon authorities. On the pressing demand of the commissioners and of a deputation from the town of Quincy, Brigham Young announced that the Mormons purposed to leave Illinois in the spring, "for some point so remote that there will not need to be a difficulty with the people and ourselves."

There can be little doubt that Douglas's advice weighed heavily with the Mormons. As a judge, he had administered the law impartially between Mormon and non-Mormon; and this was none too common in the civic history of the Mormon Church. As an aspirant for office, he had frankly courted their suffrages; but times had changed. The reply of the commissioners, though not unkindly worded, contained some wholesome advice. "We think that steps should be taken by you to make it apparent that you are actually preparing to remove in the spring. By carry-

---

[1] Linn's Story of the Mormons, Chs. 10-20, gives in great detail the facts connected with this Mormon emigration. I have borrowed freely from this account for the following episode.

ing out, in good faith, your proposition to remove, as submitted to us, we think you should be, and will be, permitted to depart peaceably next spring for your destination, west of the Rocky Mountains. . . . We recommend to you to place every possible restraint in your power over the members of your church, to prevent them from committing acts of aggression or retaliation on any citizens of the State, as a contrary course may, and most probably will, bring about a collision which will subvert all efforts to maintain the peace in this county; and we propose making a similar request of your opponents in this and the surrounding counties.''[1]

Announcing the result of their negotiations to the anti-Mormon people of Hancock County, the commissioners gave equally good advice: ''Remember, whatever may be the aggression against you, the sympathy of the public may be forfeited. It cannot be denied that the burning of the houses of the Mormons . . . . was an act criminal in itself, and disgraceful to its perpetrators . . . . A resort to, or persistence in, such a course under existing circumstances will make you forfeit all the respect and sympathy of the community.''

Unhappily this advice was not long heeded by either side. While Douglas was giving his vote for men and money for the Mexican War and the gallant Hardin was serving his country in command of a regiment, ''the last Mormon war'' broke out, which culminated in the siege and evacuation of Nauvoo. Passing westward into No-man's-land, the Mormons became eventually the founders of one of the Territories by which Douglas sought to span the continent.

[1] Linn, Story of the Mormons, pp. 340-341.

It was only in the Northwest that the cry for the re-occupation of Oregon had the ring of sincerity; elsewhere it had been thought of as a response to the re-annexation of Texas,—more or less of a vote-catching device. The sentiment in Douglas's constituency was strongly in favor of an aggressive policy in Oregon. The first band of Americans to go thither, for the single purpose of settlement and occupation, set out from Peoria.[1] These were "young men of the right sort," in whom the eternal *Wanderlust* of the race had been kindled by tales of returned missionaries. Public exercises were held on their departure, and the community sanctioned this outflow of its youthful strength. Dwellers in the older communities of the East had little sympathy with this enterprise. It was ill-timed, many hundred years in advance of the times. Why emigrate from a region but just reclaimed from barbarism, where good land was still abundant?[2] Perhaps it was in reply to such doubts that an Illinois rhymester bade his New England brother

"Scan the opening glories of the West,
    Her boundless prairies and her thousand streams,
The swarming millions who will crowd her breast,
    'Mid scenes enchanting as a poet's dreams:
And then bethink you of your own stern land,
    Where ceaseless toil will scarce a pittance earn,
And gather quickly to a hopeful band,—
    Say parting words,—and to the westward turn."[3]

Douglas tingled to his fingers' ends with the sentiment expressed in these lines. The prospect of for-

[1] Lyman, History of Oregon, III, p. 188.
[2] See the letter of a New England Correspondent in the Peoria *Register*, May, 1839.   [3] Peoria *Register*, June 8, 1839.

feiting this Oregon country,—this greater Northwest,—
to Great Britain, stirred all the belligerent blood in
his veins. Had it fallen to him to word the Democratic
platform, he would not have been able to choose a better
phrase than "re-occupation of Oregon." The elemental jealousy and hatred of the Western pioneer for
the claim-jumper found its counterpart in his hostile
attitude toward Great Britain. He was equally fearful
lest a low estimate of the value of Oregon should make
Congress indifferent to its future. He had endeavored
to have Congress purchase copies of Greenhow's *History of the Northwest Coast of North America,* so that
his colleagues might inform themselves about this El
Dorado.[1]

There was, indeed, much ignorance about Oregon,
in Congress and out. To the popular mind Oregon was
the country drained by the Columbia River, a vast
region on the northwest coast. As defined by the
authority whom Douglas summoned to the aid of his
colleagues, Oregon was the territory west of the Rocky
Mountains between the parallels of 42° and 54° 40'
north latitude.[2] Treaties between Russia and Great
Britain, and between Russia and the United States,
had fixed the southern boundary of Russian territory
on the continent at 54° 40'; a treaty between the United
States and Spain had given the forty-second parallel
as the northern boundary of the Spanish possessions;
and a joint treaty of occupation between Great Britain
and the United States in 1818,—renewed in 1827,—had
established a *modus vivendi* between the rival claimants, which might be terminated by either party on

---

[1] *Globe,* 28 Cong., 2 Sess., pp. 198 and 201.

[2] Greenhow, Northwest Coast of North America, p. 200.

twelve months' notice. Meantime Great Britain and the United States were silent competitors for exclusive ownership of the mainland and islands between Spanish and Russian America. Whether the technical questions involved in these treaties were so easily dismissed, was something that did not concern the resolute expansionist. It was enough for him that, irrespective of title derived from priority of discovery, the United States had, as Greenhow expressed it, a stronger "national right," by virtue of the process by which their people were settling the Mississippi Valley and the great West. This was but another way of stating the theory of manifest destiny.

No one knew better than Douglas that paper claims lost half their force unless followed up by vigorous action. Priority of occupation was a far better claim than priority of discovery. Hence, the government must encourage actual settlement on the Oregon. Two isolated bills that Douglas submitted to Congress are full of suggestion, when connected by this thought: one provided for the establishment of the territory of Nebraska;[1] the other, for the establishment of military posts in the territories of Nebraska and Oregon, to protect the commerce of the United States with New Mexico and California, as well as emigration to Oregon.[2] Though neither bill seems to have received serious consideration, both were to be forced upon the attention of Congress in after years by their persistent author.

A bill had already been reported by the Committee on Territories, boldly extending the government of the

---

[1] *Globe*, 28 Cong., 2 Sess., p. 41.

[2] *Ibid.*, p. 173.

United States over the whole disputed area.[1] Conservatives in both parties deprecated such action as both hasty and unwise, in view of negotiations then in progress; but the Hotspurs would listen to no prudential considerations. Sentiments such as those expressed by Morris of Pennsylvania irritated them beyond measure. Why protect this wandering population in Oregon? he asked. Let them take care of themselves; or if they cannot protect themselves, let the government defend them during the period of their infancy, and then let them form a republic of their own. He did not wish to imperil the Union by crossing barriers beyond which nature had intended that we should not go.

This frank, if not cynical, disregard of the claims of American emigrants,—"wandering and unsettled" people, Morris had called them,—brought Douglas to his feet. Memories of a lad who had himself once been a wanderer from the home of his fathers, spurred him to resent this thinly veiled contempt for Western emigrants and the part which they were manfully playing in the development of the West. The gentleman should say frankly, retorted Douglas, that he is desirous of dissolving the Union. Consistency should force him to take the ground that our Union must be dissolved and divided up into various, separate republics by the Alleghanies, the Green and the White Mountains. Besides, to cede the territory of Oregon to its inhabitants would be tantamount to ceding it to Great Britain. He, for one, would never yield an inch of Oregon either to Great Britain or any other government. He looked forward to a time when Oregon

[1] *Globe*, 28 Cong., 2 Sess., p. 63.

would become a considerable member of the great American family of States. Wait for the issue of the negotiations now pending? When had negotiations not been pending! Every man in his senses knew that there was no hope of getting the country by negotiation. He was for erecting a government on this side of the Rockies, extending our settlements under military protection, and then establishing the territorial government of Oregon. Facilitate the means of communication across the Rocky Mountains, and let the people there know and feel that they are a part of the government of the United States, and under its protection; that was his policy.

As for Great Britain: she had already run her network of possessions and fortifications around the United States. She was intriguing for California, and for Texas, and she had her eye on Cuba; she was insidiously trying to check the growth of republican institutions on this continent and to ruin our commerce. "It therefore becomes us to put this nation in a state of defense; and when we are told that this will lead to war, all I have to say is this, violate no treaty stipulations, nor any principle of the law of nations; preserve the honor and integrity of the country, but, at the same time, assert our right to the last inch, and then, if war comes, let it come. We may regret the necessity which produced it, but when it does come, I would administer to our citizens Hannibal's oath of eternal enmity, and not terminate the war until the question was settled forever. I would blot out the lines on the map which now mark our national boundaries on this continent, and make the area of liberty as broad as the continent itself. I would not suffer petty rival republics to grow up here, engendering jealousy of each other, and interfering with each other's domestic affairs, and continually endangering their peace. I do not wish to go beyond the great ocean—beyond those boundaries which the God of nature has marked out, I would limit myself only by that boundary which is so clearly defined by nature.''[1]

The vehemence of these words startled the House, although it was not the only belligerent speech on the Oregon question. Cooler heads, like J. Q. Adams, who feared the effect of such imprudent utterances falling upon British ears, remonstrated at the unseemly haste with which the bill was being ''driven through'' the House, and counselled with all the weight of years against the puerility of provoking war in this fashion. But the most that could be accomplished in the way of moderation was an amendment, which directed the President to give notice of the termination of our joint treaty of occupation with Great Britain. This precaution proved to be unnecessary, as the Senate failed to act upon the bill.

No one expected from the new President any masterful leadership of the people as a whole or of his party. Few listened with any marked attention, therefore, to his inaugural address. His references to Texas and Oregon were in accord with the professions of the Democratic party, except possibly at one point, which was not noted at the time but afterward widely commented upon. ''Our title to the country of the Oregon,'' said he, ''is clear and unquestionable.'' The text of the Baltimore platform read, ''Our title to the *whole* of the territory of Oregon is clear and unques-

[1] *Globe*, 28 Cong., 2 Sess., pp. 225-226.

tionable.'' Did President Polk mean to be ambiguous at this point? Had he any reason to swerve from the strict letter of the Democratic creed?

In his first message to Congress, President Polk alarmed staunch Democrats by stating that he had tried to compromise our clear and unquestionable claims, though he assured his party that he had done so only out of deference to his predecessor in office. Those inherited policies having led to naught, he was now prepared to reassert our title to the whole of Oregon, which was sustained ''by irrefragable facts and arguments.'' He would therefore recommend that provision be made for terminating the joint treaty of occupation, for extending the jurisdiction of the United States over American citizens in Oregon, and for protecting emigrants in transit through the Indian country. These were strong measures. They might lead to war; but the temper of Congress was warlike; and a group of Democrats in both houses was ready to take up the programme which the President had outlined. ''Fifty-four forty or fight'' was the cry with which they sought to rally the Chauvinists of both parties to their standard. While Cass led the skirmishing line in the Senate, Douglas forged to the fore in the House.[1]

It is good evidence of the confidence placed in Douglas by his colleagues that, when territorial questions of more than ordinary importance were pending, he was appointed chairman of the Committee on Territories.[2] If there was one division of legislative

---

[1] His capacity for leadership was already recognized. His colleagues conceded that he was ''a man of large faculties.'' See Hilliard, Politics and Pen Pictures, p. 129. [2] *Globe,* 29 Cong., 1 Sess., p. 25.

work in which he showed both capacity and talent, it
was in the organization of our Western domain and in
its preparation for statehood. The vision which dazzled his imagination was that of an ocean-bound republic; to that manifest destiny he had dedicated his
talents, not by any self-conscious surrender, but by
the irresistible sweep of his imagination, always impressed by things in the large and reinforced by contact with actual Western conditions. Finance, the
tariff, and similar public questions of a technical
nature, he was content to leave to others; but those
which directly concerned the making of a continental
republic he mastered with almost jealous eagerness.
He had now attained a position, which, for fourteen
years, was conceded to be indisputably his, for no
sooner had he entered the Senate than he was made
chairman of a similar committee. His career must be
measured by the wisdom of his statesmanship in the
peculiar problems which he was called upon to solve
concerning the public domain. In this sphere he laid
claim to expert judgment; from him, therefore, much
was required; but it was the fate of nearly every
territorial question to be bound up more or less intimately with the slavery question. Upon this delicate
problem was Douglas also able to bring expert testimony to bear? Time only could tell. Meantime, the
House Committee on Territories had urgent business
on hand.

Texas was now knocking at the door of the Union,
and awaited only a formal invitation to become one of
the family of States, as the chairman was wont to say
cheerily. Ten days after the opening of the session
Douglas reported from his committee a joint resolu-

tion for the admission of Texas, "on an equal footing with the original states in all respects whatever."[1] There was a certain pleonasm about this phrasing that revealed the hand of the chairman: the simple statement must be reinforced both for legal security and for rhetorical effect. Six days later, after but a single speech, the resolution went to a third reading and was passed by a large majority.[2] Voted upon with equal dispatch by the Senate, and approved by the President, the joint resolution became law, December 29, 1845.

While the belligerent spirit of Congress had abated somewhat since the last session, no such change had passed over the gentleman from Illinois. No sooner had the Texas resolution been dispatched than he brought in a bill to protect American settlers in Oregon, while the joint treaty of occupation continued. He now acquiesced, it is true, in the more temperate course of first giving Great Britain twelve months' notice before terminating this treaty; but he was just as averse as ever to compromise and arbitration. "For one," said he, "I never will be satisfied with the valley of the Columbia, nor with 49°, nor with 54° 40'; nor will I be, while Great Britain shall hold possession of one acre on the northwest coast of America. And, Sir, I never will agree to any arrangement that shall recognize her right to one inch of soil upon the northwest coast; and for this simple reason: Great Britain never did own, she never did have a valid title to one inch of the country."[3] He moved that the question of title should not be left to arbitration.[4] His countrymen, he felt sure, would never trust their interests to Euro-

---

[1] *Globe*, 29 Cong., 1 Sess., p. 39.   [2] *Ibid.*, p. 65.
[3] *Ibid.*, p. 259.   [4] *Ibid.*, p. 86.

pean arbitrators, prejudiced as they inevitably would be by their monarchical environment.[1] This feeling was, indeed, shared by the President and his cabinet advisers.

With somewhat staggering frankness, Douglas laid bare his inmost motive for unflinching opposition to Great Britain. The value of Oregon was not to be measured by the extent of its seacoast nor by the quality of its soil. "The great point at issue between us and Great Britain is for the freedom of the Pacific Ocean, for the trade of China and Japan, of the East Indies, and for the maritime ascendency on all these waters." Oregon held a strategic position on the Pacific, controlling the overland route between the Atlantic and the Orient. If this country were yielded to Great Britain—"this power which holds control over all the balance of the globe,"—it would make her maritime ascendency complete.[2]

Stripped of its rhetorical garb, Douglas's speech of January 27, 1846, must be acknowledged to have a substratum of good sense and the elements of a true prophecy. When it is recalled that recent developments in the Orient have indeed made the mastery of the Pacific one of the momentous questions of the immediate future, that the United States did not then possess either California or Alaska, and that Oregon included the only available harbors on the coast,—the pleas of Douglas, which rang false in the ears of his own generation, sound prophetic in ours. Yet all that he said was vitiated by a fallacy which a glance at a map of the Northwest will expose. The line of 49°

[1] *Globe*, 29 Cong., 1 Sess., p. 260.
[2] *Ibid.*, pp. 258-259.

eventually gave to the United States Puget Sound with its ample harbors.

Perhaps it was the same uncompromising spirit that prompted Douglas's constituents in far away Illinois to seize the moment to endorse his course in Congress. Early in January, nineteen delegates, defying the inclemency of the season, met in convention at Rushville, and renominated Douglas for Congress by acclamation.[1] History maintains an impenetrable silence regarding these faithful nineteen; it is enough to know that Douglas had no opposition to encounter in his own bailiwick.

When the joint resolution to terminate the treaty of occupation came to a vote, the intransigeants endeavored to substitute a declaration to the effect that Oregon was no longer a subject for negotiation or compromise. It was a silly proposition, in view of the circumstances, yet it mustered ten supporters. Among those who passed between the tellers, with cries of "54° 40' forever," amid the laughter of the House, were Stephen A. Douglas and four of his Illinois colleagues.[2] Against the substitute, one hundred and forty-six votes were recorded,—an emphatic rebuke, if only the ten had chosen so to regard it.

While the House resolution was under consideration in the Senate, it was noised abroad that President Polk still considered himself free to compromise with Great Britain on the line of 49°. Consternation fell upon the Ultras. In the words of Senator Hannegan, they had believed the President committed to 54° 40' in as

[1] Illinois *State Register*, Jan. 15, 1846.

[2] *Globe*, 29 Cong., 1 Sess., p. 347; Wheeler, History of Congress, pp. 114-115.

strong language as that which makes up the Holy
Book. As rumor passed into certainty, the feelings
of Douglas can be imagined, but not described. He
had committed himself, and,—so far as in him lay,—
his party, to the line of 54° 40′, in full confidence that
Polk, party man that he was, would stubbornly contest every inch of that territory. He had called on the
dogs of war in dauntless fashion, and now to find "the
standard-bearer of Democracy," "Young Hickory,"
and many of his party, disposed to compromise on
49°,—it was all too exasperating for words. In contrast to the soberer counsels that now prevailed, his
impetuous advocacy of the whole of Oregon seemed
decidedly boyish. It was greatly to his credit, however, that, while smarting under the humiliation of the
moment, he imposed restraint upon his temper and
indulged in no bitter language.

Some weeks later, Douglas intimated that some of
his party associates had proved false to the professions
of the Baltimore platform. No Democrat, he thought,
could consistently accept part of Oregon instead of
the whole. "Does the gentleman," asked Seddon,
drawing him out for the edification of the House,
"hold that the Democratic party is pledged to 54° 40′?"
Douglas replied emphatically that he thought the party
was thus solemnly pledged. "Does the gentleman,"
persisted his interrogator, "understand the President
to have violated the Democratic creed in offering to
compromise on 49°?" Douglas replied that he did
understand Mr. Polk in his inaugural address "as
standing up erect to the pledge of the Baltimore Convention." And if ever negotiations were again opened
in violation of that pledge, "sooner let his tongue

cleave to the roof of his mouth than he would defend
that party which should yield one inch of Oregon.'"[1]
Evidently he had made up his mind to maintain his
ground. Perhaps he had faint hopes that the administration would not compromise our claims. He still
clung tenaciously to his bill for extending governmental protection over American citizens in Oregon
and for encouraging emigration to the Pacific coast;
and in the end he had the empty satisfaction of seeing
it pass the House.[2]

Meantime a war-cloud had been gathering in the
Southwest. On May 11th, President Polk announced
that war existed by act of Mexico. From this moment
an amicable settlement with Great Britain was assured. The most bellicose spirit in Congress dared not
offer to prosecute two wars at the same time. The
warlike roar of the fifty-four forty men subsided into
a murmur of mild disapprobation. Yet Douglas was
not among those who sulked in their tents. To the
surprise of his colleagues, he accepted the situation,
and he was among the first to defend the President's
course in the Mexico imbroglio.

A month passed before Douglas had occasion to call
at the White House. He was in no genial temper, for
aside from personal grievances in the Oregon affair,
he had been disappointed in the President's recent appointments to office in Illinois. The President marked
his unfriendly air, and suspecting the cause, took pains
to justify his course not only in the matter of the appointments, but in the Oregon affair. If not convinced,
Douglas was at least willing to let bygones be by-

[1] *Globe*, 29 Cong., 1 Sess. p. 497.
[2] *Ibid.*, pp. 85, 189, 395, 690-691.

gones. Upon taking his departure, he assured the President that he would continue to support the administration. The President responded graciously that Mr. Douglas could lead the Democratic party in the House if he chose to do so.[1]

When President Polk announced to Congress the conclusion of the Oregon treaty with Great Britain, he recommended the organization of a territorial government for the newly acquired country, at the earliest practicable moment. Hardly had the President's message been read, when Douglas offered a bill of this tenor, stating that it had been prepared before the terms of the treaty had been made public. His committee had not named the boundaries of the new Territory in the bill, for obvious reasons. He also stated, parenthetically, that he felt so keenly the humiliation of writing down the boundary of 49°, that he preferred to leave that duty to those who had consented to compromise our claims. In drafting the bill, he had kept in mind the provisional government adopted by the people of Oregon: as they had in turn borrowed nearly all the statutes of Iowa, it was to be presumed that the people knew their own needs better than Congress.[2]

Before the bill passed the House it was amended at one notable point. Neither slavery nor involuntary servitude should ever exist in the Territory, following the provision in the Ordinance of 1787 for the Northwest Territory. Presumably Douglas was not opposed to this amendment,[3] though he voted against the

[1] Polk, MS. Diary, Entry for June 17, 1846.

[2] *Globe*, 29 Cong., 1 Sess., p. 1203.

[3] He voted for a similar amendment in 1844; see *Globe*, 28 Cong., 2 Sess., p. 236.

famous Wilmot Proviso two days later. Already Douglas showed a disposition to escape the toils of the slavery question by a *laissez faire* policy, which was compounded of indifference to the institution itself and of a strong attachment to states-rights. When Florida applied for admission into the Union with a constitution that forbade the emancipation of slaves and permitted the exclusion of free negroes, he denied the right of Congress to refuse to receive the new State. The framers of the Federal Constitution never intended that Congress should pass upon the propriety or expediency of each clause in the constitutions of States applying for admission. The great diversity of opinion resulting from diversity of climate, soil, pursuits, and customs, made uniformity impossible. The people of each State were to form their constitution in their own way, subject to the single restriction that it should be republican in character. "They are subject to the jurisdiction and control of Congress during their infancy, their minority; but when they obtain their majority and obtain admission into the Union, they are free from all restraints . . . .except such as the Constitution of the United States has imposed."[1]

The absorbing interest of Douglas at this point in his career is perfectly clear. To span the continent with States and Territories, to create an ocean-bound republic, has often seemed a gross, materialistic ideal. Has a nation no higher destiny than mere territorial bigness? Must an intensive culture with spiritual aims be sacrificed to a vulgar exploitation of physical resources? Yet the ends which this strenuous Westerner

[1] *Globe*, 28 Cong., 2 Sess., p. 284.

had in view were not wholly gross and materialistic. To create the body of a great American Commonwealth by removing barriers to its continental expansion, so that the soul of Liberty might dwell within it, was no vulgar ambition. The conquest of the continent must be accounted one of the really great achievements of the century. In this dramatic exploit Douglas was at times an irresponsible, but never a weak nor a false actor.

The session ended where it had begun, so far as Oregon was concerned. The Senate failed to act upon the bill to establish a territorial government; the earlier bill to protect American settlers also failed of adoption; and thus American caravans continued to cross the plains unprotected and ignored. But Congress had annexed a war.

CHAPTER VI

WAR AND POLITICS

A long and involved diplomatic history preceded President Polk's simple announcement that "Mexico has passed the boundary of the United States, has invaded our territory and shed American blood upon American soil." Rightly to evaluate these words, the reader should bear in mind that the mission of John Slidell to Mexico had failed; that the hope of a peaceable adjustment of the Texas boundary and of American claims against Mexico had vanished; and that General Taylor had been ordered to the Rio Grande in disregard of Mexican claims to that region. One should also know that, from the beginning of his administration, Polk had hoped to secure from our bankrupt neighbor the cession of California as an indemnity.[1] A motive for forbearance in dealing with the distraught Mexican government was thus wholly absent from the mind of President Polk.

Such of these facts as were known at the time, supplied the Whig opposition in Congress with an abundance of ammunition against the administration. Language was used which came dangerously near being unparliamentary. So the President was willing to sacrifice Oregon to prosecute this "illegal, unrighteous and damnable war" for Texas, sneered Delano. "Where did the gentleman from Illinois stand now? Was he still in favor of 61?" This sally brought

[1] See Garrison, Westward Extension, Ch. 14.

Douglas to his feet and elicited one of his cleverest extempore speeches. He believed that such words as the gentleman had uttered could come only from one who desired defeat for our arms. "All who, after war is declared, condemn the justice of our cause, are traitors in their hearts. And would to God that they would commit some overt act for which they could be dealt with according to their deserts." Patriots might differ as to the expediency of entering upon war; but duty and honor forbade divided counsels after American blood had been shed on American soil. Had he foreseen the extraordinary turn of the discussion, he assured his auditors, he could have presented "a catalogue of aggressions and insults; of outrages on our national flag—on persons and property of our citizens; of the violation of treaty stipulations, and the murder, robbery, and imprisonment of our country-men." These were all anterior to the annexation of Texas, and perhaps alone would have justified a declaration of war; but "magnanimity and forbearance toward a weak and imbecile neighbor" prevented hostilities. The recent outrages left the country no choice but war. The invasion of the country was the last of the cumulative causes for war.

But was the invaded territory properly "our country"? This was the *crux* of the whole matter. On this point Douglas was equally confident and explicit. Waiving the claims which the treaty of San Ildefonso may have given to the boundary of the Rio Grande, he rested the whole case upon "an immutable principle"— the Republic of Texas held the country on the left bank of that river by virtue of a successful revolution. The United States had received Texas as a State with all her territory, and had no right to surrender any portion of it.[1]

The evidence which Douglas presented to confirm these claims is highly interesting. The right of Texas to have and to hold the territory from the Nueces to the Rio Grande was, in his opinion, based incontrovertibly on the treaty made by Santa Anna after the battle of San Jacinto, which acknowledged the independence of Texas and recognized the Rio Grande as its boundary. To an inquiry whether the treaty was ever ratified by the government of Mexico, Douglas replied that he was not aware that it had been ratified by anyone except Santa Anna, for the very good reason that he was the government at the time. "Has not that treaty with Santa Anna been since discarded by the Mexican government?" asked the venerable J. Q. Adams. "I presume it has," replied Douglas, "for I am not aware of any treaty or compact which that government ever entered into that has not either been violated or repudiated by them afterwards." But Santa Anna, as recognized dictator, was the *de facto* government, and the acts of a *de facto* government were binding on the nation as against foreign nations. "It is immaterial, therefore, whether Mexico has or has not since repudiated Santa Anna's treaty with Texas. It was executed at the time by competent authority. She availed herself of all its benefits." Forthwith Texas established counties beyond the Nueces, even to the Rio Grande, and extended her jurisdiction over that region, while in a later armistice Mexico recognized the Rio Grande as the boundary. It was in the clear light of these facts that Congress had passed

[1] *Globe,* 29 Cong., 1 Sess., p. 815.

an act extending the revenue laws of the United States over the country between the Rio Grande and the Nueces—the very country in which American soldiers had been slain by an invading force.

All things considered, Douglas's line of argument was as well sustained as any presented by the supporters of the war. The absence of any citations to substantiate important points was of course due to the impromptu nature of the speech. Two years later,[1] in a carefully prepared speech constructed on much the same principles, he made good these omissions, but without adding much, it must be confessed, to the strength of his argument. The chain of evidence was in fact no stronger than its weakest link, which was the so-called treaty of Santa Anna with the President of the Republic of Texas. Nowhere in the articles, public or secret, is there an express recognition of the independence of the Republic, nor of the boundary. Santa Anna simply pledged himself to do his utmost to bring about a recognition of independence, and an acknowledgment of the claims of Texas to the Rio Grande as a boundary.[2] Did Douglas misinterpret these articles, or did he chance upon an unauthentic version of them? In the subsequent speech to which reference has been made, he cited specific articles which supported his contention. These citations do not tally with either the public or secret treaty. It may be doubted whether the secret articles were generally known at this time; but the open treaty had been published in Niles' *Register* correctly, and had been cited by President Polk.[3] The inference would seem

[1] February 1, 1848.

[2] See Bancroft's History of Mexico, pp. 173-174 note.

[3] Niles' *Register*, Vol. 50, p. 336.

to be that Douglas unwittingly used an unauthenticated version, and found in it a conclusive argument for the claim of Texas to the disputed territory.

Mr. John Quincy Adams had followed Douglas with the keenest interest, for with all the vigor which his declining strength permitted, he had denounced the war as an aggression upon a weaker neighbor. He had repeatedly interrupted Douglas, so that the latter almost insensibly addressed his remarks to him. They presented a striking contrast: the feeble, old man and the ardent, young Westerner. When Douglas alluded to the statement of Mr. Adams in 1819, that "our title to the Rio del Norte is as clear as to the island of New Orleans," the old man replied testily, "I never said that our title was good to the Rio del Norte from its mouth to its source." But the gentleman surely did claim the Rio del Norte in general terms as the boundary under the Louisiana treaty, persisted Douglas. "I have the official evidence over his own signature . . . . It is his celebrated dispatch to Don Onis, the Spanish minister." "I wrote that dispatch as Secretary of State," responded Mr. Adams, somewhat disconcerted by evidence from his own pen, "and endeavored to make out the best case I could for my own country, as it was my duty; but I utterly deny that I claimed the Rio del Norte in its whole extent. I only claimed it as the line a short distance up, and then took a line northward, some distance from the river." "I have heard of this line to which the gentleman refers," replied Douglas. "It followed a river near the gorge of the mountains, certainly more than a hundred miles above Matamoras. Consequently, taking the gentleman on his own claim, the position occupied by General Taylor opposite Matamoras, and every inch of the ground upon which an American soldier has planted his foot, were clearly within our own territory as claimed by him in 1819.''[1]

It seemed to an eyewitness of this encounter that the veteran statesman was decidedly worsted. ''The House was divided between admiration for the new actor on the great stage of national affairs and reverence for the retiring chief,'' wrote a friend in after years, with more loyalty than accuracy.[2] The Whig side of the chamber was certainly in no mood to waste admiration on any Democrat who defended ''Polk the Mendacious.''

Hardly had the war begun when there was a wild scramble among Democrats for military office. It seemed to the distressed President as though every Democratic civilian became an applicant for some commission. Particularly embarrassing was the passion for office that seized upon members of Congress. Even Douglas felt the spark of military genius kindling within him. His friends, too, were convinced that he possessed qualities which would make him an intrepid leader and a tactician of no mean order. The entire Illinois delegation united to urge his appointment as Brigadier Major of the Illinois volunteers. Happily for the President, his course in this instance was clearly marked out by a law, which required him to select only officers already in command of State militia.[3] Douglas was keenly disappointed. He even presented himself in person to overrule the President's objection. The

[1] *Globe*, 29 Cong., 1 Sess., pp. 816-817.

[2] Forney, Anecdotes of Public Men, I, p. 52.

[3] Polk, MS. Diary, Entry for June 22, 1846.

President was kind, but firm. He advised Douglas to withdraw his application. In his judgment, Mr. Douglas could best serve his country in Congress. Shortly afterward Douglas sent a letter to the President, withdrawing his application—"like a sensible man," commented the relieved Executive.[1] It is not likely that the army lost a great commander by this decision.

In a State like Illinois, which had been staunchly Democratic for many years, elections during a war waged by a Democratic administration were not likely to yield any surprises. There was perhaps even less doubt of the result of the election in the Fifth Congressional District. By the admission of his opponents Douglas was stronger than he had been before.[2] Moreover, the war was popular in the counties upon whose support he had counted in other years. He had committed no act for which he desired general oblivion; his warlike utterances on Oregon, which had cost him some humiliation at Washington, so far from forfeiting the confidence of his followers, seem rather to have enhanced his popularity. Douglas carried every county in his district but one, and nearly all by handsome majorities. He had been first sent to Congress by a majority over Browning of less than five hundred votes; in the following canvass he had tripled his majority; and now he was returned to Congress by a majority of over twenty-seven hundred votes.[3] He

[1] Polk, MS. Diary, Entry for June 23, 1846.

[2] Even the Alton *Telegraph*, a Whig paper, and in times past no admirer of Douglas, spoke (May 30, 1846) of the "most admirable" speech of Judge Douglas in defense of the Mexican War (May 13th).

[3] The official returns were as follows:

Douglas 9629
Vandeventer 6864
Wilson 395

had every reason to feel gratified with this showing, even though some of his friends were winning military glory on Mexican battlefields. So long as he remained content with his seat in the House, there were no clouds in his political firmament. Not even the agitation of Abolitionists and Native Americans need cause him any anxiety, for the latter were wholly a negligible political quantity and the former practically so.[1] Everywhere but in the Seventh District, from which Lincoln was returned, Democratic Congressmen were chosen; and to make the triumph complete, a Democratic State ticket was elected and a Democratic General Assembly again assured.

Early in the fall, on his return from a Southern trip, Douglas called upon the President in Washington. He was cordially welcomed, and not a little flattered by Polk's readiness to talk over the political situation before Congress met.[2] Evidently his support was earnestly desired for the contemplated policies of the administration. It was needed, as events proved. No sooner was Congress assembled than the opposition charged Polk with having exceeded his authority in organizing governments in the territory wrested from Mexico. Douglas sprang at once to the President's defense. He would not presume to speak with authority in the matter, but an examination of the accessible official papers had convinced him that the course of the President and of the commanders of the army was altogether defensible. "In conducting the war, conquest was effected, and the right growing

[1] The Abolitionist candidate in 1846 showed no marked gain over the candidate in 1844; Native Americanism had no candidates in the field.

[2] Polk. MS. Diary, Entry for September 4, 1846.

out of conquest was to govern the subdued provinces in a temporary and provisional manner, until the home government should establish a government in another form.'[1] And more to this effect, uttered in the heated language of righteous indignation.

For thus throwing himself into the breach, Douglas was rewarded by further confidences. Before Polk replied to the resolution of inquiry which the House had voted, he summoned Douglas and a colleague to the White House, to acquaint them with the contents of his message and with the documents which would accompany it, so "that they might be prepared to meet any attacks." And again, with four other members of the House, Douglas was asked to advise the President in the matter of appointing Colonel Benton to the office of lieutenant-general in command of the armies in the field. At the same time, the President laid before them his project for an appropriation of two millions to purchase peace; *i. e.* to secure a cession of territory from Mexico. With one accord Douglas and his companions advised the President not to press Benton's appointment, but all agreed that the desired appropriation should be pushed through Congress with all possible speed.[2] Yet all knew that such a bill must run the gauntlet of amendment by those who had attached the Wilmot Proviso to the two-million-dollar bill of the last session.

While Douglas was thus rising rapidly to the leadership of his party in the House, the Legislature of his State promoted him to the Senate. For six years he

[1] *Globe,* 29 Cong., 2 Sess., pp. 13-14.

[2] Polk, MS. Diary, Entry for December 14, 1846.

had been a potential candidate for the office, despite his comparative youth.[1] What transpired in the Democratic caucus which named him as the candidate of the party, history does not record. That there was jealousy on the part of older men, much heart-burning among the younger aspirants, and bargaining on all sides, may be inferred from an incident recorded in Polk's diary.[2] Soon after his election, Douglas repaired to the President's office to urge the appointment of Richard M. Young of Illinois as Commissioner of the General Land Office. This was not the first time that Douglas had urged the appointment, it would seem. The President now inquired of Senator Breese, who had accompanied Douglas and seconded his request, whether the appointment would be satisfactory to the Illinois delegation. Both replied that it would, if Mr. Hoge, a member of the present Congress, who had been recommended at the last session, could not be appointed. The President repeated his decision not to appoint members of Congress to office, except in special cases, and suggested another candidate. Neither Douglas nor Breese would consent. Polk then spoke of a diplomatic charge for Young, but they would not hear of it.

Next morning Douglas returned to the attack, and the President, under pressure, sent the nomination of Young to the Senate; before five o'clock of the same day, Polk was surprised to receive a notification from the Secretary of the Senate that the nomination had been confirmed. The President was a good deal mysti-

[1] Ford, History of Illinois, p. 390.

[2] Polk, MS. Diary, Entry for January 6, 1847.

fied by this unusual promptness, until three members of
the Illinois delegation called some hours later, in a state
of great excitement, saying that Douglas and Breese
had taken advantage of them. They had no knowledge
that Young's nomination was being pressed, and Mc-
Clernand in high dudgeon intimated that this was all
a bargain between Young and the two Senators.
Douglas and Breese had sought to prevent Young from
contesting their seats in the Senate, by securing a fat
office for him. All this is *ex parte* evidence against
Senator Douglas; but there is nothing intrinsically
improbable in the story. In these latter days, so comparatively innocent a deal would pass without comment.

Immediately upon taking his seat in the Senate,
Douglas was appointed chairman of the Committee
on Territories. It was then a position of the utmost
importance, for every question of territorial organization touched the peculiar interests of the South. The
varying currents of public opinion crossed in this
committee. Senator Bright of Indiana is well described by the hackneyed and often misapplied desig-
nation, a Northern Democrat with Southern principles; Butler was Calhoun's colleague; Clayton of
Delaware was a Whig and represented a border State
which was vacillating between slavery and freedom;
while Davis was a Massachusetts Whig. Douglas was
placed, as it appeared, in the very storm center of politics, where his well-known fighting qualities would be
in demand. It was not so clear to those who knew
him, that he possessed the not less needful qualities
of patience and tact for occasions when battles are not
won by fighting. Still, life at the capital had smoothed
his many little asperities of manner. He had learned

to conform to the requirements of a social etiquette
to which he had been a stranger; yet without losing
the heartiness of manner and genial companionable-
ness with all men which was, indeed, his greatest personal charm. His genuineness and large-hearted regard
for his friends grappled them to him and won respect
even from those who were not of his political faith.[1]

An incident at the very outset of his career in the
Senate, betrayed some little lack of self-restraint.
When Senator Cass introduced the so-called Ten Regiments bill, Calhoun asked that its consideration might
be postponed, in order to give him opportunity to discuss resolutions on the prospective annexation of
Mexico. Cass was disposed to yield for courtesy's
sake; but Douglas resented the interruption. He
failed to see why public business should be suspended
in order to discuss abstract propositions. He believed
that this doctrine of courtesy was being carried to
great lengths.[2] Evidently the young Senator, fresh
from the brisk atmosphere of the House, was restive
under the conventional restraints of the more sedate
Senate. He had not yet become acclimated.

Douglas made his first formal speech in the Senate
on February 1, 1848. Despite his disclaimers, he had
evidently made careful preparation, for his desk was
strewn with books and he referred frequently to his
authorities. The Ten Regiments bill was known to be
a measure of the administration; and for this reason,
if for no other, it was bitterly opposed. The time
seemed opportune for a vindication of the President's
policy. Douglas indignantly repelled the charge that

[1] Forney, Anecdotes of Public Men, I, pp. 146-147.
[2] *Globe*, 30 Cong., 1 Sess., p. 92.

the war had from the outset been a war of conquest. "It is a war of self-defense, forced upon us by our enemy, and prosecuted on our part in vindication of our honor, and the integrity of our territory. The enemy invaded our territory, and we repelled the invasion, and demanded satisfaction for all our grievances. In order to compel Mexico to do us justice, it was necessary to follow her retreating armies into her territory . . . . and inasmuch as it was certain that she was unable to make indemnity in money, we must necessarily take it in land. Conquest was not the motive for the prosecution of the war; satisfaction, indemnity, security, was the motive—conquest and territory the means."[1]

Once again Douglas reviewed the origin of the war re-arguing the case for the administration. If the arguments employed were now well-worn, they were repeated with an incisiveness that took away much of their staleness. This speech must be understood as complementary to that which he had made in the House at the opening of hostilities. But he had not changed his point of view, nor moderated his contentions. Time seemed to have served only to make him surer of his evidence. Douglas exhibited throughout his most conspicuous excellencies and his most glaring defects. From first to last he was an attorney, making the best possible defense of his client. Nothing could excel his adroit selection of evidence, and his disposition and massing of telling testimony. Form and presentation were admirably calculated to disarm and convince. It goes without saying that Douglas's mental attitude was the opposite of the scientific and

[1] *Globe,* 30 Cong., 1 Sess., App., p. 222.

historic spirit. Having a proposition to establish, he cared only for pertinent evidence. He rarely inquired into the character of the authorities from which he culled his data.

That this attitude of mind and these unscholarly habits often were his undoing, was inevitable. He was often betrayed by fallacies and hasty inferences. The speech before us illustrates this lamentable mental defect. With the utmost assurance Douglas pointed out that Texas had actually extended her jurisdiction over the debatable land between the Nueces and the Rio Grande, fixing by law the times of holding court in the counties of San Patricio and Bexar. This was in the year 1838. The conclusion was almost unavoidable that when Texas came into the Union, her actual sovereignty extended to the Rio Grande. But further examination would have shown Douglas, that the only inhabited portion of the so-called counties were the towns on the right bank of the Nueces: beyond, lay a waste which was still claimed by Mexico. Was he misinformed, or had he hastily selected the usable portion of the evidence? Once again, in his eagerness to show that Mexico, so recently as 1842, had tacitly recognized the Rio Grande as a boundary in her military operations, he controverted his own argument that Texas had been in undisturbed possession of the country. He corroborated the conviction of those who from the first had asserted that, in annexing Texas, the United States had annexed a war. This from the man who had formerly declared that the danger of war was remote, because there had been no war between Mexico and Texas for nine years!

Before a vote could be reached on the Ten Regi-

ments bill, the draft of the Mexican treaty had been
sent to the Senate. What transpired in executive session and what part Douglas sustained in the discussion of the treaty, may be guessed pretty accurately
by his later admissions. He was one of an aggressive
minority who stoutly opposed the provision of the fifth
article of the treaty, which was to this effect: ''The
boundary-line established by this article shall be relig-
iously respected by each of the two republics, and no
change shall ever be made therein except by the express and free consent of both nations, lawfully given
by the general government of each, in conformity with
its own Constitution.'' This statement was deemed a
humiliating avowal that the United States had wrong-
fully warred upon Mexico, and a solemn pledge that
we would never repeat the offense. The obvious retort
was that certain consciences now seemed hypersensi-
tive about the war. However that may be, eleven votes
were recorded for conscience' sake against the odious
article.

This was not the only ground of complaint. Douglas
afterward stated the feeling of the minority in this
way: ''It violated a great principle of public policy
in relation to this continent. It pledges the faith of
this Republic that our successors shall not do that
which duty to the interests and honor of the country,
in the progress of events, may compel them to do.''
But he hastened to add that he meditated no aggression upon Mexico. In short, the Republic,—such was
his hardly-concealed thought,—might again fall out
with its imbecile neighbor and feel called upon to administer punishment by demanding indemnity. There

was no knowing what "the progress of events" might make a national necessity.[1]

As yet Douglas had contributed nothing to the solution of the problem which lurked behind the Mexican cession; nor had he tried his hand at making party opinion on new issues. He seemed to have no concern beyond the concrete business on the calendar of the Senate. He classed all anticipatory discussion of future issues as idle abstraction. Had he no imagination? Had he no eyes to see beyond the object immediately within his field of vision? Had his alert intelligence suddenly become myopic?

On the subject of Abolitionism, at least, he had positive convictions, which he did not hesitate to express. An exciting episode in the Senate drew from him a sharp arraignment of the extreme factions North and South. An acrimonious debate had been precipitated by a bill introduced by that fervid champion of Abolitionism, Senator Hale of New Hampshire, which purported to protect property in the District of Columbia against rioters. A recent attack upon the office of the *National Era,* the organ of Abolitionism, at the capital, as everyone understood, inspired the bill, and inevitably formed the real subject of debate.[2] It was in the heated colloquy that ensued that Senator Foote of Mississippi earned his sobriquet of "Hangman," by inviting Hale to visit Mississippi and to "grace one of the tallest trees of the forest, with a rope around his neck." Calhoun, too, was excited beyond his wont, declaring that he would as soon argue with a maniac

---

[1] *Globe,* 32 Cong., 2 Sess., App., p. 172.

[2] The debate is reported in the *Globe,* 30 Cong., 1 Sess., App., pp. 500 ff.

from Bedlam as with the Senator from New Hampshire.

With cool audacity and perfect self-possession, Douglas undertook to recall the Senate to its wonted composure,—a service not likely to be graciously received by the aggrieved parties. Douglas remarked sarcastically that Southern gentlemen had effected just what the Senator from New Hampshire, as presidential candidate of the Abolitionists, had desired: they had unquestionably doubled his vote in the free States. The invitation of the Senator from Mississippi alone was worth not less than ten thousand votes to the Senator from New Hampshire. "It is the speeches of Southern men, representing slave States, going to an extreme, breathing a fanaticism as wild and as reckless as that of the Senator from New Hampshire, which creates Abolitionism in the North." These were hardly the words of the traditional peacemaker. Senator Foote was again upon his feet breathing out imprecations. "I must again congratulate the Senator from New Hampshire," resumed Douglas, "on the accession of the five thousand votes!" Again a colloquy ensued. Calhoun declared Douglas's course "at least as offensive as that of the Senator from New Hampshire." Douglas was then permitted to speak uninterruptedly. He assured his Southern colleagues that, as one not altogether unacquainted with life in the slave States, he appreciated their indignation against Abolitionists and shared it; but as he had no sympathy for Abolitionism, he also had none for that extreme course of Southern gentlemen which was akin to Abolitionism. "We stand up for all your constitutional rights, in which we will protect you to the last. . . . But

we protest against being made instruments—puppets—
in this slavery excitement, which can operate only to
your interest and the building up of those who wish to
put you down.''[1]

Dignified silence, however, was the last thing to be
expected from the peppery gentleman from Mississippi. He must speak "the language of just indignation.'' He gladly testified to the consideration with
which Douglas was wont to treat the South, but he
warned the young Senator from Illinois that the old
adage—''*in medio tutissimus ibis*''—might lead him
astray. He might think to reach the goal of his ambitions by keeping clear of the two leading factions
and by identifying himself with the masses, but he was
grievously mistaken.

The reply of Douglas was dignified and guarded.
He would not speak for or against slavery. The institution was local and sustained by local opinion; by
local sentiment it would stand or fall. "In the North
it is not expected that we should take the position that
slavery is a positive good—a positive blessing. If we
did assume such a position, it would be a very pertinent
inquiry, Why do you not adopt this institution? We
have moulded our institutions at the North as we have
thought proper; and now we say to you of the South,
if slavery be a blessing, it is your blessing; if it be
a curse, it is your curse; enjoy it—on you rest all
the responsibility! We are prepared to aid you in the
maintenance of all your constitutional rights; and I
apprehend that no man, South or North, has shown
more consistently a disposition to do so than myself. . . .
But I claim the privilege of pointing out to you how
you give strength and encouragement to the Abolitionists of the North.''[2]

[1] *Globe*, 30 Cong., 1 Sess., App., p. 506.   [2] *Ibid.*, p. 507.

CHAPTER VII

THE MEXICAN CESSION

When Douglas entered Washington in the fall of 1847, as junior Senator from Illinois, our troops had occupied the city of Mexico and negotiations for peace were well under way. Perplexing problems awaited Congress. President Polk sternly reminded the two Houses that peace must bring indemnity for the past and security for the future, and that the only indemnity which Mexico could offer would be a cession of territory. Unwittingly, he gave the signal for another bitter controversy, for in the state of public opinion at that moment, every accession of territory was bound to raise the question of the extension of slavery. The country was on the eve of another presidential election. Would the administration which had precipitated the war, prove itself equal to the legislative burdens imposed by that war? Could the party evolve a constructive programme and at the same time name a candidate that would win another victory at the polls?

It soon transpired that the Democratic party was at loggerheads. Of all the factions, that headed by the South Carolina delegation possessed the greatest solidarity. Under the leadership of Calhoun, its attitude toward slavery in the Territories was already clearly stated in almost syllogistic form: the States are co-sovereigns in the Territories; the general government is only the agent of the co-sovereigns; therefore, the citizens of each State may settle in the Territories with whatever is recognized as property in their own State. The corollary of this doctrine was: Congress may not exclude slavery from the Territories.

At the other pole of political thought, stood the supporters of the Wilmot Proviso, who had twice endeavored to attach a prohibition of slavery to all territory which should be acquired from Mexico, and who had retarded the organization of Oregon by insisting upon a similar concession to the principle of slavery-restriction in that Territory. Next to these Ultras were those who doubted the necessity of the Wilmot Proviso, believing that slavery was already prohibited in the new acquisitions by Mexican law. Yet not for an instant did they doubt the power of Congress to prohibit slavery in the Territories.

Between these extremes were grouped the followers of Senator Cass of Michigan, who was perhaps the most conspicuous candidate for the Democratic nomination. In his famous Nicholson letter of December 24, 1847, he questioned both the expediency and constitutionality of the Wilmot Proviso. It seemed to him wiser to confine the authority of the general government to the erection of proper governments for the new countries, leaving the inhabitants meantime to regulate their internal concerns in their own way. In all probability neither California nor New Mexico would be adapted to slave labor, because of physical and climatic conditions. Dickinson of New York carried this doctrine, which was promptly dubbed "Squatter Sovereignty," to still greater lengths. Not only by constitutional right, but by "inherent," "innate" sovereignty, were the people of the Territories vested with the power to determine their own concerns.

Beside these well-defined groups there were others which professed no doctrines and no policies. Probably the rank and file of the party were content to drift: to be non-committal was safer than to be doctrinaire; besides, it cost less effort. Such was the plight of the Democratic party on the eve of a presidential election. If harmony was to proceed out of this diversity, the process must needs be accelerated.

The fate of Oregon had been a hard one. Without a territorial government through no fault of their own, the settlers had been repeatedly visited by calamities which the prompt action of Congress might have averted.[1] The Senate had failed to act on one territorial bill; twice it had rejected bills which had passed the House, and the only excuse for delay was the question of slavery, which everybody admitted could never exist in Oregon. On January 10, 1848, for the fourth time, Douglas presented a bill to provide a territorial government for Oregon;[2] but before he could urge its consideration, he was summoned to the bed-side of his father-in-law. His absence left a dead-lock in the Committee on Territories: Democrats and Whigs could not agree on the clause in the bill which prohibited slavery in Oregon. What was the true inwardness of this unwillingness to prohibit slavery where it could never go?

The Senate seemed apathetic; but its apathy was more feigned than real. There was, indeed, great interest in the bill, but equally great reluctance to act upon it. What the South feared was not that Oregon would be free soil,—that was conceded,—but that an

[1] This was Benton's opinion; see *Globe*, 30 Cong., 1 Sess., p. 804.
[2] *Ibid.*, pp. 136, 309.

unfavorable precedent would be established. Were it conceded that Congress might exclude slavery from Oregon, a similar power could not be denied Congress in legislating for the newly acquired Territories where slavery was possible.[1]

As a last resort, a select committee was appointed, of which Senator Clayton became chairman. Within a week, a compromise was reported which embraced not only Oregon, but California and New Mexico as well. The laws of the provisional government of Oregon were to stand until the new legislature should alter them, while the legislatures of the prospective Territories of California and New Mexico were forbidden to make laws touching slavery. The question whether, under existing laws, slaves might or might not be carried into these two Territories, was left to the courts with right of appeal to the Supreme Court of the United States.[2] The Senate accepted this compromise after a prolonged debate, but the House laid it on the table without so much as permitting it to be read.[3]

Douglas returned in time to give his vote for the Clayton compromise,[4] but when this laborious effort to adjust controverted matters failed, he again pressed his original bill.[5] Hoping to make this more palatable, he suggested an amendment to the objectionable prohibitory clause: "inasmuch as the said territory is north of the parallel of 36° 30' of north latitude, usually known as the Missouri Compromise." It was the wish of his committee, he told the Senate, that "no Senator's

[1] See remarks of Mason of Virginia, *Globe*, 30 Cong., 1 Sess., p. 903.
[2] *Ibid.*, p. 950. The bill is printed on pp. 1002-1005.
[3] *Ibid.*, p. 1007.   [4] *Ibid.*, p. 1002.   [5] *Ibid.*, p. 1027.

vote on the bill should be understood as committing him on the great question.'"[1] In other words, he invited the Senate to act without creating a precedent; to extend the Missouri Compromise line without raising troublesome constitutional questions in the rest of the public domain; to legislate for a special case on the basis of an old agreement, without predicating anything about the future. When this amendment came to vote, only Douglas and Bright supported it.[2]

Douglas then proposed to extend the Missouri Compromised line to the Pacific, by an amendment which declared the old agreement "revived . . . . and in full force and binding for the future organization of the Territories of the United States, in the same sense and with the same understanding with which it was originally adopted.'"[3] This was President Polk's solution of the question. It commended itself to Douglas less on grounds of equity than of expediency. It was a compromise which then cost him no sacrifice of principle; but though the Senate agreed to the proposal, the House would have none of it.[4] In the end, after an exhausting session, the Senate gave way,[5] and the Territory of Oregon was organized with the restrictive clause borrowed from the Ordinance of 1787. All this turmoil had effected nothing except ill-feeling, for the final act was identical with the bill which Douglas had originally introduced in the House.

In the meantime, national party conventions for the nomination of presidential candidates had been held.

[1] *Globe,* 30 Cong., 1 Sess., p. 1048.
[2] *Ibid.,* p. 1061.
[3] *Ibid.,* pp. 1061-1062.
[4] *Ibid.,* pp. 1062-1063.
[5] Douglas voted finally to recede from his amendment, *Ibid.,* p. 1078.

The choice of the Democrats fell upon Cass; but his nomination could not be interpreted as an indorsement of his doctrine of squatter sovereignty. By a decisive vote, the convention rejected Yancey's resolution favoring "non-interference with the rights of property of any portion of the people of this confederation, be it in the States or in the Territories, by any other than the parties interested in them."[1] The action of the convention made it clear that traditional principles and habitual modes of political thought and action alone held the party together. The Whig party had no greater organic unity. The nomination of General Taylor, who was a doubtful Whig, was a confession that the party was non-committal on the issues of the hour. There was much opposition to both candidates. Many anti-slavery Whigs could not bring themselves to vote for Taylor, who was a slave-owner; Democrats who had supported the Wilmot Proviso, disliked the evasive doctrine of Cass.

The disaffected of both parties finally effected a fusion in the Free-Soil convention, and with other anti-slavery elements nominated Van Buren as their presidential candidate. With the cry of "Free soil, free speech, free labor, and free men," the new party threatened to upset the calculations of politicians in many quarters of the country.

The defeat of the Democratic party in the election of 1848 was attributed to the war of factions in New York. Had the Barnburners supported Cass, he would have secured the electoral vote of the State. They were accused of wrecking the party out of revenge. Certain it is that the outcome was indecisive, so far as the

[1] Stanwood, History of the Presidency, p. 236.

really vital questions of the hour were concerned. A
Whig general had been sent to the White House, but
no one knew what policies he would advocate. The
Democrats were still in control of the Senate; but
thirteen Free-Soilers held the balance of power in the
House.[1]

Curiosity was excited to know what the moribund
administration of the discredited Polk would do.
Douglas shared this inquisitiveness. He had parted
with the President in August rather angrily, owing to
a fancied grievance. On his return he called at the
White House and apologized handsomely for his "imprudent language."[2] The President was more than
glad to patch up the quarrel, for he could ill afford
now, in these waning hours of his administration, to
part company with one whom he regarded as "an
ardent and active political supporter and friend."
Cordial relations resumed, Polk read to Douglas confidentially such portions of his forthcoming message
as related to the tariff, the veto power, and the establishment of territorial governments in California and
New Mexico. In the spirit of compromise he was still
willing to approve an extension of the Missouri Compromise line through our new possessions. Should
this prove unacceptable, he would give his consent to a
bill which would leave the vexing question of slavery
in the new Territories to the judiciary, as Clayton had
proposed. Douglas was now thoroughly deferential.
He gratified the President by giving the message his
unqualified approval.[3]

[1] Garrison, Westward Extension, p. 284.
[2] Polk, MS. Diary, Entry for November 13, 1848.
[3] *Ibid.*

However, by the time Congress met, Douglas had made out his own programme; and it differed in one respect from anything that the President, or for that matter anyone else, had suggested. He proposed to admit both New Mexico and California; *i. e.* all of the territory acquired from Mexico, into the Union *as a State*. Some years later, Douglas said that he had introduced his California bill with the approval of the President;[1] but in this his memory was surely at fault. The full credit for this innovation belongs to Douglas.[2] He justified the departure from precedent in this instance, on the score of California's astounding growth in population. Besides, a territorial bill could hardly pass in this short session, "for reasons which may be apparent to all of us." Three bills had already been rejected.[3]

Now while California had rapidly increased in population, there were probably not more than twenty-six thousand souls within its borders, and of these more than a third were foreigners.[4] One would naturally suppose that a period of territorial tutelage would have been peculiarly fitting for this distant possession. Obviously, Douglas did not disclose his full thought. What he really proposed, was to avoid raising the spectre of slavery again. If the people of California could skip the period of their political minority and leap into their majority, they might then create their own institutions: no one could gainsay this right,

[1] See Douglas's Speech of December 23, 1851.

[2] Polk, MS. Diary, Entry for December 11, 1848.

[3] *Globe*, 30 Cong., 2 Sess., p. 21.

[4] Hunt, Genesis of California's First Constitution, in Johns Hopkins University Studies, XIII, pp. 16, 30.

when once California should be a "sovereign State." This was an application of squatter sovereignty at which Calhoun, least of all, could mock.

The President and his cabinet were taken by surprise. Frequent consultations were held. Douglas was repeatedly closeted with the President. All the members of the cabinet agreed that the plan of leaving the slavery question to the people of the new State was ingenious; but many objections were raised to a single State. In repeated interviews, Polk urged Douglas to draft a separate bill for New Mexico; but Douglas was obdurate.[1]

To Douglas's chagrin, the California bill was not referred to his committee, but to the Committee on the Judiciary. Perhaps this course was in accord with precedent, but it was noted that four out of the five members of this committee were Southerners, and that the vote to refer was a sectional one.[2] An adverse report was therefore to be expected. Signs were not wanting that if the people of the new province were left to work out their own salvation, they would exclude slavery.[3] The South was acutely sensitive to such signs. Nothing of this bias, however, appeared in the report of the committee. With great cleverness and circumspection they chose another mode of attack.

The committee professed to discover in the bill a radical departure from traditional policy. When had Congress ever created a State out of "an unorganized body of people having no constitution, or laws, or legitimate bond of union?" California was to be a

[1] Polk, MS. Diary, Entries for December 11, 12, 13, 14, 1848.
[2] *Globe*, 30 Cong., 2 Sess., pp. 46-49.
[3] See the petition of the people of New Mexico, *Ibid.*, p. 33.

"sovereign State," yet the bill provided that Congress should interpose its authority to form new States out of it, and to prescribe rules for elections to a constitutional convention. What sort of sovereignty was this? Moreover, since Texas claimed a part of New Mexico, endless litigations would follow. In the judgment of the committee, it would be far wiser to organize the usual territorial governments for California and New Mexico.[1]

To these sensible objections, Douglas replied ineffectively. The question of sovereignty, he thought, did not depend upon the size of a State: without doing violence to the sovereignty of California, Congress could surely carve new States out of its territory; but if there were doubts on this point, he would move to add the saving clause, "with the consent of the State." He suggested no expedient for the other obstacles in the way of State sovereignty. As for precedents, there were the first three States admitted into the Union,— Kentucky, Vermont, and Tennessee,—none of which had any organized government recognized by Congress.[2] They never furnished their constitutions to Congress for inspection. Here Douglas hit wide of the mark. No one had contended that a State must present a written constitution before being recognized, but only that the people must have some form of political organization, before they could be treated as constituting a State in a constitutional sense.[3]

At the same time, halting as this defense was, Douglas gave ample proof of his disinterestedness in

[1] *Globe*, 30 Cong., 2 Sess., pp. 190-192.
[2] *Ibid.*, pp. 192-193.
[3] *Ibid.*, p. 196; particularly the incisive reply of Westcott.

advocating a State government for California. "I think, Sir," he said, "that the only issue now presented, is whether you will admit California as a State, or whether you will leave it without government, exposed to all the horrors of anarchy and violence. I have no hope of a Territorial government this session. No man is more willing to adopt such a form of government than I would be; no man would work with more energy and assiduity to accomplish that object at this session than I would."[1] Indeed, so far from questioning his motives, the members of the Judiciary Committee quite overwhelmed Douglas by their extreme deference.[2] Senator Butler, the chairman, assured him that the committee was disposed to treat the bill with all the respect due to its author; for his own part, he had always intended to show marked respect to the Senator from Illinois.[3] Douglas responded somewhat grimly that he was quite at a loss to understand "why these assurances came so thick on this point."

Most men would have accepted the situation as thoroughly hopeless; but Douglas was nothing if not persistent. In quick succession he framed two more bills, one of which provided for a division of California and for the admission of the western part as a State;[4] and then when this failed to win support, he reverted to Polk's suggestion—the admission of New Mexico and California as two States.[5] But the Senate evinced no enthusiasm for this patch-work legislation.[6]

The difficulty of legislating for California was in-

[1] *Globe*, 30 Cong., 2 Sess., p. 193.　　[2] *Ibid.*, p. 196.
[3] *Ibid.*, p. 194.　　[4] *Ibid.*, p. 262.
[5] *Ibid.*, p. 381.　　[6] *Ibid.*, pp. 435, 551, 553.

creased by the disaffection of the Southern wing of the
Democratic party. Calhoun was suspected of foment-
ing a conspiracy to break up the Union.[1] Yet in all
probability he contemplated only the formation of a
distinctly Southern party based on common economic
and political interests.[2] He not only failed in this,
because Southern Whigs were not yet ready to break
with their Northern associates; but he barely avoided
breaking up the solidarity of Southern Democrats,
and he made it increasingly difficult for Northern and
Southern Democrats to act together in matters which
did not touch the peculiar institution of the South.[3]
Thenceforth, harmonious party action was possible
only through a deference of Northern Democrats to
Southern, which was perpetually misinterpreted by
their opponents.

Senator Hale thought the course of Northern representatives and senators pusillanimous and submis-
sive to the last degree; and no considerations of taste
prevented him from expressing his opinions on all occasions. Nettled by his taunts, and no doubt sensitive
to the grain of truth in the charge, perplexed also by
the growing factionalism in his party, Douglas retorted
that the fanaticism of certain elements at the North
was largely responsible for the growth of sectional
rancor. For the first time he was moved to state publicly his maturing belief in the efficacy of squatter
sovereignty, as a solvent of existing problems in the
public domain.

"Sir, if we wish to settle this question of slavery,

[1] Von Holst, Constitutional History of the United States, III, p.
418.   [2] Calhoun, Works, VI, pp. 290-303.
[3] Von Holst, Const. History, III, pp. 422-423.

let us banish the agitation from these halls. Let us remove the causes which produce it; let us settle the territories we have acquired, in a manner to satisfy the honor and respect the feelings of every portion of the Union. . . . Bring those territories into this Union as States upon an equal footing with the original States. Let the people of such States settle the question of slavery within their limits, as they would settle the question of banking, or any other domestic institution, according to their own will."[1]

And again, he said, "No man advocates the extension of slavery over a territory now free. On the other hand, they deny the propriety of Congress interfering to restrain, upon the great fundamental principle that the people are the source of all power; that from the people must emanate all government; that the people have the same right in these territories to establish a government for themselves that we have to overthrow our present government and establish another, if we please, or that any other government has to establish one for itself."[2]

Not the least interesting thing about these utterances, is` the fact that even Douglas could not now avoid public reference to the slavery question. He could no longer point to needed legislation quite apart from sectional interests; he could no longer treat slavery with assumed indifference; he could no longer affect to rise above such petty, local concerns to matters of national importance. He was now bound to admit that slavery stood squarely in the way of national expansion. This change of attitude was brought about in

[1] *Globe*, 30 Cong., 2 Sess., p. 208.
[2] *Ibid.*, p. 314.

part, at least, by external pressure applied by the legislature of Illinois. With no little chagrin, he was forced
to present resolutions from his own State legislature,
instructing him and his colleagues in Congress to use
their influence to secure the prohibition of slavery in
the Mexican cession.[1] It was not easy to harmonize
these instructions with the principle of non-interference which he had just enunciated.

Ten days before the close of the session, the California question again came to the fore. Senator
Walker of Wisconsin proposed a rider to the appropriations bill, which would extend the Constitution and
laws in such a way as to authorize the President to
set up a quasi-territorial government, in the country
acquired from Mexico.[2] It was a deliberate hold-up,
justified only by the exigencies of the case, as Walker
admitted. But could Congress thus extend the Constitution, by this fiat? questioned Webster. The Constitution extends over newly acquired territory *proprio
vigore,* replied Calhoun.[3] Douglas declined to enter
into the subtle questions of constitutional law thus
raised. The "metaphysics" of the subject did not
disturb him. If the Senate would not pass his statehood bill, he was for the Walker amendment. A fearful responsibility rested upon Congress. The sad fate
of a family from his own State, which had moved to
California, had brought home to him the full measure
of his responsibility. He was not disposed to quibble
over points of law, while American citizens in Cali-

---

[1] *Globe*, 30 Cong., 2 Sess., p. 394.   [2] *Ibid.*, p. 561.

[3] *Ibid*, App., pp. 253 ff. The debate summarized by Von Holst,
III, pp. 444-451.

fornia were exposed to the outrages of desperadoes, and of deserters from our own army and navy.[1]

While the Senate yielded to necessity and passed the appropriations bill, rider and all, the House stubbornly clung to its bill organizing a territorial government for California, excluding slavery.[2] The following days were among the most exciting in the history of Congress. A conference committee was unable to reach any agreement. Then Douglas tried to seize the psychological moment to persuade the Senate to accept the House bill. "I have tried to get up State bills, territorial bills, and all kinds of bills in all shapes, in the hope that some bill, in some shape, would satisfy the Senate; but thus far I have found their taste in relation to this matter too fastidious for my humble efforts. Now I wish to make another and a final effort on this bill, to see if the Senate are disposed to do anything towards giving a government to the people of California."[3]

Both Houses continued in session far into the night of March 3d. Sectional feeling ran high. Two fist-fights occurred in the House and at least one in the Senate.[4] It seemed as though Congress would adjourn, leaving our civil and diplomatic service penniless. Douglas frankly announced that for his part he would rather leave our office-holders without salaries, than our citizens without the protection of law.[5] Inauguration Day was dawning when the dead-lock was broken.

[1] *Globe,* 30 Cong., 2 Sess., App., pp. 275-276.

[2] *Ibid.,* pp. 595, 665.   [3] *Ibid.,* p. 668.

[4] Mann, Life of Horace Mann, p. 277.

[5] *Globe,* 30 Cong., 2 Sess., p. 685.

The Senate voted the appropriations bill without the rider, but failed to act on the House bill.[1] The people of California were thus left to their own devices.

The outcome was disheartening to the chairman of the Committee on Territories. His programme had miscarried at every important point. Only his bill for the organization of Minnesota became law.[2] A similar bill for Nebraska failed to receive consideration. The future of California remained problematic. Indeed, political changes in Illinois made his own future somewhat problematic.

[1] *Globe,* 30 Cong., 2 Sess., pp. 691-692.
[2] *Ibid.,* pp. 635-637; p. 693.

BOOK II
THE DOCTRINE OF POPULAR SOVEREIGNTY

CHAPTER VIII

When Douglas took his seat in Congress for the first time, an unknown man in unfamiliar surroundings, he found as his near neighbor, one David S. Reid, a young lawyer from North Carolina, who was of his own age, of his own party, and like him, serving a first term. An acquaintance sprang up between these young Democrats, which, in spite of their widely different antecedents, deepened into intimacy. It was a friendship that would have meant much to Douglas, even if it had not led to an interesting romance. Intercourse with this able young Southerner[1] opened the eyes of this Western Yankee to the finer aspects of Southern social life, and taught him the quality of that Southern aristocracy, which, when all has been said, was the truest aristocracy that America has seen. And when Reid entertained his friends and relatives in Washington, Douglas learned also to know the charm of Southern women.

Among the most attractive of these visitors was Reid's cousin, Miss Martha Denny Martin, daughter of Colonel Robert Martin of Rockingham County, North Carolina. Rumor has it that Douglas speedily fell captive to the graces of this young woman. She was not only charming in manner and fair of face, but keen-witted and intelligent. In spite of the gay

---

[1] Reid was afterward Governor of North Carolina and United States Senator.

badinage with which she treated this young Westerner, she revealed a depth and positiveness of character, to which indeed her fine, broad forehead bore witness on first acquaintance. In the give and take of small talk she more than held her own, and occasionally discomfited her admirer by sallies which were tipped with wit and reached their mark unerringly.[1] Did she know that just such treatment—strange paradox—won, while it at times wounded, the heart of the unromantic Westerner?

Colonel Robert Martin was a typical, western North Carolina planter. He belonged to that stalwart line of Martins whose most famous representative was Alexander, of Revolutionary days, six times Governor of the State. On the banks of the upper Dan, Colonel Martin possessed a goodly plantation of about eight hundred acres, upon which negro slaves cultivated cotton and such of the cereals as were needed for home consumption.[2] Like other planters, he had felt the competition of the virgin lands opened up to cotton culture in the gulf plains of Alabama, Mississippi, and Louisiana; and like his fellow planters, he had invested in these Western lands, on the Pearl River in Mississippi. This Pearl River plantation was worked by about one hundred and fifty negroes and was devoted to the raising of cotton.

When Douglas accepted Reid's invitation to visit North Carolina, the scene of the romance begun on the Potomac shifted to the banks of the Dan. Southern

[1] For many of the facts relating to Douglas's courtship and marriage, I am indebted to his son, Judge Robert Martin Douglas, of North Carolina.

[2] At the death of Colonel Martin, this plantation was worked by some seventeen slaves, according to his will.

hospitality became more than a conventional phrase on Douglas's lips. He enjoyed a social privilege which grew rarer as North and South fell apart. Intercourse like this broke down many of those prejudices unconsciously cherished by Northerners. Slavery in the concrete, on a North Carolina plantation, with a kindly master like Colonel Martin,[1] bore none of the marks of a direful tyranny. Whatever may have been his mental reservations as to slavery as a system of labor, Douglas could not fail to feel the injustice of the taunts hurled against his Southern friends by the Abolitionist press. As he saw the South, the master was not a monster of cruelty, nor the slave a victim of malevolent violence.

The romance on the banks of the Dan flowed far more clearly and smoothly toward its goal than the waters of that turbid stream. On April 7, 1847, Miss Martin became the wife of the Honorable Stephen Arnold Douglas, who had just become Senator from the State of Illinois. It was in every way a fateful alliance. Next to his Illinois environment, no external circumstance more directly shaped his career than his marriage to the daughter of a North Carolina planter. The subtle influences of a home and a wife dominated by Southern culture, were now to work upon him. Constant intercourse with Southern men and women emancipated him from the narrowness of his hereditary environment.[2] He was bound to acquire an insight into the nature of Southern life; he was compelled to comprehend, by the most tender and intimate

[1] This impression is fully confirmed by the terms of his will.

[2] He was himself fully conscious of this influence. See his speech at Raleigh, August 30, 1860.

of human relationships, the meaning and responsibility of a social order reared upon slave labor.

A year had hardly passed when the death of Colonel Martin left Mrs. Douglas in possession of all his property in North Carolina. It had been his desire to put his Pearl River plantation, the most valuable of his holdings, in the hands of his son-in-law. But Douglas had refused to accept the charge, not wishing to hold negroes. Indeed, he had frankly told Colonel Martin that the family already held more slaves than was profitable.[1] In his will, therefore, Colonel Martin was constrained to leave his Mississippi plantation and slaves to Mrs. Douglas and her children. It was characteristic of the man and of his class, that his concern for his dependents followed him to the grave. A codicil to his will provided, that if Mrs. Douglas should have no children, the negroes together with their increase were to be sent to Liberia, or to some other colony in Africa. By means of the net proceeds of the last crop, they would be able to reach Africa and have a surplus to aid them in beginning planting. "I trust in Providence," wrote this kindly master, "she will have children and if so I wish these negroes to belong to them, as nearly every head of the family have expressed to me a desire to belong to you and your children rather than go to Africa; and to set them free where they are, would entail on them a greater curse, far greater in my opinion, as well as in that of the intelligent among themselves, than to have a humane master whose duty it would be to see they

[1] The facts are so stated in Colonel Martin's will, for a transcript of which I am indebted to Judge R. M. Douglas.

were properly protected . . . . and properly provided for in sickness as well as in health."[1]

The legacy of Colonel Martin gave a handle to Douglas's enemies. It was easy to believe that he had fallen heir to slave property. That the terms of the bequest were imperfectly known, did not deter the opposition press from malevolent insinuations which stung Douglas to the quick. It was fatal to his political career to allow them to go unchallenged. In the midsummer of 1850, while Congress was wrestling with the measures of compromise, Douglas wrote to his friend, the editor of the Illinois *State Register,* "It is true that my wife does own about 150 negroes in Mississippi on a cotton plantation. My father-in-law in his lifetime offered them to me and I refused to accept them. *This fact is stated in his will,* but I do not wish it brought before the public as the public have no business with my private affairs, and besides anybody would see that the information must have come from me. My wife has no negroes except those in Mississippi. We have other property in North Carolina, but no negroes. It is our intention, however, to remove all our property to Illinois as soon as possible."[2] To correct the popular rumor, Douglas enclosed a statement which might be published editorially, or otherwise.

The dictated statement read as follows: "The Quincy *Whig* and other Whig papers are publishing an article purporting to be copied from a Mississippi paper abusing Judge Douglas as the owner of 100

[1] Extract from the will of Colonel Martin.

[2] This letter, dated August 3, 1850, is in the possession of Mrs. James W. Patton of Springfield, Illinois.

slaves and at the same time accusing him of being a Wilmot Free-soiler. That the article originated in this State, and was sent to Mississippi for publication in order that it might be re-published here we shall not question nor take the trouble to prove. The paternity of the article, the malice that prompted it, and the mis-representations it contains are too obvious to require particular notice. If it had been written by a Mississippian he would have known that the statement in regard to the ownership of the negroes was totally un-true. No one will pretend that Judge Douglas has any other property in Mississippi than that which was ac-quired in the right of his wife by inheritance upon the death of her father, and anyone who will take the trouble to examine the statutes of that State in the Secretary's office in this City will find that by the laws of Mississippi all the property of a married woman, whether acquired by will, gift or otherwise, becomes her separate and exclusive estate and is not subject to the control or disposal of her husband nor subject to his debts. We do not pretend to know whether the father of Mrs. Douglas at the time of his death owned slaves in Mississippi or not. We have heard the statement made by the Whigs but have not deemed it of sufficient importance to inquire into its truth. If it should turn out so, in no event could Judge Douglas become the owner or have the disposal of or be responsible for them. The laws of the State forbid it, and also forbid slaves under such circumstances from being removed without or emancipated within the limits of the State.''

Born a Yankee, bred a Westerner, wedded to the mistress of a Southern plantation, Douglas represented a Commonwealth whose population was made up of elements from all sections. The influences that shaped his career were extraordinarily complex. No account of his subsequent public life would be complete, without reference to the peculiar social and political characteristics of his constituency.

The people of early Illinois were drawn southward by the pull of natural forces: the Mississippi washes the western border on its gulf-ward course; and the chief rivers within the State have a general southerly trend.[1] But quite as important historically is the convergence of the Ohio, the Cumberland, and the Tennessee on the southern border of Illinois; for it was by these waterways that the early settlers reached the Illinois Territory from the States of Kentucky, Tennessee, Virginia, and North Carolina. The apex of the irregular, inverted triangle of Illinois, thrust down to the 37th parallel of latitude, brought the first settlers well within the sphere of Southern influence. Two slave States flanked this southern end. Nearly one-half of Illinois lay south of a direct, westward extension of Mason and Dixon's line.

In the early days, the possession by the Indians of the northern areas accentuated the southern connections of Illinois. At the same time the absence at the North of navigable waterways and passable highways between East and West, left the Ohio and its tributaries the only connecting lines of travel with the remote northern Atlantic States. Had Illinois been admitted into the Union with the boundaries first proposed, it would have been, by all those subtle influences which go

[1] The characteristics of Illinois as a constituency in 1850 are set forth in greater detail, in an article by the writer in the *Iowa Journal of History and Politics*, July, 1905.

to make public sentiment, a Southern State. But the extension of the northern boundary to 42° 30′ gave Illinois a frontage of fifty miles on Lake Michigan, and deflected the whole political and social history of the Commonwealth. This contact with the great waterways of the North brought to the State, in the course of time, an immense share of the lake traffic and a momentous connection with the northern central and northern Atlantic States. The passing of the Indians, the opening up of the great northern prairies to occupation, and the completion of the Illinois-Michigan canal made the northern part of Illinois fallow for New England seeding. Geographically, Illinois became the connecting link in the slender chain which bound the men of the lake and prairie plains with the men of the gulf plains. The inevitable interpenetration of Northern and Southern interests in Illinois, resulting from these contacts, is the most important fact in the social and political history of the State. It bred in Illinois statesmen a disposition to compromise for the sake of political harmony and economic progress, a passionate attachment to the Union as the *sine qua non* of State unity, and a glowing nationalism. Illinois was in short a microcosm: the larger problems of the nation existed there in miniature.

When Illinois was admitted to the Union in 1818, all the organized counties lay to the south of the projected national road between Terre Haute and Alton, hence well within the sphere of surrounding Southern influences. The society of Illinois was at this time predominantly Southern in its origin and characteristics.[1] Social life and political thought were shaped

[1] See Patterson, Early Society in Southern Illinois in the Fergus

by Southern life and Southern thought. Whatever points of contact there were with the outside world were with the Southern world. The movement to make Illinois a slave State was motived by the desire to accelerate immigration from the South.

But people had already begun to come into the State who were not of Southern origin, and who succeeded in deflecting the current of Illinois politics at this critical juncture. The fertile river bottoms and intervening prairies of southern Illinois no longer sufficed. The new comers were impelled toward the great, undulating prairies which expand above the 39th parallel. The rise of new counties marks the volume of this immigration;[1] the attitude of the older settlers toward it, fixes sufficiently its general social character. This was the beginning of the "Yankee" invasion, New York and Pennsylvania furnishing the vanguard.

As the northern prairies became accessible by the lake route and the stage roads, New England and New York poured a steady stream of homeseekers into the Commonwealth. By the middle of the century, this Northern immigration had begun to inundate the northern counties and to overflow into the interior, where it met and mingled with the counter-current. These Yankee settlers were viewed with hostility, not unmixed with contempt, by those whose culture and standards of

Historical Series, No. 14.   Also Ford, History of Illinois, pp. 38, 279-280; and Greene, Sectional forces in the History of Illinois—in the Publications of Illinois Historical Library, 1903.

[1] Between 1818 and 1840, fifty-seven new counties were organized, of which fourteen lay in the region given to Illinois by the shifting of the northern boundary. See Publications of the Illinois Historical Library, No. 8, pp. 79-80.

taste had been formed south of Mason and Dixon's line.[1]

This sectional antagonism was strengthened by the rapid commercial advance of northern Illinois. Yankee enterprise and thrift worked wonders in a decade. Governor Ford, all of whose earlier associations were with the people of southern Illinois, writing about the middle of the century, admits that although the settlers in the southern part of the State were twenty, thirty, forty, and fifty years in advance, on the score of age, they were ten years behind in point of wealth and all the appliances of a higher civilization.[2] The completion of the canal between Lake Michigan and the Illinois River, however much it might contribute to the general welfare of the State, seemed likely to profit the northern rather than the southern portion. It had been opposed at the outset by Southerners, who argued soberly that it would flood the State with Yankees;[3] and at every stage in its progress it had encountered Southern obstruction, though the grounds for this opposition were more wisely chosen.

Political ideals and customs were also a divisive force in Illinois society. True to their earlier political training, the Southern settlers had established the county as a unit of local government. The Constitution of 1818 put the control of local concerns in the hands of three county commissioners, who, though elected by the people, were not subjected to that scrutiny which selectmen encountered in the New England town meeting. To the democratic New Englander,

---

[1] Ford, History of Illinois, pp. 280-281.   [2] Ibid., p. 280.

[3] See Davidson and Stuvé, History of Illinois, Chapter on "State Policy."

every system seemed defective which gave him no opportunity to discuss neighborhood interests publicly,
and to call local officers to account before an assembly
of the vicinage. The new comers in northern Illinois
became profoundly dissatisfied with the autocratic
board of county commissioners. Since the township
might act as a corporate body for school purposes, why
might they not enjoy the full measure of township government? Their demands grew more and more insistent, until they won substantial concessions from the
convention which framed the Constitution of 1848. But
all this agitation involved a more or less direct criticism
of the system which the people of southern Illinois
thought good enough for Yankees, if it were good
enough for themselves.[1]

In the early history of Illinois, negro slavery was a
bone of contention between men of Northern and of
Southern antecedents. When Illinois was admitted as
a State, there were over seven hundred negroes held
in servitude. In spite of the Ordinance of 1787. Illinois
was practically a slave Territory. There were, to be
sure, stalwart opponents of slavery even among those
who had come from slave-holding communities; but
taken in the large, public opinion in the Territory sanctioned negro slavery as it existed under a loose system
of indenture.[2] Even the Constitution of 1818, under
which Illinois came into the Union as a free State, continued the old system of indenture with slight modification.[3]

[1] Shaw, Local Government in Illinois, in the Johns Hopkins University Studies, Vol. I; Newell, Township Government in Illinois.

[2] Harris, Negro Servitude in Illinois, Chapter II.

[3] *Ibid.*, Chapter III. See Article VI of the Constitution.

It was in the famous contest over the proposed constitutional convention of 1824 that the influence of Northern opinion respecting slavery was first felt. The contest had narrowed down to a struggle between those who desired a convention in order to draft a constitution legalizing slavery and those who, from policy or principle, were opposed to slavery in Illinois. Men of Southern birth were, it is true, among the most aggressive leaders of the anti-convention forces, but the decisive votes against the convention were cast in the seven counties recently organized, in which there was a strong Northern element.[1]

This contest ended, the anti-slavery sentiment evaporated. The "Black Laws" continued in force. Little or no interest was manifested in the fate of indentured black servants, who were to all intents and purposes as much slaves as their southern kindred. The leaven of Abolitionism worked slowly in Illinois society. By an almost unanimous vote, the General Assembly adopted joint resolutions in 1837 which condemned Abolitionism as "more productive of evil than of moral and political good." There were then not a half-dozen anti-slavery societies in the State, and these soon learned to confine their labors to central and northern Illinois, abandoning Egypt as hopelessly inaccessible to the light.[2]

The issues raised by the Mexican War and the prospective acquisition of new territory, materially changed the temper of northern Illinois. Moreover, in the later forties a tide of immigration from the northeastern States, augmented by Germans who came in increas-

[1] *Ibid.*, Chapter IV. See also Moses, History of Illinois, Vol. I, p. 324.   [2] Harris, Negro Servitude, pp. 125, 136-137

ing numbers after the European agitation of 1848, was filling the northernmost counties with men and women who held positive convictions on the question of slavery extension. These transplanted New Englanders were outspoken advocates of the Wilmot Proviso. When they were asked to vote upon that article of the Constitution of 1848 which proposed to prevent the immigration of free negroes, the fourteen northern counties voted no, only to find themselves outvoted two to one.[1] A new factor had appeared in Illinois politics.

Many and diverse circumstances contributed to the growth of sectionalism in Illinois. The disruptive forces, however, may be easily overestimated. The unifying forces in Illinois society were just as varied, and in the long run more potent. As in the nation at large so in Illinois, religious, educational, and social organizations did much to resist the strain of countervailing forces. But no organization proved in the end so enduring and effective as the political party. Illinois had by 1840 two well-developed party organizations, which enveloped the people of the State, as on a large scale they embraced the nation. These parties came to have an enduring, institutional character. Men were born Democrats and Whigs. Southern and Northern Whigs, Northern and Southern Democrats there were, of course; but the necessity of harmony for effective action tended to subordinate individual and group interests to the larger good of the whole. Parties continued to be organized on national lines, after the churches had been rent in twain by sectional forces. Of the two party organizations in Illinois, the Democratic party was numerically the larger, and in point

[1] Journal of the Constitutional Convention of 1847, pp. 453-456.

of discipline, the more efficient. It was older; it had been the first to adopt the system of State and district nominating conventions; it had the advantage of prestige and of the possession of office. The Democratic party could "point with pride" to an unbroken series of victories in State and presidential elections. By successful gerrymanders it had secured the lion's share of congressional districts. Above all it had intelligent leadership. The retirement of Senator Breese left Stephen A. Douglas the undisputed leader of the party.

The dual party system in Illinois, as well as in the nation, was seriously threatened by the appearance of a third political organization with hostility to slavery as its cohesive force. The Liberty party polled its first vote in Illinois in the campaign of 1840, when its candidate for the presidency received 160 votes.[1] Four years later its total vote in Illinois was 3,469, a notable increase.[2] The distribution of these votes, however, is more noteworthy than their number, for in no county did the vote amount to more than thirty per cent. of the total poll of all parties. The heaviest Liberty vote was in the northern counties. The votes cast in the central and southern parts of the State were indicative, for the most part, of a Quaker or New England element in the population.[3] As yet the older parties had no reason to fear for their prestige; but in 1848 the Liberty party gave place to the Free-Soil party, which developed unexpected strength in the presidential vote. It rallied anti-slavery elements by its cry of "Free Soil, Free Speech, Free Labor, and Free Men!" and for the first time broke the serried

[1] *Whig Almanac*, 1841.   [2] *Ibid.*, 1845.
[3] Smith, Liberty and Free Soil Parties, pp. 326-327.

ranks of the older parties. Van Buren, the candidate of
the Free-Soilers, received a vote of 15,774, concentrated
in the northeastern counties, but reaching formidable
proportions in the counties of the northwest and west.[1]
Of the older organizations, the Whig party seemed less
affected, Taylor having received 53,047 votes, an increase of 7,519 over the Whig vote of 1844. The Democratic candidate, Cass, received only 56,300, an absolute
decrease of 1,620. This was both an absolute and a
relative decline, for the total voting population had
increased by 24,459. Presumptive evidence points to a
wholesale desertion of the party by men of strong anti-
slavery convictions. Whither they had gone—whether
into the ranks of Whigs or Free-Soilers,—concerned
Democratic leaders less than the palpable fact that
they had gone somewhere.

At the close of this eventful year, the political situation in Illinois was without precedent. To offset Democratic losses in the presidential election, there were,
to be sure, the usual Democratic triumphs in State
and district elections. But the composition of the
legislature was peculiar. On the vote for Speaker of
the House, the Democrats showed a handsome majority: there was no sign of a third party vote. A few
days later the following resolution was carried by a
vote which threw the Democratic ranks into confusion:
"That our senators in Congress be instructed, and
our representatives requested, to use all honorable
means in their power, to procure the enactment of such
laws by Congress for the government of the countries
and territories of the United States, acquired by the
treaty of peace, friendship, limits, and settlement, with

[1] Smith, Liberty and Free Soil Parties, pp. 328-329.

the republic of Mexico, concluded February 2, A. D. 1848; as shall contain the express declaration, that there shall be neither slavery, nor involuntary servitude in said territories, otherwise than for the punishment of crimes, whereof the party shall have been duly convicted.''[1]

At least fifteen representatives of what had hitherto been Democratic constituencies, had combined with the Whigs to embarrass the Democratic delegation at Washington.[2] Their expectation seems to have been that they could thus force Senator Douglas to resign his seat, for he had been an uncompromising opponent of the Wilmot Proviso. Free-Soilers, Whigs, and Northern Democrats with anti-slavery leanings had voted for the instructions; only the Democrats from the southern counties voted solidly to sustain the Illinois delegation in its opposition to the Proviso.[3] While not a strict sectional vote, it showed plainly enough the rift in the Democratic party. A disruptive issue had been raised. For the moment a re-alignment of parties on geographical lines seemed imminent. This was precisely the trend in national politics at this moment.

There was a traditional remedy for this sectional malady—compromise. It was an Illinois senator, himself a slave-owner, who had proposed the original Missouri proviso. Senator Douglas had repeatedly proposed to extend the Missouri Compromise line to

[1] House Journal, p. 52.

[2] All these fifteen voted for the Democratic candidate for Speaker of the House.

[3] House Journal, p. 52; Senate Journal, p. 44. See also Harris, Negro Servitude in Illinois, p. 177.

the Pacific, in the same spirit in which compromise had been offered in 1820, but the essential conditions for a compromise on this basis were now wanting.

It was precisely at this time, when the Illinois legislature was instructing him to reverse his attitude toward the Wilmot Proviso, that Senator Douglas began to change his policy. Believing that the combination against him in the legislature was largely accidental and momentary, he refused to resign.[1] Events amply justified his course; but the crisis was not without its lessons for him. The futility of a compromise based on an extension of the Missouri Compromise line was now apparent. Opposition to the extension of slavery was too strong; and belief in the free status of the acquired territory too firmly rooted in the minds of his constituents. There remained the possibility of reintegrating the Democratic party through the application of the principle of "squatter sovereignty." Was it possible to offset the anti-slavery sentiment of his Northern constituents by an insistent appeal to their belief in local self-government?

The taproot from which squatter sovereignty grew and flourished, was the instinctive attachment of the Western American to local government; or to put the matter conversely, his dislike of external authority. So far back as the era of the Revolution, intense individualism, bold initiative, strong dislike of authority, elemental jealousy of the fruits of labor, and passionate attachment to the soil that has been cleared for a home, are qualities found in varying intensity among the colonists from New Hampshire to Georgia. Nowhere, however, were they so marked as along the Western

[1] See Speech in Senate, December 23, 1851.

border, where centrifugal forces were particularly strong and local attachments were abnormally developed. Under stress of real or fancied wrongs, it was natural for settlers in these frontier regions to meet for joint protest, or if the occasion were grave enough, to enter into political association, to resist encroachment upon what they felt to be their natural rights. Whenever they felt called upon to justify their course, they did so in language that repeated, consciously or unconsciously, the theory of the social contract, with which the political thought of the age was surcharged. In these frontier communities was born the political habit that manifested itself on successive frontiers of American advance across the continent, and that finally in the course of the slavery controversy found apt expression in the doctrine of squatter sovereignty.[1]

None of the Territories carved out of the original Northwest had shown greater eagerness for separate government than Illinois. The isolation of the original settlements grouped along the Mississippi, their remoteness from the seat of territorial government on the Wabash, and the consequent difficulty of obtaining legal protection and efficient government, predisposed the people of Illinois to demand a territorial government of their own, long before Congress listened to their memorials. Bitter controversy and even bloodshed attended their efforts.[2]

A generation later a similar contest occurred for the separation of the fourteen northern counties from the

[1] See the writer's article on ''The Genesis of Popular Sovereignty'' in the *Iowa Journal of History and Politics* for January, 1905.

[2] Davidson and Stuvé, History of Illinois, pp. 241-242.

State. When Congress changed the northern boundary of Illinois, it had deviated from the express provisions of the Ordinance of 1787, which had drawn the line through the southern bend of Lake Michigan. This departure from the Magna Charta of the Northwest furnished the would-be secessionists with a pretext. But an editorial in the *Northwestern Gazette and Galena Advertiser*, January 20, 1842, naïvely disclosed their real motive. Illinois was overwhelmed with debt, while Wisconsin was "young, vigorous, and free from debt." "Look at the district as it is now," wrote the editor fervidly, "the *fag end* of the State of Illinois—its interest wholly disregarded in State legislation—in short, treated as a mere *province*—taxed; laid under tribute in the form of taxation for the benefit of the South and Middle." The right of the people to determine by vote whether the counties should be annexed to Illinois, was accepted without question. A meeting of citizens in Jo Daviess County resolved, that "until the Ordinance of 1787 was altered by common consent, the free inhabitants of the region had, in common with the free inhabitants of the Territory of Wisconsin, an absolute, vested, indefeasible right to form a permanent constitution and State government."[1] This was the burden of many memorials of similar origin.

The desire of the people of Illinois to control local interests extended most naturally to the soil which nourished them. That the Federal Government should without their consent dispose of lands which they had brought under cultivation, seemed to verge on tyranny. It mattered not that the settler had taken up lands to which he had no title in law. The wilderness belonged

[1] *Northwestern Gazette,* March 19, 1842.

to him who subdued it. Therefore land leagues and claim associations figure largely in the history of the Northwest. Their object was everywhere the same, to protect the squatter against the chance bidder at a public land sale.

The concessions made by the constitutional convention of 1847, in the matter of local government, gave great satisfaction to the Northern element in the State. The new constitution authorized the legislature to pass a general law, in accordance with which counties might organize by popular vote under a township system. This mode of settling a bitter and protracted controversy was thoroughly in accord with the democratic spirit of northern Illinois. The newspapers of the northern counties welcomed the inauguration of the township system as a formal recognition of a familiar principle. Said the *Will County Telegraph:*[1] "The great principle on which the new system is based is this: that except as to those things which pertain to State unity and those which are in their nature common to the whole county, it is right that each small community should regulate its own local matters without interference." It was this sentiment to which popular sovereignty made a cogent appeal.

No man was more sensitive than Senator Douglas to these subtle influences of popular tradition, custom, and current sentiment. Under the cumulative impression of the events which have been recorded, his confidence in popular sovereignty as an integrating force in national and local politics increased, and his public utterances became more assured and positive.[2] By the

[1] September 27, 1849.

[2] Compare his utterances on the following dates: January 10, 1849;

close of the year 1850, he had the satisfaction of seeing the collapse of the Free-Soil party in Illinois, and of knowing that the joint resolutions had been repealed which had so nearly accomplished his overthrow. A political storm had been weathered. Yet the diverse currents in Illinois society might again roil local politics. So long as a bitter commercial rivalry divided northern and southern Illinois, and social differences held the sections apart, misunderstandings dangerous to party and State alike would inevitably follow. How could these diverse elements be fused into a true and enduring union? To this task Douglas set his hand. The ways and means which he employed, form one of the most striking episodes in his career.

January 22, 1849; October 23, 1849 at Springfield, Illinois; February 12, 1850; June 3, 1850.

CHAPTER IX

When Congress assembled in December, 1849, statesmen of the old school, who could agree in nothing else, were of one mind in this: the Union was in peril. In the impressive words of Webster, "the imprisoned winds were let loose. The East, the North, and the stormy South combined to throw the whole sea into commotion, to toss its billows to the skies, and disclose its profoundest depths." Clay and Calhoun were equally apprehensive. Yet there were younger men who shared none of these fears. To be sure, the political atmosphere of Washington was electric. The House spent weeks wrangling over the Speakership, so that when the serious work of legislation began, men were overwrought and excitable. California with a free constitution was knocking at the door of the Union. President Taylor gave Congress to understand that at no distant day the people of New Mexico would take similar action. And then, as though he were addressing a body of immortals, he urged Congress to await calmly the action of the people of the Territories.

Douglas was among those unimpressionable younger men who would not believe the Union to be in danger. Perhaps by his Southern connections he knew better than most Northern men, the real temper of the South. Perhaps he did not give way to the prevailing hysteria, because he was diverted from the great issues by the pressing, particular interests of his constituents. At all events, he had this advantage over Clay, Webster, and Calhoun, that when he did turn his attention to schemes of compromise, his vision was fresh, keen, and direct. He escaped that subtle distortion of mental perception from which others were likely to suffer because of long-sustained attention. To such, Douglas must have seemed unemotional, unsensitive, and lacking in spiritual fineness.

Illinois with its North and its South was also facing a crisis. To the social and political differences that bisected the State, was added a keen commercial rivalry between the sections. While the State legislature under northern control was appropriating funds for the Illinois and Michigan canal, it exhibited far less liberality in building railroads, which alone could be the arteries of traffic in southern Illinois. At a time when railroads were extending their lines westward from the Atlantic seaboard, and reaching out covetously for the produce of the Mississippi Valley, Illinois held geographically a commanding position. No roads could reach the great river, north of the Ohio at least, without crossing her borders. The avenues of approach were given into her keeping. To those who directed State policy, it seemed possible to determine the commercial destinies of the Commonwealth by controlling the farther course of the railroads which now touched the eastern boundary. Well-directed effort, it was thought, might utilize these railroads so as to build up great commercial cities on the eastern shore of the Mississippi. State policy required that none of these cross-roads should in any event touch St. Louis, and thus make it, rather than the Illinois towns now struggling toward commercial greatness, the entrepôt between East and West. With its unrivalled site at the mouth of the Missouri, Alton was as likely a competitor for the East and West traffic, and for the Mississippi commerce, as St. Louis. Alton, then, must be made the terminus of the cross-roads.[1]

The people of southern Illinois thought otherwise. Against the background of such distant hopes, they saw a concrete reality. St. Louis was already the market for their produce. From every railroad which should cross the State and terminate at St. Louis, they anticipated tangible profits. They could not see why these very real advantages should be sacrificed on the altar of northern interests. After the opening of the northern canal, they resented this exclusive policy with increased bitterness.

Upon one point, and only one, the people of northern and southern Illinois were agreed: they believed that every possible encouragement should be given to the construction of a great central railroad, which should cross the State from north to south. Such a railroad had been projected as early as 1836 by a private corporation. Subsequently the State took up the project, only to abandon it again to a private company, after the bubble of internal improvements had been pricked. Of this latter corporation,—the Great Western Railroad Company,—Senator Breese was a director and the accredited agent in Congress. It was in behalf of this corporation that he had petitioned Congress unsuccessfully for pre-emption rights on the public domain.[2]

[1] See the chapter on "State Policy" in Davidson and Stuvé, History of Illinois.

[2] Davidson and Stuvé, History of Illinois, pp. 573-574; Ackerman, Early Illinois Railroads, in Fergus Historical Series, p. 32.

Circumstances enlisted Douglas's interest powerfully in the proposed central railroad. These circumstances were partly private and personal; partly adventitious and partly of his own making. The growing sectionalism in Illinois gave politicians serious concern. It was becoming increasingly difficult to maintain the integrity of political parties, when sectional issues were thrust into the foreground of political discussion. Yankee and Southerner did not mix readily in the caldron of State politics. But a central railroad which both desired, might promote a mechanical mixture of social and commercial elements. Might it not also, in the course of time, break up provincial feeling, cause a transfusion of ideas, and in the end produce an organic union?

In the summer of 1847, Senator-elect Douglas took up his residence in Chicago, and identified himself with its commercial interests by investing in real estate.[1] Few men have had a keener instinct for speculation in land.[2] By a sort of sixth sense, he foresaw the growth of the ugly but enterprising city on Lake Michigan. He saw that commercially Chicago held a strategic position, commanding both the lake traffic eastward, and the interior waterway gulfward by means of the canal. As yet, however, these advantages were far from realization. The city was not even included within the route of the proposed central railroad. Influential business men, Eastern capitalists, and shippers along the Great Lakes were not a little exercised over this neglect. In some way the claims of Chicago must be urged upon the promoters of the rail-

[1] Letter of Breese to Douglas, Illinois *State Register*, February 6, 1851.   [2] Forney, Anecdotes, I, pp. 18-20.

road. Just here Douglas could give invaluable aid. He pointed out that if the railroad were to secure a land grant, it would need Eastern votes in Congress. The old Cairo-Galena line would seem like a sectional enterprise, likely to draw trade down the Mississippi and away from the Atlantic seaports. But if Chicago were connected with the system, as a terminal at the north, the necessary congressional support might be secured.[1]

During the summer, Douglas canvassed the State, speaking repeatedly in behalf of this larger project. For a time he hoped that Senator Breese would co-operate with him. Numerous conferences took place both before and after Congress had assembled; but Douglas found his colleague reluctant to abandon his pre-emption plan. Regardless of the memorials which poured in upon him from northern Illinois, Breese introduced his bill for pre-emption rights on the public domain, in behalf of the Holbrook Company, as the Great Western Railway Company was popularly called. Thereupon Douglas offered a bill for a donation of public lands to aid the State of Illinois in the construction of a central railroad from Cairo to Galena, with a branch from Centralia to Chicago.[2] Though Breese did not actively oppose his colleague, his lack of cordiality no doubt prejudiced Congress against a grant of any description. From the outset, Douglas's bill encountered obstacles: the opposition of those who doubted the constitutional power of Congress to grant lands for internal improvements of this sort; the opposition of landless States, which still viewed the public

---

[1] Letter of Douglas to Breese, *State Register,* January 20, 1851.

[2] *Ibid.,* January 20, 1851.

domain as a national asset from which revenue should be derived; and, finally, the opposition of the old States to the new. Nevertheless, the bill passed the Senate by a good majority. In the House it suffered defeat, owing to the undisguised opposition of the South and of the landless States both East and West. The Middle States showed distrust and uncertainty. It was perfectly clear that before such a project could pass the House, Eastern and Southern representatives would have to be won over.[1]

After Congress adjourned, Douglas journeyed to the State of Mississippi, ostensibly on a business trip to his children's plantation. In the course of his travels, he found himself in the city of Mobile—an apparent digression; but by a somewhat remarkable coincidence he met certain directors of the Mobile Railroad in the city. Now this corporation was in straits. Funds had failed and the construction of the road had been arrested. The directors were casting about in search of relief. Douglas saw his opportunity. He offered the distraught officials an alliance. He would include in his Illinois Central bill a grant of land for their road; in return, they were to make sure of the votes of their senators and representatives.[2] Such, at least, is the story told by Douglas; and some such bargain may well have been made. Subsequent events give the color of veracity to the tale.

When Douglas renewed his Illinois Central bill in a revised form on January 3, 1850, Senator Breese had been succeeded by Shields, who was well-disposed

[1] Sanborn, Congressional Grants of Land in Aid of Railways, Bulletin of the University of Wisconsin, pp. 27-30.

[2] Cutts, Constitutional and Party Questions, pp. 193-194.

toward the project.[1] The fruits of the Mobile conference were at once apparent. Senator King of Alabama offered an amendment, proposing a similar donation of public lands to his State and to Mississippi, for
the purpose of continuing the projected central railroad from the mouth of the Ohio to the port of Mobile.
Douglas afterward said that he had himself drafted
this amendment, but that he had thought best to have
Senator King present it.[2] Be that as it may, the suspicion of collusion between them can hardly be avoided,
since the amendment occasioned no surprise to the
friends of the bill and was adopted without division.

The project now before Congress was of vastly
greater consequence than the proposed grant to Illinois.
Here was a bill of truly national importance. It spoke
for itself; it appealed to the dullest imagination.
What this amended bill contemplated, was nothing less
than a trunk line connecting the Great Lakes with the
Gulf of Mexico. Now, indeed, as Douglas well said,
"nationality had been imparted to the project." At
the same time, it offered substantial advantages to
the two landless States which would be traversed by the
railroad, as well as to all the Gulf States. As thus
devised, the bill seemed reasonably sure to win votes.

Yet it must not be inferred that the bill passed
smoothly to a third reading. There was still much
shaking of heads among senators of the strict construction school. Many were conquered by expediency
and threw logic to the winds; some preferred to be

[1] Douglas renewed his bill in the short session of 1848-1849, but did
not secure action upon it.

[2] Cutts, Constitutional and Party Questions, p. 195. There is so much
brag in this account that one is disposed to distrust the details.

consistent and spoil a good cause. The bill did not sail on untroubled seas, even after it had been steered clear of constitutional shoals. It narrowly ran foul of that obstinate Western conviction, that the public lands belonged of right to the home-seeker, to whose interests all such grants were inimical, by reason of the increased price of adjoining sections of land.[1]

The real battleground, however, was not the Senate, but the House. As before, the bill passed the upper chamber by an ample margin of votes.[2] In the lower house, there was no prolonged debate upon the bill. Constitutional scruples do not seem to have been ruffled. The main difficulty was to rivet the attention of the members. Several times the bill was pushed aside and submerged by the volume of other business. Finally, on the same day that it passed the last of the compromise measures, on the 17th of September, 1850, the House passed the Illinois Central Railroad bill by a vote of 101 to 75.[3]

A comparison of this vote with that on the earlier bill shows a change of three votes in the Middle States, one in the South, ten in the Gulf States, and five in Tennessee and Kentucky.[4] This was a triumphant vindication of Douglas's sagacity, for whatever may have been the services of his colleagues in winning Eastern votes,[5] it was his bid for the vote of the Gulf

[1] Sanborn, Congressional Grants, pp. 31-34.

[2] *Globe*, 31 Cong., 1 Sess., p. 904. The vote was 26 to 14.

[3] *Ibid.*, p. 1838.   [4] Sanborn, Congressional Grants, p. 35.

[5] John Wentworth, in his *Congressional Reminiscences*, hints at some vote-getting in the East by tariff concessions; but Douglas insisted that it was the Chicago branch, promising to connect with Eastern roads, which won votes in New York, Pennsylvania and New England. See Illinois *State Register*, March 13, 1851. The subject is discussed by Sanborn, Congressional Grants, pp. 35-36.

States and of the landless, intervening States of Kentucky and Tennessee which had been most effective. But was all this anything more than the clever manœuvering of an adroit politician in a characteristic parliamentary game? A central railroad through Illinois seemed likely to quell factional and sectional quarrels in local politics; to merge Northern and Southern interests within the Commonwealth; and to add to the fiscal resources of State and nation. It was a good cause, but it needed votes in Congress. Douglas became a successful procurator and reaped his reward in increased popularity.

There is an aspect of this episode, however, which lifts it above a mere log-rolling device to secure an appropriation. Here and there it fired the imagination of men. There is abundant reason to believe that the senior Senator from Illinois was not so sordid in his bargaining for votes as he seemed. Above and apart from the commercial welfare of the Lake Region, the Mississippi Valley, and the Gulf Plains, there was an end subserved, which lay in the background of his consciousness and which came to expression rarely if ever. Practical men may see visions and dream dreams which they are reluctant to voice. There was genuine emotion beneath the materialism of Senator Walker's remarks (and he was reared in Illinois), when he said: "Anything that improves the connection between the North and the South is a great enterprise. To cross parallels of latitude, to enable the man of commerce to make up his assorted cargo, is infinitely more important than anything you can propose within the same parallels of latitude. I look upon it as a great chain to unite North and

South.''[1] Senator Shields of Illinois only voiced the inmost thought of Douglas, when he exclaimed, ''The measure is too grand, too magnificent a one to meet with such a fate at the hands of Congress. And really, as it is to connect the North and South so thoroughly, it may serve to get rid of even the Wilmot Proviso, and tie us together so effectually that the idea of separation will be impossible.''[2]

The settlement of the West had followed parallels of latitude. The men of the Lake Plains were transplanted New Englanders, New Yorkers, Pennsylvanians; the men of the Gulf Plains came from south of Mason and Dixon's line,—pioneers both, aggressive, bold in initiative, but alienated by circumstances of tremendous economic significance. If ever North should be arrayed against South, the makeweight in the balance would be these pioneers of the Northwest and Southwest. It was no mean conception to plan for the ''man of commerce'' who would cross from one region to the other, with his ''assorted cargo,''[3] for in that cargo were the destinies of two sections and his greatest commerce was to consist in the exchange of imponderable ideas. The ideal which inspired Douglas never found nobler expression, than in these words with which he replied to Webster's slighting reference to the West:

''There is a power in this nation greater than either the North or the South—a growing, increasing, swell-

[1] *Globe*, 31 Cong., 1 Sess., p. 853.   [2] *Ibid.*, p. 869.

[3] The economic significance of the Illinois Central Railroad appears in a letter of Vice-President McClellan to Douglas in 1856. The management was even then planning to bring sugar from Havana directly to the Chicago market, and to take the wheat and pork of the Northwest to the West Indies *via* New Orleans.

ing power, that will be able to speak the law to this nation, and to execute the law as spoken. That power is the country known as the great West—the Valley of the Mississippi, one and indivisible from the gulf to the great lakes, and stretching, on the one side and the other, to the extreme sources of the Ohio and Missouri—from the Alleghanies to the Rocky mountains. There, Sir, is the hope of this nation—the resting place of the power that is not only to control, but to save, the Union. We furnish the water that makes the Mississippi, and we intend to follow, navigate, and use it until it loses itself in the briny ocean. So with the St. Lawrence. We intend to keep open and enjoy both of these great outlets to the ocean, and all between them we intend to take under our especial protection, and keep and preserve as one free, happy, and united people. This is the mission of the great Mississippi Valley, the heart and soul of the nation and the continent.'"[1]

Meantime Congress was endeavoring to avert the clash of sections by other measures of accommodation. The veteran Clay, in his favorite rôle of peacemaker, had drafted a series of resolutions as a sort of legislative programme; and with his old-time vigor, was pleading for mutual forbearance. All wounds might be healed, he believed, by admitting California with her free constitution; by organizing territorial governments without any restriction as to slavery, in the region acquired from Mexico; by settling the Texas boundary and the Texas debt on a fair basis; by prohibiting the slave trade, but not slavery, in the District of Columbia; and by providing more carefully for the

[1] *Globe*, 31 Cong., 1 Sess., App., p. 365.

rendition of fugitive slaves. Clay, Calhoun, and Webster had spoken with all the weight of their years upon these propositions, before Douglas was free to address the Senate.

It was characteristic of Douglas that he chose to speak on the concrete question raised by the application of California for admission into the Union. His opening words betrayed no elevation of feeling, no alarmed patriotism transcending party lines, no great moral uplift. He made no direct reference to the state of the public mind. Clay began with an invocation; Webster pleaded for a hearing, not as a Massachusetts man, nor as a Northern man, but as an American and as a Senator, with the preservation of the Union as his theme; Douglas sprang at once to the defense of his party. With the brush of a partisan, he sketched the policy of Northern Democrats in advocating the annexation of Texas, repudiating the insinuations of Webster that Texas had been sought as a slave State. He would not admit that the whole of Texas was bound to be a slave Territory. By the very terms of annexation, provision had been made for admitting free States out of Texas. As for Webster's "law of nature, of physical geography,—the law of the formation of the earth," from which the Senator from Massachusetts derived so much comfort, it was a pity that he could not have discovered that law earlier. The "law of nature" surely had not been changed materially since the election, when Mr. Webster opposed General Cass, who had already enunciated this general principle.[1]

In his reply to Calhoun, Douglas emancipated himself successfully from his gross partisanship. Planting

[1] *Globe*, 31 Cong., 1 Sess., App., p. 366.

himself firmly upon the national theory of the Federal Union, he hewed away at what he termed Calhoun's fundamental error—"the error of supposing that his particular section has a right to have a 'due share of the territories' set apart and assigned to it." Calhoun had said much about Southern rights and Northern aggressions, citing the Ordinance of 1787 as an instance of the unfair exclusion of the South from the public domain. Douglas found a complete refutation of this error in the early history of Illinois, where slavery had for a long time existed in spite of the Ordinance. His inference from these facts was bold and suggestive, if not altogether convincing.

"These facts furnish a practical illustration of that great truth, which ought to be familiar to all statesmen and politicians, that a law passed by the national legislature to operate locally upon a people not represented, will always remain practically a dead letter upon the statute book, if it be in opposition to the wishes and supposed interests of those who are to be affected by it, and at the same time charged with its execution. The Ordinance of 1787 was practically a dead letter. It did not make the country, to which it applied, practically free from slavery. The States formed out of the territory northwest of the Ohio did not become free by virtue of the ordinance, nor in consequence of it . . . . [but] by virtue of their own will."[1]

Douglas was equally convinced that the Missouri Compromise had had no practical effect upon slavery. So far from depriving the South of its share of the West, that Compromise had simply "allayed an un-

[1] *Globe*, 31 Cong., 1 Sess., App., pp. 369-370.

fortunate excitement which was alienating the affections of different portions of the Union." "Slavery was as effectually excluded from the whole of that country, by the laws of nature, of climate, and production, before, as it is now, by act of Congress."[1] As for the exclusion of the South from the Oregon Territory, the law of 1848 "did nothing more than re-enact and affirm the law which the people themselves had previously adopted, and rigorously executed, for the period of twelve years." The exclusion of slavery was the deliberate act of the people of Oregon: "it was done in obedience to that great Democratic principle, that it is wiser and better to leave each community to determine and regulate its own local and domestic affairs in its own way."[2]

An amendment to the Constitution to establish a permanent equilibrium between slave and free States, Douglas rightly characterized as "a moral and physical impossibility." The cause of freedom had steadily advanced, while slavery had receded. "We all look forward with confidence to the time when Delaware, Maryland, Virginia, Kentucky, and Missouri, and probably North Carolina and Tennessee, will adopt a gradual system of emancipation. In the meantime," said he, with the exultant spirit of the exuberant West, "we have a vast territory, stretching from the Mississippi to the Pacific, which is rapidly filling up with a hardy, enterprising, and industrious population, large enough to form at least seventeen new free States, one half of which we may expect to see represented in this body during our day. Of these I calculate that four will be formed out of Oregon, five out of our late ac-

[1] *Globe*, 31 Cong., 1 Sess., App., p. 370.   [2] *Ibid.*

quisition from Mexico, including the present State of California, two out of the territory of Minnesota, and the residue out of the country upon the Missouri river, *including Nebraska.* I think I am safe in assuming, that each of these will be free territories and free States whether Congress shall prohibit slavery or not. Now, let me inquire, where are you to find the slave territory with which to balance these seventeen free territories, or even any one of them?"[1] Truer prophecy was never uttered in all the long controversy over the extension of slavery.

With a bit of brag, which was perhaps pardonable under the circumstances, Douglas reminded the Senate of his efforts to secure the admission of California and of his prediction that the people of that country would form a free State constitution. A few months had sufficed to vindicate his position at the last session. And yet, strangely enough, the North was still fearful lest slavery should be extended to New Mexico and Utah. "There is no ground for apprehension on this point," he stoutly contended. "If there was one inch of territory in the whole of our acquisition from Mexico, where slavery could exist, it was in the valleys of the Sacramento and San Joaquin, within the limits of the State of California. It should be borne in mind, that climate regulates this matter, and that climate depends upon the elevation above the sea as much as upon parallels of latitude." Why then leave the question open for further agitation? Give the people of California the government to which they are entitled. "The country is now free by law and in fact—it is free

[1] *Globe*, 31 Cong., 1 Sess., App., p. 371. I have italicized one phrase because of its interesting relation to the Kansas-Nebraska Act.

according to those laws of nature and of God, to which the Senator from Massachusetts alluded, and must forever remain free. It will be free under any bill you may pass, or without any bill at all.'"[1]

Though he did not discuss the compromise resolutions nor commit himself to their support, Douglas paid a noble tribute to the spirit in which they had been offered. He spoke feelingly of "the self-sacrificing spirit which prompted the venerable Senator from Kentucky to exhibit the matchless moral courage of standing undaunted between the two great hostile factions, and rebuking the violence and excesses of each, and pointing out their respective errors, in a spirit of kindness, moderation, and firmness, which made them conscious that he was right." Clay's example was already, he believed, checking the tide of popular excitement. For his part, he entertained no fears as to the future. "The Union will not be put in peril; California will be admitted; governments for the territories must be established; and thus the controversy will end, and I trust forever." A cheerful bit of Western optimism to which the country at large was not yet ready to subscribe.

With his wonted aggressiveness Douglas had a batch of bills ready by March 25th, covering the controverted question of California and the Territories. The origin of these bills is a matter of no little interest. A group of Southern Whigs in the House, led by Toombs and Stephens of Georgia, had taken a determined stand against the admission of California, until assurances were given that concessions would be made

[1] *Globe,* 31 Cong., 1 Sess., App., p. 373.

to the South in the organization of the new Territories.[1]

With both Toombs and Stephens, Douglas was on friendly terms, despite their political differences. Perhaps it was at his suggestion that McClernand of Illinois approached these gentlemen with an olive branch. At all events, a conference was arranged at the Speaker's house, at which Douglas was represented by his friends McClernand, Richardson, and Linn Boyd of Kentucky. Boyd was chairman of the House Committee on Territories; and Richardson a member of the committee. McClernand announced that he had consulted with Douglas and that they were in entire agreement on the points at issue. Douglas had thought it better not to be present in person. The Southerners stated their position frankly and fully. They would consent to the admission of California only upon condition that, in organizing the territorial governments, the power should be given to the people to legislate in regard to slavery, and to frame constitutions with or without slavery. Congress was to bind itself to admit them as States, without any restrictions upon the subject of slavery. The wording of the territorial bills, which would compass these ends, was carefully agreed upon and put in writing. On the basis of this agreement Douglas and McClernand drafted bills for both the Senate and the House Committees.[2]

But the suggestion had already been made and was growing in favor, that a select committee should be intrusted with these and other delicate questions, in

[1] Stephens, Const. View of the War between the States, II, pp. 178 ff.

[2] For an account of this interesting episode, see Stephens, War Between the States, II, pp. 202-204. Boyd, not McClernand, was chairman of the House Committee, but the latter introduced the bills by agreement with Richardson.

order to secure a basis of compromise in the spirit of
Clay's resolutions. Believing that such a course
would indefinitely delay, and even put in jeopardy, the
measure that lay nearest to his heart,—the admission
of California,—Douglas resisted the appointment of
such a committee. If it seemed best to join the California bill with others now pending, he preferred that
the Senate, rather than a committee, should decide
the conditions. But when he was outvoted, Douglas
adopted the sensible course of refusing to obstruct the
work of the Committee of Thirteen by any instructions.
He was inclined to believe the whole project a farce:
well, if it was, the sooner it was over, the better; he
was not disposed to wrangle and turn the farce into a
tragedy.[1]

Douglas was not chosen a member of the select Committee of Thirteen. He could hardly expect to be; but
he contributed not a little to its labors, if a traditional story be true. In a chance conversation, Clay,
who was chairman of the committee, told Douglas that
their report would recommend the union of his two
bills,—the California and the Territorial bills,—instead of a bill of their own. Clay intimated that the
committee felt some delicacy about appropriating
Douglas's carefully drawn measures. With a courtesy
quite equal to Clay's, Douglas urged him to use the
bills if it was deemed wise. For his part, he did not
believe that they could pass the Senate as a single bill.
In that event, he could then urge the original bills
separately upon the Senate. Then Clay, extending
his hand, said, "You are the most generous man
living. I *will* unite the bills and report them; but

[1] *Globe*, 31 Cong., 1 Sess., pp. 662, 757.

justice shall nevertheless be done you as the real author of the measures." A pretty story, and not altogether improbable. At all events, the first part of "the Omnibus Bill," reported by the Committee of Thirteen, consisted of Douglas's two bills joined together by a wafer.[1]

There was one highly significant change in the territorial bills inside the Omnibus. Douglas's measures had been silent on the slavery question; these forbade the territorial legislatures to pass any measure in respect to African slavery, restricting the powers of the territorial legislatures at a vital point. Now on this question Douglas's instructions bound him to an affirmative vote. He was in the uncomfortable and hazardous position of one who must choose between his convictions, and the retention of political office. It was a situation all the more embarrassing, because he had so often asserted the direct responsibility of a representative to his constituents. He extricated himself from the predicament in characteristic fashion. He reaffirmed his convictions; sought to ward off the question; but followed instructions when he had to give his vote. He obeyed the letter, but violated the spirit of his instructions.

In the debates on the Omnibus Bill, Douglas reiterated his theory of non-interference with the right of the people to legislate for themselves on the question of slavery. He was now forced to further interesting assertions by some pointed questions from Senator Davis of Mississippi. "The Senator says that the in-

[1] See Sheahan, Douglas, pp. 132-134. See also Douglas's speech in the Senate, Dec. 23, 1851, and the testimony of Jefferson Davis, *Globe*, 31 Cong., 1 Sess., p. 1830.

habitants of a territory have a right to decide what their institutions shall be. When? By what authority? How many of them?" Douglas replied: "Without determining the precise number, I will assume that the right ought to accrue to the people at the moment they have enough to constitute a government. . . . Your bill concedes that a representative government is necessary—a government founded upon the principles of popular sovereignty, and the right of the people to enact their own laws; and for this reason you give them a legislature constituted of two branches, like the legislatures of the different States and Territories of the Union; you confer upon them the right to legislate upon all rightful subjects of legislation, except negroes. Why except negroes?"[1] Forced to a further explanation, he added, "I am not, therefore, prepared to say that under the constitution, we have not the power to pass laws excluding negro slaves from the territories. . . . But I do say that, if left to myself to carry out my own opinions, I would leave the whole subject to the people of the territories themselves. . . . I believe it is one of those rights to be conceded to the territories the moment they have governments and legislatures established for them."[2] In short, this was a policy dictated by expediency, and not—as yet—by any constitutional necessity. Douglas was not yet ready to abandon the high national ground of supreme, Federal control over the Territories.

But the restrictive clause in the territorial bills satisfied the radical Southerners as little as it pleased Douglas. Berrien wished to make the clause more precise by forbidding the territorial legislatures "to

[1] *Globe*, 31 Cong., 1 Sess., p. 1115.   [2] *Ibid.*, p. 1116.

establish or prohibit African slavery''; but Hale, with his preternatural keenness for the supposed intrigues of the slave power, believed that even with these restrictions the legislatures might still recognize slavery as an already established institution; and he therefore moved to add the word "allow." Douglas voted consistently; first against Berrien's amendment, and then, when it carried, for Hale's, hoping thereby to discredit the former.[1] Douglas's own amendment removing all restrictions, was voted down.[2] True to his instructions, he voted for Seward's proposition to impose the Wilmot Proviso upon the Territories, but he was happy to find himself in the minority.[3] And so the battle went on, threatening to end in a draw.

A motion to abolish and prohibit peon slavery elicited an apparently spontaneous and sincere expression of detestation from Douglas of "this revolting system." Black slavery was not abhorrent to him; but a species of slavery not confined to any color or race, which might, because of a trifling debt, condemn the free white man and his posterity to an endless servitude—this was indeed intolerable. If the Senate was about to abolish black slavery, being unwilling to intrust the territorial legislature with such measures, surely it ought in all consistency to abolish also peonage. But the Senate preferred not to be consistent.[4]

By the last of July, the Omnibus—in the words of Benton—had been overturned, and all the inmates but one spilled out. The Utah bill was the lucky survivor, but even it was not suffered to pass without material alterations. Clay now joined with Douglas

[1] *Globe*, 31 Cong., 1 Sess., pp. 1134-1135.
[2] *Ibid.*, p. 1135.　　[3] *Ibid.*, p. 1134.　　[4] *Ibid.*, pp. 1143-1144.

to secure the omission of the clause forbidding the territorial legislature to touch the subject of slavery. In this they finally succeeded.[1]   The bill was thus restored to its original form.[2]

Everyone admitted that the compromise scheme had been wrecked. It was highly probable, however, that with some changes the proposals of the committee could be adopted, if they were considered separately. Such was Douglas's opinion. The eventuality had occurred which he had foreseen. He was ready for it. He had promptly called up his original California bill and had secured its consideration, when the Utah bill passed to a third reading. Then a bill to settle the Texan boundary controversy was introduced. The Senate passed many weary days discussing first one and then the other. The Texas question was disposed of on August 9th; the California bill, after weathering many storms, came to port four days later; and two days afterward, New Mexico was organized as a Territory under the same conditions as Utah. That is to say, the Senate handed on these bills with its approval to the lower house, where all were voted. It remained only to complete the compromise programme piece-meal, by abolishing the slave trade in the District of Columbia and by providing a more stringent fugitive slave law. By the middle of September, these measures had become law, and the work of Congress went to its final review before the tribunal of public opinion.

Douglas voted for all the compromise measures but

[1] *Globe*, 36 Cong., 1 Sess., App., pp. 305-306; also Cutts, Constitutional and Party Questions, pp. 80-81.

[2] *Globe*, 31 Cong., 1 Sess., App., pp. 1480-1481. Rhodes, History of the United States, I, p. 181.

the Fugitive Slave Law. This was an unfortunate omission, for many a Congressman had sought to dodge the question.[1] The partisan press did not spare him, though he stated publicly that he would have voted for the bill, had he not been forced to absent himself. Such excuses were common and unconvincing. Irritated by sly thrusts on every side, Douglas at last resolved to give a detailed account of the circumstances that had prevented him from putting himself on record in the vote. This public vindication was made upon the floor of the Senate a year later.[2] A "pecuniary obligation" for nearly four thousand dollars was about to fall due in New York. Arrangements which he had made to pay the note miscarried, so that he was compelled to go to New York at once, or suffer the note to be protested. Upon the assurance of his fellow senators that the discussion of the bill would continue at least a week, he hastened to New York. While dining with some friends from Illinois, he was astounded to hear that the bill had been ordered engrossed for a third reading. He immediately left the city for Washington, but arrived too late. He was about to ask permission then to explain his absence, when his colleague dissuaded him. Everyone knew, said Shields, that he was in favor of the bill; besides, very probably the bill would be returned from the House with amendments.

The circumstantial nature of this defense now seems quite unnecessary. After all, the best refutation of the charge lay in Douglas's reputation for courageous and manly conduct. He was true to himself when he

[1] Rhodes, History of the United States, I, pp. 182-183.
[2] *Globe*, 32 Cong., 1 Sess., App., p. 66.

said, "The dodging of votes—the attempt to avoid responsibility—is no part of my system of political tactics."

If it is difficult to distribute the credit—or discredit—of having passed the compromise measures, it verges on the impossible to fix the responsibility on any individual. Clay fathered the scheme of adjustment; but he did not work out the details, and it was just this matter of details which aggravated the situation. Clay no longer coveted glory. His dominant feeling was one of thankfulness. "It was rather a triumph for the Union, for harmony and concord." Douglas agreed with him: "No man and no party has acquired a triumph, except the party friendly to the Union." But the younger man did covet honor, and he could not refrain from reminding the Senate that he had played "an humble part in the enactment of all these great measures."[1] Oddly enough, Jefferson Davis condescended to tickle the vanity of Douglas by testifying, "If any man has a right to be proud of the success of these measures, it is the Senator from Illinois."[2]

Both Douglas and Toombs told their constituents that Congress had agreed upon a great, fundamental principle in dealing with the Territories. Both spoke with some degree of authority, for the two territorial bills had passed in the identical form upon which they had agreed in conference. But what was this principle? Toombs called it the principle which the South had unwisely compromised away in 1820—the principle of non-interference with slavery by Congress, the right of the people to hold slaves in the common Territories.

[1] *Globe*, 31 Cong., 1 Sess., pp. 1829-1830.
[2] *Ibid.*, p. 1830.

Douglas called the great principle, "the right of the people to form and regulate their own internal concerns and domestic institutions in their own way."[1] So stated the principle seems direct and simple. But was Toombs willing to concede that the people of a Territory might exclude slavery? He never said so; while Douglas conceded both the positive power· to exclude, and the negative power to permit, slavery. Here was a discrepancy.[2] And it was probably because they could not agree on this point, that a provision was added to the territorial bills, providing that cases involving title to slaves might be appealed to the Supreme Court. Whether the people of Utah and New Mexico might exclude slaves, was to be left to the judiciary. In any case Congress was not to interfere with slavery in the Territories.

One other question was raised subsequently. Was it intended that Congress should act on this principle in organizing future Territories? In other words, was the principle, newly recovered, to be applied retroactively? There was no answer to the question in 1850, for the simple reason that no one thought to ask it.

[1] See his speech in Chicago; Sheahan, Douglas, p. 169.

[2] When Douglas reported the bills, he announced that there was a difference of opinion in the committee on some points, in regard to which each member reserved the right of stating his own opinion and of acting in accordance therewith. See *Globe*, 31 Cong., 1 Sess., p. 592.

CHAPTER X

YOUNG AMERICA

When Douglas reached Chicago, immediately after the adjournment of Congress, he found the city in an uproar. The strong anti-slavery sentiment of the community had been outraged by the Fugitive Slave Law. Reflecting the popular indignation, the Common Council had adopted resolutions condemning the act as a violation of the Constitution and a transgression of the laws of God. Those senators and representatives who voted for the bill, or "who basely sneaked away from their seats and thereby evaded the question," were stigmatized as "fit only to be ranked with the traitors, Benedict Arnold and Judas Iscariot." This was indeed a sorry home-coming for one who believed himself entitled to honors.

Learning that a mass-meeting was about to indorse the action of the city fathers, Douglas determined to face his detractors and meet their charges. Entering the hall while the meeting was in progress, he mounted the platform, and announced that on the following evening he would publicly defend all the measures of adjustment. He was greeted with hisses and jeers for his pains; but in the end he had the satisfaction of securing an adjournment until his defense had been heard.

It was infinitely to his credit that when he confronted a hostile audience on the next evening, he stooped to no cheap devices to divert resentment, but

sought to approve his course to the sober intelligence
of his hearers.[1] It is doubtful if the Fugitive Slave
Law ever found a more skillful defender. The spirit
in which he met his critics was admirably calculated
to disarm prejudice. Come and let us reason together,
was his plea. Without any attempt to ignore the most
obnoxious parts of the act, he passed directly to the
discussion of the clauses which apparently denied the
writ of *habeas corpus* and trial by jury to the fugitive
from service. He reminded his hearers that this act
was supplementary to the Act of 1793. No one had
found fault with the earlier act because it had denied
these rights. Both acts, in fact, were silent on these
points; yet in neither case was silence to be construed
as a denial of constitutional obligations. On the contrary, they must be assumed to continue in full force
under the act. Misapprehension arose in these matters, because the recovery of the fugitive slave was
not viewed as a process of extradition. The act provided for the return of the alleged slave to the State
from which he had fled. Trial of the facts by jury
would then follow under the laws of the State, just as
the fugitive from justice would be tried in the State
where the alleged crime had been committed. The
testimony before the original court making the requi-
sition, would necessarily be *ex parte,* as in the case of
the escaped criminal; but this did not prevent a fair
trial on return of the fugitive. Regarding the question of establishing the identity of the apprehended
person with the fugitive described in the record, Douglas asserted that the terms of the act required proof

[1] The speech is given in part by Sheahan, Douglas, pp. 171 ff; and
at greater length by Flint, Douglas, App., pp. 3 ff.

satisfactory to the judge or commissioner, and not merely the presentment of the record. "Other and further evidence" might be insisted upon.

At various times Douglas was interrupted by questions which were obviously contrived to embarrass him. To all such he replied courteously and with engaging frankness. "Why was it," asked one of these troublesome questioners, "that the law provided for a fee of ten dollars if the commissioner decided in favor of the claimant, and for a fee of only five dollars if he decided otherwise? Was this not in the nature of an inducement, a bribe?" "I presume," said Douglas, "that the reason was that he would have more labor to perform. If, after hearing the testimony, the commissioner decided in favor of the claimant, the law made it his duty to prepare and authenticate the necessary papers to authorize him to carry the fugitive home; but if he decided against him, he had no such labor to perform."

After all, as Douglas said good-naturedly, all these objections were predicated on a reluctance to return a slave to his master under any circumstances. Did his hearers realize, he insisted, that refusal to do so was a violation of the Constitution? And were they willing to shatter the Union because of this feeling? At this point he was again interrupted by an individual, who wished to know if the provisions of the Constitution were not in violation of the law of God. "The divine law," responded Douglas, "does not prescribe the form of government under which we shall live, and the character of our political and civil institutions. Revelation has not furnished us with a constitution—a code of international law—and a system of civil and municipal jurisprudence.'' If this Constitution were to be repudiated, he begged to know, "who is to be the prophet to reveal the will of God, and establish a theocracy for us?"

At the conclusion of his speech, Douglas offered a series of resolutions expressing the obligation of all good citizens to maintain the Constitution and all laws duly enacted by Congress in pursuance of the Constitution. With a remarkable revulsion of feeling, the audience indorsed these sentiments without a dissenting voice, and subsequently repudiated in express terms the resolutions of the Common Council.[1] The triumph of Douglas was complete. It was one of those rare instances where the current of popular resentment is not only deflected, but actually reversed, by the determination and eloquence of one man.

There were two groups of irreconcilables to whom such appeals were unavailing—radical Abolitionists at the North and Southern Rights advocates. Not even the eloquence of Webster could make willing slave-catchers of the anti-slavery folk of Massachusetts. The rescue of the negro Shadrach, an alleged fugitive slave, provoked intense excitement, not only in New England but in Washington. The incident was deemed sufficiently ominous to warrant a proclamation by the President, counseling all good citizens to uphold the law. Southern statesmen of the radical type saw abundant evidence in this episode of a deliberate purpose at the North not to enforce the essential features of the compromise. Both Whig and Democratic leaders, with few exceptions, roundly denounced all attempts to nullify the Fugitive Slave Law.[2] None was

[1] Sheahan, Douglas, p. 186; Flint, Douglas, App., p. 30.
[2] *Globe*, 31 Cong., 2 Sess., Debate of February 21 and 22, 1851.

more vehement than Douglas. He could not regard
this Boston rescue as a trivial incident. He believed
that there was an organization in many States to evade
the law. It was in the nature of a conspiracy against
the government. The ring-leaders were Abolitionists,
who were exciting the negroes to excesses. He was
utterly at a loss to understand how senators, who had
sworn to obey and defend the Constitution, could
countenance these palpable violations of law.[1]

In spite of similar untoward incidents, the vast
majority of people in the country North and South were
acquiescing little by little in the settlement reached by
the compromise measures. There was an evident disposition on the part of both Whig and Democratic
leaders to drop the slavery issue. When Senator
Sumner proposed a repeal of the Fugitive Slave Act,
Douglas deprecated any attempt to "fan the flames
of discord that have so recently divided this great
people,"[2] intimating that Sumner's speech was intended to "operate upon the presidential election."
It ill became the Senator from Illinois to indulge in
such taunts, for no one, it may safely be said, was
calculating his own political chances more intently.
"Things look well," he had written to a friend, referring to his chances of securing the nomination, "and
the prospect is brightening every day. All that is
necessary now to insure success is that the northwest
should unite and speak out."[3]

When the Democrats of Illinois proposed Douglas's
name for the presidency in 1848, no one was disposed

[1] *Globe*, 31 Cong., 2 Sess., App., p. 312.
[2] *Globe*, 32 Cong., 1 Sess., App., p. 1120.
[3] MS. Letter dated December 30, 1851.

to take the suggestion seriously, outside the immediate circle of his friends. To graybeards there was something almost humorous in the suggestion that five years of service in Congress gave a young man of thirty-five a claim to consideration! Within three short years, however, the situation had changed materially. Older aspirants for the chief magistracy were forced, with no little alarm, to acknowledge the rise of a really formidable rival. By midsummer of 1851, competent observers thought that Douglas had the best chance of winning the Democratic nomination. In the judgment of certain Whig editors, he was the strongest man. It was significant of his growing favor, that certain Democrats of the city and county of New York tendered him a banquet, in honor of his distinguished services to the party and his devotion to the Union during the past two years.

Politicians of both parties shared the conviction that unless the Whigs could get together,—which was unlikely,—a nomination at the hands of a national Democratic convention was equivalent to an election. Consequently there were many candidates in the field. The preliminary canvass promised to be eager. It was indeed well under way long before Congress assembled in December, and it continued actively during the session. "The business of the session," wrote one observer in a cynical frame of mind, "will consist mainly in the manœuvres, intrigues, and competitions for the next Presidency." Events justified the prediction. "A politician does not sneeze without reference to the Presidency," observed the same writer, some weeks after the beginning of the session. "Congress does little else but intrigue for the respective candidates.''[1]

Prospective candidates who sat in Congress had at least this advantage, over their outside competitors,— they could keep themselves in the public eye by making themselves conspicuous in debate. But the wisdom of such devices was questionable. Those who could not point with confident pride to their record, wisely chose to remain non-committal on matters of personal history. Douglas was one of those who courted publicity. Perhaps as a young man pitted against older rivals, he felt that he had everything to gain thereby and not much to lose. The irrepressible Foote of Mississippi gave all his colleagues a chance to mar their reputations, by injecting into the deliberations of the Senate a discussion of the finality of the compromise measures.[2] It speedily appeared that fidelity to the settlement of 1850, from the Southern point of view, consisted in strict adherence to the Fugitive Slave Act.[3] This was the touchstone by which Southern statesmen proposed to test their Northern colleagues. Prudence whispered silence into many an ear; but Douglas for one refused to heed her admonitions. Within three weeks after the session began, he was on his feet defending the consistency of his course, with an apparent ingenuousness which carried conviction to the larger audience who read, but did not hear, his declaration of political faith.

Two features of this speech commended it to Demo-

[1] Mann, Life of Horace Mann, pp. 351, 358, 362.

[2] Senator Foote introduced the subject December 2, 1851, by a resolution pronouncing the compromise measures a ''definite adjustment and settlement.''

[3] Rhodes, History of the United States, I, p. 230.

crats: its recognition of the finality of the compromise, and its insistence upon the necessity of banishing the slavery question from politics. "The Democratic party," he asseverated, "is as good a Union party as I want, and I wish to preserve its principles and its organization, and to triumph upon its old issues. I desire no new tests—no interpolations into the old creed."[1] For his part, he was resolved never to speak again upon the slavery question in the halls of Congress.

But this was after all a negative programme. Could a campaign be successfully fought without other weapons than the well-worn blunderbusses in the Democratic arsenal? This was a do-nothing policy, difficult to reconcile with the enthusiastic liberalism which Young America was supposed to cherish. Yet Douglas gauged the situation accurately. The bulk of the party wished a return to power more than anything else. To this end, they were willing to toot for old issues and preserve the old party alignment. For four years, the Democratic office-hunters had not tasted of the loaves and fishes within the gift of the executive. They expected liberality in conduct, if not liberalism in creed, from their next President. Douglas shared this political hunger. He had always been a believer in rotation in office, and an exponent of that unhappy, American practice of using public office as the spoil of party victory. In this very session, he put himself on record against permanence in office for the clerks of the Senate, holding that such positions should fall vacant at stated intervals.[2]

[1] *Globe*, 32 Cong., 1 Sess., App., p. 68.

[2] *Globe*, 32 Cong., 1 Sess., p. 63. About this time he wrote to a friend, "I shall act on the rule of giving the offices to those who fight the battles."

But had Douglas no policy peculiarly his own, to qualify him for the leadership of his party? Distrustful Whigs accused him of being willing to offer Cuba for the support of the South.[1] Indeed, he made no secret of his desire to acquire the Pearl of the Antilles. Still, this was not the sort of issue which it was well to drag into a presidential campaign. Like all the other aspirants for the presidency, Douglas made what capital he could out of the visit of Kossuth and the question of intervention in behalf of Hungary. When the matter fell under discussion in the Senate, Douglas formulated what he considered should be the policy of the government:

"I hold that the principle laid down by Governor Kossuth as the basis of his action—that each State has a right to dispose of her own destiny, and regulate her internal affairs in her own way, without the intervention of any foreign power—is an axiom in the laws of nations which every State ought to recognize and respect. . . . It is equally clear to my mind, that any violation of this principle by one nation, intervening for the purpose of destroying the liberties of another, is such an infraction of the international code as would authorize any State to interpose, which should conceive that it had sufficient interest in the question to become the vindicator of the laws of nations."[2]

Cass had said much the same thing, but with less virility. Douglas scored on his rival in this speech: first, when he declared with a bit of Chauvinism, "I do not deem it material whether the reception of Governor Kossuth give offence to the crowned heads

[1] Mann, Life of Horace Mann, p. 354.
[2] Globe, 32 Cong., 1 Sess., p. 70.

of Europe, provided it does not violate the law of nations, and give just *cause* of offence''; and again, scorning the suggestion of an alliance with England, ''The peculiar position of our country requires that we should have an *American policy* in our foreign relations, based upon the principles of our own government, and adapted to the spirit of the age.''[1] There was a stalwart conviction in these utterances which gave promise of confident, masterful leadership. These are qualities which the people of this great democracy have always prized, but rarely discovered, in their Presidents.

It was at this moment in the canvass that the promoters of Douglas's candidacy made a false move. Taking advantage of the popular demonstration over Kossuth and the momentary diversion of public attention from the slavery question to foreign politics, they sought to thrust Douglas upon the Democratic party as the exponent of a progressive foreign policy. They presumed to speak in behalf of ''Young America,'' as against ''Old Fogyism.'' Seizing upon the *Democratic Review* as their organ, these progressives launched their boom by a sensational article in the January number, entitled ''Eighteen-Fifty-Two and the Presidency.'' Beginning with an arraignment of Webster's un-American foreign policy, the writer,—or writers,—called upon honest men to put an end to this ''Quaker policy.'' ''The time has come for strong, sturdy, clearheaded and honest men to act; and the Republic must have them, should it be compelled, as the colonies were in 1776, to drag the hero of the time out of a hole in a wild forest, [*sic*] whether in Virginia or the illimitable

[1] *Globe,* 32 Cong., 1 Sess., pp. 70-71.

West." To inaugurate such an era, the presidential chair must be filled by a man, not of the last generation, but of this. He must not be "trammeled with ideas belonging to an anterior era, or a man of merely local fame and local affections, but a statesman who can bring young blood, young ideas, and young hearts to the councils of the Republic. He must not be a mere general, a mere lawyer, a mere wire-puller. "Your beaten horse, whether he ran for a previous presidential cup as first or second," will not do. He must be 'a tried civilian, not a second and third rate general.' "Withal, a practical statesman, not to be discomfited in argument, or led wild by theory, but one who has already, in the councils and tribunals of the nation, reared his front to the dismay of the shallow conservative, to the exposure of the humanitarian incendiary, and the discomfiture of the antiquated rhetorician."

If anyone was so dense as not to recognize the portrait here painted, he had only to turn to an article entitled "Intervention," to find the name of the hero who was to usher in the new era. The author of this paper finds his sentiments so nearly identical with those of Stephen A. Douglas, that he resorts to copious extracts from his speech delivered in the Senate on the welcome of Kossuth, "entertaining no doubt that the American people, the *democracy* of the country will endorse these doctrines by an overwhelming majority." Still another article in this formidable broadside from the editors of the *Democratic Review,* deprecated Foote's efforts to thrust the slavery issue again upon Congress, and expressed the pious wish that Southern delegates might join with Northern in the Baltimore convention, to nominate a candidate who would in future "evince the most profound ignorance as to the topographical bearing of that line of discord known as 'Mason and Dixon's.'"

If all this was really the work of Douglas's friends,— and it is more than likely,—he had reason to pray to be delivered from them. At best the whole manœuvre was clumsily planned and wretchedly executed; it probably did him irreparable harm. His strength was not sufficient to confront all his rivals; yet the almost inevitable consequence of the odious comparisons in the *Review* was combinations against him. The leading article gave mortal offense in quarters where he stood most in need of support.[1] Douglas was quick to detect the blunder and appreciate its dangers to his prospects. His friends now began sedulously to spread the report that the article was a ruse of the enemy, for the especial purpose of spoiling his chances at Baltimore. It was alleged that proof sheets had been found in the possession of a gentleman in Washington, who was known to be hostile to Douglas.[2] Few believed this story: the explanation was too far-fetched. Nevertheless, one of Douglas's intimates subsequently declared, on the floor of the House, that the Judge was not responsible for anything that appeared in the *Review*, that he had no interest in or control over the magazine, and that he knew nothing about the January number until he saw it in print.[3]

In spite of this untoward incident, Douglas made a

---

[1] See speech by Breckinridge of Kentucky in *Globe*, 32 Cong., 1 Sess., App., pp. 299 ff.

[2] Pike, First Blows of the Civil War, p. 115.

[3] Statement by Richardson of Illinois in reply to J. C. Breckinridge of Kentucky, March 3, 1852. *Globe*, 32 Cong., 1 Sess., App., p. 302.

formidable showing.[1] He was himself well pleased at the outlook. He wrote to a friend, "Prospects look well and are improving every day. If two or three western States will speak out in my favor the battle is over. Can anything be done in Iowa and Missouri? That is very important. If some one could go to Iowa, I think the convention in that State would instruct for me. In regard to our own State, I will say a word. Other States are appointing a large number of delegates to the convention, ... ought not our State to do the same thing so as to ensure the attendance of most of our leading politicians at Baltimore? . . . . This large number would exert a great moral influence on the other delegates."[2]

Among the States which had led off in his favor was California; and it was a representative of California who first sounded the charge for Douglas's cohorts in the House. In any other place and at any other time, Marshall's exordium would have overshot the mark. Indeed, in indorsing the attack of the *Review* on the old fogies in the party, he tore open wounds which it were best to let heal; but gauged by the prevailing standard of taste in politics, the speech was acceptable. It so far commended itself to the editors of the much-abused *Review* that it appeared in the April number, under the caption "The Progress of Democracy vs. Old Fogy Retrograder."

To clear-headed outsiders, there was something factitious in this parade of enthusiasm for Douglas.

---

[1] "What with his Irish Organs, his Democratic reviews and an armful of other strings, each industriously pulled, he makes a formidable show." Pike, First Blows of the Civil War, p. 115.

[2] MS. Letter, February 25, 1852.

''What most surprises one,'' wrote the correspondent of the New York *Tribune,* ''is that these Congressmen, with beards and without; that verdant, flippant, smart detachment of Young America that has got into the House, propose to make a candidate for the Baltimore convention without consulting their masters, the people. With a few lively fellows in Congress and the aid of the *Democratic Review,* they fancy themselves equal to the achievement of a small job like this.''[1] As the first of June approached, the older, experienced politicians grew confident that none of the prominent candidates could command a two-thirds vote in the convention. Some had foreseen this months beforehand and had been casting about for a compromise candidate. Their choice fell eventually upon General Franklin Pierce of New Hampshire. Friends were active in his behalf as early as April, and by June they had hatched their plot. It was not their plan to present his name to the convention at the outset, but to wait until the three prominent candidates (Cass, Douglas, and Buchanan) were disposed of. He was then to be put forward as an available, compromise candidate.[2]

Was Douglas cognizant of the situation? While his supporters did not abate their noisy demonstrations, there is some ground to believe that he did not share their optimistic spirit. At all events, in spite of his earlier injunctions, only eleven delegates from Illinois attended the convention, while Pennsylvania sent fifty-five, Tennessee twenty-seven, and Indiana thirty-nine.

[1] Pike, First Blows of the Civil War, p. 118.

[2] Burke-Pierce Correspondence, printed in *American Historical Review,* X, pp. 110 ff. See also Stanwood, History of the Presidency, p. 248, and Rhodes, History of the United States, I, pp. 251-252.

Had Douglas sent home the intimation that the game was up? The first ballot told the story of his defeat. Common rumor had predicted that a large part of the Northwest would support him. Only fifteen of his twenty votes came from that quarter, and eleven of these were cast by Illinois. It was said that the Indiana delegates would divert their strength to him, when they had cast one ballot for General Lane; but Indiana cast no votes for Douglas. Although his total vote rose to ninety-two and on the thirty-first ballot he received the highest vote of any of the candidates, there was never a moment when there was the slightest prospect of his winning the prize.[1]

On the thirty-fifth ballot occurred a diversion. Virginia cast fifteen votes for Franklin Pierce. The schemers had launched their project. But it was not until the forty-ninth ballot that they started the avalanche. Pierce then received all but six votes. Two Ohio delegates clung to Douglas to the bitter end. With the frank manliness which made men forget his less admirable qualities, Douglas dictated this dispatch to the convention: "I congratulate the Democratic party upon the nomination, and Illinois will give Franklin Pierce a larger majority than any other State in the Union,"—a promise which he was not able to redeem.

If Douglas had been disposed to work out his political prospects by mathematical computation, he would have arrived at some interesting conclusions from the balloting in the convention. Indeed, very probably he drew some deductions in his own intuitive way, without any adventitious aid. Of the three rivals, Cass re-

[1] Proceedings of Democratic National Convention of 1852.

ceived the most widely distributed vote, although Douglas received votes from as many States. While they drew votes from twenty-one States, Buchanan received votes from only fifteen. Cass and Douglas obtained their highest percentages of votes from the West; Buchanan found his strongest support in the South. Douglas and Cass received least support in the Middle States; Buchanan had no votes from the West. But while Cass had, on his highest total, thirty per centum of the whole vote of the Middle States, Douglas was relatively weak in the Middle States rather than in the South. On the basis of these figures, it is impossible to justify the statement that he could expect nothing in future from New England and Pennsylvania, but would look to the South for support for the presidency.[1] On the contrary, one would say that his strong New England following would act as an equipoise, preventing too great a dip toward the Southern end of the scales. Besides, Douglas's hold on his own constituents and the West was contingent upon the favor of the strong New England element in the Northwest. If this convention taught Douglas anything, it must have convinced him that narrow, sectional policies and undue favor to the South would never land him in the White House. To win the prize which he frankly coveted, he must grow in the national confidence, and not merely in the favor of a single section, however powerful.[2]

Pledges aside, Douglas was bound to give vigorous

[1] See Rhodes, History of the United States, I, pp. 424-425.

[2] To attribute to Douglas, from this time on, as many writers have done, a purpose to pander to the South, is not only to discredit his political foresight, but to misunderstand his position in the Northwest and to ignore his reiterated assertions.

aid to the party candidates. His term as senator was about to expire. His own fortunes were inseparably connected with those of his party in Illinois. The Washington *Union* printed a list of his campaign engagements, remarking with evident satisfaction that Judge Douglas was "in the field with his armor on." His itinerary reached from Virginia to Arkansas, and from New York to the interior counties of his own State. Stray items from a speech in Richmond suggest the tenuous quality of these campaign utterances. It was quite clear to his mind that General Scott's acceptance of the Whig nomination could not have been written by that manly soldier, but by *Politician* Scott under the control of *General* Seward. Was it wise to convert a good general into a bad president? Could it be true that Scott had promised the entire patronage of his administration to the Whigs? Why, "there had never been a Democratic administration in this Union that did not retain at least one-third of their political opponents in office!"[1] And yet, when Pierce had been elected, Douglas could say publicly, without so much as a blush, that Democrats must now have the offices. "For every Whig removed there should be a competent Democrat put in his place. . . The best men should be selected, and everybody knows that the best men voted for Pierce and King."[2]

The outcome of the elections in Illinois was gratifying save in one particular. In consequence of the redistricting of the State, the Whigs had increased the number of their representatives in Congress. But the

---

[1] Richmond *Enquirer*, quoted in Illinois *Register*, August 3, 1852.

[2] Illinois *State Register*, December 23, 1852.

re-election of Douglas was assured.[1] His hold upon his constituency was unshaken. With right good will he participated in the Democratic celebration at Washington. As an influential personage in Democratic councils he was called upon to sketch in broad lines what he deemed to be sound Democratic policy; but only a casual reference to Cuba redeemed his speech from the commonplace. "Whenever the people of Cuba show themselves worthy of freedom by asserting and maintaining independence, and apply for annexation, they ought to be annexed; whenever Spain is ready to sell Cuba, with the consent of its inhabitants, we ought to accept it on fair terms; and if Spain should transfer Cuba to England or any other European power, we should take and hold Cuba anyhow."[2]

Ambition and a buoyant optimism seemed likely to make Douglas more than ever a power in Democratic politics, when a personal bereavement changed the current of his life. His young wife whom he adored, the mother of his two boys, died shortly after the new year. For the moment he was overwhelmed; and when he again took his place in the Senate, his colleagues remarked in him a bitterness and acerbity of temper which was not wonted. One hostage that he had given to Fortune had been taken away, and a certain recklessness took possession of him. He grew careless in his personal habits, slovenly in his dress, disregardful of his associates, and if possible more vehemently partisan in his public utterances.

[1] Washington *Union*, November 30, 1852. On a joint ballot of the legislature Douglas received 75 out of 95 votes. See Illinois *State Register*, January 5, 1853.

[2] Illinois *State Register*, December 23, 1852.

It was particularly regrettable that, while Douglas was passing through this domestic tragedy, he should have been drawn into a controversy relating to British claims in Central America. It was rumored that Great Britain, in apparent violation of the terms of the Clayton-Bulwer treaty, had taken possession of certain islands in the Bay of Honduras and erected them into the colony of "the Bay Islands." On the heels of this rumor came news that aroused widespread indignation. A British man-of-war had fired upon an American steamer, which had refused to pay port dues on entering the harbor of Greytown. Over this city, strategically located at the mouth of the San Juan River, Great Britain exercised an ill-disguised control as part of the Mosquito protectorate.

In the midst of the excited debate which immediately followed in Congress, Cass astonished everybody by producing the memorandum which Bulwer had given Clayton just before the signing of the treaty.[1] In this remarkable note, the British ambassador stated that his government did not wish to be understood as renouncing its existing claims to Her Majesty's settlement at Honduras and "its dependencies." And Clayton seemed to have admitted the force of this reservation. For his part, Cass made haste to say, he wished the Senate distinctly to understand that when he had voted for the treaty, he believed Great Britain was thereby prevented from establishing any such dependency. His object—and he had supposed it to be the object of the treaty—was to sweep away all British claims to Central America.

Behind this imbroglio lay an intricate diplomatic

[1] Smith, Parties and Slavery, pp. 88-93.

history which can be here only briefly recapitulated. The interest of the United States in the Central American States dated from the discovery of gold in California. The value of the control of the means of transportation across the isthmus at Nicaragua became increasingly clear, as the gold seekers sought that route to the Pacific coast. In the latter days of his administration, President Polk had sent one Elijah Hise to cultivate friendly relations with the Central American States and to offset the paramount influence of Great Britain in that region. Great Britain was already in possession of the colony of Belize and was exercising an ill-defined protectorate over the Mosquito Indians on the eastern coast of Nicaragua. In his ardor to serve American interests, Hise exceeded his instructions and secured a treaty with Nicaragua, which gave to the United States exclusive privileges over the route of the proposed canal, on condition that the sovereignty of Nicaragua were guaranteed. The incoming Whig administration would have nothing to do with the Hise *entente,* preferring to dispatch its own agent to Central America. Though Squier succeeded in negotiating a more acceptable treaty, the new Secretary of State, Clayton, was disposed to come to an understanding with Great Britain. The outcome of these prolonged negotiations was the famous Clayton-Bulwer treaty, by which both countries agreed to further the construction of a ship canal across the isthmus through Nicaragua, and to guarantee its neutrality. Other countries were invited to join in securing the neutrality of this and other regions where canals might be constructed. Both Great Britain and the United States explicitly renounced any "dominion over Nicaragua, Costa Rica, the Mosquito coast or any part of Central America.''[1]

The opposition would have been something less than human, if they had not seized upon the occasion to discredit the outgoing administration. Cass had already introduced a resolution reaffirming the terms of the famous Monroe message respecting European colonization in America, and thus furnishing the pretext for partisan attacks upon Secretary of State Clayton. But Cass unwittingly exposed his own head to a sidelong blow from his Democratic rival from Illinois, who affected the rôle of Young America once more.

It is impossible to convey in cold print the biting sarcasm, the vindictive bitterness, and the reckless disregard of justice, with which Douglas spoke on February 14th. He sneered at this new profession of the Monroe Doctrine. Why keep repeating this talk about a policy which the United States has almost invariably repudiated in fact? Witness the Oregon treaty! ''With an avowed policy, of thirty years' standing that no future European colonization is to be permitted in America—affirmed when there was no opportunity for enforcing it, and abandoned whenever a case was presented for carrying it into practical effect—is it now proposed to beat another retreat under cover of terrible threats of awful consequences when the offense shall be repeated? '*Henceforth*' no 'future' European colony is to be planted in America '*with our consent!*' It is gratifying to learn that the United States are never going to 'consent' to the repudiation

[1] MacDonald, Select Documents of the History of the United States, No. 77.

of the Monroe doctrine again. No more Clayton and Bulwer treaties; no more British 'alliances' in Central America, New Granada, or Mexico; no more resolutions of oblivion to protect 'existing rights!' Let England tremble, and Europe take warning, if the offense is repeated. 'Should the attempt be made,' says the resolution, 'it will leave the United States *free to adopt* such measures as an independent nation may justly adopt in defense of its rights and honor.' Are not the United States now *free* to adopt such measures as an independent nation may *justly adopt* in defense of its *rights and honor?* Have we not given the notice? Is not thirty years sufficient notice?"[1]

He taunted Clayton with having suppressed the Hise treaty, which secured exclusive privileges for the United States over the canal route, in order to form a partnership with England and other monarchical powers of Europe. "Exclusive privileges" were sacrificed to lay the foundation of an alliance by which European intervention in American affairs was recognized as a right!

It was generally known that Douglas had opposed the Clayton-Bulwer treaty;[2] but the particular ground of his opposition had been only surmised. Deeming the injunction of secrecy removed, he now emphatically registered his protest against the whole policy of pledging the faith of the Republic, not to do what in the future our interests, duty, and even safety, might compel us to do. The time might come when the United

---

[1] *Globe,* 32 Cong., 2 Sess., App., p. 170.

[2] Douglas declined to serve on the Senate Committee on Foreign Affairs, because he was opposed to the policy of the majority, so he afterward intimated. *Globe,* 32 Cong., 2 Sess., App., p. 268.

States would wish to possess some portion of Central America. Moreover, the agreement not to fortify any part of that region was not reciprocal, so long as Great Britain held Jamaica and commanded the entrance to the canal. He had always regarded the terms of the British protectorate over the Mosquito coast as equivocal; but the insuperable objection to the treaty was the European partnership to which the United States was pledged. The two parties not only contracted to extend their protection to any other practicable communications across the isthmus, whether by canal or railway, but invited all other powers to become parties to these provisions. What was the purport of this agreement, if it did not recognize the right of European powers to intervene in American affairs; what then became of the vaunted Monroe Doctrine?

To the undiplomatic mind of Douglas, our proper course was as clear as day. Insist upon the withdrawal of Great Britain from the Bay Islands! "If we act with becoming discretion and firmness, I have no apprehension that the enforcement of our rights will lead to hostilities." And then let the United States free itself from entangling alliances by annulling the Clayton-Bulwer treaty.[1] Surely this was simplicity itself.

The return of Clayton to the Senate, in the special session of March, brought the accused before his accusers. An acrimonious debate followed, in the course of which Douglas was forced to state his own position more explicitly. He took his stand upon the Hise treaty. Had the exclusive control of the canal been given into our hands, and the canal thrown open to the

[1] *Globe*, 32 Cong., 2 Sess., App., p. 173.

commerce of all nations upon our own terms, we would have had a right which would have been ample security for every nation under heaven to keep peace with the United States. "We could have fortified that canal at each end, and in time of war could have closed it against our enemies." But, suggested Clayton, European powers would never have consented to such exclusive control. "Well, Sir," said Douglas, "I do not know that they would have consented: but of one thing I am certain I would never have asked their consent."[1] And such was the temper of Young America that this sledge hammer diplomacy was heartily admired.

It was in behalf of Young America again, that Douglas gave free rein to his vision of national destiny. Disclaiming any immediate wish for tropical expansion in the direction of either Mexico or Central America, he yet contended that no man could foresee the limits of the Republic. "You may make as many treaties as you please to fetter the limits of this giant Republic, and she will burst them all from her, and her course will be onward to a limit which I will not venture to prescribe." Why, then, pledge our faith never to annex any more of Mexico or any portion of Central America?[2]

For this characteristic Chauvinism Douglas paid the inevitable penalty. Clayton promptly ridiculed this attitude. "He is fond of boasting . . . . that we are a *giant* Republic; and the Senator himself is said to be a 'little giant;' yes, sir, quite a *giant,* and everything that he talks about in these latter days is gigantic. He has become so magnificent of late, that he cannot con-

[1] *Globe*, 32 Cong., Special Sess., p. 261.
[2] *Ibid.*, p. 262.

sent to enter into a partnership on equal terms with any nation on earth—not he! He must have the exclusive right in himself and our noble selves!"[1]

It was inevitable, too, that Douglas should provoke resentment on his own side of the chamber. Cass was piqued by his slurs upon Old Fogyism and by his trenchant criticism of the policy of reasserting the Monroe Doctrine. Badger spoke for the other side of the house, when he declared that Douglas spoke "with a disregard to justice and fairness which I have seldom seen him exhibit." It is lamentably true that Douglas exhibited his least admirable qualities on such occasions. Hatred for Great Britain was bred in his bones. Possibly it was part of his inheritance from that grandfather who had fought the Britishers in the wars of the Revolution. Possibly, too, he had heard as a boy, in his native Vermont village, tales of British perfidy in the recent war of 1812. At all events, he was utterly incapable of anything but bitter animosity toward Great Britain. This unreasoning prejudice blinded his judgment in matters of diplomacy, and vitiated his utterances on questions of foreign policy.

Replying to Clayton, he said contemptuously, "I do not sympathize with that feeling which the Senator expressed yesterday, that it was a pity to have a difference with a nation so friendly to us as England. Sir, I do not see the evidence of her friendship. It is not in the nature of things that she can be our friend. It is impossible that she can love us. I do not blame her for not loving us. Sir, we have wounded her vanity and humbled her pride. She can never forgive us."[2]

[1] *Globe*, 32 Cong., Special Sess., p. 276.

[2] *Ibid.*, p. 262.

And when Senator Butler rebuked him for this animosity, reminding him that England was after all our
mother country, to whom we were under deeper obligations than to any other, Douglas retorted, "She is and
ever has been a cruel and unnatural mother." Yes,
he remembered the illustrious names of Hampden,
Sidney, and others; but he remembered also that "the
same England which gave them birth, and should have
felt a mother's pride and love in their virtues and services, persecuted her noble sons to the dungeon and the
scaffold." "He speaks in terms of delight and gratitude of the copious and refreshing streams which English literature and science are pouring into our country
and diffusing throughout the land. Is he not aware
that nearly every English book circulated and read in
this country contains lurking and insidious slanders
and libels upon the character of our people and the institutions and policy of our Government?"[1]

For Europe in general, Douglas had hardly more
reverence. With a positiveness which in such matters
is sure proof of provincialism, he said, "Europe is
antiquated, decrepit, tottering on the verge of dissolution. When you visit her, the objects which enlist your
highest admiration are the relics of past greatness;
the broken columns erected to departed power. It is
one vast graveyard, where you find here a tomb indi-
cating the burial of the arts; there a monument mark-
ing the spot where liberty expired; another to the
memory of a great man, whose place has never been
filled. The choicest products of her classic soil consist
in relics, which remain as sad memorials of departed
glory and fallen greatness! They bring up the mem-

[1] *Globe,* 32 Cong., Special Sess., p. 275.

ories of the dead, but inspire no hope for the living! Here everything is fresh, blooming, expanding and advancing.''[1]

And yet, soon after Congress adjourned, he set out to visit this vast graveyard. It was even announced that he proposed to spend five or six months in studying the different governments of Europe. Doubtless he regarded this study as of negative value chiefly. From the observation of relics of departed grandeur, a live American would derive many a valuable lesson. His immediate destination was the country against which he had but just thundered. Small wonder if a cordial welcome did not await him. His admiring biographer records with pride that he was not presented to Queen Victoria, though the opportunity was afforded.[2] It appears that this stalwart Democrat would not so far demean himself as to adopt the conventional court dress for the occasion. He would not stoop even to adopt the compromise costume of Ambassador Buchanan, and add to the plain dress of an American citizen, a short sword which would distinguish him from the court lackeys.

At St. Petersburg, his objections to court dress were more sympathetically received. Count Nesselrode, who found this uncompromising American possessed of redeeming qualities, put himself to no little trouble to arrange an interview with the Czar. Douglas was finally put under the escort of Baron Stoeckle, who was a member of the Russian embassy at Washington, and conducted to the field where the Czar was reviewing the army. Mounted upon a charger of huge dimen-

[1] *Globe*, 32 Cong., Special Sess., p. 273.
[2] Sheahan, Douglas, pp. 443-444.

sions, the diminutive Douglas was brought into the presence of the Czar of all the Russias.[1] It is said that Douglas was the only American who witnessed these manœuvres; but Douglas afterward confessed, with a laugh at his own expense, that the most conspicuous feature of the occasion for him was the ominous evolutions of his horse's ears, for he was too short of limb and too inexperienced a horseman to derive any satisfaction from the military pageant.[2]

We are assured by his devoted biographer, Sheahan, that Douglas personally examined *all* the public institutions of the capital during his two weeks' stay in St. Petersburg; and that he sought a thorough knowledge of the manners, laws, and government of that city and the Empire.[3] No doubt, with his nimble perception he saw much in this brief sojourn, for Russia had always interested him greatly, and he had read its history with more than wonted care.[4] He was not content to follow merely the beaten track in central and western Europe; but he visited also the Southeast where rumors of war were abroad. From St. Petersburg, he passed by carriage through the interior to the Crimea and to Sebastopol, soon to be the storm centre of war. In the marts of Syria and Asia Minor, he witnessed the contact of Orient and Occident. In the Balkan peninsula he caught fugitive glimpses of the rule of the unspeakable Turk.[5]

[1] Sheahan, Douglas, pp. 444-445.

[2] Major McConnell in the Transactions of the Illinois Historical Society, IV, p. 48; Linder, Early Bench and Bar of Illinois, pp. 80-82.

[3] Sheahan, Douglas, p. 444.

[4] Conversation with Judge R. M. Douglas.

[5] Washington *Union*, and Illinois *State Register*, May 26 and November 6, 1853.

No man with the quick apperceptive powers of Douglas could remain wholly untouched by the sights and sounds that crowd upon even the careless traveler in the East; yet such experiences are not formative in the character of a man of forty. Douglas was still Douglas, still American, still Western to the core, when he set foot on native soil in late October. He was not a larger man either morally or intellectually; but he had acquired a fund of information which made him a readier, and possibly a wiser, man. And then, too, he was refreshed in body and mind. More than ever he was bold, alert, persistent, and resourceful. In his compact, massive frame, were stored indomitable pluck and energy; and in his heart the spirit of ambition stirred mightily.

CHAPTER XI

THE KANSAS-NEBRASKA ACT

With the occupation of Oregon and of the gold fields of California, American colonization lost temporarily its conservative character. That heel-and-toe process, which had hitherto marked the occupation of the Mississippi Valley, seemed too slow and tame; the pace had lengthened and quickened. Consequently there was a great waste—No-man's-land—between the western boundary of Iowa, Missouri and Arkansas, and the scattered communities on the Pacific slope. It was a waste broken only by the presence of the Mormons in Utah, of nomadic tribes of Indians on the plains, and of tribes of more settled habits on the eastern border. In many cases these lands had been given to Indian tribes in perpetuity, to compensate for the loss of their original habitat in some of the Eastern States. With strange lack of foresight, the national government had erected a barrier to its own development.

As early as 1844, Douglas had proposed a territorial government for the region of which the Platte, or Nebraska, was the central stream.[1] The chief trail to Oregon traversed these prairies and plains. If the United States meant to assert and maintain its title to Oregon, some sort of government was needed to protect emigrants, and to supply a military basis for such forces as should be required to hold the disputed coun-

[1] House Bill No. 444; 28 Cong., 2 Sess.

try. Though the Secretary of War indorsed this view,[1] Congress was not disposed to anticipate the occupation of the prairies. Nebraska became almost a hobby with Douglas. He introduced a second bill in 1848,[2] and a third in 1852,[3] all designed to prepare the way for settled government.

The last of these was unique. Its provisions were designed, no doubt, to meet the unusual conditions presented by the overland emigration to California. Military protection for the emigrant, a telegraph line, and an overland mail were among the ostensible objects. The military force was to be a volunteer corps, which would construct military posts and at the same time provide for its own maintenance by tilling the soil. At the end of three years these military farmers were each to receive 640 acres along the route, and thus form a sort of military colony.[4] Douglas pressed the measure with great warmth; but Southerners doubted the advisability of "encouraging new swarms to leave the old hives," not wishing to foster an expansion in which they could not share,[5] nor forgetting that this was free soil by the terms of the Missouri Compromise. All sorts of objections were trumped up to discredit the bill. Douglas was visibly irritated. "Sir," he exclaimed, "it looks to me as if the design was to deprive us of everything like protection in that vast region. . . .

[1] Executive Docs., 32 Cong., 2 Sess., p. 124.
[2] House Bill, No. 170; 30 Cong., 1 Sess.
[3] *Globe*, 32 Cong., 1 Sess., p. 1161.
[4] *Ibid.*, pp. 1684-1685.
[5] *Ibid.*, p. 1760. Clingman afterward admitted that the Southern opposition was motived by reluctance to admit new free Territories. "This feeling was felt rather than expressed in words." Clingman, Speeches and Writings, p. 334.

I must remind the Senate again that the pointing out of these objections, and the suggesting of these large expenditures show us that we are to expect no protection at all; they evince direct, open hostility to that section of the country.''[1]

It was the fate of the Nebraska country to be bound up more or less intimately with the agitation in favor of a Pacific railroad. All sorts of projects were in the air. Asa Whitney had advocated, in season and out, a railroad from Lake Michigan to some available harbor on the Pacific. Douglas and his Chicago friends were naturally interested in this enterprise. Benton, on the other hand, jealous for the interests of St. Louis, advocated a ''National Central Highway'' from that city to San Francisco, with branches to other points. The South looked forward to a Pacific railroad which should follow a southern route.[2] A northern or central route would inevitably open a pathway through the Indian country and force on the settlement and organization of the territory;[3] the choice of a southern route would in all likelihood retard the development of Nebraska.

While Congress was shirking its duty toward Nebraska, the Wyandot Indians, a civilized tribe occupying lands in the fork of the Kansas and Missouri rivers, repeatedly memorialized Congress to grant them a territorial government.[4] Dogged perseverance may be an Indian characteristic, but there is reason to believe

[1] *Globe*, 32 Cong., 1 Sess., p. 1752.

[2] See Davis, Union Pacific Railway, Chap. 3.

[3] See Benton's remarks in the House, *Globe*, 31 Cong., 2 Sess., p. 56.

[4] Connelley, The Provisional Government of the Nebraska Territory, published by the Nebraska State Historical Society, pp. 23-24.

that outside influences were working upon them. Across the border, in Missouri, they had a staunch friend in ex-Senator Benton, who had reasons of his own for furthering their petitions. In 1850, the opposition, which had been steadily making headway against him, succeeded in deposing the old parliamentarian and electing a Whig as his successor in the Senate. The *coup d'état* was effected largely through the efforts of an aggressive pro-slavery faction led by Senator David R. Atchison.[1] It was while his fortunes were waning in Missouri, that Benton interested himself in the Central Highway and in the Wyandots. His project, indeed, contemplated grants of land along the route, when the Indian title should be extinguished.[2] Possibly it was Benton's purpose to regain his footing in Missouri politics by advocating this popular measure; possibly, as his opponents hinted, he looked forward to residing in the new Territory and some day becoming its first senator; at all events, he came to look upon the territorial organization of Nebraska as an integral part of his larger railroad project.

In this wise, Missouri factional quarrels, Indian titles, railroads, territorial government for Nebraska, and land grants had become hopelessly tangled, when another bill for the organization of Nebraska came before Congress in February, 1853.[3] The measure was presented by Willard P. Hall, a representative from Missouri, belonging to the Benton faction. His advocacy of the bill in the House throws a flood of light on the motives actuating both friends and opponents.

[1] Connelley, Provisional Government, p. 28.
[2] *Globe*, 31 Cong., 2 Sess., pp. 56-58.
[3] House Bill No. 353; 32 Cong., 2 Sess.

Representatives from Texas evinced a poignant concern for the rights of the poor Indian. Had he not been given these lands as a permanent home, after being driven from the hunting ground of his fathers? To be sure, there was a saving clause in the bill which promised to respect Indian claims, but zeal for the Indian still burned hotly in the breasts of these Texans. Finally, Hall retorted that Texas had for years been trying to drive the wild tribes from her borders, so as to make the northern routes unsafe and thus to force the tide of emigration through Texas.[1] "Why, everybody is talking about a railroad to the Pacific. In the name of God, how is the railroad to be made, if you will never let people live on the lands through which the road passes?"[2]

In other words, the concern of the Missourians was less for the unprotected emigrant than for the great central railroad; while the South cared less for the Indian than for a southern railroad route. The Nebraska bill passed the House by a vote which suggests the sectional differences involved in it.[3]

It was most significant that, while a bill to organize the Territory of Washington passed at once to a third reading in the Senate, the Nebraska bill hung fire. Douglas made repeated efforts to gain consideration for it; but the opposition seems to have been motived here as it was in the House.[4] On the last day of the session, the Senate entered upon an irregular, desultory debate, without a quorum. Douglas took an unwilling part. He repeated that the measure was "very dear to his' heart," that it involved "a matter of im-

[1] *Globe*, 32 Cong., 2 Sess., p. 558.
[2] *Ibid.*, p. 560.   [3] *Ibid.*, p. 565.   [4] *Ibid.*, p. 1020.

mense importance,'' that the object in view was ''to form a line of territorial governments extending from the Mississippi valley to the Pacific ocean.'' The very existence of the Union seemed to him to depend upon this policy. For eight years he had advocated the organization of Nebraska; he trusted that the favorable moment had come.[1] But his trust was misplaced. The Senate refused to consider the bill, the South voting almost solidly against it, though Atchison, who had opposed the bill in the earlier part of the session, announced his conversion,—for the reason that he saw no prospect of a repeal of the Missouri Compromise. The Territory might as well be organized now as ten years later.[2]

Disappointed by the inaction of Congress, the Wyandots took matters into their own hands, and set up a provisional government.[3] Then ensued a contest between the Missouri factions to name the territorial delegate,—who was to present the claims of the new government to the authorities at Washington. On November 7, 1853, Thomas Johnson, the nominee of the Atchison faction, was elected.[4] In the meantime Senator Atchison had again changed his mind: he was now opposed to the organization of Nebraska, unless the Missouri Compromise were repealed.[5] The motives which prompted this recantation can only be surmised. Presumably, for some reason, Atchison no longer believed the Missouri Compromise ''irremediable.''

The strangely unsettled condition of the great tract whose fate was pénding, is no better illustrated than

---

[1] *Globe*, 32 Cong., 2 Sess., pp. 1116-1117. [2] *Ibid.*, p. 1113.
[3] Connelley, Provisional Government, pp. 43 ff. [4] *Ibid.*, pp. 37-41.
[5] Pike, First Blows of the Civil War, p. 183; Connelley, pp. 76-77.

by a second election which was held on the upper Missouri. One Hadley D. Johnson, sometime member of the Iowa legislature, hearing of the proposal of the Wyandots to send a territorial delegate to Congress, invited his friends in western Iowa to cross the river and hold an election. They responded by choosing their enterprising compatriot for their delegate, who promptly set out for Washington, bearing their mandate. Arriving at the capital, he found Thomas Johnson already occupying a seat in the House in the capacity of delegate-elect. Not to be outdone, the Iowa Johnson somewhat surreptitiously secured his admission to the floor. Subsequently, "the two Johnsons," as they were styled by the members, were ousted, the House refusing very properly to recognize either. Thomas Johnson exhibited some show of temper, but was placated by the good sense of his rival, who proposed that they should strike for two Territories instead of one. Why not; was not Nebraska large enough for both?[1]

Under these circumstances, the question of Nebraska seemed likely to recur. Certain Southern newspapers were openly demanding the removal of the slavery restriction in the new Territory.[2] Yet the chairman of the Senate Committee on Territories, who had just returned from Europe, seems to have been unaware of the undercurrents whose surface indications have been pointed out. He wrote confidentially on November 11th:[3] "It [the administration] has difficulties ahead,

[1] See Hadley D. Johnson's account in the Transactions of the Nebraska Historical Society, Vol. II.

[2] Illinois *State Register*, December 22, 1853.

[3] MS. Letter to the editors of the Illinois *State Register*, dated November 11, 1853.

but it must meet them boldly and fairly. There is a surplus revenue which must be disposed of and the tariff reduced to a legitimate revenue standard. It will not do to allow the surplus to accumulate in the Treasury and thus create a pecuniary revulsion that would overwhelm the business arrangements and financial affairs of the country. The River and Harbor question must be met and decided. Now in my opinion is the time to put those great interests on a more substantial and secure basis by a well devised system of Tonnage duties. I do not know what the administration will do on this question, but I hope they will have the courage to do what we all feel to be right. The Pacific railroad will also be a disturbing element. It will never do to commence making railroads by the federal government under any pretext of necessity. We can grant alternate sections of land as we did for the Central Road, but not a dollar from the National Treasury. These are the main questions and my opinions are foreshadowed as you are entitled to know them.''

In the same letter occurs an interesting personal allusion: ''I see many of the newspapers are holding me up as a candidate for the next Presidency. I do not wish to occupy that position. I do not think I will be willing to have my name used. I think such a state of things will exist that I shall not desire the nomination. Yet I do not intend to do any act which will deprive me of the control of my own action. I shall remain entirely non-committal and hold myself at liberty to do whatever my duty to my principles and my friends may require when the time for action arrives. Our first duty is to the cause—the fate of individual politicians is of minor consequence. The party is in a distracted condition and it requires all our wisdom, prudence and energy to consolidate its power and perpetuate its principles. Let us leave the Presidency out of view for at least two years to come.''

These are not the words of a man who is plotting a revolution. Had Nebraska and the Missouri Compromise been uppermost in his thoughts, he would have referred to the subject, for the letter was written in strict confidence to friends, from whom he kept no secrets and before whom he was not wont to pose.

Those better informed, however, believed that Congress would have to deal with the territorial question in the near future. The Washington *Union,* commonly regarded as the organ of the administration, predicted that next to pressing foreign affairs, the Pacific railroad and the Territories would occupy the attention of the administration.[1] And before Congress assembled, or had been long in session, the chairman of the Committee on Territories must have sensed the situation, for on December 14, 1853, Senator Dodge of Iowa introduced a bill for the organization of Nebraska, which was identical with that of the last session.[2] The bill was promptly referred to the Committee on Territories, and the Nebraska question entered upon its last phase. Within a week, Douglas's friends of the Illinois State *Register* were sufficiently well informed of the thoughts and intents of his mind to hazard this conjecture: ''We believe they [the people of Nebraska]

---

[1] Washington *Union,* December 3, 1853. See also item showing the interest in Nebraska, in the issue of November 26.

[2] Senate Bill No. 22. The bounds were fixed at 43° on the north; 36° 30′ on the south, except where the boundary of New Mexico marked the line; the western line of Iowa and Missouri on the east; and the Rocky Mountains on the west.

may be safely left to act for themselves. . . .The territories should be admitted to exercise, as nearly as practicable, all the rights claimed by the States, and to adopt all such political regulations and institutions as their wisdom may suggest."[1] A New York correspondent announced on December 30th, that the committee would soon report a bill for three Territories on the basis of New Mexico and Utah; that is, without excluding or admitting slavery. "Climate and nature and the necessary pursuits of the people who are to occupy the territories," added the writer complacently, "will settle the question—and these will effectually exclude slavery."[2]

These rumors foreshadowed the report of the committee. The problem was to find a mode of overcoming the opposition of the South to the organization of a Territory which would not only add eventually to the number of free States, but also open up a northern route to the Pacific. The price of concession from the South on the latter point must be some apparent concession to the South in the matter of slavery. The report of January 4, 1854, and the bill which accompanied it, was Douglas's solution of the problem.[3] The principles of the compromise measures of 1850 were to be affirmed and carried into practical operation within the

[1] Illinois *State Register*, December 22, 1853.

[2] New York *Journal of Commerce*, December 30, 1853.

[3] Two years later, Douglas flatly denied that he had brought in the bill at the dictation of Atchison or any one else; and I see no good ground on which to doubt his word. His own statement was that he first consulted with Senator Bright and one other Senator from the Northwest, and then took counsel with Southern friends. See *Globe*, 34 Cong., 1 Sess., App., pp. 392-393; also Rhodes, History of the United States, I, pp. 431-432. Mr. Rhodes is no doubt correct, when he says "the committee on territories was Douglas."

limits of the new Territory of Nebraska. "In the judgment of your committee," read the report, "those
measures were intended to have a far more comprehen-
sive and enduring effect than the mere adjustment of
the difficulties arising out of the recent acquisition of
Mexican territory. They were designed to establish
certain great principles . . . . your committee have
deemed it their duty to incorporate and perpetuate, in
their territorial bill, the principles and spirit of those
measures. If any other consideration were necessary,
to render the propriety of this course imperative upon
the committee, they may be found in the fact that the
Nebraska country occupies the same relative position
to the slavery question, as did New Mexico and Utah,
when those Territories were organized."[1]

Just as it was a disputed point, the report argued,
whether slavery was prohibited by law in the country
acquired from Mexico, so it is questioned whether
slavery is prohibited in the Nebraska country by *valid*
enactment. "In the opinion of those eminent statesmen, who hold that Congress is invested with no rightful authority to legislate upon the subject of slavery in
the Territories, the 8th section of the act preparatory
to the admission of Missouri is null and void; while the
prevailing sentiment in large portions of the Union
sustains the doctrine that the Constitution of the
United States secures to every citizen an inalienable
right to move into any of the Territories with his property, of whatever kind and description, and to hold and
enjoy the same under the sanction of law. Your committee do not feel themselves called upon to enter upon
the discussion of these controverted questions. They

[1] Senate Report No. 15, 33 Cong., 1 Sess.

involve the same grave issues which produced the agitation, the sectional strife, and the fearful struggle of 1850." And just as Congress deemed it wise in 1850 to refrain from deciding the matter in controversy, so "your committee are not prepared now to recommend a departure from the course pursued on that memorable occasion either by affirming or repealing the 8th section of the Missouri act, or by any act declaratory of the meaning of the Constitution in respect to the legal points in dispute." The essential features of the Compromise of 1850, which should again be carried into practical operation, were stated as follows:

"First: That all questions pertaining to slavery in the Territories, and in the new States to be formed therefrom, are to be left to the decision of the people residing therein, by their appropriate representatives, to be chosen by them for that purpose.

"Second: That 'all cases involving title to slaves,' and 'questions of personal freedom,' are referred to the adjudication of the local tribunals, with the right of appeal to the Supreme Court of the United States.

"Third: That the provision of the Constitution of the United States, in respect to fugitives from service, is to be carried into faithful execution in all 'the organized Territories,' the same as in the States."

The substitute reported by the committee followed the Dodge bill closely, but contained the additional statement, "And when admitted as a State or States, the said Territory, or any part of the same, shall be received into the Union, with or without slavery, as their Constitution may prescribe at the time of their admission."[1] This phraseology was identical with that

[1] The northern boundary was extended to the 49th parallel.

of the Utah and New Mexico Acts. The bill also made special provision for writs of error and appeals from the territorial court to the Supreme Court of the United States, in all cases involving title to slaves and personal freedom. This feature, too, was copied from the Utah and New Mexico Acts. As first printed in the Washington *Sentinel,* January 7th, the bill contained no reference to the Missouri Compromise and no direct suggestion that the territorial legislature would decide the question of slavery. The wording of the bill and its general tenor gave the impression that the prohibition of slavery would continue during the territorial status, unless in the meantime the courts should declare the Missouri Compromise null and void. Three days later, January 10th, the *Sentinel* reprinted the bill with an additional section, which had been omitted by a "clerical error." This twenty-first section read, "In order to avoid all misconstruction, it is hereby declared to be the true intent and meaning of this act, so far as the question of slavery is concerned, to carry into practical operation the following propositions and principles, established by the compromise measures of one thousand eight hundred and fifty, to wit:" then followed the three propositions which had accompanied the report of January 4th. The last of these three propositions had been slightly abbreviated: all questions pertaining to slavery were to be left to the decision of the people through their appropriate representatives, the clause "to be chosen by them for that purpose" being omitted.

This additional section transformed the whole bill. For the first time the people of the Territory are mentioned as the determining agents in respect to slavery.

And the unavoidable inference followed, that they were not to be hampered in their choice by the restrictive feature of the Missouri Act of 1820. The omission of this weighty section was certainly a most extraordinary oversight. Whose was the "clerical error"? Attached to the original draft, now in the custody of the Secretary of the Senate, is a sheet of blue paper, in Douglas's handwriting, containing the crucial article. All evidence points to the conclusion that Douglas added this hastily, after the bill had been twice read in the Senate and ordered to be printed; but whether it was carelessly omitted by the copyist or appended by Douglas as an afterthought, it is impossible to say.[1] After his report of January 4th, there was surely no reason why Douglas should have hesitated to incorporate the three propositions in the bill; but it is perfectly obvious that with the appended section, the Nebraska bill differed essentially from its prototypes, though Douglas contended that he had only made explicit what was contained implicitly in the Utah bill.

Two years later Douglas replied to certain criticisms from Trumbull in these words: "He knew, or, if not, he ought to know, that the bill in the shape in which it was first reported, as effectually repealed the Missouri restriction as it afterwards did when the repeal was put in express terms. The only question was whether it should be done in the language of the acts of 1850,

---

[1] The first twenty sections are written on white paper, in the handwriting of a copyist. In pencil at the end are the words: "Douglas reports Bill & read 1 & to 2 reading special report Print agreed." The blue paper in Douglas's handwriting covers part of these last words. The sheet has been torn in halves, but pasted together again and attached by sealing wax to the main draft. The handwriting betrays haste.

or in the language subsequently employed, but the legal effect was precisely the same.''[1] Of course Douglas was here referring to the original bill containing the twenty-first section.

It has commonly been assumed that Douglas desired the repeal of the Missouri Compromise in order to open Nebraska to slavery. This was the passionate accusation of his anti-slavery contemporaries; and it has become the verdict of most historians. Yet there is ample evidence that Douglas had no such wish and intent. He had said in 1850, and on other occasions, that he believed the prairies to be dedicated to freedom by a law above human power to repeal. Climate, topography, the conditions of slave labor, which no Northern man knew better, forbade slavery in the unoccupied areas of the West.[2] True, he had no such horror of slavery extension as many Northern men manifested; he was probably not averse to sacrificing some of the region dedicated by law to freedom, if thereby he could carry out his cherished project of developing the greater Northwest; but that he deliberately planned to plant slavery in all that region, is contradicted by the incontrovertible fact that he believed the area of slavery to be circumscribed definitely by Nature. Man might propose but physical geography would dispose.

[1] *Globe,* 34 Cong., 1 Sess., p. 1374.

[2] See his speech of March, 1850, quoted above. In a letter to the editor of *State Capital Reporter* (Concord, N. H.), February 16, 1854, Douglas intimated as strongly as he then dared—the bill was still pending,—that ''the sons of New England'' in the West would exclude slavery from that region which lay in the same latitude as New York and Pennsylvania, and for much the same reasons that slavery had been abolished in those States; see also Transactions of Illinois S'ate Historical Society, 1900, pp. 48-49.

The regrettable aspect of Douglas's course is his attempt to nullify the Missouri Compromise by subtle indirection. This was the device of a shifty politician, trying to avert suspicion and public alarm by clever ambiguities. That he really believed a new principle had been substituted for an old one, in dealing with the Territories, does not extenuate the offense, for not even he had ventured to assert in 1850, that the compromises of that year had in any wise disturbed the status of the great, unorganized area to which Congress had applied the restrictive proviso of 1820. Besides, only so recently as 1849, he had said, with all the emphasis of sincerity, that the compromise had "become canonized in the hearts of the American people, as a sacred thing, which no ruthless hand would ever be reckless enough to disturb." And while he then opposed the extension of the principle to new Territories, he believed that it had been "deliberately incorporated into our legislation as a solemn and sacred compromise."[1]

By this time Douglas must have been aware of the covert purpose of Atchison and others to secure the repeal of the Missouri Compromise, though he hoped that they would acquiesce in his mode of doing it. He was evidently not prepared for the bold move which certain of the senators from slave States were contemplating.[2] He was therefore startled by an amendment which Dixon of Kentucky offered on January 16th, to the effect that the restrictive clause of the Act

[1] Speech before the Illinois Legislature, October 23, 1849; see Illinois *State Register*, November 8, 1849.

[2] The Southern Whigs were ready to support the Dixon Amendment, according to Clingman, Speeches and Writings, p. 335.

of 1820 should not be so construed as to apply to Nebraska or any other Territory; "but that the citizens of the several States or territories shall be at liberty to take and hold their slaves within any of the territories of the United States or of the States to be formed therefrom," as if the Missouri Act had never been passed. Douglas at once left his seat to remonstrate with Dixon, who was on the Whig side of the Senate chamber. He disliked the amendment, not so much because it wiped out the Missouri Compromise as because it seemed "affirmatively to legislate slavery into the Territory."[1] Knowing Dixon to be a supporter of the compromise measures of 1850, Douglas begged him not to thwart the work of his committee, which was trying in good faith to apply the cardinal features of those measures to Nebraska. The latter part of Dixon's amendment could hardly be harmonized with the principle of congressional non-intervention.[2]

There seems to be no reason to doubt that Dixon moved in this matter on his own initiative;[3] but he was a friend to Atchison and he could not have been wholly ignorant of the Missouri factional quarrel.[4] To be sure, Dixon was a Whig, but Southern Whigs and Democrats were at one in desiring expansion for the peculiar institution of their section. Pressure was now brought to bear upon Douglas to incorporate the direct

[1] See remarks of Douglas, January 24th, *Globe*, 33 Cong., 1 Sess., p. 240.

[2] Letter of Dixon to Foote, September 30, 1858, in Flint, Douglas, pp. 138-141.

[3] Dixon, True History of the Repeal of the Missouri Compromise.

[4] Parker, Secret History of the Kansas-Nebraska Act, in the *National Quarterly Review*, July, 1880.

repeal of the compromise in the Nebraska bill.[1] He objected strongly, foreseeing no doubt the storm of protest which would burst over his head in the North.[2] Still, if he could unite the party on the principle of non-intervention with slavery in the Territories, the risk of temporary unpopularity would be worth taking. No doubt personal ambition played its part in forming his purpose, but party considerations swayed him most powerfully.[3] He witnessed with no little apprehension the divergence between the Northern and Southern wings of the party; he had commented in private upon "the distracted condition" of the party and the need of perpetuating its principles and consolidating its power. Might this not be his opportunity?

On Sunday morning, January 22d, just before the hour for church, Douglas, with several of his colleagues, called upon the Secretary of War, Davis, stating that the Committees on Territories of the Senate and House had agreed upon a bill, for which the President's approval was desired. They pressed for an immediate interview inasmuch as they desired to report the bill on the morrow. Somewhat reluctantly, Davis arranged an interview for them, though the President was not in the habit of receiving visitors on Sunday. Yielding to their request, President Pierce took the proposed bill under consideration, giving careful heed to all explanations; and when they were done,

---

[1] Parker, Secret History of the Kansas-Nebraska Act; also Foote, Casket of Reminiscences, p. 93; also Cox, Three Decades of Federal Legislation, p. 49.

[2] Ibid. Dixon's account of his interview with Douglas is too melodramatic to be taken literally, but no doubt it reveals Douglas's agitation.

[3] This was Greeley's interpretation, Tribune, June 1, 1861.

both he and his influential secretary promised their
support.[1]

What was this momentous bill to which the President
thus pledged himself? The title indicated the most
striking feature. There were now to be two Territories: Kansas and Nebraska. Bedded in the heart
of Section 14, however, was a still more important
provision which announced that the prohibition of
slavery in the Act of 1820 had been "superseded by
the principles of the legislation of eighteen hundred
and fifty, commonly called the compromise measures,"
and was therefore "inoperative."

It has been commonly believed that Douglas contemplated making one free and one slave State out of the
Nebraska region. His own simple explanation is far
more credible: the two Johnsons had petitioned for a
division of the Territory along the fortieth parallel, and
both the Iowa and Missouri delegations believed that
their local interests would be better served by two
Territories.[2]

Again Pacific railroad interests seem to have crossed
the path of the Nebraska bill. The suspicions of
Delegate-elect Hadley Johnson had been aroused by
the neglect of the Commissioner of Indian Affairs to
extinguish the claims of the Omaha Indians, whose
lands lay directly west of Iowa. At the last session,
an appropriation had been made for the purpose of
extinguishing the Indian title to lands west of both
Missouri and Iowa; and everyone knew that this was
a preliminary step to settlement by whites. The ap-

[1] Jefferson Davis to Mrs. Dixon, September 27, 1879, in Dixon,
True History of the Repeal of the Missouri Compromise, pp. 457 ff.

[2] *Globe*, 33 Cong., 1 Sess., p. 221.

propriation had been zealously advocated by representatives from Missouri, who frankly admitted that the possession of these lands would make the Pacific railroad route available. Now as the Indian Commissioner, who had before shown himself an active partisan of Senator Atchison, rapidly pushed on the treaties with the Indians west of Missouri and dallied with the Omahas, the inference was unavoidable, that Iowa interests were being sacrificed to Missouri interests. Such was the story that the Iowa Johnson poured into the ear of Senator Douglas, to whom he was presented by Senator Dodge.[1] The surest way to safeguard the interests of Iowa was to divide the Territory of Nebraska, and give Iowa her natural outlet to the West.

Senator Dodge had also come to this conclusion. Nebraska would be to Iowa, what Iowa had been to Illinois. Were only one Territory organized, the seat of government and leading thoroughfares would pass to the south of Iowa.[2] Put in the language of the promoters of the Pacific railroad, one Territory meant aid to the central route; two Territories meant an equal chance for both northern and central routes. As the representative of Chicago interests, Douglas was not blind to these considerations.

On Monday, January 23d, Douglas reported the Kansas-Nebraska bill with a brief word of explanation. Next day Senator Dixon expressed his satisfaction with the amendment, which he interpreted as virtually repealing the Missouri Compromise. He disclaimed any other wish or intention than to secure the principle which the compromise measures of 1850 had

[1] Transactions of the Nebraska Historical Society, Vol. II, p. 90.
[2] *Globe*, 33 Cong., 1 Sess., App., p. 382.

established.[1] An editorial in the Washington *Union* threw the weight of the administration into the balance: "The proposition of Mr. Douglas is a practical execution of the principles of that compromise [of 1850], and therefore, cannot but be regarded by the administration as a test of Democratic orthodoxy."[2]

While the administration publicly wheeled into line behind Douglas, the "Appeal of the Independent Democrats in Congress to the People of the United States" summoned the anti-slavery elements to join battle in behalf of the Missouri Compromise. This memorable document had been written by Chase of Ohio and dated January 19th, but a postscript was added after the revised Kansas-Nebraska bill had been reported.[3] It was an adroitly worded paper. History has falsified many of its predictions; history then controverted many of its assumptions; but it was colored with strong emotion and had the ring of righteous indignation.

The gist of the appeal was contained in two clauses, one of which declared that the Nebraska bill would open all the unorganized territory of the Union to the ingress of slavery; the other arraigned the bill as "a gross violation of a sacred pledge; as a criminal betrayal of precious rights." In ominous words, fellow citizens were besought to observe how the blight of slavery would settle upon all this land, if this bill should become a law. Christians and Christian ministers were implored to interpose. "Let all protest, earnestly and emphatically, by correspondence, through the press, by

---

[1] *Globe,* 33 Cong., 1 Sess., pp. 239-240.
[2] Washington *Union,* January 24, 1854.
[3] *Globe,* 33 Cong., 1 Sess., p. 282.

memorials, by resolutions of public meetings and legislative bodies, and in whatever other mode may seem
expedient, against this enormous crime.'' In the postscript Douglas received personal mention. ''Not a
man in Congress or out of Congress, in 1850, pretended
that the compromise measures would repeal the Missouri prohibition. Mr. Douglas himself never advanced such a pretence until this session. His own
Nebraska bill, of last session, rejected it. It is a sheer
afterthought. To declare the prohibition inoperative,
may, indeed, have effect in law as a repeal, but it is a
most discreditable way of reaching the object. Will
the people permit their dearest interests to be thus
made the mere hazards of a presidential game, and destroyed by false facts and false inferences?''[1]

This attack roused the tiger in the Senator from
Illinois. When he addressed the Senate on January
30th, he labored under ill-repressed anger. Even in
the expurgated columns of the *Congressional Globe*
enough stinging personalities appeared to make his
friends regretful. What excited his wrath particularly was that Chase and Sumner had asked for a
postponement of discussion, in order to examine the
bill, and then, in the interval, had sent out their indictment of the author. It was certainly unworthy of him
to taunt them with having desecrated the Sabbath day
by writing their plea. The charge was not only puerile
but amusing, when one considers how Douglas himself
was observing that particular Sabbath.

It was comparatively easy to question and disprove
the unqualified statement of the *Appeal,* that ''the
original settled policy of the United States was non-

[1] *Globe,* 33 Cong., 1 Sess., pp. 281-282.

extension of slavery.'' Less convincing was Douglas's attempt to prove that the Missouri Compromise was expressly annulled in 1850, when portions of Texas and of the former Spanish province of Louisiana were added to New Mexico, and also a part of the province of Louisiana was joined to Utah. Douglas was in the main correct as to geographical data; but he could not, and did not, prove that the members of the Thirty-first Congress purposed also to revoke the Missouri Compromise restriction in all the other unorganized Territories. This contention was one of those *non-sequiturs* of which Douglas, in the heat of argument, was too often guilty. Still more regrettable, because it seemed to convict him of sophistry, was the mode by which he sought to evade the charge of the *Appeal,* that the act organizing New Mexico and settling the boundary of Texas had reaffirmed the Missouri Compromise. To establish his point he had to assume that *all* the land cut off from Texas north of 36° 30', was added to New Mexico, thus leaving nothing to which the slavery restriction, reaffirmed in the act of 1850, could apply. But Chase afterward invalidated this assumption and Douglas was forced so to qualify his original statement as to yield the point. This was a damaging admission and prejudiced his cause before the country. But when he brought his wide knowledge of American colonization to bear upon the concrete problems of governmental policy, his grasp of the situation was masterly.

''Let me ask you where you have succeeded in excluding slavery by an act of Congress from one inch of American soil? You may tell me that you did it in the northwest territory by the ordinance of 1787. I will show you by the history of the country that you did not accomplish any such thing. You prohibited slavery there by law, but you did not exclude it in fact. . . . I know of but one territory of the United States where slavery does exist, and that one is where you have prohibited it by law, and it is in this very Nebraska Territory. In defiance of the eighth section of the act of 1820, in defiance of Congressional dictation, there have been, not many, but a few slaves introduced. . . . I have no doubt that whether you organize the territory of Nebraska or not this will continue for some time to come. . . . But when settlers rush in—when labor becomes plenty, and therefore cheap, in that climate, with its productions, it is worse than folly to think of its being a slave-holding country. . . . I do not like, I never did like, the system of legislation on our part, by which a geographical line, in violation of the laws of nature, and climate, and soil, and of the laws of God, should be run to establish institutions for a people.''[1]

The fate of the bill was determined behind closed doors. After all, the Senate chamber was only a public clearing-house, where senators elucidated, or perchance befogged, the issues. The real arena was the Democratic caucus. Under the leadership of Douglas, those high in the party conclaves met, morning after morning, in the endeavor to compose the sharp differences between the Northern and the Southern wings of the party.[2] On both sides, there was a disposition to agree on the repeal of the Missouri Compromise,

[1] *Globe*, 33 Cong., 1 Sess., pp. 278-279.

[2] See remarks of Senator Bell of Tennessee, May 24, 1854, in *Globe*, 33 Cong., 1 Sess., App., pp. 939-940; also see statement of Benjamin in *Globe*, 34 Cong., 1 Sess., p. 1093.

though grave misgivings were felt. There were Southern men who believed that the repeal would be "an unavailing boon"; and there were Northern politicians who foresaw the storm of popular indignation that would break upon their heads.[1] Southern Democrats were disposed to follow the South Carolina theory to its logical extreme: as joint owners of the Territories the citizens of all the States might carry their property into the Territories without let or hindrance; only the people of the Territory in the act of framing a State constitution might exclude slavery. Neither Congress nor a territorial legislature might take away property in slaves. With equal pertinacity, Douglas and his supporters advocated the right of the people in their territorial status, to mould their institutions as they chose. Was there any middle ground?

Prolonged discussion made certain points of agreement clear to all. It was found that no one questioned the right of a State, with sufficient population and a republican constitution, to enter the Union with or without slavery as it chose. All agreed that it was best that slavery should not be discussed in Congress. All agreed that, whether or no Congress had the power to exclude slavery in the Territories, it ought not to exercise it. All agreed that if Congress had such power, it ought to delegate it to the people. Here agreement ceased. Did Congress have such power? Clearly the law of the Constitution could alone determine. Then why not delegate the power to control their domestic institutions to the people of the Territories, subject to the provisions of the Constitution? "And then," said one of the participants later, "in

[1] *Globe,* 33 Cong., 1 Sess., App. pp. 414-415; p. 943.

order to provide a means by which the Constitution could govern . . . . we of the South, conscious that we were right, the North asserting the same confidence in its own doctrines, agreed that every question touching human slavery or human freedom should be appealable to the Supreme Court of the United States for its decision.''[1]

While this compromise was being reached in caucus, the bill was under constant fire on the floor of the Senate. The *Appeal of the Independent Democrats* had bitterly arraigned the declaratory part of the Kansas-Nebraska bill, where the Missouri Compromise was said to have been superseded and therefore inoperative. Even staunch Democrats like Cass had taken exception to this phraseology, preferring to declare the Missouri Compromise null and void in unequivocal terms. To Douglas there was nothing ambiguous or misleading in the wording of the clause. What was meant was this: the acts of 1850 rendered the Missouri Compromise *inoperative* in Utah and New Mexico; but so far as the Missouri Compromise applied to territory not embraced in those acts, it was *superseded* by the great principle established in 1850. ''Superseded by'' meant ''inconsistent with'' the compromise of 1850.[2] The word ''supersede,'' however, continued to cause offense. Cass read from the dictionary to prove that the word had a more positive force than Douglas gave to it. To supersede meant

[1] *Globe*, 34 Cong., 1 Sess., p. 1093. This statement by Senator Benjamin was corroborated by Douglas and by Hunter of Virginia, during the debates, see *Globe*, 33 Cong., 1 Sess., App., p. 224. See also the letter of A. H. Stephens, May 9, 1860, in *Globe*, 36 Cong., 1 Sess., App., pp. 315-316.

[2] *Globe*, 33 Cong., 1 Sess., pp. 343-344.

to set aside: he could not bring himself to assent to this statement.[1]

By this time agreement had been reached in the caucus, so that Douglas was quite willing to modify the phraseology of the bill. "We see," said he, "that the difference here is only a difference as to the appropriate word to be used. We all agree in the principle which we now propose to establish." As he was not satisfied with the phrases suggested, he desired some time to consult with friends of the bill, as to which word would best "carry out the idea which we are intending to put into practical operation by this bill."[2]

On the following day, February 7th, Douglas reported, not merely "the appropriate word," but an entirely new clause, the product of the caucus deliberations.

The eighth section of the act preparatory to the admission of Missouri into the Union is no longer said to be superseded, but "being inconsistent with the principle of non-intervention by Congress with slavery in the States and Territories, as recognized by the legislation of 1850, (commonly called the Compromise Measures) is hereby declared inoperative and void, it being the true intent and meaning of this act not to legislate slavery into any Territory or State, nor to exclude it therefrom, but to leave the people thereof perfectly free to form and regulate their domestic institutions in their own way, subject only to the Constitution of the United States."[3]

This part of the bill had now assumed its final form. *Subject only to the Constitution of the United States.*

[1] *Globe,* 33 Cong., 1 Sess., p. 344.
[2] *Ibid.,* p. 344. [3] *Ibid.,* p. 353.

The words were clear; but what was their implication? A few days later, Douglas wrote to his Springfield confidant, "The Democratic party is committed in the most solemn manner to the principle of congressional non-interference with slavery in the States and Territories. The administration is committed to the Nebraska bill and will stand by it at all hazards. . . . The principle of this bill will form the test of parties, and the only alternative is either to stand with the Democracy or rally under Seward, John Van Buren & Co. . . . We shall pass the Nebraska bill in both Houses by decisive majorities and the party will then be stronger than ever, for it will be united upon principle."[1]

Yet there were dissentient opinions. What was in the background of Southern consciousness was expressed bluntly by Brown of Mississippi, who refused to admit that the right of the people of a Territory to regulate their domestic institutions, including slavery, was a right to destroy. "If I thought in voting for the bill as it now stands, I was conceding the right of the people in the territory, during their territorial existence, to exclude slavery, I would withhold my vote. . . . It leaves the question where I am quite willing it should be left—to the ultimate decision of the courts."[2] Chase also, though for widely different reasons, disputed the power of the people of a Territory to exclude slavery, under the terms of this bill.[3] And Senator Clayton pointed out that non-interference was a delusion, so long as it lay within the power of any member of Congress to move a repeal of any and every terri-

---

[1] MS. Letter, Douglas to Lanphier, February 13, 1854.
[2] *Globe*, 33 Cong., 1 Sess., App., p. 232.
[3] *Ibid.*, pp. 279-280.

torial law which came up for approval, for the bill expressly provided for congressional approval of territorial laws.[1]

Douglas was irritated by these aspersions on his
cherished principle. He declared again, in defiant
tones, that the right of the people to permit or exclude
was clearly included in the wording of the measure.
He was not willing to be lectured about indirectness.
He had heard cavil enough about his amendments.[2]

In the course of a debate on March 2d, another
unforeseen difficulty loomed up in the distance. If the
Missouri Compromise were repealed, would not the
original laws of Louisiana, which legalized slavery,
be revived? How then could the people of the Territories be free to legislate against slavery? It was a
knotty question, testing the best legal minds in the
Senate; and it was dispatched only by an amendment
which stated that the repeal of the Missouri Compromise should not revive any antecedent law respecting slavery.[3]

The objection raised by Clayton still remained:
how was it possible to reconcile congressional non-
intervention with the right of Congress to revise
territorial laws? Now Douglas had never contended
that the right of the people to self-government in the
Territories was complete as against the power of Congress. He had never sought to confer upon them more
than a relative degree of self-government—"the power
to regulate their domestic institutions." He could
not, and he did not, deny the truth and awkwardness
of Clayton's contention. Where, then, demanded his

[1] *Globe,* 33 Cong., 1 Sess., App., p. 391. [2] *Ibid.,* pp. 287-288.
[3] *Ibid.,* p. 296.

critics, was the guarantee that the Kansas-Nebraska bill would banish the slavery controversies from Congress? This challenge could not go unanswered. Without other explanation, Douglas moved to strike out the provision requiring all territorial laws to be submitted to Congress.[1] But did this divest Congress of the power of revision? On this point Douglas preserved a discreet silence.

Recognizing also the incongruity of giving an absolute veto power to a governor who would be appointed by the President, Douglas proposed a suspensive, in place of an absolute, veto power. A two-thirds vote in each branch of the territorial legislature would override the governor's negative.[2] Chase now tried to push Douglas one step farther on the same slippery road. "Can it be said," he asked, "that the people of a territory will enjoy self-government when they elect only their legislators and are subject to a governor, judges, and a secretary appointed by the Federal Executive?" He would amend by making all these officers elective.[3] Douglas extricated himself from this predicament by saying simply that these officers were charged with federal rather than with territorial duties.[4] The amendment was promptly negatived. Yet seven years later, this very proposition was indorsed by Douglas under peculiar circumstances. At this time in 1854, it would have effected nothing short of a revolution in American territorial policy; and it might have altered the whole history of Kansas.

Despite asseverations to the contrary, there were Southern men in Congress who nourished the tacit

---

[1] *Globe*, 33 Cong., 1 Sess., App., pp. 296-297.
[2] *Ibid.*, p. 297. [3] *Ibid.*, p. 298. [4] *Ibid.*, p. 298.

hope that another slave State might be gained west
of the Missouri. There was a growing conviction
among Southern people that the possession of Kansas
at least might be successfully contested.[1] At all events,
no barrier to Southern immigration into the Territory
was allowed to remain in the bill. Objection was raised
to the provision, common to nearly all territorial bills,
that aliens, who had declared their intention of becoming citizens, should be permitted to vote in territorial
elections. In a contest with the North for the possession of the territorial government, the South would
be at an obvious disadvantage, if the homeless aliens
in the North could be colonized in Kansas, for there
was no appreciable alien population in the Southern
States.[2] So it was that Clayton's amendment, to re-
strict the right to vote and to hold office to citizens of
the United States, received the solid vote of the South
in the Senate. It is significant that Douglas voted with
his section on this important issue. There can be no
better proof of his desire that freedom should prevail
in the new Territories. The Clayton amendment, however, passed the Senate by a close vote.[3]

On the 2d of March the Kansas-Nebraska bill went
to a third reading by a vote of twenty-nine to twelve;
its passage was thus assured.[4] Debate continued, however, during the afternoon and evening of the next day.
Friends of the bill had agreed that it should be brought
to a vote on this night. The privilege of closing the
debate belonged to the chairman of the Committee on

[1] See remarks of Bell; *Globe*, 33 Cong., 1 Sess., App., pp. 414-415;
and also later, *Globe*, 33 Cong., 1 Sess., App., p. 937.

[2] See remarks of Atchison, *Globe*, 33 Cong., 1 Sess., App., p. 302.

[3] *Ibid.*, p. 298. [4] *Ibid.*, p. 302.

Territories; but in view of the lateness of the hour, he offered to waive his privilege and let a vote be taken. Voices were raised in protest, however, and Douglas yielded to the urgent request of his friends.[1]

The speech of Douglas was a characteristic performance. It abounded in repetitions, and it can hardly be said to have contributed much to the understanding of the issues. Yet it was a memorable effort, because it exhibited the magnificent fighting qualities of the man. He was completely master of himself. He permitted interruptions by his opponents; he invited them; indeed, at times, he welcomed them; but at no time was he at a loss for a reply. Dialectically he was on this occasion more than a match for Chase and Seward. There were no studied effects in his oratory. Knowing himself to be addressing a wider audience than the Senate chamber and its crowded galleries, he appealed with intuitive keenness to certain fundamental traits in his constituents. Americans admire self-reliance even in an opponent, and the spectacle of a man fighting against personal injustice is often likely to make them forget the principle for which he stands. So Seward, who surely had no love for Douglas and no respect for his political creed, was moved to exclaim in frank admiration, "I hope the Senator will yield for a moment, because I have never had so much respect for him as I have tonight." When Chase assured Douglas that he always purposed to treat the Senator from Illinois with entire courtesy, Douglas retorted: "The Senator says that he never intended to do me injustice. . . . Sir, did he not say in the same document to which I have already alluded, that I was engaged,

[1] *Globe,* 33 Cong., 1 Sess., App., p. 325.

with others, 'in a criminal betrayal of precious rights,'
'in an atrocious plot'? . . . . Did he not say everything
calculated to produce and bring upon my head all the
insults to which I have been subjected publicly and
privately—not even excepting the insulting letters
which I have received from his constituents, rejoicing
at my domestic bereavements, and praying that other
and similar calamities may befall me?"[1]

In much the same way, he turned upon Sumner, as
the collaborator of the *Appeal*. Here was one who had
begun his career as an Abolitionist in the Senate, with
the words "Strike but hear me first," but who had
helped to close the doors of Faneuil Hall against
Webster, when he sought to speak in self-defense in
1850, and who now—such was the implication—was
denying simple justice to another patriot.[2]

Personalities aside, the burden of his speech was the
reassertion of his principle of popular sovereignty.
He showed how far he had traveled since the Fourth
of January in no way more strikingly, than when he
called in question the substantive character of the
Missouri Compromise. In his discussion of the legislative history of the Missouri acts, he easily convicted
both Chase and Seward of misapprehensions; but he
refused to recognize the truth of Chase's words, that
"the facts of the transaction taken together and as
understood by the country for more than thirty years,
constitute a compact binding in moral force," though
expressed only in the terms of ordinary statutes. So
far had Douglas gone in his advocacy of his measure
that he had lost the measure of popular sentiment.

[1] *Globe,* 33 Cong., 1 Sess., App., p. 332.
[2] *Ibid.,* p. 332.

He was so confident of himself and his cause, so well-assured that he had sacrificed nothing but an empty form, in repealing the slavery restriction, that he forgot the popular mind does not so readily cast aside its prejudices and grasp substance in preference to form. The combative instinct in him was strong. He had entered upon a quarrel; he would acquit himself well. Besides, he had supreme confidence that popular intelligence would slowly approve his course.

Perhaps Douglas's greatest achievement on this occasion was in coining a phrase which was to become a veritable slogan in succeeding years. That which had hitherto been dubbed "squatter sovereignty," Douglas now dignified with the name "popular sovereignty," and provided with a pedigree. "This was the principle upon which the colonies separated from the crown of Great Britain, the principle upon which the battles of the Revolution were fought, and the principle upon which our republican system was founded. . . . . The Revolution grew out of the assertion of the right on the part of the imperial government to interfere with the internal affairs and domestic concerns of the colonies. . . . I will not weary the Senate in multiplying evidence upon this point. It is apparent that the Declaration of Independence had its origin in the violation of the great fundamental principle which secured to the people of the colonies the right to regulate their own domestic affairs in their own way; and that the Revolution resulted in the triumph of that principle, and the recognition of the right asserted by it.'"[1]

In conclusion, Douglas said with perfect truthfulness: "I have not brought this question forward as a

[1] *Globe,* 33 Cong., 1 Sess., App., p. 337.

Northern man or as a Southern man. I am unwilling to recognize such divisions and distinctions. I have brought it forward as an American Senator, representing a State which is true to this principle, and which has approved of my action in respect to the Nebraska bill. I have brought it forward not as an act of justice to the South more than to the North. I have presented it especially as an act of justice to the people of those Territories, and of the States to be formed therefrom, now and in all time to come."[1]

Nor did he seem to entertain a doubt as to the universal appeal which his principle would make: "I say frankly that, in my opinion, this measure will be as popular at the North as at the South, when its provisions and principles shall have been fully developed and become well understood. The people at the North are attached to the principles of self-government; and you cannot convince them that that is self-government which deprives a people of the right of legislating for themselves, and compels them to receive laws which are forced upon them by a legislature in which they are not represented."[2]

The rising indignation at the North against the Kansas-Nebraska bill was felt much more directly in the House than in the Senate. So strong was the counter-current that the Senate bill was at first referred to the Committee of the Whole, and thus buried for weeks under a mass of other bills. Many believed that the bill had received a quietus for the session. Not so Douglas and his friend Richardson of Illinois, who was chairman of the Committee on Territories. With a patience born of long parliamentary experience,

[1] *Globe*, 33 Cong., 1 Sess., App., p. 338.　　[2] *Ibid.*, p. 338.

they bided their time. In the meantime, every possible influence was brought to bear upon recalcitrant Democrats. And just here the wisdom of Douglas, in first securing the support of the administration, was vindicated. All those devices were invoked which President and cabinet could employ through the use of the Federal patronage, so that when Richardson, on the 8th of May, called upon the House to lay aside one by one the eighteen bills which preceded the Kansas-Nebraska bill, he was assured of a working majority. The House bill having thus been reached, Richardson substituted for it the Senate bill, minus the Clayton amendment. When he then announced that only four days would be allowed for debate, the obstructionists could no longer contain themselves. Scenes of wild excitement followed. In the end, the friends of the bill yielded to the demand for longer discussion. Debate was prolonged until May 22d, when the bill passed by a vote of 113 to 110, in the face of bitter opposition.

Through all these exciting days, Douglas was constantly at Richardson's side, cautioning and advising. He was well within the truth when he said, in confidential chat with Madison Cutts, "I passed the Kansas-Nebraska Act myself. I had the authority and power of a dictator throughout the whole controversy in both houses. The speeches were nothing. It was the marshalling and directing of men, and guarding from attacks, and with a ceaseless vigilance preventing surprises."[1]

The refusal of the House to accept the Clayton amendment brought the Kansas-Nebraska measure again before the Senate. Knowing that a refusal to

[1] Cutts, Treatise on Constitutional and Party Questions, pp. 122-123.

concur would probably defeat the measure for the session, Southern senators were disposed to waive their objections to allowing aliens to vote in the new Territories. Even Atchison was now disposed to think the matter of little consequence. Foreigners were not the pioneers in the Territories; they followed the pioneers. He did not complete his thought, but it is unmistakable: therefore, native citizens as first-comers, rather than foreigners, would probably decide the question of slavery in the Territories forever. And so, after two days of debate, Douglas again had his way: the Senate voted to recede from the Clayton amendment. On May 30th, the President signed the Kansas-Nebraska bill and it became law.[1]

The outburst of wrath at the North which accompanied the repeal of the Missouri Compromise did not augur well for the future repose of the country. Douglas had anticipated angry demonstrations; but even he was disturbed by the vehemence of the protestations which penetrated to the Senate chamber. Had he failed to gauge the depth of Northern public opinion? Senator Everett disturbed the momentary quiet of Congress by presenting a memorial signed by over three thousand New England clergymen, who, "in the name of Almighty God," protested against the Kansas-Nebraska Act as a great moral wrong and as a breach of faith. This brought Douglas to his feet. With fierce invective he declared this whole movement was instigated by the circulars sent out by the Abolition confederates in the Senate. These preachers had been

[1] That the President believed with Douglas that the benefits of the Act would inure to freedom, is vouched for by ex-Senator Clemens of Alabama. See Illinois *State Register*, April 6, 1854.

led by an atrocious falsehood "to desecrate the pulpit, and prostitute the sacred desk to the miserable and corrupting influence of party politics." What right had these misguided men to speak in the name of Almighty God upon a political question? It was an attempt to establish in this country the doctrine that clergymen have a peculiar right to determine the will of God in legislative matters. This was theocracy.[1]

Some weeks later, Douglas himself presented another protest, signed by over five hundred clergymen of the Northwest and accompanied by resolutions which denounced the Senator from Illinois for his "want of courtesy and reverence toward man and God."[2] His comments upon this protest were not calculated to restore him to favor among these "divinely appointed ministers for the declaration and enforcement of God's will." His public letter to them, however, was much more creditable, for in it he avoided abusive language and appealed frankly to the sober sense of the clergy.[3] Of the repeal of the Missouri Compromise, he said again that it was necessary, "in order to recognize the great principle of self-government and State equality. It does not vary the question in any degree, that human slavery, in your opinion, is a great moral wrong. If so, it is not the only wrong upon which the people of each of the States and Territories of this Union are called upon to act. . . . You think you are abundantly competent to decide this question now and forever. If you should remove to Nebraska, with a view of making it your permanent home, would you be

[1] *Globe*, 33 Cong., 1 Sess., pp. 618, 621.
[2] *Ibid.*, App., p. 654.
[3] *Ibid.*, App., pp. 657-661.

any less competent to decide it when you should have arrived in the country?"[1]

The obloquy which Douglas encountered in Washington was mere child's play, as compared with the storm of abuse that met him on his return to Chicago. He afterwards said that he could travel from Boston to Chicago by the light of his own effigies.[2] "Traitor," "Arnold,"—with a suggestion that he had the blood of Benedict Arnold in his veins,—"Judas," were epithets hurled at him from desk and pulpit. He was presented with thirty pieces of silver by some indignant females in an Ohio village.[3] So incensed were the people of Chicago, that his friends advised him not to return, fearing that he would be assaulted.[4] But fear was a sensation that he had never experienced. He went to Chicago confident that he could silence opposition as he had done four years before.[5]

Three or four days after his return, he announced that on the night of September 1st, he would address his constituents in front of North Market Hall. The announcement occasioned great excitement. The opposition press cautioned their readers not to be deceived by his sophistries, and hinted broadly at the advisability of breaking up the meeting.[6] Many friends

[1] *Globe*, 33 Cong., 1 Sess., App., p. 661.

[2] Speech at Wooster, Ohio, 1859, Philadelphia *Press*, September 26, 1859.

[3] Rhodes, History of the United States, I, p. 496.

[4] Cutts, Constitutional and Party Questions, p. 98.

[5] "I speak to the people of Chicago on Friday next, September 1, on Nebraska. They threaten a mob but I have no fears. All will be right.... Come up if you can and bring our friends with you." MS. Letter, Douglas to Lanphier, August 25, 1854.

[6] Davidson and Stuvé, History of Illinois, p. 640.

of Douglas believed that personal violence was threatened. During the afternoon flags were hung at half mast on the lake boats; bells were tolled, as the crowds began to gather in the dusk of the evening; some public calamity seemed to impend. At a quarter past eight, Douglas began to address the people. He was greeted with hisses. He paused until these had subsided. But no sooner did he begin again than bedlam broke loose. For over two hours he wrestled with the mob, appealing to their sense of fairness; but he could not gain a hearing. Finally, for the first time in his career, he was forced to admit defeat. Drawing his watch from his pocket and observing that the hour was late, he shouted, in an interval of comparative quiet, "It is now Sunday morning—I'll go to church, and you may go to Hell!" At the imminent risk of his life, he went to his carriage and was driven through the crowds to his hotel.[1]

[1] Sheahan, Douglas, pp. 271-273.   Cutts, Constitutional and Party Questions, pp. 98-101.   New York *Times,* September 6, 1854.

CHAPTER XII

BLACK REPUBLICANISM

The passing of the Whig party after its defeat in
the election of 1852, must be counted among the most
momentous facts in our political history. Whatever
were its errors, whatever its shortcomings, it was at
least a national organization, with a membership that
embraced anti-slavery Northerners and slave-holding
Southerners, Easterners and Westerners. As events
proved, there was no national organization to take its
place. One of the two political ties had snapped that
had held together North and South. The Democratic
party alone could lay claim to a national organization
and membership.

Party has been an important factor in maintaining
national unity. The dangers to the Union from rapid
territorial expansion have not always been realized.
The attachment of new Western communities to the
Union has too often been taken as a matter of course.
Even when the danger of separation was small, the
isolation and provincialism of the new West was a real
menace to national welfare. Social institutions did their
part in integrating East and West; but the politically
integrating force was supplied by party. Through their
membership in national party organizations, the most
remote Western pioneers were energized to think and
act on national issues.[1] In much the same way, the

This aspect of party has been treated at greater length in an
article by the writer entitled "The Nationalizing Influence of Party,"
Yale Review, November, 1906.

great party organizations retarded the growth of sectionalism at the South. The very fact that party ties held long after social institutions had been broken asunder, proves their superior cohesion and nationalizing power. The inertia of parties during the prolonged slavery controversy was an element of strength. Because these formal organizations did not lend themselves readily to radical policies, they provided a frame-work, within which adjustments of differences were effected without danger to the Union. Had Abolitionists of the radical type taken possession of the organization of either party, can it be doubted that the Union would have been imperiled much earlier than it was, and very probably when it could not have withstood the shock?

No one who views history calmly will maintain, that it would have been well for either the radical or the conservative to have been dominant permanently. If the radical were always able to give application to his passing, restless humors, society would lose its coherence. If the conservative always had his way, civilization would stagnate. It was a fortunate circumstance that neither the Whig nor the Democratic party was composed wholly either of radicals or conservatives. Party action was thus a resultant. If it was neither so radical as the most radical could desire, nor so conservative as the ultra-conservative wished, at least it safeguarded the Union and secured the political achievements of the past. Moreover, the two great party organizations had done much to assimilate the foreign elements injected into our population. No doubt the politician who cultivated "the Irish vote" or "the German vote," was obeying no higher law than his own interests; but his activities did much to promote that fusion of heterogeneous elements which has been one of the most extraordinary phenomena of American society. With the disappearance of the Whig party, one of the two great agencies in the disciplining and educating of the immigrant was lost.

For a time the Native American party seemed likely to take the place of the moribund Whig party. Many Whigs whose loyalty had grown cold but who would not go over to the enemy, took refuge in the new party. But Native Americanism had no enduring strength. Its tenets and its methods were in flat contradiction to true American precedents. Greeley was right when he said of the new party, "It would seem as devoid of the elements of persistence as an anti-cholera or an anti-potato-rot party would be." By its avowed hostility to Catholics and foreigners, by its insistence upon America for Americans, and by its secrecy, it forfeited all real claims to succeed the Whig party as a national organization.

After the downfall of the Whig party, then, the Democratic party stood alone as a truly national party, preserving the integrity of its national organization and the bulk of its legitimate members. But the events of President Pierce's administration threatened to be its undoing. If the Kansas-Nebraska bill served to unite outwardly the Northern and Southern wings of the party, it served also to crystallize those anti-slavery elements which had hitherto been held in solution. An anti-Nebraska coalition was the outcome. Out of this opposition sprang eventually the Republican party, which was, therefore, in its inception, national neither in its organization nor in its membership.

For "Know-Nothingism," as Native Americanism was derisively called, Douglas had exhibited the liveliest antipathy. Shortly after the triumph of the Know-Nothings in the municipal elections of Philadelphia, he was called upon to give the Independence Day address in the historic Independence Square.[1] With an audacity rarely equalled, he seized the occasion to defend the great principle of self-government as incorporated in the Nebraska bill, just become law, and to beard Know-Nothingism in its den. Under guise of defending national institutions and American principles, he turned his oration into what was virtually the first campaign speech of the year in behalf of Democracy. Never before were the advantages of a party name so apparent. Under his skillful touch the cause of popular government, democracy, religious and civil liberty, became confounded with the cause of Democracy, the only party of the nation which stood opposed to "the allied forces of Abolitionism, Whigism, Nativeism, and religious intolerance, under whatever name or on whatever field they may present themselves."[2]

There can be no doubt that Douglas voiced his inmost feeling, when he declared that "to proscribe a man in this country on account of his birthplace or religious faith is revolting to our sense of justice and right."[3] In his defense of religious toleration he rose to heights of real eloquence.

Douglas paid dearly for this assault upon Know-Nothingism. The order had organized lodges also in the Northwest, and when Douglas returned to his own

[1] Sheahan, Douglas, pp. 264-265.
[2] Ibid., p. 271. [3] Ibid., p. 269.

constituency after the adjournment of Congress, he found the enemy in possession of his own redoubts. With some show of reason, he afterward attributed the demonstration against him in Chicago to the machinations of the Know-Nothings. His experience with the mob left no manner of doubt in his mind that Know-Nothingism, and not hostility to his Kansas-Nebraska policy, was responsible for his failure to command a hearing.[1]

But Douglas was mistaken, or he deceived himself, when he sought in the same fashion to explain away the opposition which he encountered as he traveled through the northern counties of the State. Malcontents from both parties, but chiefly anti-slavery Whigs, Free-Soilers, and Abolitionists, were drawing together in common hostility to the repeal of the Missouri Compromise. Mass conventions were summoned, irrespective of party, in various counties; and they gave no uncertain expression to their hatred of slavery and the slave-power. These were the counties most largely peopled by the New England immigrants. Anti-Nebraska platforms were adopted; and fusion candidates put in nomination for State and congressional office. In the central and southern counties, the fusion was somewhat less complete; but finally an anti-Nebraska State convention was held at Springfield, which nominated a candidate for State Treasurer, the only State officer to be elected.[2] For the first time in many years, the overthrow of the Democratic party seemed imminent.

However much Douglas may have misjudged the

[1] Cutts, Constitutional and Party Questions, pp. 98-99.
[2] Davidson and Stuvé, History of Illinois, pp. 641-643.

causes for this fusion movement at the outset, he was not long blind as to its implications. On every hand there were symptoms of disaffection. Personal friends turned their backs upon him; lifelong associates refused to follow his lead; even the rank and file of his followers seemed infected with the prevailing epidemic of distrust. With the instinct of a born leader of men, Douglas saw that the salvation of himself and his party lay in action. The *élan* of his forces must be excited by the signal to ride down the enemy. Sounding the charge, he plunged into the thick of the fray. For two months, he raided the country of the enemy in northern Illinois, and dashed from point to point in the central counties where his loyal friends were hard pressed.[1] It was from first to last a tempestuous conflict that exactly suited the impetuous, dashing qualities of "the Little Giant."

In the Sixth Congressional District, Douglas found his friend Harris fighting desperately with his back against the wall. His opponent, Yates, was a candidate for re-election, with the full support of anti-Nebraska men like Trumbull and Lincoln, whom the passage of the Kansas-Nebraska bill had again drawn into politics. While the State Fair was in progress at Springfield, both candidates strained every nerve to win votes. Douglas was summoned to address the goodly body of Democratic yeomen, who were keenly alive to the political, as well as to the bucolic, opportunities which the capital afforded at this interesting season. Douglas spoke to a large gathering in the State House on October 3d. Next day the Fusion-

[1] See items scattered through the Illinois *State Register* for these exciting weeks.

ists put forward Lincoln to answer him; and when Lincoln had spoken for nearly four hours, Douglas again took the stand and held his audience for an hour and a half longer.[1] Those were days when the staying powers of speakers were equalled only by the patience of their hearers.

Like those earlier encounters, whose details have passed into the haze of tradition, this lacks a trustworthy chronicler. It would seem, however, as though the dash and daring of Douglas failed to bear down the cool, persistent opposition of his antagonist. Douglas should have known that the hazards in his course were reared by his own hand. Whatever other barriers blocked his way, Nebraska-ism was the most formidable; but this he would not concede.

A curious story has connected itself with this chance encounter of the rivals. Alarmed at the effectiveness of Lincoln's attack, so runs the legend, Douglas begged him not to enter the campaign, promising that he likewise would be silent thereafter. Aside from the palpable improbability of this "Peoria truce," it should be noted that Lincoln accepted an invitation to speak at Lacon next day, without so much as referring to this agreement, while Douglas continued his campaign with unremitting energy.[2] If Douglas exhibited fear of an adversary at this time, it is the only instance in his career.

[1] See Illinois State *Register,* October 6, 1854, and subsequent issues.

[2] Nearly every biographer of Lincoln has noted this apparent breach of agreement on the part of Douglas, but none has questioned the accuracy of the story, though the unimaginative Lamon betrays some misgivings, as he records Lincoln's course after the "Peoria truce." See Lamon, Lincoln, p. 358. The statement of Irwin (in Herndon-Weik, Lincoln, II, p. 329) does not seem credible, in the light of all the attendant circumstances.

The outcome of the elections gave the Democrats food for thought. Five out of nine congressional districts had chosen anti-Nebraska or Fusion candidates; the other four returned Democrats to Congress by reduced pluralities.[1] To be sure, the Democrats had elected their candidate for the State Treasury; but this was poor consolation, if the legislature, as seemed probable, should pass from their control. A successor to Senator Shields would be chosen by this body; and the choice of an anti-Nebraska man would be as gall and wormwood to the senior senator. In the country at large, such an outcome would surely be interpreted as a vote of no confidence. In the light of these events, Democrats were somewhat chastened in spirit, in spite of apparent demonstrations of joy. Even Douglas felt called upon to vindicate his course at the banquet given in his honor in Chicago, November 9th. He was forced to admit—and for him it was an unwonted admission—that "the heavens were partially overcast."

For the moment there was a disposition to drop Shields in favor of some Democrat who was not so closely identified with the Nebraska bill. Douglas viewed the situation with undisguised alarm. He urged his friends, however, to stick to Shields. "The election of any other man," he wrote truthfully, "would be deemed not only a defeat, but an ungrateful desertion of him, when all the others who have voted with him have been sustained."[2] It was just this fine spirit of loyalty that made men his lifelong friends and steadfast followers through thick and thin. "Our

[1] *Whig Almanac* 1855.
[2] MS. Letter, Douglas to Lanphier, December 18, 1854.

friends should stand by Shields," he continued, "and throw the responsibility on the Whigs of beating him *because he was born in Ireland.* The Nebraska fight is over, and Know-Nothingism has taken its place as the chief issue in the future. If therefore Shields shall be beaten it will [be] apparent to the people & to the whole country that a gallant soldier, and a faithful public servant has been stricken down because of the place of his birth." This was certainly shrewd, and, measured by the tone of American public life, not altogether reprehensible, politics. Douglas anticipated that the Whigs would nominate Lincoln and "stick to him to the bitter end," while the Free-Soilers and anti-Nebraska Democrats would hold with equal persistence to Bissell, in which case either Bissell would ultimately get the Whig vote or there would be no election. Sounding the trumpet call to battle, Douglas told his friends to nail Shields' flag to the mast and never to haul it down. "We are sure to triumph in the end on the great issue. Our policy and duty require us to stand firm by the issues in the late election, and to make no bargains, no alliances, no concessions to any of the *allied isms.*"

When the legislature organized in January, the Democrats, to their indescribable alarm, found the Fusion forces in control of both houses. The election was postponed until February. Meantime Douglas cautioned his trusty lieutenant in no event to leave Springfield for even a day during the session.[1] On the first ballot for senator, Shields received 41 votes; Lincoln 45; Trumbull, an anti-Nebraska Democrat, 5; while three Democrats and five Fusionists scattered

[1] MS. Letter, Douglas to Lanphier, December 18, 1854.

their votes. On the seventh ballot, Shields fell out of the running, his place being taken by Matteson. On the tenth ballot, Lincoln having withdrawn, the Whig vote concentrated on Trumbull, who, with the aid of his unyielding anti-Nebraska following, received the necessary 51 votes for an election. This result left many heart-burnings among both Whigs and Democrats, for the former felt that Lincoln had been unjustly sacrificed and the latter looked upon Trumbull as little better than a renegade.[1]

The returns from the elections in other Northern States were equally discouraging, from the Democratic point of view. Only seven out of forty-two who had voted for the Kansas-Nebraska bill were re-elected. In the next House, the Democrats would be in a minority of seventy-five.[2] The anti-Nebraska leaders were not slow in claiming a substantial victory. Indeed, their demonstrations of satisfaction were so long and loud, when Congress reassembled for the short session, that many Democrats found it difficult to accept defeat good-naturedly. Douglas, for one, would not concede defeat, despite the face of the returns. Men like Wade of Ohio, who enjoyed chaffing their discomfited opponents, took every occasion to taunt the author of the bill which had been the undoing of his party. Douglas met their gibes by asking whether there was a single, anti-Nebraska candidate from the free States who did not receive the Know-Nothing vote. For every Nebraska man who had suffered defeat, two anti-Nebraska candidates were

[1] Davidson and Stuvé, History of Illinois, pp. 689-690; Sheahan, Douglas, pp. 275-276.

[2] Rhodes, History of the United States, II, p. 67.

defeated by the same causes. "The fact is, and the gentleman knows it, that in the free States there has been an alliance, I will not say whether holy or unholy, at the recent elections. In that alliance they had a crucible into which they poured Abolitionism, Maine liquor-lawism, and what there was left of Northern Whigism, and then the Protestant feeling against the Catholic, and the native feeling against the foreigner. All these elements were melted down in that crucible, and the result was what was called the Fusion party. That crucible .... was in every instance, a Know-Nothing Lodge."[1]

There was, indeed, enough or confusion in some States to give color to such assertions. Taken collectively, however, the elections indicated unmistakably a widespread revulsion against the administration of President Pierce; and it was folly to contend that the Kansas-Nebraska bill had not been the prime cause of popular resentment. Douglas was so constituted temperamentally that he both could not, and would not, confront the situation fairly and squarely. This want of sensitiveness to the force of ethical convictions stirring the masses, is the most conspicuous and regrettable aspect of his statecraft. Personally Douglas had a high sense of honor and duty; in private affairs he was scrupulously honest; and if at times he was shifty in politics, he played the game with quite as much fairness as those contemporary politicians who boasted of the integrity of their motives. He preferred to be frank; he meant to deal justly by all men. Even so, he failed to understand the impelling power of those moral ideals which border on the

[1] *Globe*, 33 Cong., 2 Sess., App., p. 216.

unattainable. For the transcendentalist in politics and philanthropy, he had only contempt. The propulsive force of an idea in his own mind depended wholly upon its appeal to his practical judgment. His was the philosophy of the attainable. Results that were approximately just and fair satisfied him. He was not disposed to sacrifice immediate advantage to future gain. His Celtic temperament made him think rapidly; and what imagination failed to supply, quick wit made good.

When, then, under the pressure of conditions for which he was not responsible, he yielded to the demand for a repeal of the Missouri Compromise, he failed to foresee that revulsion of moral sentiment that swept over the North. It was perfectly clear to his mind, that historically the prohibition of slavery by Federal law had had far less practical effect than the North believed. He was convinced that nearly all, if not all, of the great West was dedicated to freedom by a law which transcended any human enactment. Why, then, hold to a mere form, when the substance could be otherwise secured? Why should Northerner affront Southerner by imperious demands, when the same end might be attained by a compromise which would not cost either dear? Possibly he was not unwilling to let New Mexico become slave Territory, if the greater Northwest should become free by the operation of the same principle. Besides, there was the very tangible advantage of holding his party together by a sensible agreement, for the sake of which each faction yielded something.

Douglas was not blind to the palpable truth that the masses are swayed more by sentiment than logic: indeed, he knew well enough how to run through the gamut of popular emotions. What did escape him was the almost religious depth of the anti-slavery sentiment in that very stock from which he himself had sprung. It was not a sentiment that could be bargained away. There was much in it of the inexorable obstinacy of the Puritan faith. Verging close upon fanaticism at times, it swept away considerations of time and place, and overwhelmed appeals to expediency. Even where the anti-slavery spirit did not take on this extreme form, those whom it possessed were reluctant to yield one jot or tittle of the substantial gains which freedom had made.

It is probable that with the growing sectionalism, North and South would soon have been at odds over the disposition of the greater Northwest. Sooner or later, the South must have demanded the repeal of the Missouri Compromise, or have sought large concessions elsewhere. But it is safe to say that no one except Douglas could have been found in 1854, who possessed the requisite parliamentary qualities, the personal following, the influence in all sections,—and withal, the audacity, to propose and carry through the policy associated with the Kansas-Nebraska bill. The responsibility for this measure rested in a peculiar sense upon his shoulders.

It was in the course of this post-election discussion of February 23d, that Wade insinuated that mercenary motives were the key to Douglas's conduct. "Have the people of Illinois forgotten that injunction of more than heavenly wisdom, that 'Where a man's treasure is, there will his heart be also'?" To this unwarranted charge, which was current in Abolitionist circles,

Douglas made a circumstantial denial. "I am not the owner of a slave and never have been, nor have I ever received, and appropriated to my own use, one dollar earned by slave-labor." For the first time, he spoke of the will of Colonel Martin and of the property which he had bequeathed to his daughter and to her children. With very genuine emotion, which touched even his enemies, he added, "God forbid that I should be understood by anyone as being willing to cast from me any responsibility that now does, or has ever attached to any member of my family. So long as life shall last—and I shall cherish with religious veneration the memories and virtues of the sainted mother of my children—so long as my heart shall be filled with parental solicitude for the happiness of those motherless infants, I implore my enemies who so ruthlessly invade the domestic sanctuary, to do me the favor to believe, that I have no wish, no aspiration, to be considered purer or better than she, who was, or they, who are, slaveholders."[1]

When the new Congress met in the fall of 1855, the anti-Nebraska men drew closer together and gradually assumed the name "Republican." Their first victory was the election of their candidate for the Speakership. They were disciplined by astute leaders under the pressure of disorders in Kansas. Before the session closed, they developed a remarkable degree of cohesion, while the body of their supporters in the Northern States assumed alarming proportions. The party was not wholly, perhaps not mainly, the product of humanitarian sentiment. The adherence of old-line Whig politicians like Seward suggests that there

[1] *Globe*, 33 Cong., 2 Sess., App., p. 330.

was some alloy in the pure gold of Republicanism. Such leaders were willing to make political capital out of the breakdown of popular sovereignty in Kansas.[1] They were too shrewd to stake the fortune of the nascent party on a bold, constructive policy. They preferred to play a waiting game. Events in Kansas came to their aid in ways that they could not have anticipated.

While this re-alignment of parties was in progress, the presidential year drew on apace. It behooved the Democrats to gather their scattered forces. The advantage of organization was theirs; but they suffered from desertions. The morale of the party was weakened. To check further desertions and to restore confidence, was the aim of the party whips. No one had more at stake than Douglas. He was on trial with his party. Conscious of his responsibilities, he threw himself into the light skirmishing in Congress which always precedes a presidential campaign. In this partisan warfare he was clever, but not altogether admirable. One could wish that he had been less uncharitable and less denunciatory; but political victories are seldom won by unaided virtue.

From the outset his anti-Nebraska colleague was the object of his bitterest gibes, for Trumbull typified the deserter, who was causing such alarm in the ranks of the Democrats. "I understand that my colleague has told the Senate," said Douglas contemptuously, "that he comes here as a Democrat. Sir, that fact will be news to the Democracy of Illinois. I undertake to assert there is not a Democrat in Illinois who will not say that such a statement is a libel upon the De-

[1] Rhodes, History of the United States, II, pp. 97-98, 130, 196.

mocracy of that State. When he was elected he received every Abolition vote in the Legislature of Illinois. He received every Know-Nothing vote in the Legislature of Illinois. So far as I am advised and believe, he received no vote except from persons allied to Abolitionism or Know-Nothingism. He came here as the Know-Nothing-Abolition candidate, in opposition to the united Democracy of his State, and to the Democratic candidate.''[1]

When to desertion was added association with ''Black Republicans,'' Douglas found his vocabulary inadequate to express his scorn. Like most Democrats he was sensitive on the subject of party nomenclature.[2] ''Republican'' was a term which had associations with the very father of Democracy, though the party had long since dropped the hyphenated title. But this new, so-called Republican party had wisely dropped the prefix ''national,'' suggested Douglas, because ''it is a purely sectional party, with a platform which cannot cross the Ohio river, and a creed which inevitably brings the North and South into hostile collision.'' In view of the emphasis which their platform put upon the negro, Douglas thought that consistency required the substitution of the word ''Black'' for ''National.'' The Democratic party, on the other hand, had no sympathy with those who believed in making the negro the social and political equal of the white man. ''Our people are a white people; our State is a white State; and we mean to preserve the race pure, without any mixture with the negro. If you,'' turning to his Republican opponents, ''wish

[1] *Globe*, 34 Cong., 1 Sess., p. 655.
[2] *Ibid.*, App., p. 391.

your blood and that of the African mingled in the same channel, we trust that you will keep at a respectful distance from us, and not try to force that on us as one of your domestic institutions.''[1] In such wise, Douglas labored to befog and discredit the issues for which the new party stood. The demagogue in him overmastered the statesman.

Douglas believed himself—and with good reason—to be the probable nominee of his party in the approaching presidential election. Several State conventions had already declared for him. There was no other Democrat, save President Pierce, whose name was so intimately associated with the policy of the party as expressed in the Kansas-Nebraska bill. Yet, while both were in favor at the South, neither Pierce nor Douglas was likely to secure the full party vote at the North. This consideration led to a diversion in favor of James Buchanan, of Pennsylvania. The peculiar availability of this well-known Democrat consisted in his having been on a foreign mission when the Kansas-Nebraska bill was under fire. Still, Buchanan was reported ''sound'' on the essential features of this measure. Before the national convention met, a well-organized movement was under way to secure the nomination of the Pennsylvanian.[2] Equally well-organized and even more noisy and demonstrative was the following of Douglas, as the delegates began to assemble at Cincinnati during the first week in June.

The first ballot in the convention must have been a grievous disappointment to Douglas and his friends.

[1] *Globe*, 34 Cong., 1 Sess., App. p. 392.
[2] Rhodes, **History of** the United States, II, pp. 169-171.

While Buchanan received 135 votes and Pierce 122, he could muster only 33. Only the Missouri and Illinois delegations cast their full vote for him. Of the slave States, only Missouri and Kentucky gave him any support. As the balloting continued, however, both Buchanan and Douglas gained at the expense of Pierce. After the fourteenth ballot, Pierce withdrew, and the bulk of his support was turned over to Douglas. Cass, the fourth candidate before the convention, had been from the first out of the running, his highest vote being only seven. On the sixteenth ballot, Buchanan received 168 and Douglas 122. Though Buchanan now had a majority of the votes of the convention, he still lacked thirty of the two-thirds required for a nomination.[1]

It was at this juncture that Douglas telegraphed to his friend Richardson, who was chairman of the Illinois delegation and a prominent figure in the convention, instructing him to withdraw his name. The announcement was received with loud protestations. The dispatch was then read: "If the withdrawal of my name will contribute to the harmony of our party or the success of our cause, I hope you will not hesitate to take the step .... if Mr. Pierce or Mr. Buchanan, or any other statesman who is faithful to the great issues involved in the contest, shall receive a majority of the convention, I earnestly hope that all my friends will unite in insuring him two-thirds, and then making

[1] Stanwood, History of the Presidency, p. 265. Douglas received 73 votes from the slave States and Buchanan 47; Buchanan received 28 votes in New England, Douglas 13; Buchanan received 41 votes from the Northwest, Douglas 19. The loss of Buchanan in the South was more than made good by his votes from the Middle Atlantic States.

his nomination unanimous. Let no personal considerations disturb the harmony or endanger the triumph of our principles."[1] Very reluctantly the supporters of Douglas obeyed their chief, and on the seventeenth ballot, James Buchanan received the unanimous vote of the convention. For the second time Douglas lost the nomination of his party.

Douglas bore himself admirably. At a mass-meeting in Washington,[2] he made haste to pledge his support to the nominee of the convention. His generous words of commendation of Buchanan, as a man possessing "wisdom and nerve to enforce a firm and undivided execution of the laws" of the majority of the people of Kansas, were uttered without any apparent misgivings. Prophetic they certainly were not. Douglas could approve the platform unqualifiedly, for it was a virtual indorsement of the principle which he had proclaimed from the housetops for the greater part of two years. "The American Democracy," read the main article in the newly adopted resolutions, "recognize and adopt the principles contained in the organic laws establishing the Territories of Nebraska and Kansas as embodying the only sound and safe solution of the slavery question, upon which the great national idea of the people of this whole country can repose in its determined conservation of the Union, and non-interference of Congress with slavery in the Territories or in the District of Columbia."[3] Douglas deemed it a cause for

---

[1] Sheahan, Douglas, pp. 448-449; Proceedings of the National Democratic Convention, 1856.

[2] Washington *Union*, June 7, 1856.

[3] Stanwood, History of the Presidency, p. 267.

profound rejoicing that the party was at last united upon principles which could be avowed everywhere, North, South, East, and West. As the only national party in the Republic, the Democracy had a great mission to perform, for in his opinion "no less than the integrity of the Constitution, the preservation and perpetuity of the Union," depended upon the result of this election.[1]

No man could have been more magnanimous under defeat and so little resentful at a personal slight. His manly conduct received favorable comment on all sides.[2] He was still the foremost figure in the Democratic party. To be sure, James Buchanan was the titular leader, but he stood upon a platform erected by his rival. His letter of acceptance left no doubt in the minds of all readers that he indorsed the letter and the spirit of the Kansas-Nebraska Act.[3]

A fortnight later the Republican national convention met at Philadelphia, and with great enthusiasm adopted a platform declaring it to be the duty of Congress to prohibit in the Territories "those twin relics

[1] Washington *Union*, June 7, 1856.

[2] Correspondent to Cincinnati *Enquirer*, June 12, 1856.

[3] The letter read, "This legislation is founded upon principles as ancient as free government itself, and in accordance with them has simply declared that the people of a Territory like those of a State, shall decide for themselves whether slavery shall or shall not exist within their limits. The Kansas-Nebraska Act does no more than give the force of law to this elementary principle of self-government, declaring it to be 'the true intent and meaning of this act not to legislate slavery into any Territory or State, nor to exclude it therefrom, but to leave the people thereof perfectly free to form and regulate their domestic institutions in their own way, subject only to the Constitution of the United States.' How vain and illusory would any other principle prove in practice in regard to the Territories," etc. Cincinnati *Enquirer*, June 22, 1856.

of barbarism, polygamy and slavery.'' Even in this new party, availability dictated the choice of a presidential candidate. The real leaders of the party were passed over in favor of John C. Frémont, whose romantic career was believed to be worth many votes. Pitted against Buchanan and Frémont, was Millard Fillmore who had been nominated months before by the American party, and who subsequently received the indorsement of what was left of the moribund Whig party.[1]

[1] Stanwood, History of the Presidency, pp. 269-274.

CHAPTER XIII

The Testing of Popular Sovereignty

The author of the Kansas-Nebraska bill doubtless anticipated a gradual and natural occupation of the new Territories by settlers like those home-seekers who had taken up government lands in Iowa and other States of the Northwest. In the course of time, it was to be expected, such communities would form their own social and political institutions, and so determine whether they would permit or forbid slave-labor. By that rapid, and yet on the whole strangely conservative, American process the people of the Territories would become politically self-conscious and ready for statehood. Not all at once, but gradually, a politically self-sufficient entity would come into being. Such had been the history of American colonization; it seemed the part of wise statesmanship to follow the trend of that history.

Theoretically popular sovereignty, as applied in the Kansas-Nebraska Act, was not an advance over the doctrine of Cass and Dickinson. It professed to be the same which had governed Congress in organizing Utah and New Mexico. Nevertheless, popular sovereignty had an artificial quality which squatter sovereignty lacked. The relation between Congress and the people of the Territories, in the matter of slavery, was now to be determined not so much by actual conditions as by an abstract principle. Federal policy was indoctrinated.

There was, too, this vital difference between squatter sovereignty in Utah and New Mexico and popular sovereignty in Nebraska and Kansas: the former were at least partially inhabited and enjoyed some degree of social and political order; the latter were practically uninhabited. It was one thing to grant control over all domestic concerns to a population *in esse,* and another and quite different thing to grant control to a people *in posse.* In the Kansas-Nebraska Act hypothetical communities were endowed with the capacity of self-government, and told to decide for themselves a question which would become a burning issue the very moment that the first settlers set foot in the Territories. Congress attempted thus to solve an equation without a single known quantity.

Moreover, slavery was no longer a matter of local concern. Doubtless it was once so regarded; but the time had passed when the conscience of the North would acquiesce in a *laissez faire* policy. By force of circumstances slavery had become a national issue. Ardent haters of the institution were not willing that its extension or restriction should be left to a fraction of the nation, artificially organized as a Territory. The Kansas-Nebraska Act prejudiced the minds of many against the doctrine, however sound in theory it may have seemed, by unsettling what the North regarded as its vested right in the free territory north of the line of the Missouri Compromise. The Act made the political atmosphere electric. The conditions for obtaining a calm, dispassionate judgment on the domestic concern of chief interest, were altogether lacking.

It was everywhere conceded that Nebraska would

be a free Territory. The eyes of the nation were focused upon Kansas, which was from the first debatable ground. A rush of settlers from the Northwest joined by pioneers from Kentucky and Missouri followed the opening up of the new lands. As Douglas had foretold, the tide of immigration held back by Indian treaties now poured in. The characteristic features of American colonization seemed about to repeat themselves. So far the movement of population was for the most part spontaneous. Land-hunger, not the political destiny of the West, drove men to locate their claims on the Kansas and the Missouri. By midsummer colonists of a somewhat different stripe appeared. Sent out under the auspices of the Emigrant Aid Company, they were to win Kansas for freedom at the same time that they subdued the wilderness. It was a species of assisted emigration which was new in the history of American colonization, outside the annals of missionary effort. The chief promoter of this enterprise was a thrifty, Massachusetts Yankee, who saw no reason why crusading and business should not go hand in hand. Kansas might be wrested from the slave-power at the same time that returns on invested funds were secured.

The effect of these developments upon the aggressive pro-slavery people of Missouri is not easy to describe. Hitherto they had assumed that Kansas would become a slave Territory in the natural order of events. This was the prevailing Southern opinion. At once the people of western Missouri were put upon the defensive. Blue lodges were formed for the purpose of carrying slavery into Kansas. Appeals were circulated in the slave-holding States for colonists and funds. Passions were inflamed by rumors which grew as they stalked abroad. The peaceful occupation of Kansas was at an end. Popular sovereignty was to be tested under abnormal conditions.

When the election of territorial delegates to Congress occurred, in the late fall, a fatal defect in the organic law was disclosed, to which many of the untoward incidents of succeeding months may be ascribed. The territorial act conferred the right of voting at the first elections upon all free, white, male inhabitants, twenty-one years of age and actually resident in the Territory.[1] Here was an unfortunate ambiguity. What was actual residence? Every other act organizing a territorial government was definite on this point, permitting only those to vote who were living in the proposed Territory, at the time of the passage of the act. The omission in the case of Kansas and Nebraska is easily accounted for. Neither had legal residents when the act was passed. Indeed, this defect bears witness to the fact that Congress was legislating, not for actual, but for hypothetical communities. The consequences were far-reaching, for at the very first election, it was charged that frauds were practiced by bands of Missourians, who had crossed the border only to aid the pro-slavery cause. Not much was made of these charges, as no particular interest attached to the election.

Far different was the election of members of the territorial legislature in the following spring. On all hands it was agreed that this legislature would determine whether Kansas should be slave or free soil. It was regrettable that Governor Reeder postponed

[1] Section 23, United States Statutes at Large, X, p. 285.

the taking of the census until February, since by mid-winter many settlers, who had staked their claims, returned home for the cold season, intending to return with their families in the early spring. This again was a characteristic feature of frontier history.[1] In March, the governor issued his proclamation of election, giving only three weeks' notice. Of those who had returned home, only residents of Missouri and Iowa were able to participate in the election of March 30th, by hastily recrossing into Kansas. Governor Reeder did his best to guard against fraud. In his instructions to the judges of election, he warned them that a voter must be "an actual resident"; that is, "must have commenced an active inhabitancy, which he actually intends to continue permanently, and must have made the Territory his dwelling place to the exclusion of any other home."[2] Still, it was not to be expected that *bona fide* residents could be easily ascertained in communities which had sprung up like mushrooms. A hastily constructed shack served all the purposes of the would-be voter; and, in last analysis, judges of elections had to rest content with declarations of intentions. Those who crossed into Kansas after the governor's proclamation and endeavored to continue actual inhabitancy, were with difficulty distinguished from those who now crossed for the first time, under a similar pretext. As Douglas subsequently contended with much force, the number of votes cast in excess of the census returns did not in itself prove wholesale fraud.[3]

[1] See remarks of Douglas, *Globe*, 34 Cong., 1 Sess., App., pp. 360-361.
[2] Howard Report, pp. 108-109.
[3] *Globe*, 34 Cong., 1 Sess., App., pp. 360-361.

Under such liability to deception and misjudgment, the territorial authorities held the election which was likely to determine the status of Kansas with respect to slavery. Both parties were playing for great stakes; passion and violence were the almost inevitable outcome. Both parties contained desperadoes, who invariably come to the surface in the general mixing which occurs on the frontier. Both parties committed frauds at the polls. But the most serious gravamina have been laid at the door of those Blue Lodges of Missouri which deliberately sought to secure the election of pro-slavery candidates by fair means or foul. The people of western Missouri had come to believe that the fate of slavery in their own Commonwealth hinged upon the future of Kansas. It was commonly believed that after Kansas, Missouri would be abolitionized. It was, therefore, with the fierce, unreasoning energy of defenders of their own institutions, that Blue Lodges organized their crusade for Kansas.[1] On election day armed bands of Missourians crossed into Kansas and polled a heavy vote for the pro-slavery candidates, in the teeth of indignant remonstrances.[2]

The further history of popular sovereignty in Kansas must be lightly touched upon, for it is the reflex action in the halls of Congress that interests the student of Douglas's career. Twenty-eight of the thirty-nine members of the first territorial legislature were men of pronounced pro-slavery views; eleven were anti-slavery candidates. In seven districts, where protests had been filed, the governor ordered new elections. Three of those first elected were returned, six were

[1] Spring, Kansas, pp. 39-41.
[2] Ibid., pp. 43-49; Rhodes, History of the United States, II, pp. 81-82.

new men of anti-slavery proclivities. But when the
legislature met, these new elections were set aside and
the first elections were declared valid.[1]

In complete control of the legislature, the pro-
slavery party proceeded to write slavery into the
law of the Territory. In their eagerness to establish
slavery permanently, these legislative Hotspurs quite
overshot the mark, creating offenses and affixing penal-
ties of doubtful constitutionality.[2] Meanwhile the
census of February reported but one hundred ninety-
two slaves in a total population of eight thousand six
hundred.[3] Those who had migrated from the South,
were not as a rule of the slave-holding class. Those
who possessed slaves shrank from risking their property in Kansas, until its future were settled.[4] Eventually, the climate was to prove an even greater obstacle
to the transplantation of the slave-labor system into
Kansas.

Foiled in their hope of winning the territorial legislature, the free-State settlers in Kansas resolved upon
a hazardous course. Believing the legislature an illegal
body, they called a convention to draft a constitution
with which they proposed to apply for admission to
the Union as a free State. Robinson, the leader of the
free-State party, was wise in such matters by reason
of his experience in California. Reeder, who had been
displaced as governor and had gone over to the opposition, lent his aid to the project; and ex-Congressman
Lane, formerly of Indiana, gave liberally of his vehement energy to the cause. After successive conven-

---

[1] Spring, Kansas, pp. 53-56.
[2] Rhodes, History of the United States, II, p. 99.
[3] *Ibid.*, p. 100.   [4] *Ibid.*, p. 101.

tions in which the various free-State elements were worked into a fairly consistent mixture, the Topeka convention launched a constitution and a free-State government. Unofficially the supporters of the new government took measures for its defense. In the following spring, Governor Robinson sent his first message to the State legislature in session at Topeka; and Reeder and Lane were chosen senators for the inchoate Commonwealth.[1]

Meantime Governor Shannon had succeeded Reeder as executive of the territorial government at Shawnee Mission. The aspect of affairs was ominous. Popular sovereignty had ended in a dangerous dualism. Two governments confronted each other in bitter hostility. There were untamed individuals in either camp, who were not averse to a decision by wager of battle.[2]

Such was the situation in Kansas, when Douglas reached Washington in February, after a protracted illness.[3] The President had already discussed the Kansas imbroglio in a special message; but the Democratic majority in the Senate showed some reluctance to follow the lead of the administration. From the Democrats in the House not much could be expected, because of the strength of the Republicans. The party awaited its leader. Upon his appearance, all matters relating to Kansas were referred to the Committee on Territories. The situation called for unusual qualities of leadership. How would the author of the Kansas-Nebraska Act face the palpable breakdown of his policy?

[1] Spring, Kansas, Chapter V; Rhodes, II, pp. 102-103.
[2] Rhodes, History of the United States, II, p. 103.
[3] Sheahan, Douglas, p. 286.

With his customary dispatch, Douglas reported on the 12th of March.[1]   The majority report consumed two hours in the reading; Senator Collamer stated the position of the minority in half the time.[2]   Evidently the chairman was aware where the burden of proof lay. Douglas took substantially the same ground as that taken by the President in his special message, but he discussed the issues boldly in his own vigorous way. No one doubted that he had reached his conclusions independently.

The report began with a constitutional argument in defense of the Kansas-Nebraska Act.   As a contribution to the development of the doctrine of popular sovereignty, the opening paragraphs deserve more than passing notice. The distinct advance in Douglas's thought consisted in this: that he explicitly refused to derive the power to organize Territories from that provision of the Constitution which gave Congress "power to dispose of and make all needful rules and regulations respecting the territory or other property belonging to the United States." The word "territory" here was used in its geographical sense to designate the public domain, not to indicate a political community. Rather was the power to be derived from the authority of Congress to adopt necessary and proper means to admit new States into the Union.   But beyond the necessary and proper organization of a territorial government with reference to ultimate statehood, Congress might not go.   Clearly, then, Congress might not impose conditions and restrictions upon a Territory which would prevent its entering the Union on an equality

[1] Senate Reports, 34 Cong., 1 Sess., No. 34.
[2] *Globe,* 34 Cong., 1 Sess., p. 639.

with the other States. From the formation of the Union, each State had been left free to decide the question of slavery for itself. Congress, therefore, might not decide the question for prospective States. Recognizing this, the framers of the Kansas-Nebraska Act had relegated the discussion of the slavery question to the people, who were to form a territorial government under cover of the organic act.[1]

This was an ingenious argument. It was in accord with the utterances of some of the weightiest intellects in our constitutional history. But it was not in accord with precedent. There was hardly a territorial act that had emerged from Douglas's committee room, which had not imposed restrictions not binding on the older Commonwealths.

Having given thus a constitutional sanction to the principle of the Kansas-Nebraska Act, the report unhesitatingly denounced that "vast moneyed corporation," created for the purpose of controlling the domestic institutions of a distinct political community fifteen hundred miles away.[2] This was as flagrant an act of intervention as though France or England had interfered for a similar purpose in Cuba, for "in respect to everything which affects its domestic policy and internal concerns, each State stands in the relation of a foreign power to every other State." The obvious retort to this extraordinary assertion was, that Kansas was only a Territory, and not a State. Douglas then made this "mammoth moneyed corporation" the scapegoat for all that had happened in Kansas. The Missouri Blue Lodges were defensive organizations, called

[1] Senate Report, No. 34, p. 4.
[2] Ibid., p. 7.

into existence by the fear that the "abolitionizing" of Kansas was the prelude to a warfare upon slavery in Missouri. The violence and bloodshed in Kansas were "the natural and inevitable consequences of such extraordinary systems of emigration."[1]

Such *ex post facto* assertions did not mend matters in Kansas, however much they may have relieved the author of the report. It remained to deal with the existing situation. The report took the ground that the legislature of Kansas was a legal body and had been so recognized by Governor Reeder. Neither the alleged irregularity of the elections, nor other objections, could diminish its legislative authority. Protests against the election returns had been filed in only seven out of eighteen districts. Ten out of thirteen councilmen, and seventeen out of twenty-six representatives, held their seats by virtue of the governor's certificate. Even if it were assumed that the second elections in the seven districts were wrongly invalidated by the legislature, its action was still the action of a lawful legislature, possessing in either house a quorum of duly certificated members. This was a lawyer's plea. Technically it was unanswerable.

Having taken this position, Douglas very properly refused to pass judgment on the laws of the legislature. By the very terms of the Kansas-Nebraska Act, Congress had confided the power to enact local laws to the people of the Territories. If the validity of these laws should be doubted, it was for the courts of justice and not for Congress to decide the question.[2]

Throughout the report, the question was not once

[1] Senate Report, No. 34, pp. 7-9.
[2] *Ibid.*, p. 23.

raised, whether the legislature really reflected the sentiment of a majority of the settlers of Kansas. Douglas
assumed that it was truly representative. This attitude is not surprising, when one recalls his predilections and the conflict of evidence on essential points in
the controversy. Nevertheless, this attitude was unfortunate, for it made him unfair toward the free-State
settlers, with whom by temper and training he had far
more in common than with the Missouri emigrants.
Could he have cut himself loose from his bias, he would
have recognized the free-State men as the really trustworthy builders of a Commonwealth. But having
taken his stand on the legality of the territorial legislature, he persisted in regarding the free-State movement as a seditious combination to subvert the territorial government established by Congress. To the
free-State men he would not accord any inherent,
sovereign right to annul the laws and resist the authority of the territorial government.[1] The right of
self-government was derived only from the Constitution through the organic act passed by Congress. And
then he used that expression which was used with telling effect against the theory of popular sovereignty:
"The sovereignty of a Territory remains in abeyance,
suspended in the United States, in trust for the people,
until they shall be admitted into the Union as a
State."[2] If this was true, then popular sovereignty
after all meant nothing more than local self-government, the measure of which was to be determined by
Congress. If Congress left slavery to local determination, it was only for expediency's sake, and not by
reason of any constitutional obligation.

[1] Senate Report, No. 34, p. 34.   [2] *Ibid.*, p. 39.

Douglas found a vindication of his Kansas-Nebraska Act in the peaceful history of Nebraska, "to which the emigrant aid societies did not extend their operations, and into which the stream of emigration was permitted to flow in its usual and natural channels."[1] He fixed the ultimate responsibility for the disorders in Kansas upon those who opposed the principle of the Kansas-Nebraska Act, and who, "failing to accomplish their purpose in the halls of Congress, and under the authority of the Constitution, immediately resorted in their respective States to unusual and extraordinary means to control the political destinies and shape the domestic institutions of Kansas, in defiance of the wishes and regardless of the rights of the people of that Territory as guaranteed by their organic law."[2]

A practical recommendation accompanied the report. It was proposed to authorize the territorial legislature to provide for a constitutional convention to frame a State constitution, as soon as a census should indicate that there were ninety-three thousand four hundred and twenty inhabitants.[3] This bill was in substantial accord with the President's recommendations.

The minority report was equally positive as to the cause of the trouble in Kansas and the proper remedy. "Repeal the act of 1854, organize Kansas anew as a free Territory and all will be put right." But if Congress was bent on continuing the experiment, then the Territory must be reorganized with proper safeguards against illegal voting. The only alternative was to admit the Territory as a State with its free constitution.

[1] Senate Report, No. 34, p. 40.   [2] Ibid., pp. 39-40.
[3] Globe, 34 Cong., 1 Sess., p. 693.

The issue could not have been more sharply drawn. Popular sovereignty as applied in the Kansas-Nebraska Act was put upon the defensive. Republican senators made haste to press their advantage. Sumner declared that the true issue was smothered in the majority report, but stood forth as a pillar of fire in the report of the minority. Trumbull forced the attack, while Douglas was absent, without waiting for the printing of the reports. It needed only this apparent discourtesy to bring Douglas into the arena. An unseemly wrangle between the Illinois senators followed, in the course of which Douglas challenged his colleague to resign and stand with him for re-election before the next session of the legislature.[1] Trumbull wisely declined to accept the risk.

On the 20th of March, Douglas addressed the Senate in reply to Trumbull.[2] Nothing that he said shed any new light on the controversy. He had not changed his angle of vision. He had only the old arguments with which to combat the assertion that "Kansas had been conquered and a legislature imposed by violence." But the speech differed from the report, just as living speech must differ from the printed page. Every assertion was pointed by his vigorous intonations; every argument was accentuated by his forceful personality. The report was a lawyer's brief; the speech was the flexible utterance of an accomplished debater, bent upon a personal as well as an argumentative victory.

Even hostile critics were forced to yield to a certain admiration for "the Little Giant." The author of *Uncle Tom's Cabin* watched him from her seat in the

[1] *Globe*, 34 Cong., 1 Sess., p. 657.
[2] *Ibid.*, App., pp. 280 ff.

Senate gallery, with intense interest; and though writing for readers, who like herself hated the man for his supposed servility to the South, she said with unwonted objectivity, "This Douglas is the very ideal of vitality. Short, broad, and thick-set, every inch of him has its own alertness and motion. He has a good head and face, thick black hair, heavy black brows and a keen eye. His figure would be an unfortunate one were it not for the animation which constantly pervades it; as it is, it rather gives poignancy to his peculiar appearance; he has a small, handsome hand, moreover, and a graceful as well as forcible mode of using it. . . . He has two requisites of a debater—a melodious voice and a clear, sharply defined enunciation. . . . . His forte in debating is his power of mystifying the point. With the most off-hand assured airs in the world, and a certain appearance of honest superiority, like one who has a regard for you and wishes to set you right on one or two little matters, he proceeds to set up some point which is *not* that in question, but only a family connection of it, and this point he attacks with the very best of logic and language; he charges upon it horse and foot, runs it down, tramples it in the dust, and then turns upon you with—'Sir, there is your argument! Did not I tell you so? You see it is all stuff;' and if you have allowed yourself to be so dazzled by his quickness as to forget that the routed point is not, after all, the one in question, you suppose all is over with it. Moreover, he contrives to mingle up so many stinging allusions to so many piquant personalities that by the time he has done his mystification a dozen others are ready and burning to spring on their feet to repel some direct or indirect attack, all equally wide of the point.''[1]

Douglas paid dearly for some of these personal shots. He had never forgiven Sumner for his share in ''the Appeal of the Independent Democrats.'' He lost no opportunity to attribute unworthy motives to this man, whose radical views on slavery he never could comprehend. More than once he insinuated that the Senator from Massachusetts and other Black Republicans were fabricating testimony relating to Kansas for political purposes. When Sumner, many weeks later, rose to address the Senate on ''the Crime against Kansas,'' he labored under the double weight of personal wrongs and the wrongs of a people. The veteran Cass pronounced his speech ''the most un-American and unpatriotic that ever grated on the ears of the members of this high body.''[2] Even Sumner's friends listened to him with surprise and regret. Of Douglas he had this to say:

''As the Senator from South Carolina is the Don Quixote, the Senator from Illinois is the squire of slavery, its very Sancho Panza, ready to do all its humiliating offices. This Senator in his labored address, vindicating his labored report—piling one mass of elaborate error upon another mass—constrained himself, as you will remember, to unfamiliar decencies of speech. . . . I will not stop to repel the imputations which he cast upon myself. . . . Standing on this floor, the Senator issued his rescript, requiring submission to the Usurped Power of Kansas; and this was accompanied by a manner—all his own—such as befits the

[1] New York *Independent*, May 1, 1856; quoted by Rhodes II, p. 128.
[2] *Globe*, 34 Cong., 1 Sess., App. p. 544.

tyrannical threat. . . . He is bold. He shrinks from
nothing. Like Danton, he may cry, '*l'audace! l'audace!
toujours l'audace!*' but even his audacity cannot compass this work. The Senator copies the British officer,
who, with boastful swagger, said that with the hilt of
his sword he would cram the 'stamps' down the throats
of the American people, and he will meet a similar
failure.'"[1]

The retort of Douglas was not calculated to turn
away wrath. He called attention to the fact that these
gross insults were not uttered in the heat of indignation, but "conned over, written with cool, deliberate
malignity, repeated from night to night in order to
catch the appropriate grace." He ridiculed the ex-
cessive self-esteem of Sumner in words that moved
the Senate to laughter; and then completed his vindictive assault by charging Sumner with perfidy. Had
he not sworn to obey the Constitution, and then, forsooth, refused to support the enforcement of the Fugitive Slave law?[2]

Sumner replied in a passion, "Let the Senator remember hereafter that the bowie-knife and bludgeon
are not the proper emblems of senatorial debate. Let
him remember that the swagger of Bob Acres and the
ferocity of the Malay cannot add dignity to this body.
. . .No person with the upright form of a man can be
allowed, without violation of all decency, to switch out
from his tongue the perpetual stench of offensive personality. Sir, that is not a proper weapon of debate,
at least, on this floor. The noisome, squat, and nameless animal, to which I refer, is not a proper model for
an American Senator. Will the Senator from Illinois

[1] *Globe,* 34 Cong., 1 Sess., App., p. 531.   [2] *Ibid.,* p. 545.

take notice?'' And upon Douglas's unworthy retort that he certainly would not imitate the Senator in that capacity, Sumner said insultingly, ''Mr. President, again the Senator has switched his tongue, and again he fills the Senate with its offensive odor.''[1]

Two days later Brooks made his assault on Sumner in the Senate chamber. Sumner's recollection was, that on recovering consciousness, he recognized among those about him, but offering no assistance, Senators Douglas and Toombs, and between them, his assailant.[2] It was easy for ill-disposed persons to draw unfortunate inferences from this sick-bed testimony. Douglas felt that an explanation was expected from him. In a frank, explicit statement he told his colleagues that he was in the reception room of the Senate when the assault occurred. Hearing what was happening, he rose immediately to his feet to enter the chamber and put an end to the affray. But, on second thought, he realized that his motives would be misconstrued if he entered the hall. When the affair was over, he went in with the crowd. He was not near Brooks at any time, and he was not with Senator Toombs, except perhaps as he passed him on leaving the chamber. He did not know that any attack upon Mr. Sumner was purposed ''then or at any other time, here or at any other place.''[3] Still, it is to be regretted that Douglas did not act on his first, manly instincts and do all that lay in his power to end this brutal assault, regardless of possible misconstructions.

Disgraceful as these scenes in Congress were, they

[1] *Globe,* 34 Cong., 1 Sess., App., p. 547.
[2] Rhodes, History of the United States, II, p. 148.
[3] *Globe,* 34 Cong., 1 Sess., p. 1305.

were less ominous than events which were passing in
Kansas. Clashes between pro-slavery and free-State
settlers had all but resulted in civil war in the preced-
ing fall. An unusually severe winter had followed,
which not only cooled the passions of all for a while,
but convinced many a slave-holder of the futility of
introducing African slaves into a climate, where on
occasion the mercury would freeze in the thermometer.
In the spring hostilities were resumed. Under cover
of executing certain writs in Lawrence, Sheriff Jones
and a posse of ruffians took revenge upon that stronghold of the Emigrant Aid Society, by destroying the
newspaper offices, burning some public buildings, and
pillaging the town. Three days after the sack of
Lawrence, and just two days after the assault upon
Sumner in the Senate, John Brown and his sons executed the decree of Almighty God, by slaying in cold
blood five pro-slavery settlers on the Pottawatomie.
Civil war had begun in Kansas.[1]

If remedial measures for Kansas were needed at the
beginning of Congress, much more were they needed
now. The bill reported by Douglas for the eventual
admission of Kansas had commended itself neither to
the leaders, nor to the rank and file, of the party. There
was a general disposition to await the outcome of the
national party conventions, before legislating for
Kansas. Douglas made repeated efforts to expedite
his bill, but his failure to secure the Democratic nomination seemed to weaken his leadership. Pressure
from without finally spurred the Democratic members
of Congress to action. The enthusiasm of the Republicans in convention and their confident expectation of

[1] Rhodes, History of the United States, II, pp. 103-106; 154-166.

carrying many States at the North, warned the Democrats that they must make some effort to allay the disturbances in Kansas. The initiative was taken by Senator Toombs, who drafted a bill conceding far more to Northern sentiment than any yet proposed. It provided that, after a census had been taken, delegates to a constitutional convention should be chosen on the date of the presidential election in November. Five competent persons, appointed by the President with the consent of the Senate, were to supervise the census and the subsequent registration of voters. The convention thus chosen was to assemble in December to frame a State constitution and government.[1]

The Toombs bill, with several others, and with numerous amendments, was referred to the Committee on Territories. Frequent conferences followed at Douglas's residence, in which the recognized leaders of the party participated.[2] It was decided to support the Toombs bill in a slightly amended form and to make a party measure of it.[3] Prudence warned against attempting to elect Buchanan on a policy of merely negative resistance to the Topeka movement.[4] The Republican members of Congress were to be forced to make a show of hands on a measure which promised substantial relief to the people of Kansas.

In his report of June 30th, Douglas discussed the various measures that had been proposed by Whigs and Republicans, but found the Toombs bill best adapted to "insure a fair and impartial decision of the questions at issue in Kansas, in accordance with the

[1] Globe, 34 Cong., 1 Sess., p. 1439.
[2] Ibid., 35 Cong., 1 Sess., p. 22.
[3] Ibid., p. 119.
[4] Ibid., p. 119.

wishes of the *bona fide* inhabitants.'' A single paragraph from this report ought to have convinced those
who subsequently doubted the sincerity of Douglas's
course, that he was partner to no plots against the free
expression of public opinion in the Territory. "In the
opinion of your committee, whenever a constitution
shall be formed in any Territory, preparatory to its
admission into the Union as a State, justice, the genius
of our institutions, the whole theory of our republican
system imperatively demand that the voice of the
people shall be fairly expressed, and their will embodied in that fundamental law, without fraud or
violence, or intimidation, or any other improper or unlawful influence, and subject to no other restrictions
than those imposed by the Constitution of the United
States.''[1]

The Toombs bill caused Republicans grave misgivings, even while they conceded its ostensible liberality.
Could an administration that had condoned the frauds
already practiced in Kansas be trusted to appoint dis-
interested commissioners? Would a census of the
present population give a majority in the proposed
convention to the free-State party in Kansas? Everyone knew that many free-State people had been driven
away by the disorders. Douglas endeavored to re-
assure his opponents on these points; but his words
carried no weight on the other side of the chamber.
No better evidence of his good faith in the matter,
however, could have been asked than he offered, by an
amendment which extended the right of voting at the
elections to all who had been *bona fide* residents and
voters, but who had absented themselves from the Ter-

[1] Senate Report, 34 Cong., 1 Sess., No. 198.

ritory, provided they should return before October 1st.[1] If, as Republicans asserted, many more free-State settlers than pro-slavery squatters had been driven out, then here was a fair concession. But what they wanted was not merely an equal chance for freedom in Kansas, but precedence. To this end they were ready even to admit Kansas under the Topeka constitution, which, by the most favorable construction, was the work of a faction.[2]

It was afterwards alleged that Douglas had wittingly suppressed a clause in the original Toombs bill, which provided for a submission of the constitution to a popular vote. The circumstances were such as to make the charge plausible, and Douglas, in his endeavor to clear himself, made hasty and unqualified statements which were manifestly incorrect. In his own bill for the admission of Kansas, Douglas referred explicitly to "the election for the adoption of the Constitution."[3] The wording of the clause indicates that he regarded the popular ratification of the constitution to be a matter of course. The original Toombs bill had also referred explicitly to a ratification of the constitution by the people;[4] but when it was reported from Douglas's committee in an amended form, it had been stripped of this provision. Trumbull noted at the time that this amended bill made no provision for the submission of the constitution to the vote of the people and deplored the omission, though he supposed, as did most men, that such a ratification would be necessary.[5]

[1] *Globe*, 34 Cong., 1 Sess., App., p. 795.
[2] Rhodes, History of the United States, II, pp. 194-195.
[3] Senate Bill, No. 172, Section 3.   [4] Senate Bill, No. 356, Section 13.
[5] *Globe*, 34 Cong., 1 Sess., App., p. 779.

Subsequently he accused Douglas not only of having intentionally omitted the referendum clause, but of having prevented a popular vote, by adding the clause, "and until the complete execution of this Act, no other election shall be held in said Territory."[1]

Douglas cleared himself from the latter charge, by pointing out that this clause had been struck out upon his own motion, and replaced by the clause which read, "all other elections in said Territory are hereby postponed until such time as said convention shall appoint."[2] As to the other charge, Douglas said in 1857, that he knew the Toombs bill was silent on the matter of submission, but he took the fair construction to be that powers not delegated were reserved, and that of course the constitution would be submitted to the people. "That I was a party, either by private conferences at my house or otherwise, to a plan to force a constitution on the people of Kansas without submission, is not true."[3]

Still, there was the ugly fact that the Toombs bill had gone to his committee with the clause, and had emerged shorn of it. Toombs himself threw some light on the matter by stating that the clause had been stricken out because there was no provision for a second election, and therefore no proper safeguards for such a popular vote.[4] The probability is that Douglas, and in fact most men, deemed it sufficient at that time to provide a fair opportunity for the elec-

[1] Speech at Alton, Illinois, 1858.

[2] Political Debates between Lincoln and Douglas, pp. 161 ff.

[3] *Globe*, 35 Cong., 1 Sess., p. 22.

[4] *Ibid.*, App., p. 127. Toombs also stated that the submission clause had been put in his bill in the first place by accident, and that it had been stricken from the bill at his suggestion.

tion of a convention.[1]   When Trumbull preferred his charges in detail in the campaign of 1858, Douglas at first flatly denied that there was a submission clause in the original Toombs bill.   Both Trumbull and Lincoln then convicted Douglas of error, and thus put him in the light of one who had committed an offense and had sought to save himself by prevaricating.

The Toombs bill passed the Senate over the impotent Republican opposition; but in the House it encountered a hostile majority which would not so much as consider a proposition emanating from Democratic sources.[2]   Douglas charged the Republicans with the deliberate wish and intent to keep the Kansas issue alive.   "All these gentlemen want," he declared, "is to get up murder and bloodshed in Kansas for political effect.   They do not mean that there shall be peace until after the presidential election. . . . Their capital for the presidential election is blood.   We may as well talk plainly.   An angel from Heaven could not write a bill to restore peace in Kansas that would be acceptable to the Abolition Republican party previous to the presidential election."[3]

"Bleeding Kansas" was, indeed, a most effective campaign cry.   Before Congress adjourned, the Republicans had found other campaign material in the majority report of the Kansas investigating committee. The Democrats issued the minority report as a counterblast, and also circulated three hundred thousand copies of Douglas's 12th of March report, which was

---

[1] The submission of State constitutions to a popular vote had not then become a general practice.

[2] Rhodes, History of the United States, II, p. 195.

[3] *Globe*, 34 Cong., 1 Sess., App., p. 844.

held to be campaign material of the first order. Douglas himself paid for one-third of these out of his own
pocket.[1] No one could accuse him of sulking in his
tent. Whatever personal pique he may have felt at
losing the nomination, he was thoroughly loyal to his
party. He gave unsparingly of his time and strength
to the cause of Democracy, speaking most effectively
in the doubtful States. And when Pennsylvania became the pivotal State, as election day drew near,
Douglas gave liberally to the campaign fund which his
friend Forney was collecting to carry the State for
Buchanan.[2]

Illinois, too, was now reckoned as a doubtful State.
Douglas had forced the issues clearly to the fore by
pressing the nomination of Richardson for governor.[3]
Next to himself, there was no man in the State so
closely identified with Kansas-Nebraska legislation.
The anti-Nebraska forces accepted the gage of battle
by nominating Bissell, a conspicuous figure among
those Democrats who could not sanction the repeal of
the Missouri Compromise. Only the nomination of a
Know-Nothing candidate complicated the issues which
were thus drawn. Shortly before the October State
elections, Douglas saw that he had committed a tactical
blunder. Richardson was doomed to defeat. ''Would
it not be well,'' wrote Douglas to James W. Sheahan,
who had come from Washington to edit the Chicago
Times, ''to prepare the minds of your readers for
losing the State elections on the 14th of October?
Buchanan's friends expect to lose it then, but carry

[1] *Globe*, 35 Cong., 1 Sess., p. 21.
[2] Sheahan, Douglas, p. 443.
[3] Davidson and Stuvé, History of Illinois, p. 650.

the State by 20,000 in November. We may have to fight against wind and tide after the 14th. Hence our friends ought to be prepared for the worst. We must carry Illinois at all hazards and in any event.''[1]

This forecast proved to be correct. Richardson, with all that he represented, went down to defeat. In November Buchanan carried the State by a narrow margin, the total Democratic vote falling far behind the combined vote for Frémont and Fillmore.[2] The political complexion of Illinois had changed. It behooved the senior senator to take notice.

[1] MS. Letter, Douglas to Sheahan, October 6, 1856.

[2] *Tribune Almanac*, 1857. The vote was as follows:

Buchanan	105,348
Frémont	96,189
Fillmore	37,444

BOOK III
THE IMPENDING CRISIS

CHAPTER XIV

THE PERSONAL EQUATION

Vast changes had passed over Illinois since Douglas set foot on its soil, a penniless boy with his fortune to make. The frontier had been pushed back far beyond the northern boundary of the State; the Indians had disappeared; and the great military tract had been occupied by a thrifty, enterprising people of the same stock from which Douglas sprang. In 1833, the center of political gravity lay far south of the geographical center of the State; by 1856, the northern counties had already established a political equipoise. The great city on Lake Michigan, a lusty young giant, was yearly becoming more conscious of its commercial and political possibilities. Douglas had natural affinities with Chicago. It was thoroughly American, thoroughly typical of that restless, aggressive spirit which had sent him, and many another New Englander, into the great interior basin of the continent. There was no other city which appealed so strongly to his native instincts. From the first he had been impressed by its commercial potentialities. He had staked his own fortunes upon its invincible prosperity by investing in real estate, and within a few years he had reaped the reward of his faith in unseen values. His holdings both in the city and in Cook County advanced in value by leaps and bounds, so that in the year 1856, he sold approximately one hundred acres for $90,000. With his wonted prodigality, born of superb confidence in future gains, he also deeded ten acres of his valuable "Grove Property" to the trustees of Chicago University.[1] Yet with a far keener sense of honor than many of his contemporaries exhibited, he refused to speculate in land in the new States and Territories, with whose political beginnings he would be associated as chairman of the Committee on Territories. He was resolved early in his career "to avoid public suspicion of private interest in his political conduct."[2]

The gift to Chicago University was no doubt inspired in part at least by local pride; yet it was not the first nor the only instance of the donor's interest in educational matters. No one had taken greater interest in the bequest of James Smithson to the United States. At first, no doubt, Douglas labored under a common misapprehension regarding this foundation, fancying that it would contribute directly to the advancement and diffusion of the applied sciences; but his support was not less hearty when he grasped the policy formulated by the first secretary of the institution. He was the author of that provision in the act establishing the Smithsonian Institution, which called for the presentation of one copy of every copyrighted book, map, and musical composition, to the Institution and to the Congressional Library.[3] He became a member of the board of regents and retained the office until his death.

With his New England training Douglas believed profoundly in the dignity of labor; not even his Southern associations lessened his genuine admiration for

---

[1] Sheahan, Douglas, pp. 442-443; Iglehart, History of the Douglas Estate in Chicago.

[2] Letter in Chicago *Times*, August 30, 1857.

[3] *Globe*, 29 Cong., 1 Sess., pp. 749-750.

the magnificent industrial achievements of the Northern mechanic and craftsman. He shared, too, the conviction of his Northern constituents, that the inventiveness, resourcefulness, and bold initiative of the American workman was the outcome of free institutions, which permitted and encouraged free and bold thinking. The American laborer was not brought up to believe it "a crime to think in opposition to the consecrated errors of olden times."[1] It was impossible for a man so thinking to look with favor upon the slave-labor system of the South. He might tolerate the presence of slavery in the South; but in his heart of hearts he could not desire its indefinite extension.

Douglas belonged to his section, too, in his attitude toward the disposition of the public domain. He was one of the first to advocate free grants of the public lands to homesteaders. His bill to grant one hundred and sixty acres to actual settlers who should cultivate them for four years, was the first of many similar projects in the early fifties.[2] Southern statesmen thought this the best "bid" yet made for votes: it was further evidence of Northern demagogism. The South, indeed, had little direct interest in the peopling of the Western prairies by independent yeomen, native or foreign. Just here Douglas parted company with his Southern associates. He believed that the future of the great West depended upon this wise and beneficial use of the national domain. Neither could he agree with Eastern statesmen who deplored the gratuitous distribution of lands, which by sale would yield large revenues. His often-repeated reply was the quintes-

[1] *Globe,* 32 Cong., 2 Sess., p. 870.
[2] *Ibid.,* 31 Cong., 1 Sess., p. 75.

sence of Western statesmanship. The pioneer who went into the wilderness, to wrestle with all manner of hardships, was a true wealth-producer. As he cleared his land and tilled the soil, he not only himself became a tax-payer, but he increased the value of adjoining lands and added to the sum total of the national resources.[1]

Douglas gave his ungrudging support to grants of land in aid of railroads and canals. He would not regard such grants, however, as mere donations, but rather as wise provisions for increasing the value of government lands. ''The government of the United States is a great land owner; she has vast bodies of land which she has had in market for thirty or forty years; and experience proves that she cannot sell them. ... The difficulty in the way of the sale does not arise from the fact that the lands are not fertile and susceptible to cultivation, but that they are distant from market, and in many cases destitute of timber.''[2] Therefore he gave his voice and vote for nearly all land grant bills, designed to aid the construction of railroads and canals that would bring these public lands into the market; but he insisted that everything should be done by individual enterprise if possible. He shared the hostility of the West toward large grants of land to private corporations.[3] What could not be done by individual enterprise, should be done by the States; and only that should be undertaken by the Federal government which could be done in no other way.

As the representative of a constituency which was

[1] *Globe*, 31 Cong., 1 Sess., p. 266.
[2] *Ibid.*, 32 Cong., 1 Sess., pp. 350-351.   [3] *Ibid.*, p. 769.

profoundly interested in the navigation of the great interior waterways of the continent, Douglas was a vigorous advocate of internal improvements, so far as his Democratic conscience would allow him to construe the Constitution in favor of such undertakings by the Federal government. Like his constituents, he was not always logical in his deductions from constitutional provisions. The Constitution, he believed, would not permit an appropriation of government money for the construction of the ship canal around the Falls of the St. Mary's; but as landowner, the Federal government might donate lands for that purpose.[1] He was also constrained to vote for appropriations for the improvement of river channels and of harbors on the lakes and on the ocean, because these were works of a distinctly national character; but he deplored the mode by which these appropriations were made.[2]

Just when the Nebraska issue came to the fore, he was maturing a scheme by which a fair, consistent, and continuous policy of internal improvements could be initiated, in place of the political bargaining which had hitherto determined the location of government operations. Two days before he presented his famous Nebraska report, Douglas addressed a letter to Governor Matteson of Illinois in which he developed this new policy.[3] He believed that the whole question would be thoroughly aired in the session just begun.[4] Instead of making internal improvements a matter of politics, and of wasteful jobbery, he would take advan-

[1] *Globe*, 32 Cong., 1 Sess., App., p. 951.
[2] *Ibid.*, p. 952.
[3] Letter to Governor Matteson, January 2, 1854, in Sheahan, Douglas, pp. 358 ff.
[4] MS. Letter, Douglas to C. H. Lanphier, November 11, 1853.

tage of the constitutional provision which permits a State to lay tonnage duties by the consent of Congress. If Congress would pass a law permitting the imposition of tonnage duties according to a uniform rule, then each town and city might be authorized to undertake the improvement of its own harbor, and to tax its own commerce for the prosecution of the work. Under such a system the dangers of misuse and improper diversion of funds would be reduced to a minimum. The system would be self-regulative. Negligence, or extravagance, with the necessary imposition of higher duties, would punish a port by driving shipping elsewhere.

But for the interposition of the slavery issue, which no one would have more gladly banished from Congress, Douglas would have unquestionably pushed some such reform into the foreground. His heart was bound up in the material progress of the country. He could never understand why men should allow an issue like slavery to stand in the way of prudential and provident legislation for the expansion of the Republic. He laid claim to no expert knowledge in other matters: he frankly confessed his ignorance of the mysteries of tariff schedules. "I have learned enough about the tariff," said he with a sly thrust at his colleagues, who prided themselves on their wisdom, "to know that I know scarcely anything about it at all; and a man makes considerable progress on a question of this kind when he ascertains that fact."[1] Still, he grasped an elementary principle that had escaped many a protectionist, that "a tariff involves two conflicting principles which are eternally at war with each other.

[1] *Globe*, 36 Cong., 2 Sess., p. 953.

Every tariff involves the principles of protection and of oppression, the principles of benefits and of burdens. . . . The great difficulty is, so to adjust these conflicting principles of benefits and burdens as to make one compensate for the other in the end, and give equal benefits and equal burdens to every class of the community.''[1]

Douglas was wiser, too, than the children of light, when he insisted that works of art should be admitted free of duty. ''I wish we could get a model of every work of art, a cast of every piece of ancient statuary, a copy of every valuable painting and rare book, so that our artists might pursue their studies and exercise their skill at home, and that our literary men might not be exiled in the pursuits which bless mankind.''[2]

Still, the prime interests of this hardy son of the West were political. How could they have been otherwise in his environment? There is no evidence of literary refinement in his public utterances; no trace of the culture which comes from intimate association with the classics; no suggestion of inspiration quaffed in communion with imaginative and poetic souls. An amusing recognition of these limitations is vouched for by a friend, who erased a line of poetry from a manuscript copy of a public address by Douglas. Taken to task for his presumption, he defended himself by the indisputable assertion, that Douglas was never known to have quoted a line of poetry in his life.[3] Yet the unimaginative Douglas anticipated the era of aërial navigation now just dawning. On one occasion, he

[1] *Globe*, 36 Cong., 2 Sess., p. 953.   [2] *Ibid.*, p. 1050.
[3] Chicago *Times*, January 27, 1858.

urged upon the Senate a memorial from an aëronaut, who desired the aid of the government in experiments which he was conducting with dirigible balloons. When the Senate, in a mirthful mood, proposed to refer the petition to the Committee on Foreign Affairs, Douglas protested that the subject should be treated seriously.[1]

While Douglas was thus steadily growing into complete accord with the New England elements in his section—save on one vital point,—he fell captive to the beauty and grace of one whose associations were with men and women south of Mason and Dixon's line. Adèle Cutts was the daughter of Mr. J. Madison Cutts of Washington, who belonged to an old Maryland family. She was the great-niece of Dolly Madison, whom she much resembled in charm of manner. When Douglas first made her acquaintance, she was the belle of Washington society,—in the days when the capital still boasted of a genuine aristocracy of gentleness, grace, and talent. There are no conflicting testimonies as to her beauty. Women spoke of her as "beautiful as a pearl;" to men she seemed "a most lovely and queenly apparition."[1] Both men and women found her sunny-tempered, generous, warm-hearted, and sincere. What could there have been in the serious-minded, dark-visaged "Little Giant" to win the hand of this mistress of many hearts? Perhaps she saw "Othello's visage in his mind"; perhaps she yielded to the imperious will which would accept no refusal; at all events, Adèle Cutts chose this plain little man of

[1] *Globe*, 31 Cong., 2 Sess., p. 132.

[2] Mrs. Pryor, Reminiscences of Peace and War, p. 68; Villard, Memoirs, I, p. 92.

middle-age in preference to men of wealth and title.[1]
It proved to be in every respect a happy marriage.[2]
He cherished her with all the warmth of his manly
affection; she became the devoted partner of all his
toils. His two boys found in her a true mother; and
there was not a household in Washington where home-
life was graced with tenderer mutual affection.[3]

Across this picture of domestic felicity, there fell but
a single, fugitive shadow. Adèle Cutts was an ad-
herent of the Roman Church; and at a time when
Native Americanism was running riot with the sense
of even intelligent men, such ecclesiastical connections
were made the subject of some odious comment. Although Douglas permitted his boys to be educated in
the Catholic faith, and profoundly respected the
religious instincts of his tender-hearted wife, he never
entered into the Roman communion, nor in fact identified himself with any church.[4] Much of his relentless
criticism of Native Americanism can be traced to his
abhorrence of religious intolerance in any form.

This alliance meant much to Douglas. Since the
death of his first wife, he had grown careless in his
dress and bearing, too little regardful of conventionali-
ties. He had sought by preference the society of men,
and had lost those external marks of good-breeding
which companionship with gentlewomen had given
him. Insensibly he had fallen a prey to a certain
harshness and bitterness of temper, which was foreign
to his nature; and he had become reckless, so men said,

[1] Letter of Mrs. Lippincott ("Grace Greenwood") to the writer.
[2] Conversation with Stephen A. Douglas, Esq., of Chicago.
[3] The marriage took place November 20, 1856.
[4] See Philadelphia *Press*, June 8, 1861.

because of defeated ambition. But now yielding to the warmth of tender domesticity, the true nature of the man asserted itself.[1] He grew, perhaps not less ambitious, but more sensible of the obligations which leadership imposed.

No one could gainsay his leadership. He was indisputably the most influential man in his party; and this leadership was not bought by obsequiousness to party opinion, nor by the shadowy arts of the machine politician alone. True, he was a spoilsman, like all of his contemporaries. He was not above using the spoils of office to reward faithful followers. Reprehensible as the system was, and is, there is perhaps a redeeming feature in this aspect of American politics. The ignorant foreigner was reconciled to government because it was made to appear to him as a personal benefactor. Due credit must be given to those leaders like Douglas, who fired the hearts of Irishmen and Germans with loyalty to the Union through the medium of party.[2]

The hold of Douglas upon his following, however, cannot be explained by sordid appeals to their self-interest. He commanded the unbought service of thousands. In the early days of his career, he had found loyal friends, who labored unremittingly for his advancement, without hope of pecuniary reward or of any return but personal gratitude; and throughout his career he drew upon this vast fund of personal loyalty. His capacity for warm friendships was un-limited. He made men, particularly young men, feel

[1] Letter of J. H. Roberts, Esq., of Chicago to the writer; also letter of Mrs. Lippincott to the writer.

[2] See Philadelphia *Press*, November 17, 1860.

that it was an inestimable boon to be permitted to labor with him "for the cause." Far away in Asia Minor, with his mind teeming with a thousand strange sensations, he can yet think of a friend at the antipodes who nurses a grievance against him; and forthwith he sits down and writes five pages of generous, affectionate remonstrance.[1] In the thick of an important campaign, when countless demands are made upon his time, he finds a moment to lay his hand upon the shoulder of a young German ward-politician with the hearty word, "I count very much on your help in this election."[2] If this was the art of a politician, it was art reduced to artlessness.

Not least among the qualities which made Douglas a great, persuasive, popular leader, was his quite extraordinary memory for names and faces, and his unaffected interest in the personal life of those whom he called his friends. "He gave to every one of those humble and practically nameless followers the impression, the feeling, that he was the frank, personal friend of each one of them."[3] Doubtless he was well aware that there is no subtler form of flattery, than to call individuals by name who believe themselves to be forgotten pawns in a great game; and he may well have cultivated the profitable habit. Still, the fact remains, that it was an innate temperamental quality which made him frank and ingenuous in his intercourse with all sorts and conditions of men.

[1] For a copy of this letter, I am indebted to J. H. Roberts, Esq., of Chicago.

[2] Conversation with Henry Greenbaum, Esq., of Chicago.

[3] Major G. M. McConnell in the Transactions of the Illinois Historical Society, 1900; see also Forney, Anecdotes of Public Men, I, p. 147.

Those who judged the man by the senator, often failed to understand his temperament. He was known as a hard hitter in parliamentary encounters. He never failed to give a Roland for an Oliver. In the heat of debate, he was often guilty of harsh, bitter invective. His manner betrayed a lack of fineness and good-breeding. But his resentment vanished with the spoken word. He repented the barbed shaft, the moment it quitted his bow. He would invite to his table the very men with whom he had been in acrimonious controversy,—and perhaps renew the controversy next day. Greeley testified to this absence of resentment. On a certain occasion, after the New York *Tribune* had attacked Douglas savagely, a mutual acquaintance asked Douglas if he objected to meeting the redoubtable Greeley. "Not at all," was the good-natured reply, "I always pay that class of political debts as I go along, so as to have no trouble with them in social intercourse and to leave none for my executors to settle."[1]

In the round of social functions which Senator and Mrs. Douglas enjoyed, there was little time for quiet thought and reflection. Men who met him night after night at receptions and dinners, marvelled at the punctuality with which he returned to the routine work of the Senate next morning. Yet there was not a member of the Senate who had a readier command of facts germane to the discussions of the hour. His memory was a willing slave which never failed to do the bidding of master intellect. Some of his ablest and most effective speeches were made without prepara-

[1] Schuyler Colfax in the South Bend *Register*, June, 1861; Forney in his Eulogy, 1861; Greeley, Recollections of a Busy Life, p. 359.

tion and with only a few pencilled notes at hand. Truly
Nature had been lavish in her gifts to him.

To nine-tenths of his devoted followers, he was still
"Judge" Douglas. It was odd that the title, so quickly
earned and so briefly worn, should have stuck so persistently to him. In legal attainments he fell far short
of many of his colleagues in the Senate. Had he but
chosen to apply himself, he might have been a conspicuous leader of the American bar; but law was ever to
him the servant of politics, and he never cared to make
the servant greater than his lord. That he would have
developed judicial qualities, may well be doubted; advocate he was and advocate he remained, to the end
of his days. So it was that when a legal question arose,
with far-reaching implications for American politics,
the lawyer and politician, rather than the judge, laid
hold upon the points of political significance.

The inauguration of James Buchanan and the Dred
Scott decision of the Supreme Court, two days later,
marked a turning point in the career of Judge Douglas.
Of this he was of course unaware. He accepted the
advent of his successful rival with composure, and
the opinion of the Court, with comparative indifference.
In a speech before the Grand Jury of the United States
District Court at Springfield, three months later, he
referred publicly for the first time to the Dred Scott
case. Senator, and not Judge, Douglas was much in
evidence. He swallowed the opinion of the majority
of the court without wincing—the *obiter dictum* and
all. Nay, more, he praised the Court for passing, like
honest and conscientious judges, from the technicalities of the case to the real merits of the questions involved. The material, controlling points of the case

were: first, that a negro descended from slave parents could not be a citizen of the United States; second, that the Missouri Compromise was unconstitutional and void from the beginning, and thus could not extinguish a master's right to his slave in any Territory. "While the right continues in full force under .... the Constitution," he added, "and cannot be divested or alienated by an act of Congress, it necessarily remains a barren and worthless right, unless sustained, protected, and enforced by appropriate police regulations and local legislation, prescribing adequate remedies for its violation. These regulations and remedies must necessarily depend entirely upon the will and wishes of the people of the Territory, as they can only be prescribed by the local legislatures." Hence the triumphant conclusion that "the great principle of popular sovereignty and self-government is sustained and firmly established by the authority of this decision."[1]

There were acute legal minds who thought that they detected a false note in this pæan. Was this a necessary implication from the Dred Scott decision? Was it the intention of the Court to leave the principle of popular sovereignty standing upright? Was not the decision rather fatal to the great doctrine—the shibboleth of the Democratic party?

On this occasion Douglas had nothing to add to his exposition of the Dred Scott case, further than to point out the happy escape of white supremacy from African equality. And here he struck the note which put him out of accord with those Northern constituents with whom he was otherwise in complete harmony. "When

[1] The New York *Times*, June 23, 1857, published this speech of June 12th, in full.

you confer upon the African race the privileges of citizenship, and put them on an equality with white men at the polls, in the jury box, on the bench, in the Executive chair, and in the councils of the nation, upon what principle will you deny their equality at the festive board and in the domestic circle?'' In the following year, he received his answer in the homely words of Abraham Lincoln: ''I do not understand that because I do not want a negro woman for a slave I must necessarily want her for a wife.''

CHAPTER XV

THE REVOLT OF DOUGLAS

Had anyone prophesied at the close of the year 1856, that within a twelvemonth Douglas would be denounced as a traitor to Democracy, he would have been thought mad. That Douglas of all men should break with his party under any circumstances was almost unthinkable. His whole public career had been inseparably connected with his party. To be sure, he had never gone so far as to say "my party right or wrong"; but that was because he had never felt obliged to make a moral choice. He was always convinced that his party was right. Within the circumference of party, he had always found ample freedom of movement. He had never lacked the courage of his convictions, but hitherto his convictions had never collided with the dominant opinion of Democracy. He undoubtedly believed profoundly in the mission of his party, as an organization standing above all for popular government and the preservation of the Union. No ordinary circumstances would justify him in weakening the influence or impairing the organization of the Democratic party. Paradoxical as it may seem, his partisanship was dictated by a profound patriotism. He believed the maintenance of the Union to be dependent upon the integrity of his party. So thinking and feeling he entered upon the most memorable controversy of his career.

When President Buchanan asked Robert J. Walker

of Mississippi to become governor of Kansas, the choice
met with the hearty approval of Douglas. Not all the
President's appointments had been acceptable to the
Senator from Illinois. But here was one that he could
indorse unreservedly. He used all his influence to
persuade Walker to accept the uncoveted mission.
With great reluctance Walker consented, but only
upon the most explicit understanding with the administration as to the policy to be followed in Kansas. It
was well understood on both sides that a true construction of the Kansas-Nebraska Act required the submission to popular vote of any constitution which the
prospective convention might adopt. This was emphatically the view of Douglas, whom Governor Walker
took pains to consult on his way through Chicago.[1]

The call for an election of delegates to a constitutional convention had already been issued, when
Walker reached Kansas. The free-State people were
incensed because the appointment of delegates had
been made on the basis of a defective census and registration; and even the assurance of the governor, in
his inaugural, that the constitution would be submitted
to a popular vote, failed to overcome their distrust.
They therefore took no part in the election of delegates.
This course was unfortunate, for it gave the control
of the convention wholly into the hands of the pro-
slavery party, with consequences that were far-reaching for Kansas and the nation.[2] But by October the

[1] Report of the Covode Committee, pp. 105-106; Cutts, Constitutional and Party Questions, p. 111; Speech of Douglas at Milwaukee,
Wis., October 14, 1860, Chicago *Times and Herald*, October 17, 1860.

[2] Spring, Kansas, p. 213; Rhodes, History of the United States, II,
p. 274.

free-State party had abandoned its policy of abstention from territorial politics, so far as to participate in the election of a new territorial legislature. The result was a decisive free-State victory. The next legislature would have an ample majority of free-State men in both chambers. It was with the discomfiting knowledge, then, that they represented only a minority of the community that the delegates of the constitutional convention began their labors.[1] It was clear to the dullest intelligence that any pro-slavery constitution would be voted down, if it were submitted fairly to the people of Kansas. Gloom settled down upon the hopes of the pro-slavery party.

When the document which embodied the labors of the convention was made public, the free-State party awoke from its late complacence to find itself tricked by a desperate game. The constitution was not to be submitted to a full and fair vote; but only the article relating to slavery. The people of Kansas were to vote for the "Constitution with slavery" or for the "Constitution with no slavery." By either alternative the constitution would be adopted. But should the constitution with no slavery be ratified, a clause of the schedule still guaranteed "the right of property in slaves now in this Territory."[2] The choice offered to an opponent of slavery in Kansas was between a constitution sanctioning and safeguarding all forms of slave property,[3] and a constitution which guaranteed the full possession of slaves then in the Territory,

[1] Rhodes, History of the United States, II, pp. 277-278.

[2] *Ibid.*, pp. 278-279; Spring, Kansas, p. 223.

[3] See Article VII, of the Kansas constitution, Senate Reports, No. 82, 35 Cong., 1 Sess.

with no assurances as to the status of the natural increase of these slaves. Viewed in the most charitable light, this was a gambler's device for securing the stakes by hook or crook. Still further to guard existing property rights in slaves, it was provided that if the constitution should be amended after 1864, no alteration should be made to affect "the rights of property in the ownership of slaves."[1]

The news from Lecompton stirred Douglas profoundly. In a peculiar sense he stood sponsor for justice to bleeding Kansas, not only because he had advocated in abstract terms the perfect freedom of the people to form their domestic institutions in their own way, but because he had become personally responsible for the conduct of the leader of the Lecompton party. John Calhoun, president of the convention, had been appointed surveyor general of the Territory upon his recommendation. Governor Walker had retained Calhoun in that office because of Douglas's assurance that Calhoun would support the policy of submission.[2] Moreover, Governor Walker had gone to his post with the assurance that the leaders of the administration would support this course.

Was it likely that the pro-slavery party in Kansas would take this desperate course, without assurance of some sort from Washington? There were persistent rumors that President Buchanan approved the Lecompton constitution,[3] but Douglas was loth to give credence to them. The press of Illinois and of the Northwest voiced public sentiment in condemning the

[1] Schedule Section 14.
[2] Covode Report, p. 111.
[3] Chicago *Times*, November 19, 1857.

work of the Lecomptonites.[1] Douglas was soon on his way to Washington, determined to know the President's mind; his own was made up.

The interview between President Buchanan and Douglas, as recounted by the latter, takes on a dramatic aspect.[2] Douglas found his worst fears realized. The President was clearly under the influence of an aggressive group of Southern statesmen, who were bent upon making Kansas a slave State under the Lecompton constitution. Laboring under intense feeling, Douglas then threw down the gauntlet: he would oppose the policy of the administration publicly to the bitter end. "Mr. Douglas," said the President rising to his feet excitedly, "I desire you to remember that no Democrat ever yet differed from an administration of his own choice without being crushed. Beware of the fate of Tallmadge and Rives." "Mr. President," rejoined Douglas also rising, "I wish you to remember that General Jackson is dead."

The Chicago *Times,* reporting the interview, intimated that there had been a want of agreement, but no lack of courtesy or regard on either side. Douglas was not yet ready to issue an ultimatum. The situation might be remedied. On the night following this memorable encounter, Douglas was serenaded by friends and responded with a brief speech, but he did not allude to the Kansas question.[3] It was generally expected that he would show his hand on Monday, the opening day of Congress. The President's message

[1] Chicago *Times,* November 20 and 21, 1857.

[2] Speech at Milwaukee, October 14, 1860, Chicago *Times and Herald,* October 17, 1860.

[3] New York *Tribune,* December 3, 1857.

did not reach Congress, however, until Tuesday. Immediately upon its reading, Douglas offered the usual motion to print the message, adding, as he took his seat, that he totally dissented from "that portion of the message which may fairly be construed as approving of the proceedings of the Lecompton convention." At an early date he would state the reasons for his dissent.[1]

On the following day, December 9th, Douglas took the irrevocable step. For three hours he held the Senate and the audience in the galleries in rapt attention, while with more than his wonted gravity and earnestness he denounced the Lecompton constitution.[2] He began with a conciliatory reference to the President's message. He was happy to find, after a more careful examination, that the President had refrained from making any recommendation as to the course which Congress should pursue with regard to the constitution. And so, he added adroitly, the Kansas question is not to be treated as an administration measure. He shared the disappointment of the President that the constitution had not been submitted fully and freely to the people of Kansas; but the President, he conceived, had made a fundamental error in supposing that the Nebraska Act provided for the disposition of the slavery question apart from other local matters. The direct opposite was true. The main object of the Act was to remove an odious restriction by which the people had been prevented from deciding the slavery question for themselves, like all other local and domestic concerns. If the

[1] *Globe*, 35 Cong., 1 Sess., p. 5.
[2] Chicago *Times*, December 19, 1857.

President was right in thinking that by the terms of the Nebraska bill the slavery question must be submitted to the people, then every other clause of the constitution should be submitted to them. To do less would be to reduce popular sovereignty to a farce.

But Douglas could not maintain this conciliatory attitude. His sense of justice was too deeply outraged. He recalled facts which every well-informed person knew. "I know that men, high in authority and in the confidence of the territorial and National Government, canvassed every part of Kansas during the election of delegates, and each one of them pledged himself to the people that no snap judgment was to be taken. Up to the time of the meeting of the convention, in October last, the pretense was kept up, the profession was openly made, and believed by me, and I thought believed by them, that the convention intended to submit a constitution to the people, and not to attempt to put a government in operation without such submission."[1] How was this pledge redeemed? All men, forsooth, must vote for the constitution, whether they like it or not, in order to be permitted to vote for or against slavery! This would be like an election under the First Consul, when, so his enemies averred, Napoleon addressed his troops with the words: "Now, my soldiers, you are to go to the election and vote freely just as you please. If you vote for Napoleon, all is well; vote against him, and you are to be instantly shot." That was a fair election! "This election," said Douglas with bitter irony, "is to be *equally fair!* All men in favor of the constitution may vote for it—all men against it shall not vote at

[1] *Globe,* 35 Cong., 1 Sess., p. 17.

all! Why not let them vote against it? I have asked
a very large number of the gentlemen who framed
the constitution . . . . and I have received the same
answer from every one óf them. . . . They say if they
allowed a negative vote the constitution would have
been voted down by an overwhelming majority, and
hence the fellows shall not be allowed to vote at all."

"Will you force it on them against their will," he demanded, "simply because they would have voted it
down if you had consulted them? If you will, are you
going to force it upon them under the plea of leaving
them perfectly free to form and regulate their domestic institutions in their own way? Is that the mode
in which I am called upon to carry out the principle
of self-government and popular sovereignty in the
Territories?" It is no answer, he argued, that the
constitution is unobjectionable. "You have no right
to force an unexceptionable constitution on a people."
The pro-slavery clause was not the offense in the constitution, to his mind. "If Kansas wants a slave-
State constitution she has a right to it, if she wants
a free-State constitution she has a right to it. It is
none of my business which way the slavery clause is
decided. I care not whether it is voted up or down."
The whole affair looked to him "like a system of
trickery and jugglery to defeat the fair expression of
the will of the people."[1]

The vehemence of his utterance had now carried
Douglas perhaps farther than he had meant to go.[2]

[1] *Globe*, 35 Cong., 1 Sess., pp. 17-18.

[2] "I spoke rapidly, without preparation," he afterward said. *Globe*,
35 Cong., 1 Sess., p. 47.

He paused to plead for a fair policy which would redeem party pledges:

"Ignore Lecompton, ignore Topeka; treat both those party movements as irregular and void; pass a fair bill—the one that we framed ourselves when we were acting as a unit; have a fair election—and you will have peace in the Democratic party, and peace throughout the country, in ninety days. The people want a fair vote. They never will be satisfied without it. They never should be satisfied without a fair vote on their Constitution..........

"Frame any other bill that secures, a fair, honest vote, to men of all parties, and carries out the pledge that the people shall be left free to decide on their domestic institutions for themselves, and I will go with you with pleasure, and with all the energy I may possess. But if this Constitution is to be forced down our throats, in violation of the fundamental principle of free government, under a mode of submission that is a mockery and insult, I will resist it to the last. I have no fear of any party associations being severed. I should regret any social or political estrangement, even temporarily; but if it must be, if I can not act with you and preserve my faith and my honor, I will stand on the great principle of popular sovereignty, which declares the right of all people to be left perfectly free to form and regulate their domestic institutions in their own way. I will follow that principle wherever its logical consequences may take me, and I will endeavor to defend it against assault from any and all quarters. No mortal man shall be responsible for my action but myself. By my action I will compromit no man.'"[1]

The speech made a profound impression. No one could mistake its import. The correspondent of the New York *Tribune* was right in thinking that it "marked an important era in our political history."[2] Douglas had broken with the dominant pro-slavery faction of his party. How far he would carry his party with him, remained to be seen. But that a battle royal was imminent, was believed on all sides. "The struggle of Douglas with the slave-power will be a magnificent spectacle to witness," wrote one who had hitherto

[1] *Globe*, 35 Cong., 1 Sess., p. 18.
[2] New York *Tribune*, December 9, 1857.

evinced little admiration for the author of the Kansas-Nebraska Act.[1]

Douglas kept himself well in hand throughout his speech. His manner was at times defiant, but his language was restrained. At no time did he disclose the pain which his rupture with the administration cost him, except in his closing words. What he had to expect from the friends of the administration was immediately manifest. Senator Bigler of Pennsylvania sprang to the defense of the President. In an irritating tone he intimated that Douglas himself had changed his position on the question of submission, alluding to certain private conferences at Douglas's house; but as though bound by a pledge of secrecy, Bigler refrained from making the charge in so many words. Douglas, thoroughly aroused, at once absolved. him from any pledges, and demanded to know when they had agreed not to submit the constitution to the people. The reply of Bigler was still allusive and evasive. "Does he mean to say," insisted Douglas excitedly, "that I ever was, privately or publicly, in my own house or any other, in favor of a constitution without its being submitted to the people?" "I have made no such allegation," was the reply. "You have allowed it to be inferred," exclaimed Douglas in exasperated tones.[2] And then Green reminded him, that in his famous report of January 4, 1854, he had proposed to leave the slavery question to the decision of the people "by their appropriate representatives chosen by them for that purpose," with no suggestion

[1] New York *Tribune*, December 10, 1857.

[2] *Globe*, 35 Cong., 1 Sess., pp. 21-22.

of a second, popular vote. Truly, his most insidious foes were now those of his own political household.

Anti-slavery men welcomed this revolt of Douglas without crediting him with any but self-seeking motives. They could not bring themselves to believe other than ill of the man who had advocated the repeal of the Missouri Compromise. Republicans accepted his aid in their struggle against the Lecompton fraud, but for the most part continued to regard him with distrust. Indeed, Douglas made no effort to placate them. He professed to care nothing for the cause of the slave which was nearest their hearts. Hostile critics, then, were quick to point out the probable motives from which he acted. His senatorial term was drawing to a close. He was of course desirous of a re-election. But his nominee for governor had been defeated at the last election, and the State had been only with difficulty carried for the national candidates of the party. The lesson was plain: the people of Illinois did not approve the Kansas policy of Senator Douglas. Hence the weathercock obeyed the wind.

In all this there was a modicum of truth. Douglas would not have been the power that he was, had he not kept in touch with his constituency. But a sense of honor, a desire for consistency, and an abiding faith in the justice of his great principle, impelled him in the same direction. These were thoroughly honorable motives, even if he professed an indifference as to the fate of the negro. He had pledged his word of honor to his constituents that the people of Kansas should have a fair chance to pronounce upon their constitution. Nothing short of this would have been consistent with popular sovereignty as he had expounded it again and again. And Douglas was personally a man of honor. Yet when all has been said, one cannot but regret that the sense of fair play, which was strong in him, did not assert itself in the early stages of the Kansas conflict and smother that lawyer's instinct to defend a client by the technicalities of the law. Could he only have sought absolute justice for the people of Kansas in the winter of 1856, the purity of his motives would not have been questioned in the winter of 1858.

Even those colleagues of Douglas who doubted his motives, could not but admire his courage. It did, indeed, require something more than audacity to head a revolt against the administration. No man knew better the thorny road that he must now travel. No man loved his party more. No man knew better the hazard to the Union that must follow a rupture in the Democratic party. But if Douglas nursed the hope that Democratic senators would follow his lead, he was sadly disappointed. Three only came to his support —Broderick of California, Pugh of Ohio, and Stuart of Michigan,—while the lists of the administration were full. Green, Bigler, Fitch, in turn were set upon him.

Douglas bitterly resented any attempt to read him out of the party by making the Lecompton constitution the touchstone of genuine Democracy; yet each day made it clearer that the administration had just that end in view. Douglas complained of a tyranny not consistent with free Democratic action. One might differ with the President on every subject but Kansas, without incurring suspicion. Every pensioned letter writer, he complained, had been intimating for the last two weeks that he had deserted the Democratic party and gone over to the Black Republicans. He demanded to know who authorized these tales.[1] Senator Fitch warned him solemnly that the Democratic party was the only political link in the chain which now bound the States together. "None .... will hold that man guiltless, who abandons it upon a question having in it so little of practical importance .... and by seeking its destruction, thereby admits his not unwillingness that a similar fate should be visited on the Union, perhaps, to subserve his selfish purpose."[2] These attacks roused Douglas to vehement defiance. More emphatically than ever, he declared the Lecompton constitution "a trick, a fraud upon the rights of the people."

If Douglas misjudged the temper of his colleagues, he at least gauged correctly the drift of public sentiment in Illinois and the Northwest. Of fifty-six Democratic newspapers in Illinois, but one ventured to condone the Lecompton fraud.[3] Mass meetings in various cities of the Northwest expressed confidence in the course of Senator Douglas.

He now occupied a unique position at the capital. Visitors were quite as eager to see the man who had headed the revolt as to greet the chief executive.[4] His residence, where Mrs. Douglas dispensed a gracious hospitality, was fairly besieged with callers.[5] Washington society was never gayer than during this memorable winter.[6] None entertained more lavishly than Senator and Mrs. Douglas. Whatever unpopu-

---

[1] *Globe,* 35 Cong., 1 Sess., p. 120.   [2] *Ibid.,* p. 137.

[3] Chicago *Times,* December 24, 1857.   [4] *Ibid.,* December 23, 1857.

[5] Correspondent to Cleveland *Plaindealer,* quoted in Chicago *Times,* January 29, 1858.

[6] Mrs. Jefferson Davis to Mrs. Pierce, MS. Letter, April 4, 1858.

larity he incurred at the Capitol, she more than offset by her charming and gracious personality. Acknowledged as the reigning queen of the circle in which she moved, Mrs. Douglas displayed a social initiative that seconded admirably the independent, self-reliant attitude of her husband. When Adèle Cutts Douglas chose to close the shutters of her house at noon, and hold a reception by artificial light every Saturday afternoon, society followed her lead. There were no more brilliant affairs in Washington than these afternoon receptions and hops at the Douglas residence in Minnesota Block.[1] In contrast to these functions dominated by a thoroughly charming personality, the formal precision of the receptions at the White House was somewhat chilling and forbidding. President Buchanan, bachelor, with his handsome but somewhat self-contained niece, was not equal to this social rivalry.[2] Moreover, the cares of office permitted the perplexed, wearied, and timid executive no respite day or night.

Events in Kansas gave heart to those who were fighting Lecomptonism. At the election appointed by the convention, the "constitution with slavery" was adopted by a large majority, the free-State people refusing to vote; but the legislature, now in the control of the free-State party, had already provided for a fair vote on the whole constitution. On this second vote the majority was overwhelmingly against the constitution. Information from various sources corroborated the deductions which unprejudiced observers drew from the voting. It was as clear as day that the

[1] Mrs. Roger Pryor, Reminiscences of Peace and War, pp. 69-70.
[2] Ibid., Chapter 4.

people of Kansas did not regard the Lecompton constitution as a fair expression of their will.[1]

Ignoring the light which made the path of duty plain, President Buchanan sent the Lecompton constitution to Congress with a message recommending the admission of Kansas.[2] To his mind, the Lecompton convention was legally constituted and had exercised its powers faithfully. The organic act did not bind the convention to submit to the people more than the question of slavery. Meantime the Supreme Court had handed down its famous decision in the Dred Scott case. Fortified by this dictum, the President told Congress that slavery existed in Kansas by virtue of the Constitution of the United States. "Kansas is, at this moment, as much a slave State as Georgia or South Carolina"! Slavery, then, could be prohibited only by constitutional provision; and those who desired to do away with slavery would most speedily compass their ends, if they admitted Kansas at once under this constitution.

The President's message with the Lecompton constitution was referred to the Committee on Territories and gave rise to three reports: Senator Green of Missouri presented the majority report, recommending the admission of Kansas under this constitution; Senators Collamer and Wade united on a minority report, leaving Douglas to draft another expressing his dissent on other grounds.[3] Taken all in all, this must be regarded as the most satisfactory and convincing of all Douglas's committee reports. It is strong be-

[1] Rhodes, History of the United States, II, p. 289.
[2] Message of February 2, 1858.
[3] Senate Report No. 82, 35 Cong., 1 Sess., February 18, 1858.

cause it is permeated by a desire for justice, and reinforced at every point by a consummate marshalling of evidence. Rarely in his career had his conspicuous qualities as a special pleader been put so unreservedly at the service of simple justice. He planted himself firmly, at the outset, upon the incontrovertible fact that there was no satisfactory evidence that the Lecompton constitution was the act and deed of the people of Kansas.[1]

It had been argued that, because the Lecompton convention had been duly constituted, with full power to ordain a constitution and establish a government, consequently the proceedings of the convention must be presumed to embody the popular will. Douglas immediately challenged this assumption. The convention had no more power than the territorial legislature could confer. By no fair construction of the Kansas-Nebraska Act could it be assumed that the people of the Territory were authorized, "at their own will and pleasure, to resolve themselves into a sovereign power, and to abrogate and annul the organic act and territorial government established by Congress, and to ordain a constitution and State government upon their ruins, without the consent of Congress." Surely, then, a convention which the territorial legislature called into being could not abrogate or impair the authority of that territorial government established by Congress. Hence, he concluded, the Lecompton constitution, formed without the consent of Congress, must be considered as a memorial or petition, which Congress may accept or reject. The convention was the creature of the territorial legislature. "Such being the case,

[1] Minority Report, p. 52.

whenever the legislature ascertained that the convention whose existence depended upon its will, had devised a scheme to force a constitution upon the people without their consent, and without any authority from Congress, ... it became their imperative duty to interpose and exert the authority conferred upon them by Congress in the organic act, and arrest and prevent the consummation of the scheme before it had gone into operation."[1] This was an unanswerable argument.

In the prolonged debate upon the admission of Kansas, Douglas took part only as some taunt or challenge brought him to his feet. While the bill for the admission of Minnesota, also reported by the Committee on Territories, was under fire, Senator Brown of Mississippi elicited from Douglas the significant concession, that he did not deem an enabling act absolutely essential, so long as the constitution clearly embodied the will of the people. Neither did he think a submission of the constitution always essential; it was, however, a fair way of ascertaining the popular will, when that will was disputed. "Satisfy me that the constitution adopted by the people of Minnesota is their will, and I am prepared to adopt it. Satisfy me that the constitution adopted, or said to be adopted, by the people of Kansas, is their will, and I am prepared to take it. . . . I will never apply one rule to a free State and another to a slave-holding State."[2] Nevertheless, even his Democratic colleagues continued to believe that slavery had something to do with his opposition. In the classic phraseology of Toombs, "there was a 'nigger' in it."

[1] Minority Report, p. 64.
[2] *Globe,* 35 Cong., 1 Sess., p. 502.

The opposition of Douglas began to cause no little uneasiness. Brown paid tribute to his influence, when he declared that if the Senator from Illinois had stood with the administration, "there would not have been a ripple on the surface." "Sir, the Senator from Illinois gives life, he gives vitality, he gives energy, he lends the aid of his mighty genius and his powerful will to the Opposition on this question."[1] But Douglas paid a fearful price for this power. Every possible ounce of pressure was brought to bear upon him. The party press was set upon him. His friends were turned out of office. The whole executive patronage was wielded mercilessly against his political following. The Washington *Union* held him up to execration as a traitor, renegade, and deserter.[2] "We cannot affect indifference at the treachery of Senator Douglas," said a Richmond paper. "He was a politician of considerable promise. Association with Southern gentlemen had smoothed down the rugged vulgarities of his early education, and he had come to be quite a decent and well-behaved person."[3] To political denunciation was now to be added the sting of mean and contemptible personalities.

Small wonder that even the vigorous health of "the Little Giant" succumbed to these assaults. For a fortnight he was confined to his bed, rising only by sheer force of will to make a final plea for sanity, before his party took its suicidal plunge. He spoke on the 22d of March under exceptional conditions. In the expectation that he would speak in the forenoon, people

---

[1] *Globe*, 35 Cong., 1 Sess., pp. 572-573.
[2] Washington *Union*, February 26, 1858.
[3] Richmond *South*, quoted in Chicago *Times*, December 18, 1857.

thronged the galleries at an early hour, and refused to give up their seats, even when it was announced that the Senator from Illinois would not address the Senate until seven o'clock in the evening. When the hour came, crowds still held possession of the galleries, so that not even standing room was available. The door-keepers wrestled in vain with an impatient throng without, until by motion of Senator Gwin, ladies were admitted to the floor of the chamber. Even then, Douglas was obliged to pause several times, for the confusion around the doors to subside.[1] He spoke with manifest difficulty, but he was more defiant than ever. His speech was at once a protest and a personal vindication. Denial of the right of the administration to force the Lecompton constitution upon the people of Kansas, went hand in hand with a defense of his own Democracy. Sentences culled here and there suggest not unfairly the stinging rebukes and defiant challenges that accentuated the none too coherent course of his speech:

"I am told that this Lecompton constitution is a party test, a party measure; that no man is a Democrat who does not sanction it.........
Sir, who made it a party test? Who made it a party measure?........
Who has interpolated this Lecompton constitution into the party platform?........Oh! but we are told it is an Administration measure.
Because it is an Administration measure, does it therefore follow that it is a party measure?"........"I do not recognize the right of the President or his Cabinet....to tell me my duty in the Senate Chamber."
"Am I to be told that I must obey the Executive and betray my State, or else be branded as a traitor to the party, and hunted down by all the newspapers that share the patronage of the government, and every man who holds a petty office in any part of my State to have the question put to him, 'Are you Douglas's enemy? if not, your head comes off.'"

[1] Sheahan, Douglas, p. 328; *Globe*, 35 Cong., 1 Sess., App., pp. 193-194.

THE REVOLT OF DOUGLAS

I intend to perform my duty in accordance with my own convictions. Neither the frowns of power nor the influence of patronage will change my action, or drive me from my principles. I stand firmly, immovably upon those great principles of self-government and state sovereignty upon which the campaign was fought and the election won.........If, standing firmly by my principles, I shall be driven into private life, it is a fate that has no terrors for me. I prefer private life, preserving my own self-respect and manhood, to abject and servile submission to executive will. If the alternative be private life or servile obedience to executive will, I am prepared to retire. Official position has no charms for me when deprived of that freedom of thought and action which becomes a gentleman and a senator.'"

On the following day, the Senate passed the bill for the admission of Kansas under the Lecompton constitution, having rejected the amendment of Crittenden to submit that constitution to a vote of the people of Kansas. A similar amendment, however, was carried in the House. As neither chamber would recede from its position, a conference committee was appointed to break the deadlock.[2] It was from this committee, controlled by Lecomptonites, that the famous English bill emanated. Stated briefly, the substance of this compromise measure—for such it was intended to be—was as follows: Congress was to offer to Kansas a conditional grant of public lands; if this land ordinance should be accepted by a popular vote, Kansas was to be admitted to the Union with the Lecompton constitution by proclamation of the President; if it should be rejected, Kansas was not to be admitted until the Territory had a population equal to the unit of representation required for the House of Representatives.

Taken all in all, the bill was as great a concession as

---

[1] *Globe,* 35 Cong., 1 Sess., App., pp. 194-201, *passim.*

[2] Rhodes, History of the United States, II, pp. 297-299.

could be expected from the administration. Not all were willing to say that the bill provided for a vote on the constitution, but Northern adherents could point to the vote on the land ordinance as an indirect vote upon the constitution. It is not quite true to say that the land grant was a bribe to the voters of Kansas. As a matter of fact, the amount of land granted was only equal to that usually offered to the Territories, and it was considerably less than the area specified in the Lecompton constitution. Moreover, even if the land ordinance were defeated in order to reject the constitution, the Territory was pretty sure to secure as large a grant at some future time. It was rather in the alternative held out, that the English bill was unsatisfactory to those who loved fair play. Still, under the bill, the people of Kansas, by an act of self-denial, could defeat the Lecompton constitution. To that extent, the supporters of the administration yielded to the importunities of the champion of popular sovereignty.

Under these circumstances it would not be strange if Douglas "wavered."[1] Here was an opportunity to close the rift between himself and the administration, to heal party dissensions, perhaps to save the integrity of the Democratic party and the Union. And the price which he would have to pay was small. He could assume, plausibly enough,—as he had done many times before in his career,—that the bill granted all that he had ever asked. He was morally sure that the people of Kansas would reject the land grant to rid themselves of the Lecompton fraud. Why hesitate

[1] Wilson, Rise and Fall of the Slave Power, II, p. 563.

then as to means, when the desired end was in clear view?

Douglas found himself subjected to a new pressure, harder even to resist than any he had yet felt. Some of his staunch supporters in the anti-Lecompton struggle went over to the administration, covering their retreat by just such excuses as have been suggested. Was he wiser and more conscientious than they? A refusal to accept the proffered olive branch now meant,—he knew it well,—the irreconcilable enmity of the Buchanan faction. And he was not asked to recant, but only to accept what he had always deemed the very essence of statesmanship, a compromise. His Republican allies promptly evinced their distrust. They fully expected him to join his former associates. From them he could expect no sympathy in such a dilemma.[1] His political ambitions, no doubt, added to his perplexity. They were bound up in the fate of the party, the integrity of which was now menaced by his revolt. On the other hand, he was fully conscious that his Illinois constituency approved of his opposition to Lecomptonism and would regard a retreat across this improvised political bridge as both inglorious and treacherous. Agitated by conflicting emotions, Douglas made a decision which probably cost him more anguish than any he ever made; and when all has been said to the contrary, love of fair play would seem to have been his governing motive.[2]

When Douglas rose to address the Senate on the English bill, April 29th, he betrayed some of the emo-

[1] Wilson, Rise and Fall of the Slave Power, II, pp. 566-567.

[2] This cannot, of course, be demonstrated, but it accords with his subsequent conduct.

tion under which he had made his decision. He confessed an "anxious desire" to find such provisions as would permit him to support the bill; but he was painfully forced to declare that he could not find the principle for which he had contended, fairly carried out. He was unable to reconcile popular sovereignty with the proposed intervention of Congress in the English bill. "It is intervention with inducements to control the result. It is intervention with a bounty on the one side and a penalty on the other."[1] He frankly admitted that he did not believe there was enough in the bounty nor enough in the penalty to influence materially the vote of the people of Kansas; but it involved "the principle of freedom of election and .... the great principle of self-government upon which our institutions rest." And upon this principle he took his stand. "With all the anxiety that I have had," said he with deep feeling, "to be able to arrive at a conclusion in harmony with the overwhelming majority of my political friends in Congress, I could not bring my judgment or conscience to the conclusion that this was a fair, impartial, and equal application of the principle."[2]

As though to make reconciliation with the administration impossible, Douglas went on to express his distrust of the provision of the bill for a board of supervisors of elections. Instead of a board of four, two of whom should represent the Territory and two the Federal government, as the Crittenden bill had provided, five were to constitute the board, of whom three were to be United States officials. "Does not this change," asked Douglas significantly, "give

[1] *Globe*, 35 Cong., 1 Sess., p. 1869.
[2] *Ibid.*, p. 1870.

ground for apprehension that you may have the Oxford, the Shawnee, and the Delaware Crossing and Kickapoo frauds re-enacted at this election?'"[1] The most suspicious Republican could hardly have dealt an unkinder thrust.

There could be no manner of doubt as to the outcome of the English bill in the Senate. Douglas, Stuart, and Broderick were the only Democrats to oppose its passage, Pugh having joined the majority. The bill passed the House also, nine of Douglas's associates in the anti-Lecompton fight going over to the administration.[2] Douglas accepted this defection with philosophic equanimity, indulging in no vindictive feelings.[3] Had he not himself felt misgivings as to his own course?

By midsummer the people of Kansas had recorded nearly ten thousand votes against the land ordinance and the Lecompton constitution. The administration had failed to make Kansas a slave State. Yet the Supreme Court had countenanced the view that Kansas was legally a slave Territory. What, then, became of the great fundamental principle of popular sovereignty? This was the question which Douglas was now called upon to answer.

[1] *Globe*, 35 Cong., 1 Sess., p. 1870.
[2] Rhodes, History of the United States, II, p. 300.
[3] Cox, Three Decades of Federal Legislation, p. 58.

CHAPTER XVI

The Joint Debates With Lincoln

National politics made strange bed-fellows in the winter of 1857-8. Douglas consorting with Republicans and flouting the administration, was a rare spectacle. There was a moment in this odd alliance when it seemed likely to become more than a temporary fusion of interests. The need of concerted action brought about frequent conferences, in which the distrust of men like Wilson and Colfax was, in a measure, dispelled by the engaging frankness of their quondam opponent.[1] Douglas intimated that in all probability he could not act with his party in future.[2] He assured Wilson that he was in the fight to stay—in his own words, "he had checked his baggage and taken a through ticket."[3] There was an odd disposition, too, on the part of some Republicans to indorse popular sovereignty, now that it seemed likely to exclude slavery from the Territories.[4] There was even a rumor afloat that the editor of the New York *Tribune* favored Douglas for the presidency.[5] On at least two occasions, Greeley was in conference with Senator Douglas at the latter's residence. To the gossiping public this was evidence enough that the rumor was correct. And it may well be that Douglas dallied with the hope that a great

[1] Hollister, Life of Colfax pp. 119 ff; Wilson, Rise and Fall of the Slave Power, II, p. 567.

[2] Hollister, Colfax, p. 121.　　　　[3] Wilson, p. 567.

[4] Bancroft, Life of Seward, I, pp. 449-450.

[5] Pike, First Blows of the Civil War, p. 403.

Constitutional Union party might be formed.[1] But he could hardly have received much encouragement from the Republicans, with whom he was consorting, for so far from losing their political identity, they calculated upon bringing him eventually within the Republican fold.[2]

A Constitutional Union party, embracing Northern and Southern Unionists of Whig or Democratic antecedents, might have supplied the gap left by the old Whig party. That such a party would have exercised a profound nationalizing influence can scarcely be doubted. Events might have put Douglas at the head of such a party. But, in truth, such an outcome of the political chaos which then reigned, was a remote possibility.

The matter of immediate concern to Douglas was the probable attitude of his allies toward his re-election to the Senate. There was a wide divergence among Republican leaders; but active politicians like Greeley and Wilson, who were not above fighting the devil with his own weapons, counselled their Illinois brethren not to oppose his return.[3] There was no surer way to disrupt the Democratic party. In spite of these admonitions, the Republicans of Illinois were bent upon defeating Douglas. He had been too uncompromising and bitter an opponent of Trumbull and other ''Black Republicans'' to win their confidence by a few months of conflict against Lecomptonism. ''I see his tracks all over our State,'' wrote the editor of the Chicago *Tribune*, ''they point only in one direction; not a single toe is turned toward the Republican

[1] Hollister, Colfax, p. 119.   [2] *Ibid.*, p. 121.
[3] Wilson, II, p 567; Greeley, Recollections of a Busy Life, p. 397.

camp. Watch him, use him, but do not trust him—not an inch.'"[1] Moreover, a little coterie of Springfield politicians had a candidate of their own for United States senator in the person of Abraham Lincoln.[2]

The action of the Democratic State convention in April closed the door to any reconciliation with the Buchanan administration. Douglas received an unqualified indorsement. The Cincinnati platform was declared to be "the only authoritative exposition of Democratic doctrine." No power on earth except a similar national convention had a right "to change or interpolate that platform, or to prescribe new or different tests." By sound party doctrine the Lecompton constitution ought to be "submitted to the direct vote of the actual inhabitants of Kansas at a fair election."[3] Could any words have been more explicit? The administration responded by a merciless proscription of Douglas office-holders and by unremitting efforts to create an opposition ticket. Under pressure from Washington, conventions were held to nominate candidates for the various State offices, with the undisguised purpose of dividing the Democratic vote for senator.[4]

On the 16th of June, the Republicans of Illinois threw advice to the winds and adopted the unusual course of naming Lincoln as "the first and only choice of the Republicans of Illinois for the United States Senate." It was an act of immense political significance. Not only did it put in jeopardy the political life of Douglas, but it ended for all time to come any

[1] Hollister, Colfax, p. 120.
[2] Herndon-Weik, Life of Lincoln, II, pp. 59 ff.
[3] Sheahan, Douglas, p. 394.
[4] Foote, Casket of Reminiscences, p. 135.

coalition between his following and the Republican party.

The subsequent fame of Lincoln has irradiated every phase of his early career. To his contemporaries in the year 1858, he was a lawyer of recognized ability, an astute politician, and a frank aspirant for national honors. Those who imagine him to have been an un-ambitious soul, upon whom honors were thrust, fail to understand the Lincoln whom Herndon, his partner, knew. Lincoln was a seasoned politician. He had been identified with the old Whig organization; he had repeatedly represented the Springfield district in the State legislature; and he had served one term without distinction in Congress. Upon the passage of the Kansas-Nebraska Act he had taken an active part in fusing the opposing elements into the Republican party. His services to the new party made him a candidate for the senatorship in 1855, and received recognition in the national Republican convention of 1856, when he was second on the list of those for whom the convention balloted for Vice-President. He was not unknown to Republicans of the Northwest, though he was not in any sense a national figure. Few men had a keener insight into political conditions in Illinois. None knew better the ins and outs of political campaigning in Illinois.

Withal, Lincoln was rated as a man of integrity. He had strong convictions and the courage of his convictions. His generous instincts made him hate slavery, while his antecedents prevented him from loving the negro. His anti-slavery sentiments were held strongly in check by his sound sense of justice. He had the temperament of a humanitarian with the intellect of a lawyer. While not combative by nature, he possessed the characteristic American trait of measuring himself by the attainments of others. He was solicitous to match himself with other men so as to prove himself at least their peer. Possessed of a cause that enlisted the service of his heart as well as his head, Lincoln was a strong advocate at the bar and a formidable opponent on the stump. Douglas bore true witness to Lincoln's powers when he said, on hearing of his nomination, "I shall have my hands full. He is the strong man of his party—full of wit, facts, dates—and the best stump speaker, with his droll ways and dry jokes, in the West. He is as honest as he is shrewd; and if I beat him, my victory will be hardly won."[1]

The nomination of Lincoln was so little a matter of surprise to him and his friends, that at the close of the convention he was able to address the delegates in a carefully prepared speech. Wishing to sound a dominant note for the campaign, he began with these memorable words:

"If we could first know where we are, and whither we are tending, we could better judge what to do and how to do it. We are now far into the fifth year, since a policy was initiated with the avowed object, and confident promise, of putting an end to slavery agitation. Under the operation of that policy, that agitation has not only not ceased, but has constantly augmented. In my opinion, it will not cease, until a crisis shall have been reached and passed. 'A house divided against itself cannot stand.' I believe this government cannot endure permanently half slave and half free. I do not expect the Union to be dissolved—I do not expect

[1] Forney, Anecdotes, II, p. 179.

the house to fall—but I do expect it will cease to be divided. It will become all one thing, or all the other. Either the opponents of slavery will arrest the further spread of it, and place it where the public mind shall rest in the belief that it is in the course of ultimate extinction, or its advocates will push it forward, till it shall become alike lawful in all the States, old as well as new—North as well as South.'"[1]

All evidence, continued Lincoln, pointed to a design to make slavery national. The Kansas-Nebraska Act, the popular indorsement of Buchanan, and the Dred Scott decision, were so many parts of a plot. Only one part was lacking; *viz.* another decision declaring it unconstitutional for a State to exclude slavery. Then the fabric would be complete for which Stephen, Franklin, Roger, and James had each wrought his separate piece with artful cunning. It was impossible not to believe that these Democratic leaders had labored in concert. To those who had urged that Douglas should be supported, Lincoln had only this to say: Douglas could not oppose the advance of slavery, for he did not care whether slavery was voted up or down. His avowed purpose was to make the people care nothing about slavery. The Republican cause must not be intrusted to its adventitious allies, but to its undoubted friends.

A welcome that was truly royal awaited Douglas in Chicago. On his way thither, he was met by a delegation which took him a willing captive and conducted him on a special train to his destination. Along the route there was every sign of popular enthusiasm. He entered the city amid the booming of cannon; he

[1] Lincoln-Douglas Debates (Edition of 1860), p. 1.

was conveyed to his hotel in a carriage drawn by six horses, under military escort; banners with flattering inscriptions fluttered above his head; from balconies and windows he heard the shouts of thousands.[1]

Even more flattering if possible was the immense crowd that thronged around the Tremont House in the early evening to hear his promised speech. Not only the area in front of the hotel, but the adjoining streets were crowded. Illuminations and fireworks cast a lurid light on the faces which were upturned to greet the "Defender of Popular Sovereignty," as he appeared upon the balcony. A man of far less vanity would have been moved by the scene. Just behind the speaker but within the house, Lincoln was an attentive listener.[2] The presence of his rival put Douglas on his mettle. He took in good part a rather discourteous interruption by Lincoln, and referred to him in generous terms, as "a kind, amiable, and intelligent gentleman, a good citizen, and an honorable opponent."[3]

The address was in a somewhat egotistical vein— pardonably egotistical, considering the extraordinary circumstances. Douglas could not refrain from referring to his career since he had confronted that excited crowd in Chicago eight years before, in defense of the compromise measures. To his mind the events of those eight years had amply vindicated the great principle of popular sovereignty. Knowing that he was in a Republican stronghold, he dwelt with particular complacency upon the manful way in which the Republican party had come to the support of that principle,

---

[1] Sheahan, Douglas, pp. 398-400.

[2] Sheahan, Douglas, p. 400; Mr. Horace White in Herndon-Weik, Life of Lincoln, II, p. 93.   [3] Debates, p. 9.

in the recent anti-Lecompton fight. It was this fundamental right of self-government that he had cham-
pioned through good and ill report, all these years.
It was this, and this alone, which had governed his
action in regard to the Lecompton fraud. It was not
because the Lecompton constitution was a slave constitution, but because it was not the act and deed of
the people of Kansas that he had condemned it.
"Whenever," said he, "you put a limitation upon the
right of a people to decide what laws they want, you
have destroyed the fundamental principle of self-government."

With Lincoln's house-divided-against-itself proposition, he took issue unqualifiedly. "Mr. Lincoln as-
serts, as a fundamental principle of this government,
that there must be uniformity in the local laws and
domestic institutions of each and all the States of the
Union, and he therefore invites all the non-slavehold-
ing States to band together, organize as one body, and
make war upon slavery in Kentucky, upon slavery in
Virginia, upon slavery in the Carolinas, upon slavery
in all of the slave-holding States in this Union, and
to persevere in that war until it shall be exterminated.
He then notifies the slave-holding States to stand
together as a unit and make an aggressive war upon
the free States of this Union with a view of establishing slavery in them all; of forcing it upon Illinois, of
forcing it upon New York, upon New England, and
upon every other free State, and that they shall keep
up the warfare until it has been formally established
in them all. In other words, Mr. Lincoln advocates
boldly and clearly a war of sections, a war of the North
against the South, of the free States against the slave

States—a war of extermination—to be continued relentlessly until the one or the other shall be subdued, and all the States shall either become free or become slave."[1]

But such uniformity in local institutions would be possible only by blotting out State Sovereignty, by merging all the States in one consolidated empire, and by vesting Congress with plenary power to make all the police regulations, domestic and local laws, uniform throughout the Republic. The framers of our government knew well enough that differences in soil, in products, and in interests, required different local and domestic regulations in each locality; and they organized the Federal government on this fundamental assumption.[2]

With Lincoln's other proposition Douglas also took issue. He refused to enter upon any crusade against the Supreme Court. "I do not choose, therefore, to go into any argument with Mr. Lincoln in reviewing the various decisions which the Supreme Court has made, either upon the Dred Scott case, or any other. I have no idea of appealing from the decision of the Supreme Court upon a constitutional question to the decision of a tumultuous town meeting."[3]

Neither could Douglas agree with his opponent in objecting to the decision of the Supreme Court because it deprived the negro of the rights, privileges, and immunities of citizenship, which pertained only to the white race. Our government was founded on a white basis. "It was made by the white man, for the benefit of the white man, to be administered by white men." To be sure, a negro, an Indian, or any other

<hr />

[1] Debates, p. 9. [2] *Ibid.*, p. 10. [3] *Ibid.*, p. 11.

man of inferior race should be permitted to enjoy all
the rights, privileges, and immunities consistent with
the safety of society; but each State should decide for
itself the nature and extent of these rights.

On the next evening, Republican Chicago greeted
its protagonist with much the same demonstrations, as
he took his place on the balcony from which Douglas
had spoken. Lincoln found the flaw in Douglas's
armor at the outset. "Popular sovereignty! Everlasting popular sovereignty! What is popular sovereignty"? How could there be such a thing in the
original sense, now that the Supreme Court had decided that the people in their territorial status might
not prohibit slavery? And as for the right of the
people to frame a constitution, who had ever disputed
that right? But Lincoln, evidently troubled by Douglas's vehement deductions from the house-divided-
against-itself proposition, soon fell back upon the
defensive, where he was at a great disadvantage. He
was forced to explain that he did not favor a war by
the North upon the South for the extinction of slavery;
nor a war by the South upon the North for the national-
ization of slavery. "I only said what I expected
would take place. I made a prediction only,—it may
have been a foolish one, perhaps. I did not even say
that I desired that slavery should be put in course of
ultimate extinction. I do say so now, however."[1] He
believed that slavery had endured, because until the
Nebraska Act the public mind had rested in the conviction that slavery would ultimately disappear. In
affirming that the opponents of slavery would arrest
its further extension, he only meant to say that they

[1] Debates, p. 18.

would put it where the fathers originally placed it. He was not in favor of interfering with slavery where it existed in the States. As to the charge that he was inviting people to resist the Dred Scott decision, Lincoln responded rather weakly—again laying himself open to attack—"We mean to do what we can to have the court decide the other way."[1]

Lincoln also betrayed his fear lest Douglas should draw Republican votes. Knowing the strong antislavery sentiment of the region, he asked when Douglas had shown anything but indifference on the subject of slavery. Away with this quibbling about inferior races! "Let us discard all these things and unite as one people throughout this land, until we shall once more stand up declaring that all men are created equal."[2]

From Chicago Douglas journeyed like a conquering hero to Bloomington. At every station crowds gathered to see his gaily decorated train and to catch a glimpse of the famous senator. A platform car bearing a twelve-pound gun was attached to the train and everywhere "popular sovereignty," as the cannon was dubbed, heralded his arrival.[3] On the evening of July 16th he addressed a large gathering in the open air; and again he had among his auditors, Abraham Lincoln, who was hot upon his trail.[4] The county and district in which Bloomington was situated had once been strongly Whig; but was now as strongly Republican. With the local conditions in mind, Douglas made an artful plea for support. He gratefully acknowl-

---

[1] Debates, p. 20. [2] Ibid., p. 24.
[3] Flint, Douglas, pp. 114-117; Chicago Times, July 18, 1858.
[4] Debates, p. 24.

edged the aid of the Republicans in the recent anti-Lecompton fight, and of that worthy successor of the immortal Clay, John J. Crittenden of Kentucky. After all, was it not a common principle for which they had been contending? "My friends," said Douglas with engaging ingenuousness, "when I am battling for a great principle, I want aid and support from whatever quarter I can get it." Pity, then, that Republican politicians, in order to defeat him, should form an alliance with Lecompton men and thus betray the cause![1]

Douglas called attention to Lincoln's explanation of his house-divided-against-itself argument. It still seemed to him to invite a war of sections. Mr. Lincoln had said that he had no wish to see the people *enter into* the Southern States and interfere with slavery: for his part, he was equally opposed to a sectional agitation to control the institutions of other States.[2] Again, Mr. Lincoln had said that he proposed, so far as in him lay, to secure a reversal of the Dred Scott decision. How, asked Douglas, will he accomplish this? There can be but one way: elect a Republican President who will pack the bench with Republican justices. Would a court so constituted command respect?[3]

As to the effect of the Dred Scott decision upon slavery in the Territories, Douglas had only this to say: "With or without that decision, slavery will go just where the people want it, and not one inch further." "Hence, if the people of a Territory want slavery, they will encourage it by passing affirmatory laws, and the necessary police regulations, patrol laws, and slave code; if they do not want it they will withhold

[1] Debates, p. 27.   [2] *Ibid.*, p. 30.   [3] *Ibid.*, pp. 33-34.

that legislation, and by withholding it slavery is as dead as if it was prohibited by a constitutional prohibition, especially if, in addition, their legislation is unfriendly, as it would be if they were opposed to it. They could pass such local laws and police regulations as would drive slavery out in one day, or one hour, if they were opposed to it, and therefore, so far as the question of slavery in the Territories is concerned, so far as the principle of popular sovereignty is concerned, in its practical operation, it matters not how the Dred Scott case may be decided with reference to the Territories.''[1]

The closing words of the speech approached dangerously near to bathos. Douglas pictured himself standing beside the deathbed of Clay and pledging his life to the advocacy of the great principle expressed in the compromise measures of 1850, and later in the Kansas-Nebraska Act. Strangely enough he had given the same pledge to ''the god-like Webster.''[2] This filial reverence for Clay and Webster, whom Douglas had fought with all the weapons of partisan warfare, must have puzzled those Whigs in his audience who were guileless enough to accept such statements at their face value.

Devoted partisans accompanied Douglas to Springfield, on the following day. In spite of the frequent downpours of rain and the sultry atmosphere, their enthusiasm never once flagged. On board the same train, surrounded by good-natured enemies, was Lincoln, who was also to speak at the capital.[3] Douglas again found a crowd awaiting him. He had much the

[1] Debates, p. 35.　　　[2] Ibid., p. 39.
[3] Sheahan, Douglas, p. 417; Chicago Times, July 21, 1858.

same things to say. Perhaps his arraignment of Lincoln's policy was somewhat more severe, but he turned the edges of his thrusts by a courteous reference to his opponent, "with whom he anticipated no personal collision." For the first time he alluded to Lincoln's charge of conspiracy, but only to remark casually, "If Mr. Lincoln deems me a conspirator of that kind, all I have to say is that I do not think so badly of the President of the United States, and the Supreme Court of the United States, the highest judicial tribunal on earth, as to believe that they were capable in their actions and decision of entering into political intrigues for partisan purposes."[1]

Meantime Lincoln, addressing a Republican audience, was relating his recent experiences in the enemy's camp. Believing that he had discovered the line of attack, he sought to fortify his position. He did not contemplate the abolition of State legislatures, nor any such radical policy, any more than the fathers of the Republic did, when they sought to check the spread of slavery by prohibiting it in the Territories.[2] He did not propose to resist the Dred Scott decision except as a rule of political action.[3] Here in Sangamon County, he was somewhat less insistent upon negro equality. The negro was not the equal of the white man in all respects, to be sure; "still, in the right to put into his mouth the bread that his own hands have earned, he is the equal of every other man, white or black."[4]

As matters stood, Douglas had the advantage of Lincoln, since with his national prominence and his

[1] Debates, p. 44.   [2] Ibid., p. 60.
[3] Ibid., p. 61.   [4] Ibid., p. 63.

great popularity, he was always sure of an audience, and could reply as he chose to the attacks of his antagonist. Lincoln felt that he must come to close terms with Douglas and extort from him admissions which would discredit him with Republicans. With this end in view, Lincoln suggested that they "divide time, and address the same audiences the present canvass."[1] It was obviously to Douglas's interest to continue the campaign as he had begun. He had already mapped out an extensive itinerary. He therefore replied that he could not agree to such an arrangement, owing to appointments already made and to the possibility of a third candidate with whom Lincoln might make common cause. He intimated, rather unfairly, that Lincoln had purposely waited until he was already bound by his appointments. However, he would accede to the proposal so far as to meet Lincoln in a joint discussion in each congressional district except the second and sixth, in which both had already spoken.[2]

It was not such a letter as one would expect from a generous opponent. But politics was no pastime to the writer. He was sparring now in deadly earnest, for every advantage. Not unnaturally Lincoln resented the imputation of unfairness; but he agreed to the proposal of seven joint debates. Douglas then named the times and places; and Lincoln agreed to the terms, rather grudgingly, for he would have but three openings and closings to Douglas's four.[3] Still, as he had followed Douglas in Chicago, he had no reason to complain.

The next three months may be regarded as a prolonged debate, accentuated by the seven joint discus-

[1] Debates, p. 64.   [2] Ibid., pp. 64-65.   [3] Ibid., p. 66.

sions. The rival candidates traversed much the same territory, and addressed much the same audiences on successive days. At times, chance made them fellow-passengers on the same train or steamboat. Douglas had already begun his itinerary, when Lincoln's last note reached him in Piatt County.[1] He had just spoken at Clinton, in De Witt County, and again he had found Lincoln in the audience.

No general ever planned a military campaign with greater regard to the topography of the enemy's country, than Douglas plotted his campaign in central Illinois. For it was in the central counties that the election was to be won or lost. The Republican strength lay in the upper, northern third of the State; the Democratic strength, in the southern third. The doubtful area lay between Ottawa on the north and Belleville on the south; Oquawka on the northwest and Paris on the east. Only twice did Douglas make any extended tour outside this area: once to meet his appointment with Lincoln at Freeport; and once to engage in the third joint debate at Jonesboro.

The first week in August found Douglas speaking at various points along the Illinois River to enthusiastic crowds. Lincoln followed closely after, bent upon weakening the force of his opponent's arguments by lodging an immediate demurrer against them. On the whole, Douglas drew the larger crowds; but it was observed that Lincoln's audiences increased as he proceeded northward. Ottawa was the objective point for both travelers, for there was to be held the first joint debate on August 21st.

An enormous crowd awaited them. From sunrise

[1] Debates, p. 66.

to mid-day men, women, and children had poured into town, in every sort of conveyance. It was a typical midsummer day in Illinois. The prairie roads were thoroughly baked by the sun, and the dust rose, like a fine powder, from beneath the feet of horses and pedestrians, enveloping all in blinding clouds. A train of seventeen cars had brought ardent supporters of Douglas from Chicago. The town was gaily decked; the booming of cannon resounded across the prairie; bands of music added to the excitement of the occasion. The speakers were escorted to the public square by two huge processions. So eager was the crowd that it was with much difficulty, and no little delay, that Lincoln and Douglas, the committee men, and the reporters, were landed on the platform.[1]

For the first time in the campaign, the rival candidates were placed side by side. The crowd instinctively took its measure of the two men. They presented a striking contrast:[2] Lincoln, tall, angular, and long of limb; Douglas, short, almost dwarfed by comparison, broad-shouldered and thick-chested. Lincoln was clad in a frock coat of rusty black, which was evidently not made for his lank, ungainly body. His sleeves did not reach his wrists by several inches, and his trousers failed to conceal his huge feet. His long, sinewy neck emerged from a white collar, drawn over a black tie. Altogether, his appearance bordered upon the grotesque, and would have provoked mirth in any other than an Illinois audience, which knew and

---

[1] Mr. Horace White in Herndon-Weik, Lincoln, II, pp. 104-105.

[2] For the following description I have drawn freely from the narratives of eye-witnesses. I am particularly indebted to the graphic account by Mr. Carl Schurz in McClure's Magazine, January, 1907.

respected the man too well to mark his costume. Douglas, on the contrary, presented a well-groomed figure. He wore a well-fitting suit of broadcloth; his linen was immaculate; and altogether he had the appearance of a man of the world whom fortune had favored.

The eyes of the crowd, however, sought rather the faces of the rival candidates. Lincoln looked down upon them with eyes in which there was an expression of sadness, not to say melancholy, until he lost himself in the passion of his utterance. There was not a regular feature in his face. The deep furrows that seamed his countenance bore unmistakable witness to a boyhood of grim poverty and grinding toil. Douglas surveyed the crowd from beneath his shaggy brows, with bold, penetrating gaze. Every feature of his face bespoke power. The deep-set eyes; the dark, almost sinister, line between them; the mouth with its tightly-drawn lips; the deep lines on his somewhat puffy cheeks —all gave the impression of a masterful nature, accustomed to bear down opposition. As men observed his massive brow with its mane of abundant, dark hair; his strong neck; his short, compact body; they instinctively felt that here was a personality not lightly to be encountered. He was "the very embodiment of force, combativeness, and staying power."[1]

When Douglas, by agreement, opened the debate, he was fully conscious that he was addressing an audience which was in the main hostile to him. With the instinct of a born stump speaker, he sought first to find common ground with his hearers. Appealing to the history of parties, he pointed out the practical

[1] Mr. Schurz in *McClure's,* January, 1907.

agreement of both Whig and Democratic parties on the slavery question down to 1854. It was when, in accordance with the Compromise of 1850, he brought in the Kansas-Nebraska bill, that Lincoln and Trumbull entered into an agreement to dissolve the old parties in Illinois and to form an Abolition party under the pseudonym "Republican." The terms of the alliance were that Lincoln should have Senator Shields' place in the Senate, and that Trumbull should have Douglas's, when his term should expire.[1] History, thus interpreted, made not Douglas, but his opponent, the real agitator in State politics.

Douglas then read from the first platform of the Black Republicans. "My object in reading these resolutions," he said, "was to put the question to Abraham Lincoln this day, whether he now stands and will stand by each article in that creed and carry it out. I desire to know whether Mr. Lincoln to-day stands, as he did in 1854, in favor of the unconditional repeal of the Fugitive Slave law. I desire him to answer whether he stands pledged to-day, as he did in 1854, against the admission of any more slave States into the Union, even if the people want them. I want to know whether he stands pledged against the admission of a new State into the Union with such a Constitution as the people of that State may see fit to make. I want to know whether he stands to-day pledged to the abolition of slavery in the District of Columbia. I desire him to answer whether he stands pledged to the prohibition of the slave trade between the different States. I desire to know whether he stands pledged to prohibit slavery in all the Territories of the United States,

[1] Debates, p. 67.

North as well as South of the Missouri Compromise line. I desire him to answer whether he is opposed to the acquisition of any more territory, unless slavery is prohibited therein."[1]

In all this there was a rude vehemence and coarse insinuation that was regrettable; yet Douglas sought to soften the asperity of his manner, by adding that he did not mean to be disrespectful or unkind to Mr. Lincoln. He had known Mr. Lincoln for twenty-five years. While he was a school-teacher, Lincoln was a flourishing grocery-keeper. Lincoln was always more successful in business; Lincoln always did well whatever he undertook; Lincoln could beat any of the boys wrestling or running a foot-race; Lincoln could ruin more liquor than all the boys of the town together. When in Congress, Lincoln had distinguished himself by his opposition to the Mexican War, taking the side of the enemy against his own country.[2] If this disparagement of an opponent seems mean and ungenerous, let it be remembered that in the rough give-and-take of Illinois politics, hard hitting was to be expected. Lincoln had invited counter-blows by first charging Douglas with conspiracy. No mere reading of cold print can convey the virile energy with which Douglas spoke. The facial expression, the animated gesture, the toss of the head, and the stamp of the foot, the full, resonant voice—all are wanting.

To a man of Lincoln's temperament, this vigorous invective was indescribably irritating. Rather unwisely he betrayed his vexation in his first words. His manner was constrained. He seemed awkward and ill at ease, but as he warmed to his task, his face became

[1] Debates, p. 68.   [2] *Ibid.*, p. 69.

more animated, he recovered the use of his arms, and he pointed his remarks with forceful gestures. His voice, never pleasant, rose to a shrill treble in moments of excitement. After the familiar manner of Western speakers of that day, he was wont to bend his knees and then rise to his full height with a jerk, to enforce some point.[1] Yet with all his ungraceful mannerisms, Lincoln held his hearers, impressing most men with a sense of the honesty of his convictions.

Instead of replying categorically to Douglas's questions, Lincoln read a long extract from a speech which he had made in 1854, to show his attitude then toward the Fugitive Slave Act. He denied that he had had anything to do with the resolutions which had been read. He believed that he was not even in Springfield at the time when they were adopted.[2] As for the charge that he favored the social and political equality of the black and white races, he said, "Anything that argues me into his idea of perfect social and political equality with the negro, is but a specious and fantastic arrangement of words, by which a man can prove a horse-chestnut to be a chestnut horse. . . . .I have no purpose to introduce political and social equality between the white and the black races. There is a physical difference between the two, which, in my judgment, will probably forever forbid their living together upon the footing of perfect equality . . . . notwithstanding all this, there is no reason in the world why the negro is not entitled to all the natural rights enumerated in the Declaration of Independence,—the

---

[1] Herndon in Herndon-Weik, Lincoln, II, pp. 76-77; Mr. Carl Schurz in *McClure's*, January, 1907.

[2] Debates, p. 73.

right to life, liberty, and the pursuit of happiness.'"[1]
Slavery had always been, and would always be, "an
apple of discord and an element of division in the
house." He disclaimed all intention of making war
upon Southern institutions, yet he was still firm in the
belief that the public mind would not be easy until
slavery was put where the fathers left it. He reminded
his hearers that Douglas had said nothing to clear himself from the suspicion of having been party to a conspiracy to nationalize slavery. Judge Douglas was
not always so ready as now to yield obedience to judicial decisions, as anyone might see who chose to
inquire how he earned his title.[2]

In his reply, Douglas endeavored to refresh Lincoln's
memory in respect to the resolutions. They were
adopted while he was in Springfield, for it was the
season of the State Fair, when both had spoken at the
Capitol. He had not charged Mr. Lincoln with having
helped to frame these resolutions, but with having
been a responsible leader of the party which had
adopted them as its platform. Was Mr. Lincoln trying to dodge the questions? Douglas refused to allow
himself to be put upon the defensive in the matter of
the alleged conspiracy, since Lincoln had acknowledged
that he did not know it to be true. He would brand it
as a lie and let Lincoln prove it if he could.[3]

At the conclusion of the debate, two young farmers,
in their exuberant enthusiasm, rushed forward, seized
Lincoln in spite of his remonstrances, and carried him
off upon their stalwart shoulders. "It was really a

[1] Debates, p. 75.
[2] *Ibid.*, p. 82.
[3] *Ibid.*, p. 86.

ludicrous sight," writes an eye-witness,[1] "to see the grotesque figure holding frantically to the heads of his supporters, with his legs dangling from their shoulders, and his pantaloons pulled up so as to expose his underwear almost to his knees." Douglas was not slow in using this incident to the discomfiture of his opponent. "Why," he said at Joliet, "the very notice that I was going to take him down to Egypt made him tremble in his knees so that he had to be carried from the platform. He laid up seven days, and in the meantime held a consultation with his political physicians,"[2] etc. Strangely enough, Lincoln with all his sense of humor took this badinage seriously, and accused Douglas of telling a falsehood.[3]

The impression prevailed that Douglas had cornered Lincoln by his adroit use of the Springfield resolutions of 1854. Within a week, however, an editorial in the Chicago *Press and Tribune* reversed the popular verdict, by pronouncing the resolutions a forgery. The Republicans were jubilant. "The Little Dodger" had cornered himself. The Democrats were chagrined. Douglas was thoroughly nonplussed. He had written to Lanphier for precise information regarding these resolutions, and he had placed implicit confidence in the reply of his friend. It now transpired that they were the work of a local convention in Kane County.[4] Could any blunder have been more unfortunate?

When the contestants met at Freeport, far in the

---

[1] Henry Villard, Memoirs, I, p. 93; Mr. Horace White in Herndon-Weik, Lincoln, II, p. 108.

[2] Debates, p. 129.   [3] *Ibid.*, p. 130.

[4] Holland, Lincoln, p. 185; Tarbell, Lincoln, *McClure's Magazine*, VII, pp. 408-409.

solid Republican counties of the North, Lincoln was ready with his answers to the questions propounded by Douglas at Ottawa. In most respects Lincoln was clear and explicit. While not giving an unqualified approval of the Fugitive Slave Law, he was not in favor of its repeal; while believing that Congress possessed the power to abolish slavery in the District of Columbia, he favored abolition only on condition that it should be gradual, acceptable to a majority of the voters of the District, and compensatory to unwilling owners; he would favor the abolition of the slave-trade between the States only upon similar conservative principles; he believed it, however, to be the right and duty of Congress to prohibit slavery in all the Territories; he was not opposed to the honest acquisition of territory, provided that it would not aggravate the slavery question. The really crucial questions, Lincoln did not face so unequivocally. Was he opposed to the admission of more slave States? Would he oppose the admission of a new State with such a constitution as the people of that State should see fit to make?

Lincoln answered hesitatingly: "In regard to the other question, of whether I am pledged to the admission of any more slave States into the Union, I state to you very frankly that I would be exceedingly sorry ever to be put in a position of having to pass upon that question. I should be exceedingly glad to know that there would never be another slave State admitted into the Union; but I must add, that if slavery shall be kept out of the Territories during the territorial existence of any one given Territory, and then the people shall, having a fair chance and a clear field, when they come to adopt the Constitution, do such an extraordinary thing as to adopt a slave Constitution, uninfluenced by the actual presence of the institution among them, I see no alternative, if we own the country, but to admit them into the Union.''[1]

It was now Lincoln's turn to catechise his opponent. He had prepared four questions, the second of which caused his friends some misgivings.[2] It read: ''Can the people of a United States Territory, in any lawful way, against the wish of any citizen of the United States, exclude slavery from its limits prior to the formation of a State Constitution?''

Lincoln knew well enough that Douglas held to the power of the people practically to exclude slavery, regardless of the decision of the Supreme Court; Douglas had said as much in his hearing at Bloomington. What he desired to extort from Douglas was his opinion of the legality of such action in view of the Dred Scott decision. Should Douglas answer in the negative, popular sovereignty would become an empty phrase; should he answer in the affirmative, he would put himself, so Lincoln calculated, at variance with Southern Democrats, who claimed that the people of a Territory were now inhibited from any such power over slave property. In the latter event, Lincoln proposed to give such publicity to Douglas's reply as to make any future evasion or retraction impossible.[3]

Douglas faced the critical question without the slightest hesitation. ''It matters not what way the

[1] Debates, p. 89.

[2] Holland, Lincoln, pp. 188-189; Mr. Horace White in Herndon-Weik, Lincoln, II, p. 109.

[3] Herndon-Weik, Lincoln, II, p. 109.

Supreme Court may hereafter decide as to the abstract question whether slavery may or may not go into a Territory under the Constitution, the people have the lawful means to introduce it or exclude it as they please, for the reason that slavery cannot exist a day or an hour anywhere, unless it is supported by local police regulations. Those police regulations can only be established by the local legislature; and if the people are opposed to slavery, they will elect representatives to that body who will by unfriendly legislation effectually prevent the introduction of it into their midst. If, on the contrary, they are for it, their legislation will favor its extension. Hence, no matter what the decision of the Supreme Court may be on that abstract question, still the right of the people to make a slave Territory or a free Territory is perfect and complete under the Nebraska Bill. I hope Mr. Lincoln deems my answer satisfactory on that point ''[1]

The other three questions involved less risk for the advocate of popular sovereignty. He would vote to admit Kansas without the requisite population for representation in Congress, if the people should frame an unobjectionable constitution. He would prefer a general rule on this point, but since Congress had decided that Kansas had enough people to form a slave State, she surely had enough to constitute a free State. He scouted the imputation in the third question, that the Supreme Court could so far violate the Constitution as to decide that a State could not exclude slavery from its own limits. He would always vote for the acquisition of new territory, when it was needed, irrespective of the question of slavery.[2]

[1] Debates, p. 95.   [2] Debates, pp. 94-97.

Smarting under Lincoln's animadversions respecting the Springfield resolutions, Douglas explained his error by quoting from a copy of the Illinois *State Register,* which had printed the resolutions as the work of the convention at the capital. He gave notice that he would investigate the matter, "when he got down to Springfield." At all events there was ample proof that the resolutions were a faithful exposition of Republican doctrine in the year 1854. Douglas then read similar resolutions adopted by a convention in Rockford County. One Turner, who was acting as one of the moderators, interrupted him at this point, to say that he had drawn those very resolutions and that they were the Republican creed exactly. "And yet," exclaimed Douglas triumphantly, "and yet Lincoln denies that he stands on them. Mr. Turner says that the creed of the Black Republican party is the admission of no more slave States, and yet Mr. Lincoln declares that he would not like to be placed in a position where he would have to vote for them. All I have to say to friend Lincoln is, that I do not think there is much danger of his being placed in such a position. . . . I propose, out of mere kindness, to relieve him from any such necessity."[1]

As he continued, Douglas grew offensively denunciatory. His opponents were invariably Black Republicans; Lincoln was the ally of rank Abolitionists like Giddings and Fred Douglass; of course those who believed in political and social equality for blacks and whites would vote for Lincoln. Lincoln had found fault with the resolutions because they were not adopted on the right spot. Lincoln and his friends were great

[1] Debates, pp. 100-101.

on "spots." Lincoln had opposed the Mexican War because American blood was not shed on American soil in the right spot. Trumbull and Lincoln were like two decoy ducks which lead the flock astray. Ambition, personal ambition, had led to the formation of the Black Republican party. Lincoln and his friends were now only trying to secure what Trumbull had cheated them out of in 1855, when the senatorship fell to Trumbull. Under this savage attack the crowd grew restive. As Douglas repeated the epithet "Black" Republican, he was interrupted by indignant cries of "White," "White." But Douglas shouted back defiantly, "I wish to remind you that while Mr. Lincoln was speaking there was not a Democrat vulgar and blackguard enough to interrupt him," and browbeat his hearers into quiet again.[1]

Realizing, perhaps, the immense difficulty of exposing the fallacy of Douglas's reply to his questions, in the few moments at his disposal, Lincoln did not refer to the crucial point. He contented himself with a defense of his own consistency. His best friends were dispirited, when the half-hour ended. They could not shake off the impression that Douglas had saved himself from defeat by his adroit answers to Lincoln's interrogatories.[2]

The next joint debate occurred nearly three weeks later down in Egypt. By slow stages, speaking incessantly at all sorts of meetings, Douglas and Lincoln made their several ways through the doubtful central counties to Jonesboro in Union County. This was the enemy's country for Lincoln; and by reason of the

[1] Debates, p. 101.
[2] Mr. Horace White in Herndon-Weik, Lincoln, p. 110.

activities of United States Marshal Dougherty, a Buchanan appointee, the county was scarcely less hostile to Douglas. The meeting was poorly attended. Those who listened to the speakers were chary of applause and appeared politically apathetic.[1]

Douglas opened the debate by a wild, unguarded appeal to partisan prejudices. Knowing his hearers, he was personally vindictive in his references to Black Republicans in general and to Lincoln in particular. He reiterated his stock arguments, giving new vehemence to his charge of corrupt bargain between Trumbull and Lincoln by quoting Matheny, a Republican and "Mr. Lincoln's especial and confidential friend for the last twenty years."[2]

Lincoln begged leave to doubt the authenticity of this new evidence, in view of the little episode at Ottawa, concerning the Springfield resolutions. At all events the whole story was untrue, and he had already declared it to be such.[3] Why should Douglas persist in misrepresenting him? Brushing aside these lesser matters, however, Lincoln addressed himself to what had now come to be known as Douglas's Freeport doctrine. "I hold," said he, "that the proposition that slavery cannot enter a new country without police regulations is historically false. . . . There is enough vigor in slavery to plant itself in a new country even against unfriendly legislation. It takes not only law but the enforcement of law to keep it out." Moreover, the decision of the Supreme Court in the Dred Scott case had created constitutional obligations. Now that the right of property in slaves was affirmed by the Constitution, according to the Court, how could a mem-

[1] Mr. Horace White in Herndon-Weik, Lincoln, p. 118.
[2] Debates, pp. 113-114.   [3] Ibid., p. 120.

ber of a territorial legislature, who had taken the oath to support the Constitution, refuse to give his vote for laws necessary to establish slave property? And how could a member of Congress keep his oath and withhold the necessary protection to slave property in the Territories?[1]

Of course Lincoln was well aware that Douglas held that the Court had decided only the question of jurisdiction in the Dred Scott case; and that all ·else was a mere *obiter dictum.* Nevertheless, "the Court did pass its opinion. . . . If they did not decide, they showed what they were ready to decide whenever the matter was before them. They used language to this effect: That inasmuch as Congress itself could not exercise such a power [*i. e.,* pass a law prohibiting slavery in the Territories], it followed as a matter of course that it could not authorize a Territorial Government to exercise it; for the Territorial Legislature can do no more than Congress could do."[2]

The only answer of Douglas to this trenchant analysis was a reiterated assertion: "I assert that under the Dred Scott decision [taking Lincoln's view of that decision] you cannot maintain slavery a day in a Territory where there is an unwilling people and unfriendly legislation. If the people are opposed to it, our right is a barren, worthless, useless right; and if they are for it, they will support and encourage it."[3]

Douglas made much of Lincoln's evident unwillingness to commit himself on the question of admitting more slave States. In various ways he sought to trip his adversary, believing that Lincoln had pledged himself to his Abolitionist allies in 1855 to vote against the

[1] Debates, p. 127.   [2] *Ibid.,* p. 129.   [3] *Ibid.,* p. 135.

admission of more slave States, if he should be elected senator. "Let me tell Mr. Lincoln that his party in the northern part of the State hold to that Abolition platform [no more slave States], and if they do not in the South and in the center, they present the extraordinary spectacle of a house-divided-against-itself.' "[1]

Douglas turned the edge of Lincoln's thrust at the duties of legislators under the Dred Scott decision by saying, "Well, if you are not going to resist the decision, if you obey it, and do not intend to array mob law against the constituted authorities, then, according to your own statement, you will be a perjured man if you do not vote to establish slavery in these Territories."[2] And it did not save Lincoln from the horns of this uncomfortable dilemma to repeat that he did not accept the Dred Scott decision as a rule for political action, for he had just emphasized the moral obligation of obeying the law of the Constitution.

From the darkness of Egypt, Douglas and Lincoln journeyed northward toward Charleston in Coles County, where the fourth debate was to be held. Both paused *en route* to visit the State Fair, then in full blast at Centralia. Curious crowds followed them around the fair grounds, deeming the rival candidates quite as worthy of close scrutiny as the other exhibits.[3]

---

[1] Debates, p. 133. Lamon is authority for the statement that Lincoln pledged himself to Lovejoy and his faction to favor the exclusion of slavery from all the territory of the United States. Douglas did not know of this pledge, but suspected an understanding to this effect. If Lamon may be believed, this statement explains the persistence of Douglas on this point and the evasiveness of Lincoln. See Lamon, Lincoln, pp. 361-365.   [2] *Ibid.*, p. 135.

[3] Mr. Horace White in Herndon-Weik, Lincoln, p. 119.

Ten miles from Charleston, they left the train to be escorted by rival processions along the dusty highway to their destination. From all the country-side people had come to town to cheer on their respective champions.[1] This twenty-fifth district, comprising Coles and Moultrie counties, had been carried by the Democrats in 1856, but was now regarded as doubtful. The uncertainty added piquancy to the debate.

It was Lincoln's turn to open the joust. At the outset he tried to allay misapprehensions regarding his attitude toward negro equality. "I will say, then, that I am not, nor ever have been, in favor of bringing about in any way the social and political equality of the white and black races; that I am not, nor ever have been, in favor of making voters or jurors of negroes, nor of qualifying them to hold office, nor to intermarry with white people; and I will say in addition to this, that there is a physical difference between the white and black races which I believe will forever forbid the two races living together on terms of social and political equality. And inasmuch as they cannot so live, while they do remain together there must be the position of superior and inferior, and I as much as any other man am in favor of having the superior position assigned to the white race. I say upon this occasion I do not perceive that because the white man is to have the superior position the negro should be denied everything. I do not understand that because I do not want a negro woman for a slave I must necessarily want her for a wife. My understanding is that I can just let her alone."[2] This was by far the most explicit statement that he had yet made on the hazardous subject.

[1] Mr. Horace White in Herndon-Weik, Lincoln, p. 121.
[2] Debates, p. 136.

Lincoln then turned upon his opponent, with more aggressiveness than he had hitherto exhibited, to drive home the charge which Trumbull had made earlier in the campaign. Prompted by Trumbull, probably, Lincoln reviewed the shadowy history of the Toombs bill and Douglas's still more enigmatical connection with it. The substance of the indictment was, that Douglas had suppressed that part of the original bill which provided for a popular vote on the constitution to be drafted by the Kansas convention. In replying to Trumbull, Douglas had damaged his own case by denying that the Toombs bill had ever contained such a provision. Lincoln proved the contrary by the most transparent testimony, convicting Douglas not only of the original offense but of an untruth in connection with it.[1]

This was not a vague charge of conspiracy which could be treated with contempt, but an indictment, accompanied by circumstantial evidence. While a dispassionate examination of the whole incident will acquit Douglas of any part in a plot to prevent the fair adoption of a constitution by the people of Kansas, yet he certainly took a most unfortunate and prejudicial mode of defending himself.[2] His personal retorts were so vindictive and his attack upon Trumbull so full of venom, that his words did not carry conviction to the minds of his hearers. It was a matter of common observation that Democrats seemed ill at ease after the debate.[3] "Judge Douglas is playing cuttle-fish," remarked Lincoln, noting with satisfaction the very evident discomfiture of his opponent, "a

[1] Debates, pp. 137-143. [2] See above pp. 303-304.
[3] Mr. Horace White in Herndon-Weik, Lincoln, p. 122.

small species of fish that has no mode of defending itself when pursued except by throwing out a black fluid, which makes the water so dark the enemy cannot see it, and thus it escapes.''[1]

Douglas, however, did his best to recover his ground by accusing Lincoln of shifting his principles as he passed from the northern counties to Egypt; the principles of his party in the north were ''jet-black,'' in the center, ''a decent mulatto,'' and in lower Egypt ''almost white.'' Lincoln then dared him to point out any difference between his speeches. Blows now fell thick and fast, both speakers approaching dangerously near the limit of parliamentary language. Reverting to his argument that slavery must be put in the course of ultimate extinction, Lincoln made this interesting qualification: ''I do not mean that when it takes a turn toward ultimate extinction it will be in a day, nor in a year, nor in two years. I do not suppose that in the most peaceful way ultimate extinction would occur in less than a hundred years at least; but that it will occur in the best way for both races, in God's own good time, I have no doubt.''[2]

Douglas was now feeling the full force of the opposition within his own party. The Republican newspapers of the State had seized upon his Freeport speech to convince the South and the administration that he was false to their creed. The Washington *Union* had from the first denounced him as a renegade, with whom no self-respecting Democrat would associate.[3] Slidell was active in Illinois, spending money

[1] Debates, p. 159.   [2] *Ibid.*, p. 157.

[3] Rhodes, History of the United States, II, p. 342.

freely to defeat him.[1] The Danites in the central counties plotted incessantly to weaken his following. Daniel S. Dickinson of New York sent "a Thousand Greetings" to a mass-meeting of Danites in Springfield,—a liberal allowance, commented some Douglasite, as each delegate would receive about ten greetings.[2] Yet the dimensions of this movement were not easily ascertained. The declination of Vice-President Breckinridge to come to the aid of Douglas was a rebuff not easily laughed down, though to be sure, he expressed a guarded preference for Douglas over Lincoln. The coolness of Breckinridge was in a measure offset by the friendliness of Senator Crittenden, who refused to aid Lincoln, because he believed Douglas's re-election "necessary as a rebuke to the administration and a vindication of the great cause of popular rights and public justice."[3] The most influential Republican papers in the East gave Lincoln tardy support, with the exception of the New York *Times*.[4]

Unquestionably Douglas drew upon resources which Lincoln could not command. The management of the Illinois Central Railroad was naturally friendly toward him, though there is no evidence that it countenanced any illegitimate use of influence on his behalf. If Douglas enjoyed special train service, which Lincoln did not, it was because he drew upon funds that exceeded Lincoln's modest income. How many thousands of dollars Douglas devoted from his own exchequer to

---

[1] Foote, Casket of Reminiscences, p. 135; Herndon-Weik, Lincoln, II, p. 127.

[2] Mr. Horace White in Herndon-Weik, Lincoln, II, p. 129.

[3] Coleman, Life of Crittenden, II, p. 163.

[4] Rhodes, History of the United States, II, p. 341.

his campaign, can now only be conjectured. In all probability, he spent all that remained from the sale of his real estate in Chicago, and more which he borrowed in New York by mortgaging his other holdings in Cook County.[1] And not least among his assets was the constant companionship of Mrs. Douglas, whose tact, grace, and beauty placated feelings which had been ruffled by the rude vigor of "the Little Giant."[2]

When the rivals met three weeks later at Galesburg, they were disposed to drop personalities. Indeed, both were aware that they were about to address men and women who demanded an intelligent discussion of the issues of the hour. Lincoln had the more sympathetic hearing, for Knox County was consistently Republican; and the town with its academic atmosphere and New England traditions shared his hostility to slavery. Vast crowds braved the cold, raw winds of the October day to listen for three hours to this debate.[3] From a platform on the college campus, Douglas looked down somewhat defiantly upon his hearers, though his words were well-chosen and courteous. The circumstances were much the same as at Ottawa; and he spoke in much the same vein. He rang the changes upon his great fundamental principle; he defended his course in respect to Lecomptonism; he denounced the Republican party as a sectional organization whose leaders were bent upon "outvoting, conquering, gov-

---

[1] Rhodes, History of the United States, II, p. 338, note 3. The record of the Circuit Court of Cook County, December term, 1867, states that the entire lien upon the estate in 1864 exceeded $94,000. The mortgages were held by Fernando Wood and others of New York.

[2] Villard, Memoirs, I, p. 92.

[3] Mr. Horace White in Herndon-Weik, Lincoln, II, p. 123.

erning, and controlling the South." Douglas laid
great stress upon this sectional aspect of Republicanism, which made its southward extension impossible.
"Not only is this Republican party unable to proclaim
its principles alike in the North and in the South, in
the free States and in the slave States, but it cannot
even proclaim them in the same forms and give them
the same strength and meaning in all parts of the same
State. My friend Lincoln finds it extremely difficult
to manage a debate in the center part of the State,
where there is a mixture of men from the North and
the South."[1]

Here Douglas paused to read from Lincoln's
speeches at Chicago and at Charleston, and to ask his
hearers to reconcile the conflicting statements respecting negro equality. He pronounced Lincoln's doctrine,
that the negro and the white man are made equal by
the Declaration of Independence and Divine Providence, "a monstrous heresy."

Lincoln protested that nothing was farther from
his purpose than to "advance hypocritical and deceptive and contrary views in different portions of the
country." As for the charge of sectionalism, Judge
Douglas was himself fast becoming sectional, for his
speeches no longer passed current south of the Ohio
as they had once done. "Whatever may be the result
of this ephemeral contest between Judge Douglas and
myself, I see the day rapidly approaching when his
pill of sectionalism, which he has been thrusting down
the throats of Republicans for years past, will be
crowded down his own throat."[2]

And Lincoln again scored on his opponent, when he

[1] Debates, p. 173.   [2] Ibid., p. 180.

pointed out that his political doctrine rested upon the major premise, that there was no wrong in slavery. "If you will take the Judge's speeches, and select the short and pointed sentences expressed by him,—as his declaration that he 'don't care whether slavery is voted up or down'—you will see at once that this is perfectly logical, if you do not admit that slavery is wrong. . . . Judge Douglas declares that if any community wants slavery they have a right to have it. He can say that logically, if he says that there is no wrong in slavery; but if you admit that there is a wrong in it, he cannot logically say that anybody has a right to do wrong."[1]

Those who now read these memorable debates dispassionately, will surely acquit Lincoln of inconsistency in his attitude toward the negro. His speech at Charleston supplements the speech at Chicago; at Galesburg, he made an admirable re-statement of his position. Nevertheless, there was a marked difference in point of emphasis between his utterances in Northern and in Southern Illinois. Even the casual reader will detect subtle omissions which the varying character of his audience forced upon Lincoln. In Chicago he said nothing about the physical inferiority of the negro; he said nothing about the equality of the races in the Declaration of Independence, when he spoke at Charleston. Among men of anti-slavery leanings, he had much to say about the moral wrong of slavery; in the doubtful counties, Lincoln was solicitous that he should not be understood as favoring social and political equality between whites and blacks.

Feeling keenly this diplomatic shifting of emphasis, Douglas persisted in accusing Lincoln of inconsistency:

[1] Debates, p. 181.

"He has one set of principles for the Abolition counties and another set for the counties opposed to Abolitionism." If Lincoln had said in Coles County what he has to-day said in old Knox, Douglas complained, "it would have settled the question between us in that doubtful county."[1] And in this Douglas was probably correct.

At Quincy, Douglas was in his old bailiwick. Three times the Democrats of this district had sent him to Congress; and though the bounds of the congressional district had since been changed, Adams County was still Democratic by a safe majority. Among the people who greeted the speakers, however, were many old-time Whigs, for whose special benefit the Republicans of the city carried on a pole, at the head of their procession, a live raccoon. With a much keener historic sense, the Democrats bore aloft a dead raccoon, suspended by its tail.[2]

Lincoln again harked back to his position that slavery was "a moral, a social, and a political wrong" which the Republican party proposed to prevent from growing any larger; and that "the leading man—I think I may do my friend Judge Douglas the honor of calling him such—advocating the present Democratic policy, never himself says it is wrong."[3]

The consciousness that he was made to seem morally obtuse, cut Douglas to the quick. Even upon his tough constitution this prolonged campaign was beginning to tell. His voice was harsh and broken; and he gave unmistakable signs of nervous irritability,

---

[1] Debates, p. 188.
[2] Mr. Horace White in Herndon-Weik, Lincoln, II, pp. 123-124.
[3] Debates, p. 198.

brought on by physical fatigue. When he rose to reply to Lincoln, his manner was offensively combative. At the outset, he referred angrily to Lincoln's "gross personalities and base insinuations."[1] In his references to the Springfield resolutions and to his mistake, or rather the mistake of his friends at the capital, he was particularly denunciatory. "When I make a mistake," he boasted, "as an honest man, I correct it without being asked to, but when he, Lincoln, makes a false charge, he sticks to it and never corrects it."[2]

But Douglas was too old a campaigner to lose control of himself, and no doubt the rude charge and counter-charge were prompted less by personal ill-will than by controversial exigencies. Those who have conceived Douglas as the victim of deep-seated and abiding resentment toward Lincoln, forget the impulsive nature of the man. There is not the slightest evidence that Lincoln took these blows to heart. He had himself dealt many a vigorous blow in times past. It was part of the game.

Douglas found fault with Lincoln's answers to the Ottawa questions: "I ask you again, Lincoln, will you vote to admit New Mexico, when she has the requisite population with such a constitution as her people adopt, either recognizing slavery or not, as they shall determine?" He was well within the truth when he asserted that Lincoln's answer had been purposely evasive and equivocal, "having no reference to any territory now in existence."[3] Of Lincoln's Republican policy of confining slavery within its present limits, by prohibiting it in the Territories, he said, "When he

[1] Debates, p. 199; *McClure's Magazine*, January, 1907.
[2] Debates, p. 201.   [3] *Ibid.*, p. 201.

gets it thus confined, and surrounded, so that it cannot
spread, the natural laws of increase will go on until
the negroes will be so plenty that they cannot live on
the soil. He will hem them in until starvation seizes
them, and by starving them to death, he will put slavery
in the course of ultimate extinction."[1]   A silly argument which Douglas's wide acquaintance with Southern conditions flatly contradicted and should have kept
him from repeating.

To the charge of moral obliquity on the slavery question, Douglas made a dignified and worthy reply. "I
hold that the people of the slave-holding States are
civilized men as well as ourselves; that they bear consciences as well as we, and that they are accountable
to God and their posterity, and not to us. It is for
them to decide, therefore, the moral and religious
right of the slavery question for themselves within
their own limits."[2]

On the following day both Lincoln and Douglas took
passage on a river steamer for Alton. The county of
Madison had once been Whig in its political proclivities. In the State legislature it was now represented
by two representatives and a senator who were Native
Americans; and in the present campaign, the county
was classed as doubtful. In Alton and elsewhere there
was a large German vote which was likely to sway the
election.

Douglas labored under a physical disadvantage. His
voice was painful to hear, while Lincoln's betrayed no
sign of fatigue.[3] Both fell into the argument *ad homi-
nem*. Lincoln advocated holding the Territories open

[1] Debates, p. 204.   [2] *Ibid.*, p. 209.
[3] Mr. Horace White in Herndon-Weik, Lincoln, II, p. 124.

to "free white people" the world over—to "Hans, Baptiste, and Patrick." Douglas contended that the equality referred to in the Declaration of Independence, was the equality of white men—"men of European birth and European descent." Both conjured with the revered name of Clay. Douglas persistently referred to Lincoln as an Abolitionist, knowing that his auditors had "strong sympathies southward," as Lincoln shrewdly guessed; while Lincoln sought to unmask that "false statesmanship that undertakes to build up a system of policy upon the basis of caring nothing about the very thing that everybody does care the most about."[1]

Douglas made a successful appeal to the sympathy of the crowd, when he said of his conduct in the Lecompton fight, "Most of the men who denounced my course on the Lecompton question objected to it, not because I was not right, but because they thought it expedient at that time, for the sake of keeping the party together, to do wrong. I never knew the Democratic party to violate any one of its principles, out of policy or expediency, that it did not pay the debt with sorrow. There is no safety or success for our party unless we always do right, and trust the consequences to God and the people. I chose not to depart from principle for the sake of expediency on the Lecompton question, and I never intend to do it on that or any other question."[2]

Both at Quincy and at Alton, Douglas paid his respects to the "contemptible crew" who were trying to break up the party and defeat him. At first he had avoided direct attacks upon the administration; but

[1] Debates, p. 231.   [2] *Ibid.*, p. 218.

the relentless persecution of the Washington *Union* made him restive. Lincoln derived great satisfaction from this intestine warfare in the Democratic camp. "Go it, husband! Go it, bear!" he cried.

In this last debate, both sought to summarize the issues. Said Lincoln, "You may turn over everything in the Democratic policy from beginning to end, . . . it everywhere carefully excludes the idea that there is anything wrong in it [slavery].

"That is the real issue. That is the issue that will continue in this country when these poor tongues of Judge Douglas and myself shall be silent. It is the eternal struggle between these two principles—right and wrong—throughout the world. . . . I was glad to express my gratitude at Quincy, and I re-express it here, to Judge Douglas,—*that he looks to no end of the institution of slavery.* That will help the people to see where the struggle really is."[1]

To the mind of Douglas, the issue presented itself in quite another form. "He [Lincoln] says that he looks forward to a time when slavery shall be abolished everywhere. I look forward to a time when each State shall be allowed to do as it pleases. If it chooses to keep slavery forever, it is not my business, but its own; if it chooses to abolish slavery, it is its own business,—not mine. I care more for the great principle of self-government, the right of the people to rule, than I do for all the negroes in Christendom. I would not endanger the perpetuity of this Union, I would not blot out the great inalienable rights of the white men, for all the negroes that ever existed."[2]

With this encounter at Alton, the joint debates, but

[1] Debates, p. 234.   [2] *Ibid.*, p. 238.

not the campaign closed. Douglas continued to speak at various strategic points, in spite of inclement weather and physical exhaustion, up to the eve of the election.[1] The canvass had continued just a hundred days, during which Douglas had made one hundred and thirty speeches.[2] During the last weeks of the campaign, election canards designed to injure Douglas were sedulously circulated, adding no little uncertainty to the outcome in doubtful districts. The most damaging of these stories seems to have emanated from Senator John Slidell of Louisiana, whose midsummer sojourn in Illinois has already been noted. A Chicago journal published the tale that Douglas's slaves in the South were "the subjects of inhuman and disgraceful treatment—that they were hired out to a factor at fifteen dollars per annum each—that he, in turn, hired them out to others in lots, and that they were ill-fed, over-worked, and in every way so badly treated that they were spoken of in the neighborhood where they are held as a disgrace to all slave-holders and the system they support." The explicit denial of the story came from Slidell some weeks after the election, when the slander had accomplished the desired purpose.[3]

All signs pointed to a heavy vote for both tickets. As the campaign drew to a close, the excitement reached a pitch rarely equalled even in presidential elections. Indeed, the total vote cast exceeded that of 1856 by many thousands,—an increase that cannot be wholly accounted for by the growth of population in these years.[4] The Republican State ticket was

[1] Sheahan, Douglas, p. 432.

[2] Nicolay and Hay, Lincoln, II, p. 146 note.

[3] Sheahan, Douglas, pp. 439-442; Herndon-Weik, Lincoln, II, p. 128.

[4] It has not been generally observed that the Democrats gained more

elected by less than four thousand votes over the Democratic ticket. The relative strength of the rival candidates for the senatorship, however, is exhibited more fully in the vote for the members of the lower house of the State legislature. The avowed Douglas candidates polled over 174,000, while the Lincoln men received something over 190,000. Administration candidates received a scant vote of less than 2,000. Notwithstanding this popular majority, the Republicans secured only thirty-five seats, while the Democratic minority secured forty. Out of fifteen contested senatorial seats, the Democrats won eight with a total of 44,826 votes, while the Republicans cast 53,784 votes and secured but seven. No better proof could be offered of Lincoln's contention that the State was gerrymandered in favor of the Democrats. Still, this was part of the game; and had the Republicans been in office, they would have undoubtedly used an advantage which has proved too tempting for the virtue of every American party.

When the two houses of the Illinois Legislature met in joint session, January 6, 1859, not a man ventured, or desired, to record his vote otherwise than as his party affiliations dictated. Douglas received fifty-four votes and Lincoln forty-six. "Glory to God and the Sucker Democracy," telegraphed the editor of the *State Register* to his chief. And back over the wires from Washington was flashed the laconic message, "Let the voice of the people rule." But had the *will* of the people ruled?

than their opponents over the State contest of 1856. The election returns were as follows:

Democratic ticket in 1856, 106,643; in 1858, 121,609; gain, 14,966.
Republican ticket in 1856, 111,375; in 1858, 125,430; gain, 14,055.

CHAPTER XVII

THE AFTERMATH

Douglas had achieved a great personal triumph. Not even his Republican opponents could gainsay it. In the East, the Republican newspapers .applauded him undisguisedly, not so much because they admired him or lacked sympathy with Lincoln, as because they regarded his re-election as a signal. condemnation of the Buchanan administration. Moreover, there was a general expectation in anti-slavery circles to which Theodore Parker gave expression when he wrote, "Had Lincoln succeeded, Douglas would be a ruined man. . . . But now in place for six years more, with his own personal power unimpaired and his positional influence much enhanced, he can do the Democratic party a world of damage."[1] There was cheer in this expectation even for those who deplored the defeat of Lincoln.

As Douglas journeyed southward soon after the November elections, he must have felt the poignant truth of Lincoln's shrewd observation that he was himself becoming sectional. Though he was received with seeming cordiality at Memphis and New Orleans, he could not but notice that his speeches, as Lincoln predicted, "would not go current south of the Ohio River as they had formerly." Democratic audiences applauded his bold insistence upon the universality of the principles of the party creed, but the tone of the

[1] Weiss, Life and Correspondence of Theodore Parker, II, p. 243.

Southern press was distinctly unfriendly to him and his Freeport doctrine.[1] He told his auditors at Memphis that he indorsed the decision of the Supreme Court; he believed that the owners of slaves had the same right to take them into the Territories as they had to take other property; but slaves once in the Territory were then subject to local laws for protection, on an equal footing with all other property. If no local laws protecting slave property were passed, slavery would be practically excluded. "Non-action is exclusion." It was a matter of soil, climate, interests, whether a Territory would permit slavery or not. "You come right back to the principle of dollars and cents... If old Joshua R. Giddings should raise a colony in Ohio and settle down in Louisiana, he would be the strongest advocate of slavery in the whole South; he would find when he got there, his opinion would be very much modified; he would find on those sugar plantations that it was not a question between the white man and the negro, but between the negro and the crocodile." "The Almighty has drawn the line on this continent, on one side of which the soil must be cultivated by slave labor; on the other by white labor."[2]

At New Orleans, he repeated more emphatically much the same thought. "There is a line, or belt of country, meandering through the valleys and over the mountain tops, which is a natural barrier between free territory and slave territory, on the south of which are to be found the productions suitable to slave labor, while on the north exists a country adapted to free

---

[1] Rhodes, History of the United States, II, p. 355.

[2] Memphis *Avalanche*, November 30, 1858, quoted by Chicago *Times*, December 8, 1858.

labor alone. . . . But in the great central regions, where there may be some doubt as to the effect of natural causes, who ought to decide the question except the people residing there, who have all their interests there, who have gone there to live with their wives and children?''[1]

It was characteristic of the man that he thought politics even when he was in pursuit of health. Advised to take an ocean voyage, he decided to visit Cuba so that even his recreative leisure might be politically profitable, for the island was more than ever coveted by the South and he wished to have the advantage of first-hand information about this unhappy Spanish province. Landing in New York upon his return, he was given a remarkable ovation by the Democracy of the city; and he was greeted with equal warmth in Philadelphia and Baltimore.[2] Even a less ambitious man might have been tempted to believe in his own capacity for leadership, in the midst of these apparently spontaneous demonstrations of regard. At the capital, however, he was less cordially welcomed. He was not in the least surprised, for while he was still in the South, the newspapers had announced his deposition from the chairmanship of the Committee on Territories. He knew well enough what he had to expect from the group of Southern Democrats who had the ear of the administration.[3] Nevertheless, his removal from a position which he had held ever since he entered the Senate was a bitter pill.

[1] New Orleans *Delta*, December 8, 1858, quoted by Chicago *Times*, December 19, 1858.

[2] Rhodes, History of United States, II, p. 355.

[3] See reported conversation of Douglas with the editor of the Chicago *Press and Tribune*, Hollister, Life of Colfax, p. 123.

For the sake of peace Douglas smothered his resentment, and, for a brief time at least, sought to demonstrate his political orthodoxy in matters where there was no conflict of opinion. As a member of the Committee on Foreign Affairs, he cordially supported the bill for the purchase of Cuba, even though the chairman, Slidell, had done more to injure him in the recent campaign than any other man. There were those who thought he demeaned himself by attending the Democratic caucus and indorsing the Slidell project.[1]

It was charged that the proposed appropriation of $30,000,000 was to be used to bribe Spanish ministers to sell Cuba; that the whole project was motived by the desire of the South to acquire more slave territory; and that Douglas was once more cultivating the South to secure the presidency in 1860. The first of these charges has never been proved; the second is probably correct; but the third is surely open to question. As long ago as Polk's administration, Douglas had expressed his belief that the Pearl of the Antilles must some day fall to us; and on various occasions he had advocated the annexation of Cuba, with the consent of Spain and the inhabitants. At New Orleans, he had been called upon to express his views regarding the acquisition of the island; and he had said, without hesitation, "It is folly to debate the acquisition of Cuba. It naturally belongs to the American continent. It guards the mouth of the Mississippi River, which is the heart of the American continent and the body of the American nation." At the same time he was care-

---

[1] Letcher to Crittenden; Coleman. Life of John J. Crittenden, II, p. 171; Hollister, Colfax, p. 124.

ful to add that he was no filibuster: he desired Cuba only upon terms honorable to all concerned.[1]

Subsequent events acquit Douglas of truckling to the South at this time. No doubt he would have been glad to let bygones be bygones, to close up the gap of unpleasant memories between himself and the administration, and to restore Democratic harmony. For Douglas loved his party and honored its history. To him the party of Jefferson and Jackson was inseparably linked with all that made the American Commonwealth the greatest of democracies. Yet where men are acutely conscious of vital differences of opinion, only the hourly practice of self-control can prevent clashing. Neither Douglas nor his opponents were prepared to undergo any such rigid self-discipline.

On February 23d, the pent-up feeling broke through all barriers and laid bare the thoughts and intents of the Democratic factions. The Kansas question once more recurring, Brown of Mississippi now demanded adequate protection for property; that is, "protection sufficient to protect animate property." Any other protection would be a delusion and a cheat. If the territorial legislature refused such protection, he for one would demand it of Congress. He dissented altogether from the doctrine of the Senator from Illinois, that by non-action, or unfriendly legislation a Territory could annul a decision of the Supreme Court and exclude slavery. That was mistaking power for right. "What I want to know is, whether you will interpose against power and in favor of right. . . . If the Territorial Legislature refuses to act, will you act? . . . . If it pass laws hostile to slavery, will you annul them,

[1] New Orleans *Delta*, December 8, 1858.

and substitute laws favoring slavery in their stead?"
"What I and my people ask is action; positive, unqualified action. Our understanding of the doctrine
of non-intervention was, that you were not to intervene against us, but I never understood that we could
have any compromise or understanding here which
could release Congress from an obligation imposed
on it by the Constitution of the United States."[1]

Reluctant as Douglas must have been to accentuate
the differences between himself and the Southern Democrats, he could not remain silent, for silence would be
misconstrued. With all the tact which he could muster
out of a not too abundant store, he sought to conciliate,
without yielding his own opinions. It was a futile
effort. At the very outset he was forced to deny the
right of slave property to other protection than common property. Thence he passed with wider and
wider divergence from the Southern position over the
familiar ground of popular sovereignty. To the specific demands which Brown had voiced, he replied that
Congress had never passed an act creating a criminal
code for any organized Territory, nor any law protecting any species of property. Congress had left
these matters to the territorial legislatures. Why,
then, make an exception of slave property? The Supreme Court had made no such distinction. "I know,"
said Douglas, in a tone little calculated to soothe the
feelings of his opponents, "I know that some gentlemen do not like the doctrine of non-intervention as
well as they once did. It is now becoming fashionable
to talk sneeringly of 'your doctrine of non-intervention.' Sir, that doctrine has been a fundamental

[1] *Globe,* 35 Cong., 2 Sess., p. 1243.

article in the Democratic creed for years." "If you repudiate the doctrine of non-intervention and form a slave code by act of Congress, when the people of a Territory refuse it, you must step off the Democratic platform. . . . I tell you, gentlemen of the South, in all candor, I do not believe a Democratic candidate can ever carry any one Democratic State of the North on the platform that it is the duty of the Federal government to force the people of a Territory to have slavery when they do not want it."[1]

What Brown had asserted with his wonted impulsiveness, was then reaffirmed more soberly by his colleague, Jefferson Davis, upon whom more than any other Southerner the mantle of Calhoun had fallen. State sovereignty was also his major premise. The Constitution was a compact. The Territories were common property of the States. The territorial legislatures were mere instruments through which the Congress of the United States "executed its trust in relation to the Territories." If, as the Senator from Illinois insisted, Congress had granted full power to the inhabitants of the Territories to legislate on all subjects not inconsistent with the Constitution, then Congress had exceeded its authority. Turning to Douglas, Davis said, "Now, the senator asks, will you make a discrimination in the Territories? I say, yes, I would discriminate in the Territories wherever it is needful to assert the right of citizens. . . . I have heard many a siren's song on this doctrine of non-intervention; a thing shadowy and fleeting, changing its color as often as the chameleon."[2]

[1] *Globe*, 35 Cong., 2 Sess., p. 1245.
[2] *Ibid.*, pp. 1247-1248.

When Douglas could again get the floor, he retorted sharply, "The senator from Mississippi says, if I am not willing to stand in the party on his platform, I can go out. Allow me to inform him that I stand on the platform, and those that jump off must go out of the party."

Hot words now passed between them. Davis spoke disdainfully of men who seek to build up a political reputation by catering to the prejudice of a majority, to exclude the property of the minority. And Douglas retorted, "I despise to see men from other sections of the Union pandering to a public sentiment against what I conceive to be common rights under the Constitution." "Holding the views that you do," said Davis, "you would have no chance of getting the vote of Mississippi to-day." The senator has "confirmed me in the belief that he is now as full of heresy as he once was of adherence to the doctrine of popular sovereignty, correctly construed; that he has gone back to his first love of squatter sovereignty, a thing offensive to every idea of conservatism and sound government."

Davis made repeated efforts to secure an answer to the question whether, in the event that slavery should be excluded by the people of a Territory and the Supreme Court should decide against such action, Douglas would maintain the rights of the slave-holders. Douglas replied, somewhat evasively, that when the Supreme Court should decide upon the constitutionality of the local laws, he would abide by the decision. "That is not the point," rejoined Davis impatiently; "Congress must compel the Territorial Legislature to perform its proper functions"; i. e. actively protect slave property. "Well," said Douglas with exasperating coolness, "on that point, the Senator and I differ. If the Territorial Legislature will not pass such laws as will encourage mules, I will not force them to have them." Again Davis insisted that his question had not been answered. Douglas repeated, "I will vote against any law by Congress attempting to interfere with a regulation made by the Territories, with respect to any kind of property whatever, whether horses, mules, negroes, or anything else."[1]

But there was a flaw in Douglas's armor which Green of Missouri detected. Had the Senator from Illinois not urged the intervention of Congress to prevent polygamy in Utah? "Not at all," replied Douglas; "the people of that Territory were in a state of rebellion against the Federal authorities." What he had urged was the repeal of the organic act of the Territory, so that the United States might exercise absolute jurisdiction and protect property in that region. "But if the people of a Territory took away property in slaves, were they not also defying the Federal authorities?" persisted Green. Unquestionably Congress might revoke the Kansas-Nebraska Act, Douglas admitted; but it should be remembered that the act was bottomed upon an agreement. There was a distinct understanding that the question whether territorial laws affecting the right of property in slaves were constitutional, should be referred to the Supreme Court. "If constitutional, they were to remain in force until repealed by the Territorial Legislature; if not, they were to become void not by action of Congress but by the decision of the court."[2] And Douglas quoted at

[1] *Globe*, 35 Cong., 2 Sess., p. 1259.
[2] *Ibid.*, p. 1258.

length from a speech by Senator Benjamin in 1856, to prove his point. But it was precisely this agreement of 1854, which was now being either repudiated or construed in the interest of the South. Jefferson Davis frankly deprecated the "great hazard" which representatives from his section ran in 1854; but, he added, "I take it for granted my friends who are about me must have understood at that time clearly that this was the mere reference of a right; and that if decided in our favor, congressional legislation would follow in its train, and secure to us the enjoyment of the right thus defined."[1]

The wide divergence of purpose and opinion which this debate revealed, dashed any hope of a united Democratic party in 1860. Men who looked into the future were sobered by the prospect. If the Democratic party were rent in twain,—the only surviving national party,—if Northerners and Southerners could no longer act together within a party of such elastic principles, what hope remained for the Union? The South was already boldly facing the inevitable. Said Brown, passionately, "If I cannot obtain the rights guaranteed to me and my people under the Constitution, as expounded by the Supreme Court, then, Sir, I am prepared to retire from the concern. . . . When our constitutional rights are denied us, we *ought* to retire from the Union. . . . If you are going to convert the Union into a masked battery from behind which to make war on me and my property, in the name of all the gods at once, why should I not retire from it?"[2]

After the 23d of February, Douglas neither gave

---

[1] *Globe*, 35 Cong., 2 Sess., p. 1256.
[2] *Ibid.*, p. 1243.

nor expected quarter from the Southern faction led by Jefferson Davis. So far from avoiding conflict, he seems rather to have forced the fighting. He flaunted his views in the faces of the fire-eaters. Prudence would have suggested silence, when a convention of Southern States met at Vicksburg and resolved that "all laws, State and Federal, prohibiting the African slave-trade, ought to be repealed,"[1] but Douglas, who knew something of the dimensions which this illicit traffic had already assumed, at once declared himself opposed to it. He said privately in a conversation, which afterwards was reported by an anonymous correspondent to the New York *Tribune,* that he believed fifteen thousand Africans were brought into the country last year. He had seen "with his own eyes three hundred of those recently imported miserable beings in a slave-pen at Vicksburg, Mississippi, and also large numbers at Memphis, Tennessee."[2]

In a letter which speedily became public property, Douglas said that he would not accept the nomination of the Democratic party, if the convention should interpolate into the party creed "such new issues as the revival of the African slave-trade, or a congressional slave code for the Territories."[3] And to leave no doubt as to his attitude he wrote a second letter, devoted exclusively to this subject; it also found its way, as the author probably intended it should, into the newspapers. He opposed the revival of the African slave-trade because it was abolished by one of the compromises which had made the Federal Union and the

---

[1] Rhodes, History of the United States, II, p. 371.
[2] *Ibid.,* pp. 369-370.
[3] Letter to J. B. Dorr, June 22, 1859; Flint, Douglas, pp. 168-169.

Constitution. "In accordance with this compromise, I am irreconcilably opposed to the revival of the African slave-trade, in any form and under any circumstances."[1] How deeply this unequivocal condemnation lacerated the feelings of the South, will never be known until the economic necessities and purposes of the large plantation owners are more clearly revealed.

The captious criticism of the Freeport doctrine by Southerners of the Calhoun-Jefferson Davis school was less damaging, from a legal point of view, than the sober analysis of Lincoln. The emphasis in Lincoln's famous question at Freeport fell upon the word *lawful:* "Can the people of a United States Territory, in any lawful way," etc. Douglas had replied to the question of legal right by an assertion of the power of the people of the Territories. This answer, as Lincoln pointed out subsequently, was equivalent to saying that "a thing may be lawfully driven away from where it has the lawful right to be."[2] As a prediction, Douglas's simple statement, that if the people of a Territory wanted slavery they would have it, and if they did not, they would not let it be forced on them, was fully justified by the facts of American history. It has been characteristic of the American people that, without irreverence for law, they have not allowed it to stand in the way of their natural development: they have not, as a rule, driven rough-shod over law, but have quietly allowed undesirable laws to fall into innocuous desuetude.

[1] Letter to J. L. Peyton, August 2, 1859; Sheahan, Douglas, pp. 465-466.

[2] Speech at Columbus, Ohio, September, 1859; see Debates, p. 250.

But such an answer was unworthy of a man who prided himself upon his fidelity to the obligation of the Constitution and the laws. Feeling the full force of Lincoln's inexorable logic,[1] but believing that it was bottomed on a false premise, Douglas endeavored to give his Freeport doctrine its proper constitutional setting. During the summer, he elaborated an historical and constitutional defense of popular sovereignty. The editors of *Harper's Magazine* so far departed from the traditions of that popular periodical as to publish this long and tedious essay in the September number. Douglas probably calculated that through this medium better than almost any other, he would reach those readers to whom Lincoln made his most effective appeal.[2]

The essay bore the title "The Dividing Line between Federal and Local Authority," with the sub-caption, "Popular Sovereignty in the Territories." In his interpretation of history, the author proved himself rather a better advocate than historian. He had traversed much the same ground in his speeches—and with far more vivacity and force. Douglas searched the colonial records, and found—one is tempted to say, to find—our fathers contending unremittingly for "the inalienable right, when formed into political communi-

[1] On his return to Washington after the debates, Douglas said to Wilson, "He [Lincoln] is an able and honest man, one of the ablest of the nation. I have been in Congress sixteen years, and there is not a man in the Senate I would not rather encounter in debate." Wilson, Slave Power in America, II, p. 577.

[2] It does not seem likely that Douglas hoped to reach the people of the South through *Harper's Magazine*, as it never had a large circulation south of Mason and Dixon's line. See Smith, Parties and Slavery, p. 292.

ties, to exercise exclusive power of legislation in their local legislatures in respect to all things affecting their internal polity—slavery not excepted.''[1]

Douglas took issue with the fundamental postulate of Lincoln's syllogism—that a Territory is the mere creature of Congress and cannot be clothed with powers not possessed by the creator. He denied that such an inference could be drawn from that clause in the Constitution which permits Congress to dispose of, and make all needful rules for, the territory or other property belonging to the United States. Names were deceptive. The word ''territory'' in this connection was not used in a political, but in a geographical sense. The power of Congress to organize governments for the Territories must be inferred rather from the power to admit new States into the Union. The Federal government possessed only expressly delegated powers; and the absence of any explicit authority to interfere in local territorial affairs must be held to inhibit any exercise of such power. It was on these grounds that the Supreme Court had ruled that Congress was not authorized by the Constitution to prohibit slavery in the Territories.

It had been erroneously held by some, continued the essayist, that the Court decided in the Dred Scott case that a territorial legislature could not legislate in respect to slave property like other property. He understood the Court to speak only of forbidden powers—powers denied to Congress, to State legislatures and to territorial legislatures alike. But if ever slavery should be decided to be one of these forbidden subjects of legislation, then the conclusion

[1] *Harper's Magazine*, XIX, p. 527.

would be inevitable that the Constitution established slavery in the Territories beyond the power of the people to control it by law, and guaranteed to every citizen the right to go there and be protected in the enjoyment of his slave property; then every member of Congress would be in duty bound to supply adequate protection, if the rights of property should be invaded. Not only so, but another conclusion would follow,— if the Constitution should be held to establish slavery in the Territories beyond the power of the people to control it,—Congress would be bound to provide adequate protection for slave property everywhere, *in the States* as well as in the Territories.

Douglas immediately went on to show that such was not the decision of the Court in the Dred Scott case. The Court had held that "the right of property in slaves is distinctly and expressly affirmed in the Constitution." Yes, but where? Why in that provision which speaks of persons "held to service or labor in one State, under the laws thereof"; not under the Constitution, not under the laws of Congress, Douglas emphasized, but *under the laws of the particular State where such service is due.* And so, when the Court declared that "the government, in express terms, is pledged to protect it [slave property] in all future time," it added "if the slave escapes from his owner." "This is the only contingency," Douglas maintained, "in which the Federal Government is authorized, required, or permitted to interfere with slavery in the States or Territories; and in that case only for the purpose of 'guarding and protecting the owner in his rights' to reclaim his slave property." Slave-owners, therefore, who moved with their property to a Territory, must hold it like all other property, subject to local law, and look to local authorities for its protection.

One other question remained: was the word "State," as used in the clause just cited, intended to include Territories? Douglas so contended. Otherwise, "the Territories must become a sanctuary for all fugitives from service and justice." In numerous clauses in the Constitution, the Territories were recognized as *States*.

Clever as this reasoning was, it clearly was not a fair exposition of the opinion of the Court in the case of Dred Scott. If the Court did not deny the right of a territorial legislature to interfere with slave property, it certainly left that proposition open to fair inference by the phrasing and emphasis of the critical passages. It should be noted that Douglas, in quoting the decision, misplaced the decisive clause so as to bring it in juxtaposition to the reference to the fugitive slave clause of the Constitution, thus redistributing the emphasis and confusing the real significance of the foregoing paragraph.[1] Douglas stated subsequently that he did not believe the decision of the Court reached the power of a territorial legislature, because there was no territorial legislature in the record nor any allusion to one; because there was no territorial enactment before the Court; and because there was no fact in the case alluding to or connected with territorial legislation.[2] All this was perfectly true.

[1] Compare the quotation in *Harper's*, p. 531, with the opinion of the Court, U. S. Supreme Court Reports, 19 How., p. 720. The clause beginning "And if the Constitution recognizes" is taken from its own paragraph and put in the middle of the following paragraph.

[2] *Globe*, 36 Cong., 1 Sess., p. 2152. This statement was confirmed

The opinion of the Court was *obiter dicens;* but the Court expressed its opinion nevertheless. As Lincoln said, men knew what to expect of the Court when a territorial act prohibiting slavery came before it. Yet this was what Douglas would not concede. He would not admit the inference. Congress could confer powers upon a territorial legislature which it could not itself exercise. The dividing line between Federal and local authority was so drawn as to permit Congress to institute governments with legislative, judicial, and executive functions but without permitting Congress to exercise those functions itself. From Douglas's point of view, a Territory was not a dependency of the Federal government, but an inchoate Commonwealth, endowed with many of the attributes of sovereignty possessed by the full-fledged States.

So unusual an event as a political contribution by a prominent statesman to a popular magazine, created no little excitement.[1] Attorney-General Black came to the defense of the South with an unsigned contribution to the Washington *Constitution,* the organ of the administration.[2] And Douglas, who had meantime gone to Ohio to take part in the State campaign, replied caustically to this critique in his speech at Wooster, September 16th. Black rejoined in a pamphlet under his own name. Whereupon Douglas returned to the attack with a slashing pamphlet, which he sent to the printer in an unfinished form and which did him little credit.[3]

by Reverdy Johnson, who was one of the lawyers that argued the case. See the speech of Reverdy Johnson, June 7, 1860.

[1] Rhodes, History of the United States, II., p. 374.

[2] Washington *Constitution,* September 10, 1859. The article was afterward published in a collection of his essays and speeches.

[3] Flint, Douglas, p. 181.

This war of pamphlets was productive of no results. Douglas and Black were wide apart upon their major premises, and diverged inevitably in their conclusions. Holding fast to the premise that a Territory was not sovereign but a "subordinate dependency," Black ridiculed the attempts of Douglas to clothe it, not with complete sovereignty but with "the attributes of sovereignty."[1] Then Douglas denounced in scathing terms the absurdity of Black's assumption that property in the Territories would be held by the laws of the State from which it came, while it must look for redress of wrongs to the law of its new domicile.[2]

The Ohio campaign attracted much attention throughout the country, not only because the gubernatorial candidates were thoroughgoing representatives of the Republican party and of Douglas Democracy, but because both Lincoln and Douglas were again brought into the arena.[3] While the latter did not meet in joint debate, their successive appearance at Columbus and Cincinnati gave the campaign the aspect of a prolongation of the Illinois contest. Lincoln devoted no little attention to the *Harper's Magazine* article, while Douglas defended himself and his doctrine against all comers. There was a disposition in many quarters to concede that popular sovereignty, whether theoretically right or wrong, would settle the question of slavery in the Territories.[4] Apropos of Douglas's

[1] One of the most interesting commentaries on Black's argument is his defense of the people of Utah, many years later, against the Anti-Polygamy Laws, when he used Douglas's argument without the slightest qualms. See Essays and Speeches, pp. 603, 604, 609.

[2] Flint, Douglas, pp. 172-181 gives extracts from these pamphlets.

[3] Rhodes History of United States, II, p. 381.

[4] *Ibid.*, p. 382.

speech at Columbus, the New York *Times* admitted that at least his principles were "definite" and uttered in a "frank, gallant and masculine" spirit;[1] and his speeches were deemed of enough importance to be printed entire in the columns of this Republican journal. "He means to go to Charleston," guessed the editor shrewdly, "as the unmistakable representative of the Democratic party of the North and to bring this influence to bear upon Southern delegates as the only way to secure their interests against anti-slavery sentiment represented by the Republicans. He will claim that not a single Northern State can be carried on a platform more pro-slavery than his. The Democrats of the North have yielded all they will."[2]

While Douglas was in Ohio, he was saddened by the intelligence that Senator Broderick of California, his loyal friend and staunch supporter in the Lecompton fight, had fallen a victim to the animosity of the Southern faction in his State. The Washington *Constitution* might explain his death as an affair of honor —he was shot in a duel—but intelligent men knew that Broderick's assailant had desired to rid Southern "chivalry" of a hated political opponent.[3] A month later, on the night of October 16th, John Brown of Kansas fame marshalled his little band of eighteen men and descended upon the United States arsenal at Harper's Ferry. What did these events portend?

[1] New York *Times*, September 9, 1859.
[2] *Ibid.*, September 9, 1859.
[3] Rhodes, History of the United States, II, pp. 374-379.

CHAPTER XVIII

The Campaign of 1860

Deeds of violence are the inevitable precursors of an approaching war. They are so many expressions of that estrangement which is at the root of all sectional conflicts. The raid of John Brown upon Harper's Ferry, like his earlier lawless acts in Kansas, was less the crime of an individual than the manifestation of a deep social unrest. Occurring on the eve of a momentous presidential election, it threw doubts upon the finality of any appeal to the ballot. The antagonism between North and South was such as to make an appeal to arms seem a probable last resort. The political question of the year 1860 was whether the law-abiding habit of the American people and the traditional mode of effecting changes in governmental policy, would be strong enough to withstand the primitive instinct to decide the question of right by an appeal to might. To actors in the drama the question assumed this simple, concrete form: could the national Democratic party maintain its integrity and achieve another victory over parties which were distinctly sectional?

The passions aroused by the Harper's Ferry episode had no time to cool before Congress met. They were again inflamed by the indorsement of Helper's "Impending Crisis" by influential Republicans. As the author was a poor white of North Carolina who hated slavery and desired to prove that the institution was

412

inimical to the interests of his class, the book was regarded by slave-holders as an incendiary publication, conceived in the same spirit as John Brown's raid. The contest for the Speakership of the House turned upon the attitude of candidates toward this book. At the North "The Impending Crisis" had great vogue, passing through many editions. All events seemed to conspire to prevent sobriety of judgment and moderation in speech.

From a legislative point of view, this exciting session of Congress was barren of results. The paramount consideration was the approaching party conventions. What principles and policies would control the action of the Democratic convention at Charleston, depended very largely upon who should control the great body of delegates. Early in January various State conventions in the Northwest expressed their choice. Illinois took the lead with a series of resolutions which rang clear and true on all the cardinal points of the Douglas creed.[1] Within the next sixty days every State in the greater Northwest had chosen delegates to the national Democratic convention, pledged to support the nomination of Stephen A. Douglas.[2] It was with the knowledge, then, that he spoke for the Democracy of the Northwest that Douglas took issue with those Southern senators who plumed themselves on their party orthodoxy.

In a debate which was precipitated by a resolution of Senator Pugh, the old sores were rent open. Senator Davis of Mississippi was particularly irritating in his allusions to the Freeport, and other recent, heresies of the Senator from Illinois. In the give and

[1] Flint, Douglas, pp. 205-207.   [2] Ibid., pp. 207-209.

take which followed, Douglas was beset behind and before. But his fighting blood was up and he promised to return blow for blow, with interest. Let every man make his assault, and when all were through, he would "fire into the lump."[1] "I am not seeking a nomination," he declared, "I am willing to take one provided I can assume it on principles that I believe to be sound; but in the event of your making a platform that I could not conscientiously execute in good faith if I were elected, I will not stand upon it and be a candidate." For his part he would like to know "who it is that has the right to say who is in the party and who not?" He believed that he was backed by two-thirds of the Democracy of the United States. Did one-third of the Democratic party propose to read out the remaining two-thirds? "I have no grievances, but I have no concessions. I have no abandonment of position or principle; no recantation to make to any man or body of men on earth."[2]

Some days later Douglas made it equally clear that he had no recantation to make for the sake of Republican support. Speaking of the need of some measure by which the States might be protected against acts of violence like the Harper's Ferry affair, he roundly denounced that outrage as "the natural, logical, inevitable result of the doctrines and teachings of the Republican party, as explained and enforced in their platform, their partisan presses, their pamphlets and books, and especially in the speeches of their leaders in and out of Congress."[3] True, they disavowed the *act* of John Brown, but they should also repudiate and

---

[1] *Globe,* 36 Cong., 1 Sess., p. 421.
[2] *Ibid.,* pp. 424-425. [3] *Ibid.,* p. 553.

denounce the doctrines and teachings which produced the act. Fraternal peace was possible only upon "that good old golden principle which teaches all men to mind their own business and let their neighbors' alone." When men so act, the Union can endure forever as the fathers made it, composed of free and slave States.[1] "Then the senator is really indifferent to slavery, as he is reported to have said?" queried Fessenden. "Sir," replied Douglas, "I hold the doctrine that a statesman will adapt his laws to the wants, conditions, and interests of the people to be governed by them. Slavery may be very essential in one climate and totally useless in another. If I were a citizen of Louisiana I would vote for retaining and maintaining slavery, because I believe the good of the people would require it. As a citizen of Illinois I am utterly opposed to it, because our interests would not be promoted by it."[2]

The lines upon which the Charleston convention would divide, were sharply drawn by a series of resolutions presented to the Senate by Jefferson Davis. They were intended to serve as an ultimatum, and they were so understood by Northern Democrats. They were deliberately wrought out in conference as the final expression of Southern conviction. In explicit language the right of either Congress or a territorial legislature to impair the constitutional right of property in slaves, was denied. In case of unfriendly legislation, it was declared to be the duty of Congress to provide adequate protection to slave property. Popular sovereignty was completely discarded by the assertion that

[1] *Globe,* 36 Cong., 1 Sess., pp. 554-555.
[2] *Ibid.,* p. 559.

the people of a Territory might pass upon the question of slavery only when they formed a State constitution.[1]

As the delegates to the Democratic convention began to gather in the latter part of April, the center of political interest shifted from Washington to Charleston. Here the battle between the factions was to be fought out, but without the presence of the real leaders. The advantages of organization were with the Douglas men. The delegations from the Northwest were devoted, heart and soul, to their chief. As they passed through the capital on their journey to the South, they gathered around him with noisy demonstrations of affection; and when they continued on their way, they were more determined than ever to secure his nomination.[2] From the South, too, every Douglas man who was likely to carry weight in his community, was brought to Charleston to labor among the Ultras of his section.[3] The Douglas headquarters in Hibernian Hall bore witness to the business-like way in which his candidacy was being promoted. Not the least striking feature within the committee rooms was the ample supply of Sheahan's *Life of Stephen A. Douglas,* fresh from the press.[4]

Recognized leader of the Douglas forces was Colonel Richardson of Illinois, a veteran in convention warfare, seasoned by years of congressional service and by long practice in managing men.[5] It was he who had led the Douglas cohorts in the Cincinnati convention. The memory of that defeat still rankled, and he was not disposed to yield to like contingencies. Indeed,

[1] *Globe*, 36 Cong., 1 Sess., p. 658. For the final version, see p. 935.

[2] Halstead, Political Conventions of 1860, p. 59.

[3] *Ibid.*, p. 29.   [4] *Ibid.*, p. 5.   [5] *Ibid.*, pp. 9 and 20.

the spirit of the delegates from the Northwest,—and they seemed likely to carry the other Northern delegates with them,—was offensively aggressive; and their demonstrations of enthusiasm assumed a minatory aspect, as they learned of the presence of Slidell, Bigler, and Bright, and witnessed the efforts of the administration to defeat the hero of the Lecompton fight.[1]

Those who observed the proceedings of the convention could not rid themselves of the impression that opposing parties were wrestling for control, so bitter and menacing was the interchange of opinion. It was matter of common report that the Southern delegations would withdraw if Douglas were nominated.[2] Equally ominous was the rumor that Richardson was authorized to withdraw the name of Douglas, if the platform adopted should advocate the protection of slavery in the Territories.[3] The temper of the convention was such as to preclude an amicable agreement, even if Douglas withdrew.

The advantages of compact organization and conscious purpose were apparent in the first days of the convention. At every point the Douglas men forced the fighting. On the second day, it was voted that where a delegation had not been instructed by a State convention how to give its vote, the individual delegates might vote as they pleased. This rule would work to the obvious advantage of Douglas.[4] On the third day, the convention refused to admit the contest-

[1] Halstead, Political Conventions of 1860, pp. 12-13.

[2] *Ibid.*, p. 8.   [3] *Ibid.*, p. 36.

[4] Especially in securing votes from the delegations of Massachusetts, Pennsylvania and New Jersey, where the influence of the administration was strong. Halstead, Political Conventions of 1860, pp. 25-28.

ing delegations from New York and Illinois, represented by Fernando Wood and Isaac Cook respectively.[1]

Meantime the committee on resolutions, composed of one delegate from each State, was in the throes of platform-making. Both factions had agreed to frame a platform before naming a candidate. But here, as in the convention, the possibility of amiable discussion and mutual concession was precluded. The Southern delegates voted in caucus to hold to the Davis resolutions; the Northern, with equal stubbornness, clung to the well-known principles of Douglas. On the fifth day of the convention, April 27th, the committee presented a majority report and two minority reports. The first was essentially an epitome of the Davis resolutions; the second reaffirmed the Cincinnati platform, at the same time pledging the party to abide by the decisions of the Supreme Court on those questions of constitutional law which should affect the rights of property in the States or Territories; and the third report simply reaffirmed the Cincinnati platform without additional resolutions.[2] The defense of the main minority report fell to Payne of Ohio. In a much more conciliatory spirit than Douglas men had hitherto shown, he assured the Southern members of the convention that every man who had signed the report felt that "upon the result of our deliberations and the action of this convention, in all human probability, depended the fate of the Democratic party and the destiny of the Union." The North was devoted to the principle of popular sovereignty, but "we ask nothing

[1] Halstead, Political Conventions of 1860, p. 36.
[2] Stanwood, History of the Presidency, pp. 283-288.

for the people of the territories but what the Constitution allows them.'"[1]   The argument of Payne was cogent and commended itself warmly to Northern delegates; but it struck Southern ears as a tiresome reiteration of arguments drawn from premises which they could not admit.

It was Yancey of Alabama, chief among fire-eaters, who, in the afternoon of the same day, warmed the cockles of the Southern heart.   Gifted with all the graces of Southern orators, he made an eloquent plea for Southern rights.   Protection was what the South demanded: protection in their constitutional rights and in their sacred rights of property.   The proposition contained in the minority report would ruin the South.   "You acknowledged that slavery did not exist by the law of nature or by the law of God—that it only existed by State law; that it was wrong, but that you were not to blame.   That was your position, and it was wrong.   If you had taken the position directly that slavery was right, and therefore ought to be . . . . you would have triumphed, and anti-slavery would now have been dead in your midst. . . . I say it in no disrespect, but it is a logical argument that your admission that slavery is wrong has been the cause of all this discord.'"[2]

These words brought Senator Pugh to his feet. Wrought to a dangerous pitch of excitement, he thanked God that a bold and honest man from the South had at last spoken, and had told the whole of the Southern demands. The South demanded now nothing less than that Northern Democrats should declare slavery to be

[1] Rhodes, History of the United States, II, p. 446.
[2] *Ibid.*, p. 448.

right. "Gentlemen of the South," he exclaimed, "you mistake us—you mistake us—we will not do it."[1] The convention adjourned before Pugh had finished; but in the evening he told the Southern delegates plainly that Northern Democrats were not children at the bidding of the South. If the gentlemen from the South could stay only on the terms they proposed, they must go. For once the hall was awed into quiet, for Senator Pugh stood close to Douglas and the fate of the party hung in the balance.[2]

Sunday intervened, but the situation remained unchanged. Gloom settled down upon the further deliberations of the convention. On Monday, the minority report (the Douglas platform) was adopted by a vote of 165 to 138. Thereupon the chairman of the Alabama delegation protested and announced the formal withdrawal of his State from the convention. The crisis had arrived. Mississippi, Louisiana, South Carolina, Florida, Texas, and Arkansas followed in succession, with valedictories which seemed directed less to the convention than to the Union. Indeed, more than one face blanched at the probable significance of this secession. Southerners of the Yancey following, however, were jubilant and had much to say about an independent Southern Republic.[3]

On the following day, what Yancey scornfully dubbed the "Rump Convention," proceeded to ballot, having first voted that two-thirds of the full vote of the convention should be necessary to nominate. On the first ballot, Douglas received 145½, Hunter of Virginia 42, Guthrie of Kentucky 35½, and the remaining thirty

---

[1] Halstead, Political Conventions of 1860, p. 49.
[2] Ibid., p. 50.   [3] Ibid., pp. 74-75.

were divided among several candidates. As 202 votes were necessary for a choice, the hopelessness of the outlook was apparent to all. Nevertheless, the balloting continued, the vote of Douglas increasing on four ballots to 152½. After the thirty-sixth ballot, he failed to command more than 151½. In all, fifty-seven ballots were taken.[1] On the tenth day of the convention, it was voted to adjourn to meet at Baltimore, on the 18th of June.

The followers of Douglas left Charleston with wrath in their hearts. Chagrin and disappointment alternated with bitterness and resentment toward their Southern brethren. Moreover, contact with the South, so far from having lessened their latent distrust of its culture and institutions, had widened the gulf between the sections. Such speeches as that of Goulden of Georgia, who had boldly advocated the re-opening of the African slave-trade, saying coarsely that "the African slave-trade man is the Union man—the Christian man," caused a certain ethical revolt in the feelings of men, hitherto not particularly susceptible to moral appeals on the slavery question.[2] Added to all these cumulative grievances was the uncomfortable probability, that the next President was about to be nominated in the Republican convention at Chicago.

What were the feelings of the individual who had been such a divisive force in the Charleston convention? The country was not long left in doubt. Douglas was quite ready to comment upon the outcome; and it needed only the bitter arraignment of his theories by Davis, to bring him armed *cap-a-pie* into the arena.

[1] Proceedings of the National Democratic Convention, pp. 46-53.
[2] Halstead, Political Conventions of 1860, p. 78.

Aided by his friend Pugh, who read long extracts from letters and speeches, Douglas made a systematic review of Democratic principles and policy since 1848. His object, of course, was to demonstrate his own consistency, and at the same time to convict his critics of apostasy from the party creed. There was, inevitably, much tiresome repetition in all this. It was when he directed his remarks to the issues at Charleston that Douglas warmed to his subject. He refused to recognize the right of a caucus of the Senate or of the House, to prescribe new tests, to draft party platforms. That was a task reserved, under our political system, for national conventions, made up of delegates chosen by the people. Tried by the standard of the only Democratic organization competent to pronounce upon questions of party faith, he was no longer a heretic, no longer an outlaw from the Democratic party, no longer a rebel against the Democratic organization. "The party decided at Charleston also, by a majority of the whole electoral college, that I was the choice of the Democratic party of America for the Presidency of the United States, giving me a majority of fifty votes over all other candidates combined; and yet my Democracy is questioned!" "But," he added, and there is no reason to doubt his sincerity, "my friends who know me best know that I have no personal desire or wish for the nomination; . . . . know that my name never would have been presented at Charleston, except for the attempt to proscribe me as a heretic, too unsound to be the chairman of a committee in this body, where I have held a seat for so many years without a suspicion resting on my political fidelity. I was forced to allow my name to go there in self-defense;

and I will now say that had any gentleman, friend or foe, received a majority of that convention over me, the lightning would have carried a message withdrawing my name from the convention."[1]

Douglas was ready to acquit his colleagues in the Senate of a purpose to dissolve the Union, but he did not hesitate to assert that such principles as Yancey had advocated at Charleston would lead "directly and inevitably" to a dissolution of the Union. Why was the South so eager to repudiate the principle of non-intervention? By it they had converted New Mexico into slave Territory; by it, in all probability, they would extend slavery into the northern States of Mexico, when that region should be acquired. "Why," he asked, "are you not satisfied with these practical results? The only difference of opinion is on the judicial question, about which we agreed to differ—which we never did decide; because, under the Constitution, no tribunal on earth but the Supreme Court could decide it." To commit the Democratic party to intervention was to make the party sectional and to invite never-ceasing conflict. "Intervention, North or South, means disunion; non-intervention promises peace, fraternity, and perpetuity to the Union, and to all our cherished institutions."[2]

The challenge contained in these words was not permitted to pass unanswered. Davis replied with offensive references to the "swelling manner" and "egregious vanity" of the Senator from Illinois. He resented such dictation.[3] On the following day, May 17th, an exciting passage-at-arms occurred between these rep-

---

[1] *Globe,* 36 Cong., 1 Sess., App., p. 313.
[2] *Ibid.,* p. 316.   [3] *Globe,* 36 Cong., 1 Sess., p. 2120.

resentatives of the Northwest and the Southwest. Douglas repeated his belief that disunion was the prompting motive which broke up the Charleston convention. Davis resented the insinuation, with fervent protestations of affection for the Union of the States. It was the Senator from Illinois, who, in his pursuit of power, had prevented unanimity, by trying to plant his theory upon the party. The South would have no more to do with the "rickety, double-construed platform" of 1856. "The fact is," said Davis, "I have a declining respect for platforms. I would sooner have an honest man on any sort of a rickety platform you could construct, than to have a man I did not trust on the best platform which could be made. A good platform and an honest man on it is what we want."[1] Douglas reminded his opponent sharply that the bolters at Charleston seceded, not on the candidate, but on the platform. "If the platform is not a matter of much consequence, why press that question to the disruption of the party? Why did you not tell us in the beginning of this debate that the whole fight was against the man, and not upon the platform?"[2]

In the interval between the Charleston and the Baltimore conventions, the Davis resolutions were pressed to a vote in the Senate, with the purpose of shaping party opinion. They passed by votes which gave a deceptive appearance of Democratic unanimity. Only Senator Pugh parted company with his Democratic colleagues on the crucial resolution; yet he represented the popular opinion at the North.[3] The futility of these resolutions, so far as practical results were con-

[1] *Globe*, 36 Cong., 1 Sess., p. 2155.   [2] *Ibid.*, p. 2156.
[3] Rhodes, History of the United States, II, p. 456.

cerned, was demonstrated by the adoption of Clingman's resolution, that the existing condition of the
Territories did not require the intervention of Congress
for the protection of property in slaves.[1] In other
words, the South was insisting upon rights which were
barren of practical significance. Slave-holders were
insisting upon the right to carry their slaves where
local conditions were unfavorable, and where therefore they had no intention of going.[2]

The nomination of Lincoln rather than Seward, at
the Republican convention in Chicago, was a bitter
disappointment to those who felt that the latter was
the real leader of the party of moral ideas, and that
the rail-splitter was simply an "available" candidate.[3]
But Douglas, with keener insight into the character of
Lincoln, said to a group of Republicans at the Capitol,
"Gentlemen, you have nominated a very able and a
very honest man.'"[4] For the candidate of the new Constitutional Union party, which had rallied the politically unattached of various opinions in a convention
at Baltimore, Douglas had no such words of praise,
though he recognized John Bell as a Unionist above
suspicion and as an estimable gentleman.

These nominations rendered it still less prudent for
Northern Democrats to accept a candidate with
stronger Southern leanings than Douglas. No Northern Democrat could carry the Northern States on a
Southern platform; and no Southern Democrat would
accept a nomination on the Douglas platform. Unless

---

[1] *Globe,* 36 Cong., 1 Sess., p. 2344.
[2] See Wise, Life of Henry A. Wise, pp. 264-265.
[3] Rhodes, History of the United States, II, p. 472.
[4] *Ibid.,* p. 472.

some middle ground could be found,—and the debates in the Senate had disclosed none,—the Democrats of the North were bound to adhere to Douglas as their first and only choice in the Baltimore convention.

When the delegates reassembled in Baltimore, the factional quarrel had lost none of its bitterness. Almost immediately the convention fell foul of a complicated problem of organization. Some of the original delegates, who had withdrawn at Charleston, desired to be re-admitted. From some States there were contesting delegations, notably from Louisiana and Alabama, where the Douglas men had rallied in force. Those anti-Douglas delegates who were still members of the convention, made every effort to re-admit the delegations hostile to him. The action of the convention turned upon the vote of the New York delegation, which would be cast solidly either for or against the admission of the contesting delegations. For three days the fate of Douglas was in the hands of these thirty-five New Yorkers, in whom the disposition to bargain was not wanting.[1] It was at this juncture that Douglas wrote to Dean Richmond, the *Deus ex machina* in the delegation,[2] "If my enemies are determined to divide and destroy the Democratic party, and perhaps the country, rather than see me elected, and if the unity of the party can be preserved, and its ascendancy perpetuated by dropping my name and uniting upon some reliable non-intervention and Union-loving Democrat, I beseech you, in consultation with my friends, to pursue that course which will save the country, without regard to my individual interests. I mean all this

[1] Halstead, Political Conventions of 1860, pp. 227-228.
[2] *Ibid.*, pp. 194-195.

letter implies. Consult freely and act boldly for the right.'"[1]

It was precisely the "if's" in this letter that gave the New Yorkers most concern. Where was the candidate who possessed these qualifications and who would be acceptable to the South? On the fifth day of the convention, the contesting Douglas delegations were admitted. The die was cast. A portion of the Virginia delegation then withdrew, and their example was followed by nearly all the delegates from North Carolina, Tennessee, Kentucky and Maryland. If the first withdrawal at Charleston presaged the secession of the cotton States from the Union, this pointed to the eventual secession of the border States.

On June 23d, the convention proceeded to ballot. Douglas received 173½ votes; Guthrie 10; and Breckinridge 5; scattering 3. On the second ballot, Douglas received all but thirteen votes; whereupon it was moved and carried unanimously with a tremendous shout that Douglas, having received "two-thirds of all votes given in this convention," should be the nominee of the party.[2] Colonel Richardson then begged leave to have the Secretary read a letter from Senator Douglas. He had carried it in his pocket for three days, but the course of the bolters, he said, had prevented him from using it.[3] The letter was of the same tenor as that written to Dean Richmond. There is little likelihood that an earlier acquaintance with its contents would have changed the course of events,

[1] The letter was written at Washington, June 22d, at 9:30 a. m.

[2] Stanwood, History of the Presidency, p. 286; Halstead, Political Conventions of 1860, p. 211.

[3] Halstead, p. 216.

since so long as the platform stood unaltered, the choice of Douglas was a logical and practical necessity. Douglas and the platform were one and inseparable.

Meantime the bolters completed their destructive work by organizing a separate convention in Baltimore, by adopting the report of the majority in the Charleston convention as their platform, and by nominating John C. Breckinridge as their candidate for the presidency. Lane of Oregon was named for the second place on the ticket for much the same reason that Fitzpatrick of Alabama, and subsequently Herschel V. Johnson of Georgia, was put upon the Douglas ticket. Both factions desired to demonstrate that they were national Democrats, with adherents in all sections. In his letter of acceptance Douglas rang the changes on the sectional character of the doctrine of intervention either for or against slavery. "If the power and duty of Federal interference is to be conceded, two hostile sectional parties must be the inevitable result—the one inflaming the passions and ambitions of the North, the other of the South."[1] Indeed, his best,—his only,—chance of success lay in his power to appeal to conservative, Union-loving men, North and South. This was the secret purpose of his frequent references to Clay and Webster, who were invoked as supporters of "the essential, living principle of 1850"; i. e. his own doctrine of non-intervention by Congress with slavery in the Territories. But the Constitutional Union party was quite as likely to attract the remnant of the old Whig party of Clay and Webster.

[1] Flint, Douglas, pp. 213-215.

Douglas began his campaign in excellent spirits. His only regret was that he had been placed in a position where he had to look on and see a fight without taking a hand in it.[1] The New York *Times,* whose editor followed the campaign of Douglas with the keenest interest, without indorsing him, frankly conceded that popular sovereignty had a very strong hold upon the instinct of nine-tenths of the American people.[2] Douglas wrote to his Illinois confidant in high spirits after the ratification meeting in New York.[3] Conceding South Carolina and possibly Mississippi to Breckinridge, and the border slave States to Bell, he expressed the firm conviction that he would carry the rest of the Southern States and enough free States to be elected by the people. Richardson had just returned from New England, equally confident that Douglas would carry Maine, New Hampshire, Rhode Island, and Connecticut. If the election should go to the House of Representatives, Douglas calculated that Lincoln, Bell, and he would be the three candidates. In any event, he was sure that Breckinridge and Lane had "no show." He enjoined his friends everywhere to treat the Bell and Everett men in a friendly way and to cultivate good relations with them, "for they are Union men." But, he added, "we can have no partnership with the Bolters." "Now organize and rally in Illinois and the Northwest. The chances in our favor are immense in the East. Organize the State!"

Buoyed up by these sanguine expectations, Douglas

---

[1] New York *Times,* July 3, 1860.   [2] *Ibid.,* June 26.

[3] MS. letter, Douglas to C. H. Lanphier, July 5, 1860. He wrote in a similar vein to a friend in Missouri, July 4, 1860.

undertook a tour through New England, not to make stump speeches, he declared, but to visit and enhearten his followers. Yet at every point on the way to Boston, he was greeted with enthusiasm; and whenever time permitted he responded with brief allusions to the political situation. As the guest of Harvard University, at the alumni dinner, he was called upon to speak— not, to be sure, as a candidate for the presidency, but as one high in the councils of the nation, and as a generous contributor to the founding of an educational institution in Chicago.[1] A visit to Bunker Hill suggested the great principle for which our Revolutionary fathers fought and for which all good Democrats were now contending.[2] At Springfield, too, he harked back to the Revolution and to the beginnings of the great struggle for control of domestic concerns.[3]

Along the route from Boston to Saratoga, he was given ovations, and his diffidence about making stump speeches lessened perceptibly.[4] At Troy, he made a political speech in his own vigorous style, remarking apologetically that if he did not return home soon, he would "get to making stump speeches before he knew it."[5] Passing through Vermont, he visited the grave of his father and the scenes of his childhood; and here and there, as he told the people of Concord with a twinkle in his eye, he spoke "a little just for exercise." Providence recalled the memory of Roger Williams and the principles for which he suffered— principles so nearly akin to those for which Democrats to-day were laboring. By this time the true nature

---

[1] New York *Times*, July 20, 1860.
[2] *Ibid.*, July 21.   [3] *Ibid.*, July 21.
[4] *Ibid.*, July 24.   [5] *Ibid.*, July 28.

of this pilgrimage was apparent to everybody. It was the first time in our history that a presidential candidate had taken the stump in his own behalf. There was bitter criticism on the part of those who regretted the departure from decorous precedent.[1] When Douglas reached Newport for a brief sojourn, the expectation was generally entertained that he would continue in retirement for the remainder of the campaign.

Except for this anomaly of a candidate canvassing in his own behalf, the campaign was devoid of exciting incidents. The personal canvass of Douglas was indeed almost the only thing that kept the campaign from being dull and spiritless.[2] Republican politicians were somewhat at a loss to understand why he should manoeuvre in a section devoted beyond question to Lincoln. Indeed, a man far less keen than Douglas would have taken note of the popular current in New England. Why, then, this expenditure of time and effort? In all probability Douglas gauged the situation correctly. He is said to have conceded frankly that Lincoln would be elected.[3] His contest was less with Republicans and Constitutional Unionists now, than with the followers of Breckinridge. He hoped to effect a reorganization of the Democratic party by crushing the disunion elements within it. With this end in view he could not permit the organization to go to pieces in the North. A listless campaign on his part would not only give the election to Lincoln, but leave his own followers to wander leaderless into other organizations. For the sake of discipline and future

---

[1] New York *Times*, July. 24.

[2] Rhodes, History of the United States, II, pp. 482-483.

[3] Wilson, Slave Power in America, II, p. 699.

success, he rallied Northern Democrats for a battle that was already lost.[1]

Well assured that Lincoln would be elected, Douglas determined to go South and prepare the minds of the people for the inevitable.[2] The language of Southern leaders had grown steadily more menacing as the probability of Republican success increased. It was now proclaimed from the house-tops that the cotton States would secede, if Lincoln were elected. Republicans might set these threats down as Southern gasconade, but Douglas knew the animus of the secessionists better than they.[3] This determination of Douglas was warmly applauded where it was understood.[4] Indeed, that purpose was dictated now alike by politics and patriotism.

On August 25th, Douglas spoke at Norfolk, Virginia. In the course of his address, an elector on the Breckinridge ticket interrupted him with two questions. Though taken somewhat by surprise, Douglas with unerring sagacity detected the purpose of his interrogator and answered circumstantially.[5] "First, If Abraham Lincoln be elected President of the United States, will the Southern States be justified in seceding from the Union?" "To this I emphatically answer no. The election of a man to the presidency by the American people in conformity with the Constitution of the United States *would not justify any attempt at dis-*

---

[1] This was the view of a well-informed correspondent of the New York *Times*, August 10, 14, 16, 1860. From this point of view, Douglas's tour through Maine in August takes on special significance.

[2] Wilson, Slave Power in America, II, 699.

[3] Rhodes, History of the United States, II, pp. 487, 489.

[4] New York *Times*, August 16, 1860.

[5] *Ibid.*, August 29, 1860.

solving this glorious confederacy." "Second, If they
secede from the Union upon the inauguration of Abraham Lincoln, before an overt act against their constitutional rights, will you advise or vindicate resistance to the decision?" "I answer emphatically, that
it is the duty of the President of the United States and
of all others in authority under him, to enforce the
laws of the United States, passed by Congress and as
the Courts expound them; and I, as in duty bound by
my oath of fidelity to the Constitution, *would do all in
my power to aid the government of the United States
in maintaining the supremacy of the laws against all
resistance to them, come from whatever quarter it
might*. ... I hold that the Constitution has a remedy for
every grievance that may arise within the limits of the
Union. . . . The mere inauguration of a President of
the United States, whose political opinions were, in
my judgment, hostile to the Constitution and safety
of the Union, without an overt act on his part, without
striking a blow at our institutions or our rights, is not
such a grievance as would justify revolution or secession." But for the disunionists at the South, Douglas went on to say, "I would have beaten Lincoln in
every State but Vermont and Massachusetts. As it is
I think I will beat him in almost all of them yet.'"[1]
And now these disunionists come forward and ask aid
in dissolving the Union. "I tell them 'no—never on
earth!' "

Widely quoted, this bold defiance of disunion made a

---

[1] This can hardly be regarded as a sober opinion. Clingman had become convinced by conversation with Douglas that he was not making
the canvass in his own behalf, but in order to weaken and divide the
South, so as to aid Lincoln. Clingman, Speeches and Writings, p. 513.

profound impression through the South. At Raleigh,
North Carolina, Douglas entered into collusion with a
friend, in order to have the questions repeated.[1] And
again he stated his attitude in unequivocal language.
"I am in favor of executing, in good faith, every
clause and provision of the Constitution, and of protecting every right under it, and then hanging every
man who takes up arms against it. Yes, my friends,
I would hang every man higher than Haman who
would attempt to resist by force the execution of any
provision of the Constitution which our fathers made
and bequeathed to us."[2]

He touched many hearts when he reminded his hearers that in the great Northwest, Northerners and
Southerners met and married, bequeathing the choice
gifts of both sections to their children. "When their
children grow up, the child of the same parents has a
grandfather in North Carolina and another in Vermont,
and that child does not like to hear either of those
States abused. . . . He will never consent that this
Union shall be dissolved so that he will be compelled
to obtain a passport and get it *viséd* to enter a foreign
land to visit the graves of his ancestors. You cannot
sever this Union unless you cut the heart strings that
bind father to son, daughter to mother, and brother to
sister, in all our new States and territories." And the
heart of the speaker went out to his kindred and his
boys, who were almost within hearing of his voice. "I
love my children," he exclaimed, "but I do not desire
to see them survive this Union."

At Richmond, Douglas received an ovation which

[1] Clingman, Speeches and Writings, p. 513.
[2] North Carolina *Standard*, September 5, 1860.

recalled the days when Clay was the idol of the Whigs;[1] but as he journeyed northward he felt more and more the hostility of Breckinridge men, and marked the disposition of many of his own supporters to strike an alliance with them. Unhesitatingly he threw the weight of his personal influence against fusion. At Baltimore, he averred that while Breckinridge was not a disunionist, every disunionist was a Breckinridge man.[2] And at Reading, he said, "For one, I can never fuse, and never will fuse with a man who tells me that the Democratic creed is a dogma, contrary to reason and to the Constitution. . . . I have fought twenty-seven pitched battles, since I entered public life, and never yet traded with nominations or surrendered to treachery."[3] With equal pertinacity he refused to countenance any attempts at fusion in North Carolina.[4] Even more explicitly he declared against fusion in a speech at Erie: "No Democrat can, without dishonor, and a forfeiture of self-respect and principle, fuse with anybody who is in favor of intervention, either for or against slavery. . . . As Democrats we can never fuse either with Northern Abolitionists or Southern Bolters and Secessionists."[5]

In spite of these protests and admonitions, Douglas men in several of the doubtful States entered into more or less definite agreement with the supporters

[1] Correspondent to New York *Times*, September 5, 1860.

[2] *Ibid.*, September 7, 1860.

[3] New York *Tribune*, September 10, 1860. Greeley did Douglas an injustice when he accused him of courting votes by favoring a protective tariff in Pennsylvania. The misapprehension was doubtless due to a garbled associated press dispatch.

[4] Clingman, Speeches and Writings, p. 513.

[5] New York *Times*, September 27, 1860.

of Breckinridge. The pressure put upon him in New York by those to whom he was indebted for his nomination, was almost too strong to be resisted. Yet he withstood all entreaties, even to maintain a discreet silence and let events take their course. Hostile newspapers expressed his sentiments when they represented him as opposed to fusion, "all the way from Maine to California."[1] "Douglas either must have lost his craft as a politician," commented Raymond, in the editorial columns of the *Times,* "or be credited with steadfast convictions."[2]

Adverse comment on Douglas's personal canvass had now ceased. Wise men recognized that he was preparing the public mind for a crisis, as no one else could. He set his face westward, speaking at numerous points.[3] Continuous speaking had now begun to tell upon him. At Cincinnati, he was so hoarse that he could not address the crowds which had gathered to greet him, but he persisted in speaking on the following day at Indianapolis. He paused in Chicago only long enough to give a public address, and then passed on into Iowa.[4] Among his own people he unbosomed himself as he had not done before in all these weeks of incessant public speaking. "I am no alarmist. I believe that this country is in more danger now than at any other moment since I have known anything of public life. It is not personal ambition that has induced me to take the stump this year. I say to you who know me, that the presidency has no charms

---

[1] New York *Times,* September 13, 1860.   [2] *Ibid.*

[3] His movements were still followed by the New York *Times,* which printed his list of appointments.

[4] Chicago *Times* and *Herald,* October 9, 1860.

for me. I do not believe that it is my interest as an ambitious man, to be President this year if I could. But I do love this Union. There is no sacrifice on earth that I would not make to preserve it."[1]

While Douglas was in Cedar Rapids, Iowa, he received a dispatch from his friend, Forney, announcing that the Republicans had carried Pennsylvania in the October State election. Similar intelligence came from Indiana. The outcome in November was thus clearly foreshadowed. Recognizing the inevitable, Douglas turned to his Secretary with the laconic words, "Mr. Lincoln is the next President. We must try to save the Union. I will go South."[2] He at once made appointments to speak in Tennessee, Alabama, and Georgia, as soon as he should have met his Western engagements. His friends marvelled at his powers of endurance. For weeks he had been speaking from hotel balconies, from the platform of railroad coaches, and in halls to monster mass-meetings.[3] Not infrequently he spoke twice and thrice a day, for days together. It was often said that he possessed the constitution of the United States; and he caught up the jest with delight, remarking that he believed he had. Small wonder if much that he said was trivial and unworthy of his attention;[4] in and through all his utterance, nevertheless, coursed the passionate current of his love for the Union, transfiguring all that was paltry and commonplace. From Iowa he passed into Wisconsin and

---

[1] Chicago *Times and Herald*, October 6, 1860.

[2] Wilson, Rise and Fall of the Slave Power in America, II, p. 700; see also Forney's Eulogy of Douglas, 1861.

[3] Rhodes, History of the United States, II, p. 493.

[4] *Ibid.*

Michigan, finally entering upon his Southern mission at St. Louis, October 19th. "I am not here to-night," he told his auditors, with a shade of weariness in his voice, "to ask your votes for the presidency. I am not one of those who believe that I have any more personal interest in the presidency than any other good citizen in America. I am here to make an appeal to you in behalf of the Union and the peace of the country."[1]

It was a courageous little party that left St. Louis for Memphis and the South. Mrs. Douglas was still with her husband, determined to share all the hardships that fell to his lot; and besides her, there was only James B. Sheridan, Douglas's devoted secretary and stenographer. The Southern press had threatened Douglas with personal violence, if he should dare to invade the South with his political heresies.[2] But Luther bound for Worms was not more indifferent to personal danger than this modern intransigeant. His conduct earned the hearty admiration of even Republican journals, for no one could now believe that he courted the South in his own behalf. Nor was there any foolish bravado in this adventure. He was thoroughly sobered by the imminence of disunion. When he read, in a newspaper devoted to his interests, that it was "the deep-seated fixed determination on the part of the leading Southern States to go out of the Union, peaceably and quietly," he knew that these words were no cheap rhetoric, for they were penned by a man of Northern birth and antecedents.[3]

---

[1] Chicago *Times and Herald*, October 24, 1860.

[2] Philadelphia *Press*, October 29, 1860.

[3] Savannah (Ga.) *Express*, quoted by Chicago *Times and Herald*, October 25, 1860.

The history of this Southern tour has never been written. It was the firm belief of Douglas that at least one attempt was made to wreck his train. At Montgomery, while addressing a public gathering, he was made the target for nameless missiles.[1] Yet none of these adventures were permitted to find their way into the Northern press. And only his intimates learned of them from his own lips after his return.

The news of Mr. Lincoln's election overtook Douglas in Mobile. He was in the office of the Mobile *Register*, one of the few newspapers which had held to him and his cause through thick and thin. It now became a question what policy the paper should pursue. The editor asked his associate to read aloud an article which he had just written, advocating a State convention to deliberate upon the course of Alabama in the approaching crisis. Douglas opposed its publication; but he was assured that the only way to manage the secession movement was to appear to go with it, and by electing men opposed to disunion, to control the convention. With his wonted sagacity, Douglas remarked that if they could not prevent the calling of a convention, they could hardly hope to control its action. But the editors determined to publish the article, "and Douglas returned to his hotel more hopeless than I had ever seen him before," wrote Sheridan.[2]

On his return to the North, Douglas spoke twice, at New Orleans and at Vicksburg, urging acquiescence in the result of the election.[3] He put the case most

[1] There was a bare reference to the Montgomery incident in the Chicago *Times and Herald*, November 12, 1860.

[2] Wilson, Slave Power in America, II, p. 700.

[3] Chicago *Times and Herald*, November 13, 1860; Philadelphia *Press*, November 28, 1860.

cogently in a letter to the business men of New Orleans, which was widely published. No one deplored the election of an Abolitionist as President more than he. Still, he could not find any just cause for dissolving the Federal Union in the mere election of any man to the presidency, in accordance with the Constitution. Those who apprehended that the new President would carry out the aggressive policy of his party, failed to observe that his party was in a minority. Even his appointments to office would have to be confirmed by a hostile Senate. Any invasion of constitutional rights would be resented in the North, as well as in the South. In short, the election of Mr. Lincoln could only serve as a pretext for those who purposed to break up the Union and to form a Southern Confederacy.[1]

On the face of the election returns, Douglas made a sorry showing; he had won the electoral vote of but a single State, Missouri, though three of the seven electoral votes of New Jersey fell to him as the result of fusion. Yet as the popular vote in the several States was ascertained, defeat wore the guise of a great personal triumph. Leader of a forlorn hope, he had yet received the suffrages of 1,376,957 citizens, only 489,495 less votes than Lincoln had polled. Of these 163,525 came from the South, while Lincoln received only 26,430, all from the border slave States. As compared with the vote of Breckinridge and Bell at the South, Douglas's vote was insignificant; but at the North, he ran far ahead of the combined vote of both.[2] It goes without saying that had Douglas secured the full Democratic vote in the free States, he would have

[1] Chicago *Times and Herald*, November 19, 1860.
[2] Stanwood, History of the Presidency, p. 297.

pressed Lincoln hard in many quarters. From the national standpoint, the most significant aspect of the popular vote was the failure of Breckinridge to secure a majority in the slave States.[1] Union sentiment was still stronger than the secessionists had boasted. The next most significant fact in the history of the election was this: Abraham Lincoln had been elected to the presidency by the vote of a section which had given over a million votes to his rival, the leader of a faction of a disorganized party.

[1] Douglas and Bell polled 135,057 votes more than Breckinridge; see Greeley, American Conflict, I, p. 328.

CHAPTER XIX

The Merging of the Partisan in the Patriot

On the day after the election, the palmetto and lone star flag was thrown out to the breeze from the office of the Charleston *Mercury* and hailed with cheers by the populace. "The tea has been thrown overboard— the revolution of 1860 has been initiated," said that ebullient journal next morning.[1] On the 10th of November, the legislature of South Carolina called a convention of the people to consider the relations of the Commonwealth "with the Northern States and the government of the United States." The instantaneous approval of the people of Charleston, the focus of public opinion in the State, left no doubt that South Carolina would secede from the Union soon after the 17th of December, when the convention was to assemble. On November 23d, Major Robert Anderson, in command of Fort Moultrie in Charleston harbor, urged the War Department to reinforce his garrison and to occupy also Fort Sumter and Castle Pinckney, saying, "I need not say how anxious I am—indeed, determined, so far as honor will permit—to avoid collision with the citizens of South Carolina. Nothing, however, will be better calculated to prevent bloodshed than our being found in such an attitude that it would be madness and folly to attack us." "That there is a settled determination," he continued, "to leave the Union, and to obtain possession of this work, is

[1] Rhodes, History of the United States, III, pp. 116 ff.

apparent to all."[1]   No sane man could doubt that a crisis was imminent.   Unhappily, James Buchanan was still President of the United States.

To those who greeted Judge Douglas upon his return to Washington, he seemed to be in excellent health, despite rumors to the contrary.[2]   Demonstrative followers insisted upon hearing his voice immediately upon his arrival, and he was not unwilling to repeat what he had said at New Orleans, here within hearing of men of all sections.   The burden of his thought was contained in a single sentence: "Mr. Lincoln, having been elected, must be inaugurated in obedience to the Constitution."   "Fellow citizens," he said, in his rich, sonorous voice, sounding the key-note of his subsequent career, "I beseech you, with reference to former party divisions, to lay aside all political asperities, all personal prejudices, to indulge in no criminations or recriminations, but to unite with me, and all Union-loving men, in a common effort to save the country from the disasters which threaten it."[3]

In the midst of forebodings which even the most optimistic shared, Congress reassembled.   Feeling was tense in both houses, but it was more noticeable in the Senate, where, hitherto, political differences had not been a barrier to social intercourse.   Senator Iverson put into words what all felt: "Look at the spectacle exhibited on this floor.   How is it?   There are Republican Northern senators upon that side. Here are Southern senators on this side.   How much social intercourse is there between us?   You sit upon

---

[1] Rhodes, History of the United States, III, pp. 131-132.

[2] Chicago *Times and Herald*, December 7, 1860.

[3] *Ibid.*

your side, silent and gloomy; we sit upon ours with knit brows and portentous scowls. . . . Here are two hostile bodies on this floor; and it is but a type of the feeling that exists between the two sections.''[1]

Southern senators hastened to lay bare their grievances. However much they might differ in naming specific, tangible ills, they all agreed upon the great cause of their apprehension and uneasiness. Davis voiced the common feeling when he said, ''I believe the true cause of our danger to be that a sectional hostility has been substituted for a general fraternity.''[2] And his colleague confirmed this opinion. Clingman put the same thought more concretely when he declared that the South was apprehensive, not because a dangerous man had been elected to the presidency; but because a President had been elected who was known to be a dangerous man and who had declared his purpose to war upon the social system of the South.[3]

With the utmost boldness, Southern senators announced the impending secession of their States. ''We intend,'' said Iverson of Georgia speaking for his section, ''to go out peaceably if we can, forcibly if we must. . . . In this state of feeling, divided as we are by interests, by a geographical feeling, by everything that makes two people separate and distinct, I ask why we should remain in the same Union together?''[4]

No Northern senator had better reason than Douglas to believe that these were not merely idle threats. The knowledge sobered him. In this hour of peril,

---

[1] *Globe*, 36 Cong., 2 Sess., p. 12.

[2] *Ibid.*, p. 29.   [3] *Ibid.*, p. 3.   [4] *Ibid.*, pp. 11-12.

his deep love for the Union welled up within him, submerging the partisan and the politician. "I trust," he said, rebuking a Northern senator, "we may lay aside all party grievances, party feuds, partisan jealousies, and look to our country, and not to our party, in the consequences of our action. Sir, I am as good a party man as anyone living, when there are only party issues at stake, and the fate of political parties to be provided for. But, Sir, if I know myself, I do not desire to hear the word party, or to listen to any party appeal, while we are considering and discussing the questions upon which the fate of the country now hangs."[1]

In this spirit Douglas welcomed from the South the recital of special grievances. "Give us each charge and each specification. . . . I hold that there is no grievance growing out of a nonfulfillment of constitutional obligations, which cannot be remedied under the Constitution and within the Union."[2] And when the Personal Liberty Acts of Northern States were cited as a long-standing grievance, he heartily denounced them as in direct violation of the letter and the spirit of the Constitution. At the same time he contended that these acts existed generally in the States to which few fugitives ever fled, and that the Fugitive Slave Act was enforced nineteen out of twenty times. It was the twentieth case that was published abroad through the press, misleading the South. In fact, the present excitement was, to his mind, due to the inability of the extremes of North and South to understand each other. "Those of us that live upon the border, and have

[1] *Globe*, 36 Cong., 2 Sess., p. 28.
[2] *Ibid.*, p. 57.

commercial intercourse and social relations across the line, can live in peace with each other.'' If the border slave States and the border free States could arbitrate the question of slavery, the Union would last forever.[1]

Arbitration and compromise—these were the words with which the venerable Crittenden of Kentucky, successor to Clay, now endeavored to rally Union-loving men. He was seconded by his colleague, Senator Powell, who had already moved the appointment of a special committee of thirteen, to consider the grievances between the slave-holding and non-slave-holding States. Douglas put himself unreservedly at the service of the party of compromise. It seemed, for the moment, as though the history of the year 1850 were to be repeated. Now, as then, the initiative was taken by a senator from the border-State of Kentucky. Again a committee of thirteen was to prepare measures of adjustment. The composition of the committee was such as to give promise of a settlement, if any were possible. Seward, Collamer, Wade, Doolittle, and Grimes, were the Republican members; Douglas, Rice, and Bigler represented the Democracy of the North. Davis and Toombs represented the Gulf States; Powell, Crittenden, and Hunter, the border slave States.[2]

On the 22d of December, the committee took under consideration the Crittenden resolutions, which proposed six amendments to the Constitution and four joint resolutions. The crucial point was the first amendment, which would restore the Missouri Compromise line ''in all the territory of the United States

---

[1] *Globe,* 36 Cong., 2 Sess., p. 52.
[2] Rhodes, History of the United States, III, pp. 151-153.

now held, or hereafter acquired." Could this disposition of the vexing territorial question have been agreed upon, the other features of the compromise would probably have commanded assent. But this and all the other proposed amendments were defeated by the adverse vote of the Republican members of the committee.[1]

The outcome was disheartening. Douglas had firmly believed that conciliation, or concession, alone could save the country from civil war.[2] When the committee first met informally[3] the news was already in print that the South Carolina convention had passed an ordinance of secession. Under the stress of this event, and of others which he apprehended, Douglas had voted for all the Crittenden amendments and resolutions, regardless of his personal predilections. "The prospects are gloomy," he wrote privately, "but I do not yet despair of the Union. *We can never acknowledge the right of a State to secede and cut us off from the ocean and the world, without our consent.* But in view of impending civil war with our brethren in nearly one-half of the States of the Union, I will not consider the question of force and war until all efforts at peaceful adjustment have been made and have failed. The fact can no longer be disguised that many of the Republican leaders desire war and disunion under pretext of saving the Union. They wish to get rid of the Southern senators in order to have a majority in the Senate to confirm Lincoln's appointments; and many of them think they can hold a permanent Republican

---

[1] Report of the Committee of Thirteen, pp. 11-12.

[2] *Globe*, 36 Cong., 2 Sess., p. 158.

[3] December 21st.

ascendancy in the Northern States, but not in the whole Union. For partisan reasons, therefore, they are anxious to dissolve the Union, if it can be done without making them responsible before the people. I am for the Union, and am ready to make any reasonable sacrifice to save it. No adjustment will restore and preserve peace *which does not banish the slavery question from Congress forever* and place it beyond the reach of Federal legislation. Mr. Crittenden's proposition to extend the Missouri line accomplishes this object, and hence I can accept it now for the same reasons that I proposed it in 1848. I prefer our own plan of non-intervention and popular sovereignty, however.'"[1]

The propositions which Douglas laid before the committee proved to be even less acceptable than the Crittenden amendments. Only a single, insignificant provision relating to the colonizing of free negroes in distant lands, commended itself to a majority of the committee.[2] All hope of an agreement had now vanished. Sad at heart, Douglas voted to report the inability of the committee to agree upon any general plan of adjustment.[3] Yet he did not abandon all hope; he was not yet ready to admit that the dread alternative must be accepted. He joined with Crittenden in replying to a dispatch from the South: "We have hopes that the rights of the South, and of every State and section, may be protected within the Union. Don't give up the ship. Don't despair of the Republic."[4]

[1] MS. Letter, Douglas to C. H. Lanphier, December 25, 1860.
[2] Report of the Committee of Thirteen, p. 16.
[3] *Ibid.,* p. 18.
[4] McPherson, Political History of the Rebellion, p. 38.

And when Crittenden proposed to the Senate that the people at large should be allowed to express their approval, or disapproval, of his amendments by a vote, Douglas cordially indorsed the suggested referendum in a speech of great power.

There was dross mingled with the gold in this speech of January 3d. Not all his auditors by any means were ready to admit that the attempt of the Federal government to control the slavery question in the Territories, regardless of the wishes of the inhabitants, was the real cause of Southern discontent. Nor were all willing to concede that "whenever Congress had refrained from such interference, harmony and fraternal feeling had been restored."[1] The history of Kansas was still too recent. Yet from these premises, Douglas drew the conclusion "that the slavery question should be banished forever from the Halls of Congress and the arena of Federal politics by an irrepealable constitutional provision."[2]

The immediate occasion for revolution in the South was no doubt the outcome of the presidential election; but that it furnished a just cause for the dissolution of the Union, he would not for an instant admit. No doubt Mr. Lincoln's public utterances had given some ground for apprehension. No one had more vigorously denounced these dangerous, revolutionary doctrines than he; but neither Mr. Lincoln nor his party would have the power to injure the South, if the Southern States remained in the Union and maintained full delegations in Congress. "Besides," he added, "I still indulge the hope that when Mr. Lincoln shall assume the high responsibilities which will soon devolve upon

[1] *Globe*, 36 Cong., 2 Sess., App., p. 35.   [2] *Ibid.*, p. 38.

him, he will be fully impressed with the necessity of sinking the politician in the statesman, the partisan in the patriot, and regard the obligations which he owes to his country as paramount to those of his party."[1]

No one brought the fearful alternatives into view, with such inexorable logic, as Douglas in this same speech. While he denounced secession as "wrong, unlawful, unconstitutional, and criminal," he was bound to recognize the fact of secession. "South Carolina had no right to secede; *but she has done it.* The rights of the Federal government remain, but possession is lost. How can possession be regained, by arms or by a peaceable adjustment of the matters in controversy? *Are we prepared for war?* I do not mean that kind of preparation which consists of armies and navies, and supplies, and munitions of war; but are we prepared IN OUR HEARTS for war with our own brethren and kindred? I confess I am not."[2]

These were not mere words for oratorical effect. They were expressions wrung from a tortured heart, bound by some of the tenderest of human affections to the people of the South. Buried in the land of her birth rested the mother of his two boys, whom he had loved tenderly and truly. There in the Southland were her kindred, the kindred of his two boys, and many of his warmest personal friends. The prospect

---

[1] *Globe* 36 Cong., 2 Sess., App., p. 39. It is not unlikely that Douglas may have been reassured on this point by some communication from Lincoln himself. The Diary of a Public Man (*North American Review*, Vol. 129,) p. 130, gives the impression that they had been in correspondence. Personal relations between them had been cordial even in 1859, just after the debates; See Publication No. 11, of the Illinois Historical Library, p. 191.

[2] *Globe*, 36 Cong., 2 Sess., App., p. 39.

of war brought no such poignant grief to men whose associations for generations had been confined to the North.

Returning to the necessity of concession and compromise, he frankly admitted that he had thrown consistency to the winds. The preservation of the Union was of more importance than party platforms or individual records. "I have no hesitation in saying to senators on all sides of this Chamber, that I am prepared to act on this question with reference to the present exigencies of the case, as if I had never given a vote, or uttered a word, or had an opinion upon the subject."[1]

Nor did he hesitate to throw the responsibility for disagreement in the Committee of Thirteen upon the Republican members. In the name of peace he pled for less of party pride and the pride of individual opinion. "The political party which shall refuse to allow the people to determine for themselves at the ballot-box the issue between revolution and war on the one side, and obstinate adherence to a party platform on the other, will assume a fearful responsibility. A war upon a political issue, waged by the people of eighteen States against the people and domestic institutions of fifteen sister-States, is a fearful and revolting thought."[2] But Republican senators were deaf to all warnings from so recent a convert to non-partisan politics.

While the Committee of Thirteen was in session, Major Anderson moved his garrison from Fort Moultrie to Fort Sumter in Charleston harbor, urging re-

---

[1] *Globe*, 36 Cong., 2 Sess., App., p. 41.
[2] *Ibid.*, p. 42.

peatedly the need of reinforcements. At the beginning of the new year, President Buchanan was inspired to form a good resolution. He resolved that Anderson should not be ordered to return to Moultrie but should be reinforced. On the 5th of January, the "Star of the West," with men, arms and ammunition, was dispatched to Charleston harbor. On the 9th the steamer was fired upon and forced to return without accomplishing its mission. Then came the news of the secession of Mississippi. In rapid succession Florida, Alabama, and Georgia passed ordinances of secession.[1] Louisiana and Texas were sure to follow the lead of the other cotton States.

In spite of these untoward events, the Republican senators remained obdurate. Their answer to the Crittenden referendum proposition was the Clark resolution, which read, "The provisions of the Constitution are ample for the preservation of the Union, and the protection of all the material interests of the country; it needs to be obeyed rather than amended."[2] On the 21st of the month, the senators of the seceding States withdrew; yet Douglas could still say to anxious Union men at the South, "There is hope of adjustment, and the prospect has never been better than since we first assembled."[3] And Senator Crittenden concurred in this view. On what could they have grounded their hopes?

Douglas still believed in the efficacy of compromise to preserve the Union. Through many channels he

---

[1] January 10th, 11th, and 19th.

[2] The resolution was carried, 25 to 23, six Southern Senators refusing to vote. *Globe*, 36 Cong., 2 Sess., p. 409.

[3] McPherson, Political History of the Rebellion, p. 39.

received intelligence from the South, and he knew well that the leaders of public opinion were not of one mind. Some, at least, regarded the proposed Southern confederacy as a means of securing a revision of the Constitution. Men like Benjamin of Louisiana were still ready to talk confidentially of a final adjustment.[1] Moreover, there was a persistent rumor that Seward was inclining to the Crittenden Compromise; and Seward, as the prospective leader of the incoming administration, would doubtless carry many Republicans with him. Something, too, might be expected from the Peace Convention, which was to meet on February 4th, in Washington.

Meantime Douglas lent his aid to such legislative labors as the exigencies of the hour permitted. Once again, he found himself acting with the Republicans to do justice to Kansas, for Kansas was now a suppliant for admission into the Union with a free constitution. Again specious excuses were made for denying simple justice. Toward the obstructionists, his old enemies, Douglas showed no rancor: there was no time to lose in personalities. "The sooner we close up this controversy the better, if we intend to wipe out the excited and irritated feelings that have grown out of it. It will have a tendency to restore good feelings."[2] But not until the Southern senators had withdrawn, was Kansas admitted to the Union of the States, which was then hanging in the balance.

Whenever senators from the slave States could be

---

[1] Diary of a Public Man, pp. 133-134. Douglas was on terms of intimacy with the writer, and must have shared these communications. Besides, Douglas had independent sources of information.

[2] Globe, 36 Cong., 2 Sess., pp. 445-446.

induced to name their tangible grievances, and not to
dwell merely upon anticipated injuries, they were wont
to cite the Personal Liberty Acts. In spite of his good
intentions, Douglas was drawn into an altercation
with Mason of Virginia, in which he cited an historic
case where Virginia had been the offender. Recovering himself, he said ingenuously, "I hope we are not
to bandy these little cases backwards and forwards for
the purpose of sectional irritation. Let us rather meet
the question, and give the Constitution the true construction, and allow all criminals to be surrendered
according to the law of the State where the offense was
committed."[1]

As evidence of his desire to remove this most
tangible of Southern gravamina, Douglas introduced
a supplementary fugitive slave bill on January 28th.[2]
Its notable features were the provision for jury trial
in a Federal court, if after extradition a fugitive
should persist in claiming his freedom; and the provisions for the payment of damages to the claimant,
if he should lose through violence a fugitive slave to
whom he had a valid title. The Federal government
in turn might bring suit against the county where
the rescue had occurred, and the county might reim-
burse itself by suing the offenders to the full amount
of the damages paid.[3] Had this bill passed, it would
have made good the most obvious defects in the much-
defamed legislation of 1850; but the time had long
since passed, when such concessions would satisfy the
South.

Douglas had to bear many a gibe for his publicly

[1] *Globe*, 36 Cong., 2 Sess., p. 508.   [2] *Ibid.*, p. 586.
[3] Senate Bill, No. 549, 36 Cong., 2 Sess.

expressed hopes of peace. Mason denounced his letter
to Virginia gentlemen as a "puny, pusillanimous attempt to hoodwink" the people of Virginia. But
Douglas replied with an earnest reiteration of his expectations. Yet all depended, he admitted, on the
action of Virginia and the border States. For this
reason he deprecated the uncompromising attitude of
the senator from Virginia, when he said, "We want
no concessions." Equally deplorable, he thought, was
the spirit evinced by the senator from New Hampshire
who applauded that regrettable remark. "I never
intend to give up the hope of saving this Union so long
as there is a ray left," he cried.[1] Why try to force
slavery to go where experience has demonstrated that
climate is adverse and where the people do not want it?
Why prohibit slavery where the government cannot
make it exist? "Why break up the Union upon an
abstraction?" Let the one side give up its demand
for protection and the other for prohibition; and let
them unite upon an amendment to the Constitution
which shall deny to Congress the power to legislate
upon slavery everywhere, except in the matter of
fugitive slaves and the African slave-trade. "Do
that, and you will have peace; do that, and the Union
will last forever; do that, and you do not extend
slavery one inch, nor circumscribe it one inch; you do
not emancipate a slave, and do not enslave a free-
man."[2]

In the course of his eloquent plea for mutual concession, Douglas was repeatedly interrupted by Wigfall of Texas, whose State was at the moment prepar-

[1] *Globe*, 36 Cong., 2 Sess., p. 661.
[2] *Ibid.*

ing to leave the Union. In ironical tones, Wigfall begged to be informed upon what ground the senator based his hope and belief that the Union would be preserved. Douglas replied, "I see indications every day of a disposition to meet this question now and consider what is necessary to save the Union." And then, anticipating the sneers of his interrogator, he said sharply, "If the senator will just follow me, instead of going off to Texas; sit here, and act in concert with us Union men, we will make him a very efficient agent in accomplishing that object."[1] But to the obdurate mind of Wigfall this Union talk was "the merest balderdash." Compromise on the basis of non-intervention, he pronounced "worse than 'Sewardism,' for it had hypocrisy and the other was bold and open." There was, unhappily, only too much truth in his pithy remark that "the apple of discord is offered to us as the fruit of peace."

It was a sad commentary on the state of the Union that while the six cotton States were establishing the constitution and government of a Southern Confederacy, the Federal Senate was providing for the territorial organization of that great domain whose acquisition had been the joint labor of all the States. Three Territories were projected. In one of these, Colorado, a provisional government had already been set up by the mining population of the Pike's Peak country. To the Colorado bill Douglas interposed serious objections. By its provisions, the southern boundary cut off a portion of New Mexico, which was slave Territory, and added it to Colorado. At the same time a provision in the bill prevented the territorial legislature

[1] *Globe*, 36 Cong., 2 Sess., pp. 669.

from passing any law to destroy the rights of private property. Was the new Territory of Colorado to be free or slave? Another provision debarred the territorial legislature from condemning private property for public uses. How, then, could Colorado construct even a public road? Still another provision declared that there should be no discrimination in the rate of taxation between different kinds of property. How, then, could Colorado make those necessary exemptions which were to be found on all statute books?[1]

In his encounter with Senator Green, who had succeeded him as chairman of the Committee on Territories, Douglas did not appear to good advantage. It was easy to prove his first objection idle, as there was no slave property in northern New Mexico. As for the other objectionable provisions, all—by your leave! —were to be found in the Washington Territory Act, which had passed through Douglas's committee without comment.[2]

Douglas proposed a substitute for the Colorado bill, nevertheless, which, besides rectifying these errors,— for such he still deemed them to be,—proposed that the people of the Territory should elect their own officers. He reminded the Senate that the Kansas-Nebraska bill had been sharply criticised, because while professing to recognize popular sovereignty, it had withheld this power. At that time, however, the governor was also an Indian agent and a Federal officer; now, the two functions were separated. He proposed that, henceforth, the President and Senate should appoint only such officers as performed Federal

[1] *Globe*, 36 Cong., 2 Sess., p. 764.
[2] *Ibid.*

duties.[1] When Senator Wade suggested that Douglas had experienced a conversion on this point, because he happened to be in opposition to the incoming administration, which would appoint the new territorial officers, Douglas referred to his utterances in the last session, as proof of his disinterestedness in the matter.[2]

Even in his rôle of peace-maker, Douglas could not help remarking that the bill contained not a word about slavery. "I am rejoiced," he said, somewhat ironically, "to find that the two sides of the House, representing the two sides of the 'irrepressible conflict,' find it impossible when they get into power, to practically carry on the government without coming to non-intervention, and saying nothing upon the subject of slavery. Although they may not vote for my proposition, the fact that they have to avow the principle upon which they have fought me for years is the only one upon which they can possibly agree, is conclusive evidence that I have been right in that principle, and that they have been wrong in fighting me upon it."[3]

In the House the Colorado bill was amended by the excision of the clause providing for appeals to the United States Supreme Court in all cases involving title to slaves. Douglas promptly pointed out the significance of this omission. The decisions of the territorial court regarding slavery would now be final. The question of whether the territorial legislature might, or might not, exclude slavery, would now be decided by territorial judges who would be appointed

[1] *Globe*, 36 Cong., 2 Sess., p. 764.
[2] *Ibid.*, p. 765.
[3] *Ibid.*, p. 766.

by a Republican President.[1]   The Republicans now in
control of the Senate were eager to press their advantage.   And Douglas had to acquiesce.   After all, the
practical importance of the matter was not great.   No
one anticipated that slavery ever would exist in these
new Territories.

The substitute which Douglas offered for the Colorado bill, and subsequently for the other territorial
bills, deserves more than a passing allusion.   Not only
was it his last contribution to territorial legislation,
but it suggested a far-reaching change in our colonial
policy.   It was the logical conclusion of popular sovereignty practically applied.[2]   Congress was invited to
abdicate all but the most meagre power in organizing
new Territories.   The task of framing an organic act
for the government of a Territory was to be left to a
convention chosen by adult male citizens who were in
actual residence; but this organic law must be republican in form, and in every way subordinate to the Constitution and to all laws and treaties affecting the Indians and the public lands.   A Territory so organized
was to be admitted into the Union whenever its population should be equal to the unit required for representation in the lower house of Congress.   The initiative in
taking a preliminary census and calling a territorial
convention, was to be taken by the judge of the Federal
court in the Territory.   The tutelage of the Federal
government was thus to be reduced to lowest terms.

Congress was to confine itself to general provisions
applicable to all Territories, leaving the formation of
new Territories to the caprice of the people in actual

[1] *Globe,* 36 Cong., 2 Sess., p. 1205.
[2] It is printed in full in *Globe,* 36 Cong., 2 Sess., p. 1207.

residence. This was a generous concession to popular sovereignty; but even so, the paramount authority was still vested in Congress. Congress, and not the people, was to designate the bounds of the Territory; Congress was to pass judgment upon the republicanism of the organic law, and a Federal judge was to set the machinery of popular sovereignty in motion. Obviously the time had passed when Congress would make so radical a departure from precedent. Least of all were the Republican members disposed to weaken the hold of the Federal government upon Territories where the question of slavery might again become acute.

While the House was unwilling to vote for a submission of the Crittenden propositions to a popular vote, it did propose an amendment denying to Congress the power to interfere with the domestic institutions of any State. Not being in any sense a concession, but only an affirmation of a widely accepted principle, this amendment passed the House easily enough. Yet in his rôle of compromiser, Douglas made much of this vote. He called Senator Mason's attention to two great facts—"startling, tremendous facts—that they [the Republicans] have abandoned their aggressive policy in the Territories and are willing to give guarantees in the States." These "ought to be accepted as an evidence of a salutary change in public opinion at the North."[1] Now if the Republican party would only offer a similar guarantee, by a constitutional amendment, that they would never revive their aggressive policy toward slavery in the Territories!

As the February days wore away, Douglas became

[1] *Globe,* 36 Cong., 2 Sess., p. 1391.

less hopeful of peaceable adjustment through compromise. If he had counted upon large concessions from Seward, he was disappointed. If he had entertained hopes of the Peace Conference, he had also erred grievously. He became more and more assured that the forces making against peace were from the North as well as the South. He told the Senate on February 21st, that there was "a deliberate plot to break up this Union under pretense of preserving it."[1] Privately he feared the influence of some of Mr. Lincoln's advisers, who were hostile to Seward. "What the Blairs really want," he said hotly to a friend, "is a civil war."[2] With many another well-wisher he deplored the secret entrance of Mr. Lincoln into the capital. It seemed to him both weak and undignified, when the situation called for a conciliatory, but firm, front.[3]

With an absence of personal pique which did him credit, he determined to take the first opportunity to warn Mr. Lincoln of the dangers of his position. Douglas knew Lincoln far better than the average Washington politician. To an acquaintance who lamented the apparent weakness of the President-elect, Douglas said emphatically, "No, he is not that, Sir; but he is eminently a man of the atmosphere which surrounds him. He has not yet got out of Springfield, Sir. . . . He he does not know that he is President-elect of the United States, Sir, he does not see that the shadow he casts is any bigger now than it was last year. It will not take him long to find it out when he has got established in the White House."[4]

[1] *Globe*, 36 Cong., 2 Sess., p. 1081.
[2] Diary of a Public Man, p. 261.
[3] *Ibid.*, p. 260.   [4] *Ibid.*, p. 261.

The ready tact of Mrs. Douglas admirably seconded the initiative of her husband. She was among the first to call upon Mrs. Lincoln, thereby setting the example for the ladies of the opposition.[1] A little incident, to be sure; but in critical hours, the warp and woof of history is made up of just such little acts of thoughtful courtesy. Washington society understood and appreciated the gracious spirit of Adèle Cutts Douglas; and even the New York press commented upon the incident with satisfaction.

That Seward and his friends were no less alarmed than Douglas, at the prospect of Lincoln's falling under the influence of the coercionists, is a matter of record.[2] There were, indeed, two factions contending for mastery over the incoming administration. So far as an outsider could do so, Douglas was willing to lend himself to the schemes of the Seward faction, for in so doing he was obviously promoting the cause of peace.[3] Three days after Lincoln's arrival Douglas called upon him; and on the following evening (February 27th) he sought another private interview.[4] They had long known each other; and politics aside, Lincoln entertained a high opinion of Douglas's fairmindedness and common sense.[5] They talked earnestly about the Peace Conference and the efforts of extremists in Congress to make it abortive.[6] Each knew the other to be a genuine lover of the Union. Upon this common basis of sentiment they could converse without reservations.

[1] Correspondent of the New York *Times*, February 25, 1861.
[2] Diary of a Public Man, pp. 260-261.   [3] *Ibid.*, p. 264.
[4] *Ibid.*, pp. 264, 268; the interview of February 26th was commented upon by the Philadelphia *Press*, February 28.
[5] Herndon-Weik, Lincoln, II, p. 73, note.
[6] Diary of a Public Man, p. 268.

Douglas was agitated and distressed.[1] Compromise was now impossible in Congress. He saw but one hope. With great earnestness he urged Lincoln to recommend the instant calling of a national convention to amend the Constitution. Upon the necessity of this step Douglas and Seward agreed. But Lincoln would not commit himself to this suggestion, without further consideration.[2] "It is impossible not to feel," wrote an old acquaintance, after hearing Douglas's account of this interview, "that he [Douglas] really and truly loves his country in a way not too common, I fear now, in Washington."[3]

The Senate remained in continuous session from Saturday, March 2d, until the oath of office was taken by Vice-President Hamlin on Monday morning. During these eventful hours, the Crittenden amendments were voted down;[4] and when the venerable senator from Kentucky made a final effort to secure the adoption of the resolution of the Peace Congress, which was similar to his own, it too was decisively defeated.[5] In the closing hours of the session, however, in spite of the opposition of irreconcilables like Sumner, Wade, and Wilson, the Senate adopted the amendment which had passed the House, limiting the powers of Congress in the States.[6]

While Union-loving men were thus wrestling with a forlorn hope, Douglas was again closeted with Lincoln. It is very probable that Douglas was invited to call, in order to pass judgment upon certain passages in the

---

[1] Diary of a Public Man, p. 268.
[2] Ibid., p. 268.   [3] Ibid., p. 268.
[4] Globe, 36 Cong., 2 Sess., p. 1405.
[5] Ibid., p. 1405.   [6] Ibid., p. 1403.

inaugural address, which would be delivered on the morrow. At all events, Douglas exhibited a familiarity with portions of the address, which can hardly be accounted for in other ways. He expressed great satisfaction with Lincoln's statement of the invalidity of secession. It would do, he said, for all constitutional Democrats to "brace themselves against."[1] He frankly announced that he would stand by Mr. Lincoln in a temperate, resolute Union policy.[2]

On the forenoon of Inauguration Day, Douglas told a friend that he meant to put himself as prominently forward in the ceremonies as he properly could, and to leave no doubt in any one's mind of his determination to stand by the administration in the performance of its first great duty to maintain the Union. "I watched him carefully," records this same acquaintance. "He made his way not without difficulty—for there was literally no sort of order in the arrangements—to the front of the throng directly beside Mr. Lincoln, when he prepared to read his address. A miserable little rickety table had been provided for the President, on which he could hardly find room for his hat, and Senator Douglas, reaching forward, took it with a smile and held it during the delivery of the address. It was a trifling act, but a symbolical one, and not to be forgotten, and it attracted much attention all around me."[3]

At least one passage in the inaugural address was framed upon suggestions made by Douglas. Contrary to his original intention, Lincoln went out of his way to say, "I cannot be ignorant of the fact that many worthy and patriotic citizens are desirous of having

[1] Diary of a Public Man, p. 380.
[2] Ibid., p. 379.   [3] Ibid., p. 383.

the National Constitution amended. While I make no recommendation of amendments, I fully recognize the rightful authority of the people over the whole subject, to be exercised in either of the modes prescribed in the instrument itself; and I should, under existing circumstances, favor rather than oppose a fair opportunity being afforded the people to act upon it. I will venture to add that to me the convention mode seems preferable, in that it allows amendments to originate with the people themselves, instead of only permitting them to take or reject propositions originated by others, not especially chosen for the purpose, and which might not be precisely such as they would wish to either accept or refuse. I understand a proposed amendment to the Constitution—which amendment, however, I have not seen—has passed Congress, to the effect that the Federal Government shall never interfere with the domestic institutions of the States, including that of persons held to service. To avoid misconstruction of what I have said, I depart from my purpose, not to speak of particular amendments, so far as to say that, holding such a provision to now be implied constitutional law, I have no objection to its being made express and irrevocable.''[1]

In the original draft of his address, written before he came to Washington, Lincoln had dismissed with scant consideration the notion of a constitutional amendment: ''I am not much impressed with the belief that the present Constitution can be improved. I am rather for the old ship, and the chart of the old pilots.''[2]

---

[1] Nicolay and Hay, Lincoln, III, pp. 340-341. These authors note that Lincoln rewrote this paragraph, but take it for granted that he did so upon his own motion, after rejecting Seward's suggestion.

[2] Nicolay and Hay, Lincoln, III, p. 340, note.

Sometime after his interview with Douglas, Lincoln
struck out these words and inserted the paragraph
already quoted, rejecting at the same time a suggestion
from Seward.[1]

The curious and ubiquitous correspondents of the
New York press, always on the alert for straws to
learn which way the wind was blowing, made much
of Douglas's conspicuous gallantry toward Mrs. Lincoln. He accompanied her to the inaugural ball and
unhesitatingly defended his friendliness with the
President's household, on the ground that Mr. Lincoln "meant to do what was right." To one press
agent, eager to have his opinion of the inaugural,
Douglas said, "I defend the inaugural if it is as I
understand it, namely, an emanation from the brain
and heart of a patriot, and as I mean, if I know myself,
to act the part of a patriot, I endorse it."[2]

On March 6th, while Republican senators maintained
an uncertain and discreet silence respecting the inaugural address, Douglas rose to speak in its defense.
Senator Clingman had interpreted the President's
policy in terms of his own emotions: there was no
doubt about it, the inaugural portended war. "In no
wise," responded Douglas with energy: "It is a
peace-offering rather than a war message." In all
his long congressional career there is nothing that
redounds more to Douglas's everlasting credit than
his willingness to defend the policy of his successful
rival, while men of Lincoln's own party were doubting

---

[1] Seward's letter was written on the evening of February 24th. Douglas called upon the President February 26th. See Nicolay and Hay,
Lincoln, III, p. 319; Diary of a Public Man, pp. 264, 268.

[2] New York *Times*, March 6, 1861.

what manner of man the new President was and what his policy might mean. Nothing could have been more adroit than Douglas's plea for the inaugural address. He did not throw himself into the arms of the administration and betray his intimate acquaintance with the plans of the new President. He spoke as the leader of the opposition, critically and judiciously. He had read the inaugural with care; he had subjected it to a critical analysis; and he was of the opinion that it was characterized by ability and directness on certain points, but by lack of explicitness on others. He cited passages that he deemed equivocal and objectionable. Nevertheless he rejoiced to read one clause which was evidently the key to the entire document:

"The course here indicated will be followed unless current events and experience shall show a modification or change to be proper, and in every case and exigency my best discretion will be exercised according to circumstances actually existing, and with a view and a hope of a peaceful solution of the national troubles, and the restoration of fraternal sympathies and affections."[1]

By the terms of his message, too, the President was pledged to favor such amendments as might originate with the people for the settlement of the slavery question,—even if the settlement should be repugnant to the principles of his party. Mr. Lincoln should receive the thanks of all Union-loving men for having "sunk the partisan in the patriot." The voice of Douglas never rang truer than when he paid this tribute to his rival's honesty and candor.

"I do not wish it to be inferred," he said in con-

[1] *Globe*, 36 Cong., Special Sess., p. 1437.

clusion, ... "that I have any political sympathy with his administration, or that I expect any contingency can happen in which I may be identified with it. I expect to oppose his administration with all my energy on those great principles which have separated parties in former times; but on this one question—that of preserving the Union by a peaceful solution of our present difficulties; that of preventing any future difficulties by such an amendment of the Constitution as will settle the question by an express provision—if I understand his true intent and meaning, I am with him."[1]

But neither President Lincoln nor Douglas had committed himself on the concrete question upon which hung peace or war—what should be done about Fort Sumter and Fort Pickens. The point was driven home with relentless vigor by Wigfall, who still lingered in the Senate after the secession of his State. "Would the Senator who is speaking for the administration say explicitly, whether he would advise the withdrawal of the troops from the forts?" The reply of Douglas was admirable: "As I am not in their counsels nor their confidence, I shall not tender them my advice until they ask it. . . . I do not choose either, to proclaim what my policy would be, in view of the fact that the Senator does not regard himself as the guardian of the honor and interests of my country, but is looking to the interests of another, which he thinks is in hostility to this country. It would hardly be good policy or wisdom for me to reveal what I think ought to be our policy, to one who may so soon be in the counsels of the enemy, and the command of its armies."[2]

[1] *Globe*, 36 Cong., Special Sess., p. 1438. [2] *Ibid.*, p. 1442.

Douglas did admit, however, that since the garrison of Fort Sumter had provisions for only thirty days, he presumed no attempt would be made to reinforce it. Under existing circumstances the President had no power to collect the revenues of the government and no military force sufficient to reinforce Sumter. Congress was not in session to supply either the necessary coercive powers or troops. He therefore drew the conclusion that not only the President himself was pacific in his policy, but the Republican party as well, despite the views of individual members. "But," urged Mason of Virginia, "I ask the Senator, then, what is to be done with the garrison if they are in a starving condition?" "If the Senator had voted right in the last presidential election," replied Douglas good-naturedly, "I should have been in a condition, perhaps, to tell him authoritatively what ought to be done."

From this moment on, Douglas enjoyed the confidence of President Lincoln to an extraordinary degree. No one knew better than Lincoln the importance of securing the coöperation of so influential a personage. True, by the withdrawal of Southern senators, the Democratic opposition had been greatly reduced; but Douglas was still a power in this Democratic remnant. Besides, the man who could command the suffrages of a million voters was not a force lightly to be reckoned with. After this speech of the 6th, Lincoln again sent for Douglas, to express his entire agreement with its views and with its spirit.[1] He gave Douglas the impression that he desired to gain time for passions to cool by removing the causes

[1] Diary of a Public Man, p. 493.

of irritation. He felt confident that there would soon be a general demand for a national convention where all existing differences could be radically treated. "I am just as ready," Douglas reported him to have said, "to reinforce the garrisons at Sumter and Pickens or to withdraw them, as I am to see an amendment adopted protecting slavery in the Territories or prohibiting slavery in the Territories. What I want is to get done what the people desire to have done, and the question for me is how to find that out exactly."[1] On this point they were in entire accord.

The patriotic conduct of Douglas earned for him the warm commendation of Northern newspapers, many of which had hitherto been incapable of ascribing honorable motives to him.[2] No one who met him at the President's levees would have suspected that he had been one of his host's most relentless opponents. A correspondent of the New York *Times* described him as he appeared at one of these functions. "Here one minute, there the next—now congratulating the President, then complimenting Mrs. Lincoln, bowing and scraping, and shaking hands, and smiling, laughing, yarning and saluting the crowd of people whom he knew." More soberly, this same observer added, "He has already done a great deal of good to the administration."[3] It is impossible to find the soured and discomfited rival in this picture.

The country was anxiously awaiting the development of the policy of the new Executive, for to eight

[1] Diary of a Public Man, p. 493.

[2] New York *Times*, March 8, 1861; also the Philadelphia *Press*, March 11, 1861.

[3] New York *Times*, March 10, 1861.

out of every ten men, Lincoln was still an unknown man. Rumors were abroad that both Sumter and Pickens would be surrendered.[1] Seward was known to be conciliatory on this point; and the man on the street never once doubted that Seward would be the master-mind in the cabinet. Those better informed knew—and Douglas was among them—that Seward's influence was menaced by an aggressive faction in the cabinet.[2] Behind these official advisers, giving them active support, were those Republican senators who from the first had doubted the efficacy of compromise.

Believing the country should have assurances that President Lincoln did not meditate war,—did not, in short, propose to yield to the aggressive wing of his party,—Douglas sought to force a show of hands.[3] On March 13th, he offered a resolution which was designed to draw the fire of Republican senators. The Secretary of War was requested to furnish information about the Southern forts now in possession of the Federal government; to state whether reinforcements were needed to retain them; whether under existing laws the government had the power and means to reinforce them, and whether it was wise to retain military possession of such forts and to recapture those that had been lost, except for the purpose of subjugating and occupying the States which had seceded; and finally, if such were the motives, to supply estimates of the military force required to reduce the seceding States and to protect the national capital.[4] The word-

[1] Rhodes History of the United States, III, p. 332.

[2] Diary of a Public Man, p. 493.

[3] *Ibid.*, pp. 495-496.

[4] *Globe,* 36 Cong., Special Sess., p. 1452.

ing of the resolution was purposely involved. Douglas hoped that it would precipitate a discussion which would disclose the covert wish of the aggressives, and force an authoritative announcement of President Lincoln's policy. Doubtless there was a political motive behind all this. Douglas was not averse to putting his bitter and implacable enemies in their true light, as foes of compromise even to the extent of disrupting the Union.[1]

Not receiving any response, Douglas took the floor in defense of his resolution. He believed that the country should have the information which his resolution was designed to elicit. The people were apprehensive of civil war. He had put his construction upon the President's inaugural; but "the Republican side of the Chamber remains mute and silent, neither assenting nor dissenting." The answer which he believed the resolution would call forth, would demonstrate two points of prime importance: "First, that the President does not meditate war; and, secondly, that he has no means for prosecuting a warfare upon the seceding States, even if he desired."

With his wonted dialectic skill Douglas sought to establish his case. The existing laws made no provision for collecting the revenue on shipboard. It was admitted on all sides that collection at the port of entry in South Carolina was impossible. The President had no legal right to blockade the port of Charleston. He could not employ the army to enforce the laws in the seceded States, for the military could be used only to aid a civil process; and where was the marshal in South Carolina to execute a writ? The

[1] Diary of a Public Man, pp. 495-496.

President must have known that he lacked these powers. He must have referred to the future action of Congress, then, when he said that he should execute the laws in all the States, unless the "requisite means were withheld." But Congress had not passed laws empowering the Executive to collect revenue or to gain possession of the forts. What, then, was the inference? Clearly this, that the Republican senators did not desire to confer these powers.

If this inference is not correct, if this interpretation of the inaugural address is faulty, urged Douglas, why preserve this impenetrable silence? Why not let the people know what the policy of the administration is? They have a right to know. "The President of the United States holds the destiny of this country in his hands. I believe he means peace, and war will be averted, unless he is overruled by the disunion portion of his party. We all know the irrepressible conflict is going on in their camp. . . . Then, throw aside this petty squabble about how you are to get along with your pledges before election; meet the issues as they are presented; do what duty, honor, and patriotism require, and appeal to the people to sustain you. Peace is the only policy that can save the country or save your party."[1]

On the Republican side of the chamber, this appeal was bitterly resented. It met with no adequate response, because there was none to give; but Wilson roundly denounced it as a wicked, mischief-making utterance.[2] Unhappily, Douglas allowed himself to be drawn into a personal altercation with Fessenden,

[1] *Globe*, 36 Cong., Special Sess., p 1461.
[2] *Ibid.*, p. 1461.

in which he lost his temper and marred the effect of his patriotic appeal. There was probably some truth in Douglas's charge that both senators intended to be personally irritating.[1] Under the circumstances, it was easier to indulge in personal disparagement of Douglas, than to meet his embarrassing questions.

How far Douglas still believed in the possibility of saving the Union through compromise, it is impossible to say. Publicly he continued to talk in an optimistic strain.[2] On March 25th, he expressed his satisfaction in the Senate that only one danger-point remained; Fort Sumter, he understood, was to be evacuated.[3] But among his friends no one looked into the future with more anxiety than he. Intimations from the South that citizens of the United States would probably be excluded from the courts of the Confederacy, wrung from him the admission that such action would be equivalent to war.[4] He noted anxiously the evident purpose of the Confederated States to coerce Kentucky and Virginia into secession.[5] Indeed, it is probable that before the Senate adjourned, his ultimate hope was to rally the Union men in the border States.[6]

When President Lincoln at last determined to send supplies to Fort Sumter, the issue of peace or war rested with Jefferson Davis and his cabinet at Montgomery. Early on the morning of April 12th, a shell, fired from a battery in Charleston harbor, burst directly over Fort Sumter, proclaiming to anxious ears the close of an era.

---

[1] *Globe*, 36 Cong., Special Sess., p. 1465.
[2] *Ibid.*, pp. 1460, 1501, 1504. [3] *Ibid.*, p. 1501.
[4] Diary of a Public Man, p. 494. [5] *Ibid.*, p. 494.
[6] *Globe*, 36 Cong., Special Sess., pp. 1505, 1511.

CHAPTER XX

THE SUMMONS

The news of the capitulation of Fort Sumter reached Washington on Sunday morning, April 14th. At a momentous cabinet meeting, President Lincoln read the draft of a proclamation calling into service seventy-five thousand men, to suppress combinations obstructing the execution of the laws in the Southern States. The cabinet was now a unit. Now that the crisis had come, the administration had a policy. Would it approve itself to the anxious people of the North? Could it count upon the support of those who had counselled peace, peace at any cost?

Those who knew Senator Douglas well could not doubt his loyalty to the Union in this crisis; yet his friends knew that Union-loving men in the Democratic ranks would respond to the President's proclamation with a thousandfold greater enthusiasm, could they know that their leader stood by the administration. Moved by these considerations, Hon. George Ashmun of Massachusetts ventured to call upon Douglas on this Sunday evening, and to suggest the propriety of some public statement to strengthen the President's hands. Would he not call upon the President at once and give him the assurance of his support? Douglas demurred: he was not sure that Mr. Lincoln wanted his advice and aid. Mr. Ashmun assured him that the President would welcome any advances, and he spoke advisedly as a friend to both men. The peril of the country was grave; surely this was not a time when men should let personal and partisan considerations stand between them and service to their country. Mrs. Douglas added her entreaties, and Douglas finally yielded. Though the hour was late, the two men set off for the White House, and found there the hearty welcome which Ashmun had promised.[1]

Of all the occurrences of this memorable day, this interview between Lincoln and Douglas strikes the imagination with most poignant suggestiveness. Had Douglas been a less generous opponent, he might have reminded the President that matters had come to just that pass which he had foreseen in 1858. Nothing of the sort passed Douglas's lips. The meeting of the rivals was most cordial and hearty. They held converse as men must when hearts are oppressed with a common burden. The President took up and read aloud the proclamation summoning the nation to arms. When he had done, Douglas said with deep earnestness, "Mr. President, I cordially concur in every word of that document, except that instead of the call for seventy-five thousand men, I would make it two hundred thousand. You do not know the dishonest purposes of those men as well as I do."[2] Why has not some artist seized upon the dramatic moment when they rose and passed to the end of the room to examine a map which hung there? Douglas, with animated face and impetuous gesture, pointing out the strategic places in the coming contest; Lincoln, with the suggestion of brooding melancholy upon his careworn face, listening in rapt attention to the quick, penetrat-

[1] Holland, Life of Lincoln, p. 301.
[2] Ibid., p. 302.

ing observations of his life-long rival. But what no artist could put upon canvas was the dramatic absence of resentment and defeated ambition in the one, and the patient teachableness and self-mastery of the other. As they parted, a quick hearty grasp of hands symbolized this remarkable consecration to a common task.

As they left the executive mansion, Ashmun urged his companion to send an account of this interview to the press, that it might accompany the President's message on the morrow. Douglas then penned the following dispatch: "Senator Douglas called upon the President, and had an interesting conversation on the present condition of the country. The substance of it was, on the part of Mr. Douglas, that while he was unalterably opposed to the administration in all its political issues, he was prepared to fully sustain the President in the exercise of all his constitutional functions, to preserve the Union, maintain the government, and defend the Federal capital. A firm policy and prompt action was necessary. The capital was in danger, and must be defended at all hazards, and at any expense of men and money. He spoke of the present and future without any reference to the past."[1] When the people of the North read the proclamation in the newspapers, on the following morning, a million men were cheered and sustained in their loyalty to the Union by the intelligence that their great leader had subordinated all lesser ends of party to the paramount duty of maintaining the Constitution of the fathers. To his friends in Washington, Douglas said unhesitatingly,

[1] Arnold, Lincoln, pp. 200-201. The date of this dispatch should be April 14, and not April 18.

"We must fight for our country and forget all differences. There can be but two parties—the party of patriots and the party of traitors. We belong to the first."[1] And to friends in Missouri where disunion sentiment was rife, he telegraphed, "I deprecate war, but if it must come I am with my country, and for my country, under all circumstances and in every contingency. Individual policy must be subordinated to the public safety."[2]

From this day on, Douglas was in frequent consultation with the President. The sorely tried and distressed Lincoln was unutterably grateful for the firm grip which this first of "War Democrats" kept upon the progress of public opinion in the irresolute border States. It was during one of these interviews, after the attack upon the Sixth Massachusetts Regiment in the streets of Baltimore, that Douglas urged upon the President the possibility of bringing troops by water to Annapolis, thence to Washington, thus avoiding further conflict in the disaffected districts of Maryland.[3] Eventually the Eighth Massachusetts and the Seventh New York reached Washington by this route, to the immense relief of the President and his cabinet.

Before this succor came to the alarmed capital, Douglas had left the city for the West. He had received intimations that Egypt in his own State showed marked symptoms of disaffection. The old ties of blood and kinship of the people of southern Illinois with their neighbors in the border States were proving stronger than Northern affiliations. Douglas wielded an influence in these southern, Democratic counties,

---

[1] Forney, Anecdotes, I, p. 224.   [2] New York *Tribune*, April 18.
[3] Forney, Anecdotes, I, p. 225.

such as no other man possessed. Could he not best
serve the administration by bearding disunionism in
its den? Believing that Cairo, at the confluence of
the Mississippi and the Ohio, was destined to be a
strategic point of immense importance in the coming
struggle, and that the fate of the whole valley depended
upon the unwavering loyalty of Illinois, Douglas laid
the matter before Lincoln. He would go or stay in
Washington, wherever Lincoln thought he could do the
most good. Probably neither then realized the tremendous nature of the struggle upon which the country had entered; yet both knew that the Northwest
would be the makeweight in the balance for the Union;
and that every nerve must be strained to hold the
border States of Kentucky and Missouri. Who could
rouse the latent Unionism of the Northwest and of the
border States like Douglas? Lincoln advised him to
go. There was a quick hand-grasp, a hurried farewell,
and they parted never to meet again.[1]

Rumor gave strange shapes to this "mission" which
carried Douglas in such haste to the Northwest. Most
persistent of all is the tradition that he was authorized
to raise a huge army in the States of the upper Mississippi Valley, and to undertake that vast flanking movement which subsequently fell to Grant and Sherman
to execute. Such a project would have been thoroughly consonant with Douglas's conviction of the
inevitable unity and importance of the great valley;
but evidence is wanting to corroborate this legend.[2]

[1] Herndon-Weik, Lincoln, II, p. 249 note; Forney, Anecdotes, I,
p. 225.

[2] Many friends of Douglas have assured me of their unshaken belief in this story.

Its frequent repetition, then and now, must rather be taken as a popular recognition of the complete accord between the President and the greatest of War Democrats. Colonel Forney, who stood very near to Douglas, afterward stated "by authority," that President Lincoln would eventually have called Douglas into the administration or have placed him in one of the highest military commands.[1] Such importance may be given to this testimony as belongs to statements which have passed unconfirmed and unchallenged for half a century.

On his way to Illinois, Douglas missed a train and was detained half a day in the little town of Bellaire, Ohio, a few miles below Wheeling in Virginia.[2] It was a happy accident, for just across the river the people of northwestern Virginia were meditating resistance to the secession movement, which under the guidance of Governor Letcher threatened to sever them from the Union-loving population of Ohio and Pennsylvania It was precisely in this region, nearly a hundred years before, that popular sovereignty had almost succeeded in forming a fourteenth State of the Confederacy. There had always been a disparity between the people of these transmontane counties and the tide-water region. The intelligence that Douglas was in Bellaire speedily brought a throng about the hotel in which he was resting. There were clamors for a speech. In the afternoon he yielded to their importunities. By this time the countryside was aroused. People came across the river from Virginia and many

---

[1] Forney, Anecdotes, I, pp. 121, 226.

[2] Philadelphia *Press*, April 26, 1861.

came down by train from Wheeling.[1] Men who were torn by a conflict of sentiments, not knowing where their paramount allegiance lay, hung upon his words.

Douglas spoke soberly and thoughtfully, not as a Democrat, not as a Northern man, but simply and directly as a lover of the Union. "If we recognize the right of secession in one case, we give our assent to it in all cases; and if the few States upon the Gulf are now to separate themselves from us, and erect a barrier across the mouth of that great river of which the Ohio is a tributary, how long will it be before New York may come to the conclusion that she may set up for herself, and levy taxes upon every dollar's worth of goods imported and consumed in the Northwest, and taxes upon every bushel of wheat, and every pound of pork, or beef, or other productions that may be sent from the Northwest to the Atlantic in search of a market?" Secession meant endless division and sub-division, the formation of petty confederacies, appeals to the sword and the bayonet instead of to the ballot.

"Unite as a band of brothers," he pleaded, "and rescue your government and its capital and your country from the enemy who have been the authors of your calamity." His eye rested upon the great river. "Ah!" he exclaimed, a great wave of emotion checking his utterance, "This great valley must never be divided. The Almighty has so arranged the mountain and the plain, and the water-courses as to show that this valley in all time shall remain one and indissoluble. Let no man attempt to sunder what Divine Providence has rendered indivisible."[2]

[1] Philadelphia *Press*, April 26, 1861.

[2] The Philadelphia *Press*, April 26, 1861, reprinted the speech from the Wheeling *Intelligencer* of April 21, 1861.

As he concluded, anxious questions were put to him, regarding the rumored retirement of General Scott from the army. "I saw him only Saturday," replied Douglas. "He was at his desk, pen in hand, writing his orders for the defense and safety of the American Capital." And as he repeated the words of General Scott declining the command of the forces of Virginia— " 'I have served my country under the flag of the Union for more than fifty years, and as long as God permits me to live, I will defend that flag with my sword; even if my own State assails it,' "—the crowds around him broke into tumultuous cheers. Within thirty days the Unionists of western Virginia had rallied, organized, and begun that hardy campaign which brought West Virginia into the Union. On the very day that Douglas was making his fervent plea for the Union, Robert E. Lee cast in his lot with the South.

At Columbus, Douglas was again forced to break his journey; and again he was summoned to address the crowd that gathered below his window. It was already dark; the people had collected without concert; there were no such trappings as had characterized public demonstrations in the late campaign. Douglas appeared half-dressed at his bedroom window, a dim object to all save to those who stood directly below him. Out of the darkness came his solemn, sonorous tones, bringing relief and assurance to all who listened, for in the throng were men of all parties, men who had followed him through all changes of political weather, and men who had been his persistent foes. There was little cheering. As Douglas pledged anew his hearty support to President Lincoln, "it was rather a deep 'Amen' that went up from the crowd," wrote one who had distrusted hitherto the mighty power of this great popular leader.[1]

On the 25th of April, Douglas reached Springfield, where he purposed to make his great plea for the Union. He spoke at the Capitol to members of the legislature and to packed galleries. Friend and foe alike bear witness to the extraordinary effect wrought by his words. "I do not think that it is possible for a human being to produce a more prodigious effect with spoken words," wrote one who had formerly detested him.[2] "Never in all my experience in public life, before or since," testified the then Speaker of the House, now high in the councils of the nation, "have I been so impressed by a speaker."[3] Douglas himself was thrilled with his message. As he approached the climax, the veins of his neck and forehead were swollen with passion, and the perspiration ran down his face in streams. At times his clear and resonant voice reverberated through the chamber, until it seemed to shake the building.[4] While he was in the midst of a passionate invective, a man rushed into the hall bearing an American flag. The trumpet tones of the speaker and the sight of the Stars and Stripes roused the audience to the wildest pitch of excitement.[5] Men and women became hysterical with the divine madness of patriotism. "When hostile armies," he exclaimed with amazing force, "When hostile armies are marching under new and odious banners against the govern-

[1] J. D. Cox, Military Reminiscences of the Civil War, I, pp. 5-6.

[2] Mr. Horace White in Herndon-Weik, Lincoln, II, pp. 126-127.

[3] Senator Cullom of Illinois, quoted in Arnold, Lincoln, p. 201, note.

[4] Mr. Horace White in Herndon-Weik, Lincoln, II, pp. 126-127.

[5] Arnold, Lincoln, p. 201, note.

ment of our country, the shortest way to peace is the most stupendous and unanimous preparation for war. We in the great valley of the Mississippi have peculiar interests and inducements in the struggle. . . . I ask every citizen in the great basin between the Rocky Mountains and the Alleghanies . . . . to tell me whether he is ever willing to sanction a line of policy that may isolate us from the markets of the world, and make us dependent provinces upon the powers that thus choose to isolate us? . . . . Hence, if a war does come, it is a war of self-defense on our part. It is a war in defense of the Government which we have inherited as a priceless legacy from our patriotic fathers, in defense of those great rights of freedom of trade, commerce, transit and intercourse from the center to the circumference of our great continent.''[1]

The voice of the strong man, so little given to weak sentiment, broke, as he said, ''I have struggled almost against hope to avert the calamities of war and to effect a reunion and reconciliation with our brethren in the South. I yet hope it may be done, but I am not able to point out how it may be. Nothing short of Providence can reveal to us the issues of this great struggle. Bloody—calamitous—I fear it will be. May we so conduct it, if a collision must come, that we will stand justified in the eyes of Him who knows our hearts, and who will justify our every act. We must not yield to resentments, nor to the spirit of vengeance, much less to the desire for conquest or ambition. I see no path of ambition open in a bloody struggle for triumphs over my countrymen. There is no path of

[1] The speech was printed in full in the New York *Tribune,* May 1, 1861.

ambition open for me in a divided country. . . . My friends, I can say no more. To discuss these topics is the most painful duty of my life. It is with a sad heart—with a grief I have never before experienced— that I have to contemplate this fearful struggle; but I believe in my conscience that it is a duty we owe to ourselves and to our children, and to our God, to protect this Government and that flag from every assailant, be he who he may.''

Thereafter treason had no abiding place within the limits of the State of Illinois. And no one, it may be safely affirmed, could have so steeled the hearts of men in Southern Illinois for the death grapple. In a manly passage in his speech, Douglas said, ''I believe I may with confidence appeal to the people of every section of the country to bear witness that I have been as thoroughly national as any man that has lived in my day. And I believe if I should make an appeal to the people of Illinois, or of the Northern States, to their impartial verdict; they would say that whatever errors I have committed have been in leaning too far to the Southern section of the Union against my own. . . . I have never pandered to the prejudice and passion of my section against the minority section of the Union.'' It was precisely this truth which gave him a hearing through the length and breadth of Illinois and the Northwest during this crisis.

The return of Douglas to Chicago was the signal for a remarkable demonstration of regard. He had experienced many strange home-comings. His Democratic following, not always discriminating, had ever accorded him noisy homage. His political opponents had alternately execrated him and given him grudging praise. But never before had men of all parties, burying their differences, united to do him honor. On the evening of his arrival, he was escorted to the Wigwam, where hardly a year ago Lincoln had been nominated for the presidency. Before him were men who had participated jubilantly in the Republican campaign, with many a bitter gibe at the champion of "squatter sovereignty." Douglas could not conceal his gratification at this proof that, however men had differed from him on political questions, they had believed in his loyalty. And it was of loyalty, not of himself, that he spoke. He did not spare Southern feelings before this Chicago audience. He told his hearers unequivocally that the slavery question, the election of Lincoln, and the territorial question, were so many pretexts for dissolving the Union. "The present secession movement is the result of an enormous conspiracy formed more than a year since, formed by leaders in the Southern Confederacy more than twelve months ago." But this was no time to discuss pretexts and causes. "The conspiracy is now known. Armies have been raised, war is levied to accomplish it. There are only two sides to the question. Every man must be for the United States or against it. There can be no neutrals in this war; *only patriots—or traitors.*"[1] It was the first time he had used the ugly epithet.

Hardly had he summoned the people of Illinois to do battle, when again he touched that pathetic note that recurred again and again in his appeal at Springfield. Was it the memory of the mother of his boys that moved him to say, "But we must remember

[1] The New York *Tribune,* June 13th, and the Philadelphia *Press,* June 14th, published this speech in full.

certain restraints on our action even in time of war.
We are a Christian people, and the war must be prosecuted in a manner recognized by Christian nations.
We must not invade Constitutional rights. The innocent must not suffer, nor women and children be the
victims.'' Before him were some who felt toward the
people of the South as Greek toward barbarian. But
Douglas foresaw that the horrors of war must invade
and desolate the homes of those whom he still held
dear. There is no more lovable and admirable side
of his personality than this tenderness for the helpless
and innocent. Had he but lived to temper justice with
mercy, what a power for good might he not have been
in the days of reconstruction!

The summons had gone forth. Already doubts and
misgivings had given way, and the North was now
practically unanimous in its determination to stifle
rebellion. There was a common belief that secession
was the work of a minority, skillfully led by designing
politicians, and that the loyal majority would rally
with the North to defend the flag. Young men who
responded jubilantly to the call to arms did not doubt
that the struggle would be brief. Douglas shared the
common belief in the conspiracy theory of secession,
but he indulged no illusion as to the nature of the war,
if war should come. Months before the firing upon
Fort Sumter, in a moment of depression, he had
prophesied that if the cotton States should succeed in
drawing the border States into their schemes of secession, the most fearful civil war the world had ever seen
would follow, lasting for years. ''Virginia,'' said he,
pointing toward Arlington, ''over yonder across the
Potomac, will become a charnel-house. . . . Washington

will become a city of hospitals, the churches will be used for the sick and wounded. This house 'Minnesota Block,' will be devoted to that purpose before the end of the war.'[1] He, at least, did not mistake the chivalry of the South. Not for an instant did he doubt the capacity of the Southern people to suffer and endure, as well as to do battle. And he knew—Ah! how well—the self-sacrifice and devotion of Southern women.

The days following the return of Douglas to Chicago were filled also with worries and anxieties of a private nature. The financial panic of 1857 had been accompanied by a depression of land values, which caused Douglas grave concern for his holdings in Chicago, and no little immediate distress. Unable and unwilling to sacrifice his investments, he had mortgaged nearly all of his property in Cook County, including the valuable "Grove Property" in South Chicago. Though he was always lax in pecuniary matters, and, with his buoyant generous nature, little disposed to take anxious thought for the morrow, these heavy financial obligations began now to press upon him with grievous weight. The prolonged strain of the previous twelve months had racked even his constitution. He had made heavy drafts on his bodily health, with all too little regard for the inevitable compensation which Nature demands. As in all other things, he had been prodigal with Nature's choicest gift.

Not long after his public address Douglas fell ill and developed symptoms that gave his physicians the gravest concern. Weeks of illness followed. The dis-

[1] Arnold, Lincoln, p. 193. See also his remarks in the Senate, January 3, 1861.

ease, baffling medical skill, ran its course. Yet never in his lucid moments did Douglas forget the ills of his country; and even when delirium clouded his mind, he was still battling for the Union. "Telegraph to the President and let the column move on," he cried, wrestling with his wasting fever. In his last hours his mind cleared. Early on the morning of June 3d, he seemed to rally, but only momentarily. It was evident to those about him that the great summons had come. Tenderly his devoted wife leaned over him to ask if he had any message for his boys, "Robbie" and "Stevie." With great effort, but clearly and emphatically, he replied, "Tell them to obey the laws and support the Constitution of the United States." Not long after, he grappled with the great Foe, and the soul of a great patriot passed on.

> "I was ever a fighter, so—one fight more,
>   The best and the last!
> I would hate that death bandaged my eyes, and forbore,
>   And bade me creep past.
> No! let me taste the whole of it, fare like my peers
>   The heroes of old,
> Bear the brunt, in a minute pay glad life's arrears
>   Of pain, darkness and cold."

With almost royal pomp, the earthly remains of Stephen Arnold Douglas were buried beside the inland sea that washes the shores of the home of his adoption. It is a fitting resting place. The tempestuous waters of the great lake reflect his own stormy career. Yet they have their milder moods. There are hours when sunlight falls aslant the subdued surface and irradiates the depths.

INDEX

Abolitionism, debate in the Senate on, 124-126.

Abolitionists, in Illinois, 156, 158-160; agitation of, 194-195.

Adams, John Quincy, on Douglas, 72, 76, 89, 98; catechises Douglas, 111, 113.

Albany Regency, 10.

Anderson, Robert, dispatch to War Department, 442; moves garrison to Fort Sumter, 451.

Andrews, Sherlock J., 11.

Anti-Masonry, in New York, 10.

Anti-Nebraska party. *See* Republican party.

"Appeal of the Independent Democrats," origin, 240; assails motives of Douglas, 241.

Arnold, Mar'' a, grandmother of Stephen A. Douglas, 4.

Arnold, William, ancestor of Stephen A. Douglas, 4.

Ashmun, George, 475, 476, 477.

Atchison, David R., pro-slavery leader in Missouri, 223; favors Nebraska bill (1853), 225; and repeal of Missouri Compromise, 225, 235; and Kansas-Nebraska bill, 256.

Badger, George E., 215.

"Barnburners," 132.

Bay Islands, Colony of, 209, 213.

Bell, John, presidential candidate, 425, 429, 440.

Benjamin, Judah P., quoted, 402, 453.

Benton, Thomas H., 44, 117, 223.

Berrien, John M., 185.

Bigler, William, 333, 335, 417, 446.

Bissell, William H., 305.

Black, Jeremiah S., controversy with Douglas, 409-410.

"Black Republicans," origin of epithet, 275; arraigned by Douglas, 296, 297, 304, 374-375.

"Blue Lodges" of Missouri, 283, 286.

Boyd, Linn, 182.

Brandon, birthplace of Douglas, 5, 9, 69.

Brandon Academy, 7, 9.

Breckinridge, John C., 382; presidential candidate (1860), 427, 428, 435, 440-441.

Breese, Sidney, judge of Circuit Court, 52; elected Senator, 62; and Federal patronage, 118-119; director of Great Western Railroad Company, 168-170; retirement, 158, 171.

Bright, Jesse D., 119, 417.

Broderick, David C., and Lecompton constitution, 335; and English bill, 347; killed, 411.

Brooks, S. S., editor of Jacksonville *News*, 19, 20, 25, 40.

Brooks, Preston, assaults Sumner, 298.

Brown, Albert G., 247, 340, 341, 397-398, 402.

Brown, John, Pottawatomie massacre, 299; Harper's Ferry raid, 411, 412.

490

208n.; death of his wife, 208;
on Clayton-Bulwer treaty, 211-
214; hostility to Great Britain,
215-216; travels abroad, 217-219;
proposes military colonization
of Nebraska, 221; urges organization of Nebraska, 224-225;
report of January 4, 1854,
229ff.; offers substitute for
Dodge bill, 231-232; interprets
new bill, 233-234; and Dixon,
235-236; drafts Kansas-Nebraska bill, 237; secures support of administration, 237-238;
reports bill, 239; arraigned by
Independent Democrats, 241;
replies to ''Appeal,'' 241-243;
proposes amendments to Kansas-Nebraska bill, 246, 249;
closes debate, 251-254; answers
protests, 256-257; faces mob in
Chicago, 258-259; denounces
Know-Nothings, 263; in campaign of 1854, 264 ff.; debate
with Lincoln, 265-266; and
Shields, 267, 268; on the elections, 269-272; and Wade, 272-
273; on ''Black Republicanism,''
275-276; candidacy at Cincinnati, 276-278; supports Buchanan, 278; reports on Kansas,
289-293; proposes admission of
Kansas, 293; replies to Trumbull, 294; and Sumner, 296-298;
reports Toombs bill, 300-301;
omits referendum provision, 302;
subsequent defense, 303-304; in
campaign of 1856, 304-306; second marriage, 316; on Dred
Scott decision, 321-323; interview with Walker, 325; and
Buchanan, 327-328; denounces

Lecompton constitution, 329-332;
report on Kansas, 338-340;
speech on Lecomptonism, 341-
343; rejects English bill, 345-
347; Republican ally, 348; re-
election opposed, 349-350; in
Chicago, 352-354; opening
speech of campaign, 354-357;
speech at Bloomington, 358-
360; speech at Springfield, 360-
361; agrees to joint debate,
362; first debate at Ottawa,
363-370; Springfield resolutions,
370; Freeport debate, 370-375;
debate at Jonesboro, 375-378;
debate at Charleston, 378-381;
friends and foes, 381-382; resources, 382-383; debate at
Galesburg, 383-386; debate at
Quincy, 386-388; debate at Alton, 388-390; the election, 391-
392; journey to South and Cuba,
393-395; deposed from chairmanship of Committee on Territories, 395; supports Slidell
project, 396; debate of February 23, 1859, 397 ff.; opposes
slave-trade, 403-404; *Harper's
Magazine* article, 405-409; controversy with Black, 409-410;
in Ohio, 410-411; presidential
candidate of Northwest, 413,
416; and the South, 414; and
Republicans, 414-415; candidate
at Charleston, 416 ff.; defends
his orthodoxy, 422-424; nominated at Baltimore, 427; letter
of acceptance, 428; personal
canvass, 429-439; on election of
Lincoln, 439 ff.; and Crittenden
compromise, 446-448; speech of
January 3, 1861, 449 ff.; ef-